THE RISE OF THE

CHINESE REPUBLIC

From the Last Emperor to Deng Xiaoping

EDWIN P. HOYT

New foreword by the author

A DA CAPO PAPERBACK

Library of Congress Cataloging in Publication Data

Hoyt, Edwin Palmer.
  The rise of the Chinese republiuc: from the last emperor to Deng Xiaoping /
Edwin P. Hoyt: new foreword by the author.
      p.   cm. —(A Da Capo paperback)
  Includes bibliographical references and index.
  ISBN 0-306-80426-3
  1. China—History—20th century. I. Title.
DS774.H62   1991   90-26754
951—dc20   CIP

This Da Capo Press paperback edition of *The Rise of the Chinese Republic* is an
unabridged republication of the edition published in New York in 1989, supplemented
with a new foreword by the author. It is here reprinted by arrangement
with McGraw-Hill Publishing Company.

Published by Da Capo Press, Inc.
A Subsidiary of Plenum Publishing Corporation
233 Spring Street, New York, N.Y. 10013

Contents

Foreword to the Da Capo Edition

The original edition of *The Rise of the Chinese Republic* was published in 1989, months before the Tiananmen Square students' demonstrations in Beijing that led to the June massacre and consequent repression of dissent in China. What had been a promising future of orderly change and liberalization of thought suddenly came to a stop. The man responsible for both the liberalization campaign and the end of it was Deng Xiaoping, the virtual dictator of China in the days since the fall of the Gang of Four and the gradual abolition of Maoism.

So what will take place in China now with the new "white terror," as the students describe it? The answer, from the record since June 1989, seems to be that the terror will continue until a number of deaths have occurred, although it may take just one, the death of Deng Xiaoping. What is happening within the army is a matter of great interest, because the Red Army is the only institution capable of changing the power structure. The Communist Party has retreated to cronyism and corruption, and it has lost the respect of the youth it once tried to attract. The army has not really been heard from since Tiananmen Square; one can only assume that the factionalism that always existed therein has continued. Since that May day when a group of senior generals published a letter to the government in the *People's Daily* warning against "killing the people," nothing has been heard from any segment of the army. It is known, however, that during the demonstrations several divisions refused to fire on the students, whereupon Li Peng and his associates brought in a Mongol division to do the job. Those troops performed well; the Beijing government is still picking up the pieces of their wild terrorizing ride through the foreign ghetto, shooting up the houses of businessmen and diplomats. Foreign investors continue to be very leery—even the Japanese, who were quickest to return. In the spring of 1990 their government was still debating the matter of loans, and businessmen were going slow on the joint ventures that were so enormously popular a few years ago.

Without a question China has been set back a whole generation, for the nation now finds itself alone in the world in its rejection of liberalization and the sharing of power by the Communist Party. Just three years ago Deng Xiaoping was calling for precisely that. In 1990 he paid little but lip service to "reform" and there was no real reform. Once Deng advocated the embracement of Taiwan—"one China, two systems"—but that, like his other reformist ideas, has gone by the boards, and when in May Taiwan President Lee Teng Hui proposed an end to hostility toward Beijing, there was no indication that Beijing was moved.

What is apparent from all that occurred in China since June 1989 is that the Communist Party and the Communist government are afraid of their own people. Under such conditions there can be no positive change.

I happened to be in Beijing in that Spring of 1989 and it seemed to me that the students had won their point in the middle of May, when such luminaries as Zhao Ziyang came out to the square to talk to them. I felt too that the student leaders, by continuing their protest, provoked the repression. It would have been interesting to see the outcome had the students disbanded and waited for the government and party to carry out promised reforms.

But one cannot solve problems with speculations. The students played into the hands of the old radicals of the Communist Party, the Maoists, the hardliners who saw themselves gradually being deprived of influence and power. Now they are having their last fling, but how long it will continue is debatable.

The greatest gain of the student demonstrations was the evident solidarity of intellectuals, workers, and bureaucrats in favor of liberalization. That spirit will not die; for one thing, it is being kept alive abroad. The great loss to China will be if the party and government delay too long in reversing policy, and thus lose the interest and allegiance of a whole generation of students.

What the world awaits is the death of Deng Xiaoping, for the struggle that will ensue could conceivably bring some welcome change. One hopes for the elimination of the vestiges of Maoism and the sacrifice of a few salient characters such as Li Peng, who gained infamy with the cognomen "the butcher of Beijing."

Hallieford, Virginia
July 1990

Introduction

As the world approaches the twenty-first century, it seems apparent that the Chinese revolution has stabilized, and it is possible now for the first time to assess the changes that have come to China in the twentieth century.

Napoleon's shrewd observation in the nineteenth century that China was a sleeping giant has proved to be true. China has awakened, and a world that was very afraid of what would happen when finally that country did awaken can now be confident and share Gen. Omar Bradley's assessment that the Chinese People's Republic is not a danger to international peace. Further, the development of the Chinese revolution shows that the Chinese are not trying to export their brand of communism.

A revolution, said Mao Zedong, is not like a dinner party—it is a violent overthrow of one class by another; and that is what happened in China. The common people, the *laobaixing*, rose up and threw out the aristocracy and the landed gentry. The fact that the revolution was led by Communists is more or less incidental. A century before, a similar revolution was led by a group of people from Guangdong Province who based their philosophy on their interpretation of Christianity. That was the Taiping Rebellion, which failed because of foreign intervention in China's affairs.

The original people's revolution of the twentieth century was planned by Dr. Sun Yatsen, who was not a Communist, and his Guomindang party was every bit as "red" and revolutionary as the Russian Bolshevik party was in 1917. Any assessment of the Chinese revolution that does not accept the popular nature of that upheaval or its beginnings cannot be valid.

In 1900, following the Boxer Rebellion, China was ripe for revolution. The Qing dynasty had lost all its vigor; the dowager empress was a venal old woman without a thought for the welfare of the people. As is noted in the text, Yuan Shikai, her trusted general and minister, who later became president of the first Chinese Republic, had ambitions of becoming emperor himself and tried to do so. Thus the original revolution of 1911 failed. It was not until Dr. Sun Yatsen set up his government in Guangzhou (Canton) that the Chinese revolution began to succeed, and it was not until after Dr. Sun's death, when Gen. Chiang Kaishek marched out on his northern expedition, that the Republic of China became national in character. Even so, several years elapsed before the Republic of China secured recognition by the imperial powers.

One of the important factors in the Chinese revolution's change of direction in the late 1920s was Chiang's campaign to exterminate the Communists. In 1927 the Comintern in Moscow advised the Chinese Communists to seize control of the revolution. The Communists had already moved into the three-city Wuhan complex. Although the government there was labeled "Nationalist," it was controlled by the Communists. Chiang Kaishek learned of the Communists' plans, and quite rightly deduced that the Communists would insist on establishing a government controlled by the Communist party. He broke with them and pledged to drive them out of China. After he began that struggle, the western powers became more comfortable, hoping that under the Republic of China they would retain their old imperialist positions. The deal was made; Chiang sacrificed the people's revolution in a bid for power and assistance in destroying the Communists.

This trade-off is one of the basic reasons that Chiang Kaishek's Guomindang government failed: The people of China were sick of foreign imperialism and wanted their country back. The victory of the Communists gave it to them.

During World War II some well-meaning Americans referred to the Chinese Communists as "no more than agrarian reformers," but that description was never accurate. Only for the purposes of national unity during the war against the Japanese did the Communists temporarily stop their land-reform program and their policy of dispossessing landlords. They never promised that they would change their basic policy, and they did not.

The fact is, however, that until the agrarian reform—dispossessing landlords and placing the land into the hands of the people who worked it— there was no chance that any revolution in China would succeed or that the people would have a better life than they had had for thousands of years before the twentieth century.

Certainly the Chinese revolution cost many lives; the Communists killed millions of people in their various campaigns of terror. Yet the Qing dynasty killed many people, too, as did the Guomindang government. The government specialized in killing Communists and hoped to wipe out every last one of them from Chinese soil. But by the 1940s, when the war raged in the Pacific, the Guomindang had lost its faith in the revolution, and the people of China had lost their faith in the Guomindang.

Americans have never bothered to understand the Chinese revolution. Because of that lack of interest, American policy in the late 1940s went completely astray as the United States was unable to comprehend the basic needs and fears of China. For example, China could not possibly have allowed an unfriendly government to exist in Korea, which was right next to the northeastern provinces and, because of Japanese control of both Korea and Manchuria in the past, was an area linked to China. Korea had always been linked to China; before the Japanese took control of it, the Korean kingdom had been a Chinese vassal state. Had President Harry S. Truman understood China, he would never have allowed Gen. Douglas MacArthur to turn the Korean police action into a vendetta against Communist governments, and there would not have been a Chinese-American war in the framework of the Korean war.

That is all behind us now, and the Chinese have become most forgiving about American stupidities of the past. There are areas of friction between the two governments, but there will always be areas of friction between any governments—some even exist between the United States and its closest ally, the United Kingdom. What is important about Chinese-American relations is that they are, by and large, good and growing better; there is enormous goodwill on both sides, now that the people of the United States have begun to shed their paranoia about communism.

In assessing those relations and China's internal policies, it would be a serious mistake to expect the emergence of a western-style democracy. China's government is Communist, and the Communist party has no intention of giving up control. Within the party there are still left and right factions, although their public character has been changing. The major dilemma of the Chinese Communist party (CCP) is how to achieve economic advances, as it has been proved that the Marxist-Leninist policies do not bring about economic progress. From the left wing's point of view, every economic and political reform is a danger to Communist control. This attitude will continue for some years, and it will bring about convolutions in China's internal policies. The thing to watch is not the government's rhetoric but its actions in opening doors and enforcing restrictions. As this is written, a number of the author's young Chinese friends are convinced that a new era marked by repression of intellectuals on political grounds is about to begin. The situation will be similar to that in the troubled years of 1986 and 1987. Already, the government has refused to permit many young people to travel abroad for study.

This policy is ultimately self-defeating, and the governors of China know it. Without education and exposure to foreign developments, China's economic progress will grind to a halt. That is the party's dilemma, and it is not an easy one to face. Yet the fact remains that despite the convolutions, the demand for reforms has lasted and grows stronger. The Deng Xiaoping leadership has proved this point.

In 1988 it seems most likely that the time is soon coming when China and Taiwan will be reunited, and that will end a difficult era for Americans. Deng Xiaoping has offered a "one-China, two-economic-systems" policy that appeals to many people on Taiwan. Also, there is a growing nostalgia among the transplanted mainland Chinese for reunion with their friends and relatives on the mainland. At the time of the recent Thirteenth Congress of the CCP in Beijing (Peking), the Nationalist government of Taiwan offered the people an olive branch: permission for Nationalist Chinese to visit the mainland.

China has many problems, and they will not be solved easily. When they are solved, it will be in a Chinese fashion, just as the Communist revolution took on a peculiarly Chinese pattern despite the efforts of the Comintern and the Kremlin.

CHINA'S ADMINISTRATIVE DIVISIONS

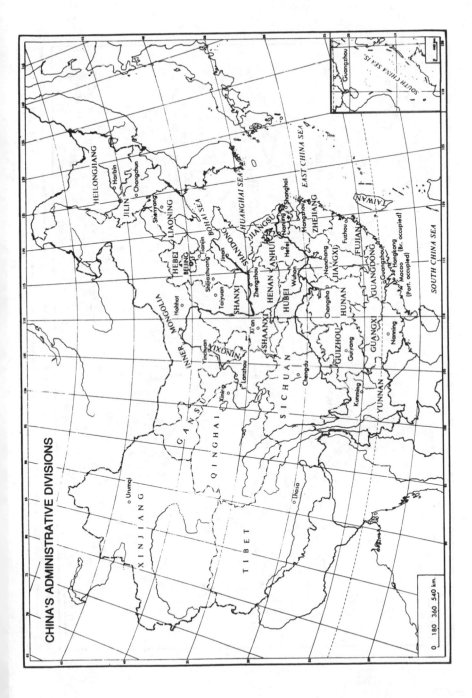

HEILONGJIANG		
Harbin		
JILIN		
Changchun		

SHENYANG

LIAONING

BOHAI SEA

INNER MONGOLIA

Hohhot

NINGXIA

Yinchuan

HEBEI
BEIJING
Tianjin

SHANDONG

Shijiazhuang

Jinan

HUANGHAI SEA

JIANGSU

Taiyuan

SHANXI

Zhengzhou

HENAN

ANHUI

Nanjing

Shanghai

Hangzhou

ZHEJIANG

EAST CHINA SEA

Xi'an

SHAANXI

Wuhan

HUBEI

Hefei

Lanzhou

GANSU

Xining

QINGHAI

Chengdu

SICHUAN

Changsha

HUNAN

Nanchang

JIANGXI

Fuzhou

FUJIAN

TAIWAN

GUIZHOU

Guiyang

Kunming

YUNNAN

GUANGXI

Nanning

GUANGDONG

Guangzhou

Hongkong (Br. occupied)

Macao (Port. occupied)

SOUTH CHINA SEA

Urumqi

XINJIANG

Lhasa

TIBET

0   180   360   540 km.

Guangzhou

SOUTH CHINA SEA IS.

0   240   480 km.

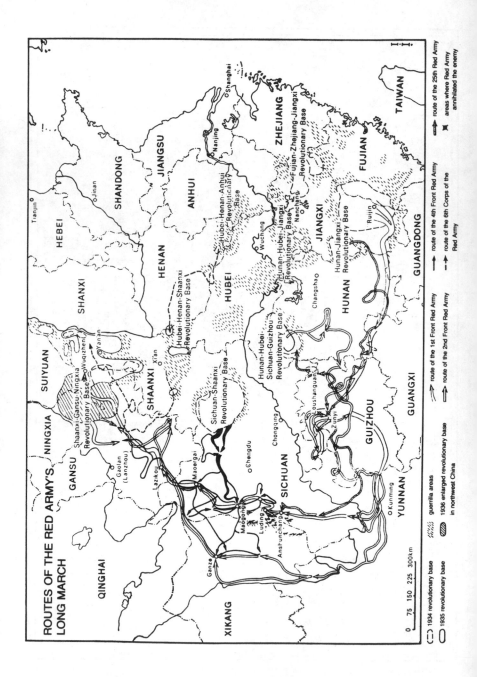

ROUTES OF THE RED ARMY'S LONG MARCH

Legend

- ⊏⊐ 1934 revolutionary base
- ◯ 1935 revolutionary base
- ∷∷ guerrilla areas
- ▨ 1936 enlarged revolutionary base in northwest China

- ⇒ route of the 1st Front Red Army
- → route of the 2nd Front Red Army
- ⇒ route of the 4th Front Red Army
- ⟶ route of the 6th Corps of the Red Army
- ⟹ route of the 25th Red Army
- ✳ areas where Red Army annihilated the enemy

Scale: 0 75 150 225 300km

Provinces and places

QINGHAI, XIKANG, YUNNAN, SICHUAN, GUIZHOU, GUANGXI, HUNAN, GUANGDONG, JIANGXI, FUJIAN, ZHEJIANG, JIANGSU, ANHUI, HENAN, HUBEI, SHANXI, SHAANXI, GANSU, NINGXIA, SUIYUAN, HEBEI, SHANDONG, TAIWAN

Tianjin, Jinan, Shanghai, Nanjing, Nanchang, Ruijin, Wuchang, Changsha, Chongqing, Chengdu, Kunming, Zunyi, Xi'an, Yan'an, Wuqizhen, Gaolan (Lanzhou), Lazikou, Maoergai, Maogong, Luding, Anshunchang, Ganzi, Loushanguan

Shaanxi-Gansu-Ningxia Revolutionary Base

Sichuan-Shaanxi Revolutionary Base

Hubei-Henan-Shaanxi Revolutionary Base

Hubei-Henan-Anhui Revolutionary Base

Hunan-Hubei-Jiangxi Revolutionary Base

Hunan-Hubei-Sichuan-Guizhou Revolutionary Base

Hunan-Jiangxi Revolutionary Base

Fujian-Zhejiang-Jiangxi Revolutionary Base

1
Collapse of the Old

The officials fear the foreigners, but the foreigners fear the people.

—Chinese saying, nineteenth century

Until the cultural revolution of the 1960s at least, the Chinese considered their society to be far superior to that of the west. When Europeans were running around in bearskins and fleeing the saber-toothed tiger, the Chinese said, China's civilization was producing art and literature.

It is true that by the sixteenth century (Ming dynasty) Chinese technological development was far superior to that of the west and had been for a long time. Joseph Needham's massive study of Chinese science and technology certainly proved that. In fact, this superiority had existed since the Song dynasty (960–1279), but Chinese technology stabilized after that and did not move much further.

That, of course, was the problem. In 1600 the Chinese had a far higher standard of living than the Europeans. Marco Polo and those westerners who followed him were dazzled, and with good reason. By 1800 China was, on the surface, the same, but the western world was not. The social system of China had ceased to be upwardly mobile, and beneath the calm facade was a powder keg. Economic problems prevented the improvement of the scene. The Qing dynasty, outwardly so powerful, proved totally unable to cope with the incursions from a dynamic western world, and by 1750 the end of China's Imperial rule was in sight. The military establishment had deteriorated so much that the westerners were able to dominate the country and actually wrench off chunks of China as colonies.

The problem was essentially an internal one. The rulers of China, bemused by the good life, forgot the basic precept that the only good government is one which brings constant improvement to the living and social standards of its people.

In the days of the Tang (618–907) and thereafter, the emperor's councillors would sit with him to discuss the problems of the empire. In the days of Song, the councillors stood at attention before their emperor at all times. Gone was every semblance of the old camaraderie. By 1400, the time of Ming, the emperor had become so lordly that his vassals kowtowed before him as he sat on his elevated throne. The atmosphere of Ming was truly oppressive; the court of Ming Taizu was so deadly that officials said goodbye to their families in the mornings before they went to court, and if they came home at night, they were congratulated for having survived one more day.

In this sense, the Qing dynasty, which began in 1644, was a decided improvement. The early Qing emperors returned to consultation with their officials and no longer let the eunuchs run the court. China was reunified, on the surface. Yet by this time the damage had been done, and popular resistance raised its head. In 1721 Zhu Yigui staged an armed uprising in Taiwan, and before it ended he had 300,000 men under arms.

Fifty years later Wang Lun, a leader of a revolutionary group called "The White Lotus," started a rebellion in western Shandong Province. He captured several cities, including Lingqing. This city, on the bank of the Grand Canal, was very important to the empire—it controlled the passage of goods up the canal to Beijing—so no time was lost by the Imperial government in suppressing the rebellion. Wang Lun died in the flames of his burning house, but the rebellion seethed on beneath the ashes. The next three-quarters of a century was marked by a number of revolutionary attempts, most of them regional, in Gansu, Taiwan, Guizhou, Henan, Sichuan. Some of the leaders, by the way, were women. One of them, Wang Conger, led a rebellion at Xiangyang for two years until, surrounded in the mountain area of Yunxi, she jumped from a cliff to her death. This period of rebellion by the White Lotus society lasted nine years and caused the Imperial government to spend 220 million *taels* of silver.*

The rebellions were staged, for the most part, by elements representing

---

*A tael equals 1.5 ounces. A tael of silver was the equivalent of 1,000 cash (copper coins on a string). A *picul* of rice (100 *catties*, or 33.5 pounds) sold for three taels of silver.

the common people, who suffered badly from the Imperial refusal to change an outmoded social system. Each decade the rebellions became more numerous and more serious. In 1813 Lin Qing, leader of the Sect of Heavenly Reason, had the audacity to attack the Imperial Palace in Beijing. His uprising was put down, but it represented a new trend: a blow at the Imperial system itself.

The Imperial answer to popular rebellion was to tighten the noose of control. Under the Song dynasty the *baojia* system had been established. Ten households in every community made up a *jia*, and ten jia made up a *bao*. Each jia was commanded by a person known to be loyal to the regime, and he reported to the bao chief, whose loyalty was also secure. Thus the people were under a very tight control which increased in the Qing period.

Qing Emperor Qian Long was particularly noted for his corrupt and dissolute life. So dedicated was he to the ultimate in luxury that he built seventy-two summer palaces throughout the empire. His reign was marked by new heights of corruption. He Shen, a minister of the privy council, amassed an enormous fortune by taking bribes. He had 120,000 acres of farmland and kept 184,000 taels of gold and 55,000 taels of silver in his household vault. Secretly, he also had an additional million taels of silver, as well as jewels, furs, and other valuables worth another 9 million taels, plus 600 pounds of ginseng. He owned forty lending houses, at which he charged usurious rates, and seventy-five pawnshops.

Corruption was the order of the day. By the end of Qian Long's rule, it was not even kept secret. When Emperor Jia Qing came to power, he announced that in 1811 more than half the annual budget of 30 million taels of silver appropriated for water control throughout the empire by his predecessor had been dissipated in bribes and corruption without a single benefit to the people.

The breakdown of public morality was accompanied by a breakdown in government. For example, in the enormously important matter of water control, the superintendents often destroyed the dykes in their regions to create an emergency and then requested huge outlays of funds to repair them. But the dykes were often not properly repaired, and the canal and water systems decayed rapidly. Such corruption festered in every aspect of the Imperial government.

So by the middle of the nineteenth century, when adventurers from Europe were surging around the world, the Chinese were set in a pattern of life and government that admitted little improvement. They acknowledged European technological advances with lip service only. The Mings and Qings employed modern firearms, but in so desultory a fashion that their military forces could not stand up against a European attack. There had been forecasts of the coming disaster: In 1533 the Portuguese occupied Macao; the Dutch seized Taiwan early in the seventeenth century; and a few years later the Russians invaded the Heilongjiang River region. But to the vast majority of Chinese, these events were almost unknown, occurring as they did on the fringes of empire.

Then late in the eighteenth century the privy council of King George III suggested to Qing Emperor Qian Long that Britain be allowed to send merchants to China and open trading establishments there. The Emperor replied in lordly fashion:

"The Celestial Empire possesses all things in prolific abundance and lacks no product within its borders. There is therefore no need to import the manufactures of outside barbarians in exchange for our own products."

This attitude meant that if the British wanted Chinese goods (which they did), they would have to pay for them in hard currency. The British East India Company, which enjoyed the monopoly of Chinese trade, found this restriction was draining its resources, so it searched for a way to change the system of trade. Soon enough the company learned that many Chinese were addicted to opium smoking, and it set about enlarging the vice in China. The company subsidized the growing of opium poppies in its India colony, and in 1781 made its first shipment of opium to China. The opium trade flourished from the beginning.

In 1800 Emperor Jia Qing banned the opium trade, but the Qing government by that time was so corrupt that the ban had little effect. It was a long way from Guangzhou, where the British traded, to Beijing, where the Qing government sat, and the local officials in the south were eager to enrich themselves. The import of opium into China soon reached 300 tons per year, or 4000 opium chests, each chest containing more than 100 pounds of poppy gum. Since a fraction of an ounce would put a strong man into dreamland, this figure represented an enormous drug trade. In fewer than 40 years, the figure had been multiplied ten times, and opium had become a national disaster in China. So great was the demand that opium constituted 57 percent of all Chinese imports from abroad. Emperor Qian Long may have been right when he said China did not need the produce of the barbarians. But by appealing to vice, the British (and the Americans) broke into the trade market.

In 1838 Qing Emperor Dao Guang became so alarmed at the drain of silver from the Chinese economy for opium that he appointed a special commissioner to deal with the problem. Lin Zexu was his name, and he was an honest official. He went to Guangzhou and immediately confiscated all the opium stock of British and American traders and burned it in a public bonfire on the beach.

The greasy black smoke was a signal to the British merchants that their livelihood was threatened. So in 1840, on the pretext that trade in vice was still legitimate trade, the British government sent troops and ships to China to enforce the principle of "free trade."

China then had its first major lesson in dealings with the outside world: the First Opium War.

From the outset the result was predictable. The western powers had been steadily building up their armed forces; China had not. Although a number of Chinese generals fought sturdily for two years, British power triumphed, and in the end China was forced to accept the Treaty of Nanjing on August 29, 1842. It was the first humiliation of the Imperial Dragon Throne in history. The British were given possession of Hong Kong island, and the Chinese government paid an "indemnity" of 21 million silver dollars. The humiliation was devastating, and would never be forgotten by the Chinese, but at the moment that factor seemed unimportant. The westerners had broken through the Chinese defenses against exploitation. That was the real message of the First Opium War: China was ripe for conquest.

The first moves came through five treaty ports. Guangzhou, Xiamen, Fuzhou, Ningbo, and Shanghai were opened to foreign trade. For the first time, barbarian ships could sail freely into these ports without special permission. Once they got there, the rates of tariff on the goods they brought in were established—not by the Chinese Imperial government but by mutual consent, which meant constant haggling. The Chinese government had given up its right to tax, and within a year the British had forced on China a limit of 5 percent on import duties. This meant that Chinese consumers could buy British goods more cheaply than similar goods produced in China. Thus there was no way the textile and metals factories could survive, except for those in such specialized areas as silk production. Cotton and steel, the sinews of civilization, were henceforth to be imported.

At the same time, the Imperial Chinese government sacrificed its sovereignty in another way. British nationals accused of crimes and misdemeanors in China would no longer be subject to Chinese law; they were to be turned over to British consuls and treated under British law. Thus the foreigners could do as they pleased in China. The humiliation of the *laobaixing*, the Chinese people, was enormous. It would last for a whole century, creating an antiforeign backlash that was still manifest in the years of the People's Republic.

The Americans were close on the British tail. In 1843 the American minister, Caleb Cushing, was sent to make a trade treaty that would give American merchants all the privileges that the British had. Using the same tactic that the British had employed—the threat of war—the Americans secured their treaty, the Treaty of Wangxia. They were to have equal treatment with the British. In fact, the American treaty further undermined Chinese independence, for the extraterritoriality provisions were extended (to protect American missionaries who were eager to exploit China for their religion). Soon enough France, Belgium, Sweden, and Norway, all demanded treaties, and they received them. China had lost control of its own external affairs.

2

The Taiping Rebellion

All the land under Heaven should be cultivated by the people under Heaven.

—Slogan of the Taiping rebels

The Europeans had so destroyed the power of the Qing dynasty, and caused the Imperial government to become so oppressive to the peasants, that a major rebellion was inevitable. It began in 1851. It was called the Taiping Rebellion, and it came close to overthrowing the Imperial government after more than a thousand years of virtually uninterrupted Imperial rule. It is safe to say that had it not been for foreign intervention, the Taiping Rebellion would have succeeded, and the history of China would have been advanced by at least fifty years.

In a sense the Ming and Qing dynasties had brought new ways to China, and with those ways came a respect for capitalism. But this was spotty, and in the south in particular the people who attempted to go into business were often ruined, usually by the government, through its policies of taxation and repression. Yet the concept of enterprise remained, even where it was in fact denied.

By the 1850s the breakdown of Chinese society had speeded up. In 1853, 80,000 chests of opium were sold in China, and the problem distressed many loyal Chinese. One of them, Zeng Guofan, wrote a memorial to the throne, suggesting that something should be done.

He warned of the widening distress of the people. Formerly, he said, by delivering three pecks of rice (¾ bushel) a peasant could pay the land tax on a *mu* (⅙ acre) of land. But in 1852 six pecks of rice (1.5 bushels) would not produce enough money to pay the tax. So the peasants had to borrow from their landlords, and the landlords charged usurious rates of interest. If the peasants borrowed in the spring, they had to repay by fall with 100 percent interest. Each year more families had to desert the land

7

and go begging. Others became bandits and revolutionaries, and many times they were both.

The cheap imports of cloth and metal goods from Europe wrecked the Chinese cottage-industry system. Within twenty years millions of weavers were unemployed. So were palmers. The transport of foreign goods in big ships wrecked the Chinese inland transportation system, and thousands of boatmen and porters were thrown out of work. Meanwhile, to keep up its expensive lifestyle, the Qing dynasty raised the people's taxes, the land tax in particular. The government also had to pay an annual indemnity to Britain, and soon enough that tax was doubled.

Out of the inequities, over the years, came the banding together of rebels, and in 1851 a full-scale people's rebellion broke out. It was the Rebellion of the Taiping Heavenly Kingdom, led by a rural intellectual of Guangdong Province named Hong Xiuquan. Oddly enough, it owed its genesis to a Christian tract, *Good Words for Exhorting the Age*, though Hong Xiuquan's interpretation of the text was not precisely that of the missionaries who had distributed it. After studying the book, Hong fell ill and had a vision: He was the second son of God, the brother of Jesus Christ, and he had been given instructions from Heaven to save mankind. He organized the Bai Shang Di Hui ("Society for the Worship of God"), gathered some friends around him, and went into Guangxi Province to organize and propagandize for the revolution. One of the precepts of the society was: "All men under Heaven are brothers and all women are sisters." The concept is not unlike that professed by John Locke, who had offered revolutionary ideas in England two centuries earlier.

Guangxi Province became the center of the rebellion. In 1850 the region was hit hard by drought, and the result was famine. After Qing Emperor Xian Feng succeeded Emperor Dao Guang, peasants in the area erupted in anger at the harsh strictures of the Imperial rule. By this time the Bai Shang Di Hui was well organized. On January 11, 1851, Hong Xiuquan led an insurrection in Jintian village and set himself up as "Heavenly King of the Kingdom of Taiping." In a short time the Taiping army held control of much of Guangxi. The Qing government reacted by sending in a large military force. The Imperial troops encircled the city of Yong'an, but the Taiping broke out and moved northward. A series of battles was fought across the route, from Guangxi to Hunan and into Hubei Province. The Taiping troops suffered losses (two of the generals were killed), but they laid waste to the Qing Imperial system, killing local officials and landlords and burning title deeds and loan papers referring to land. They robbed the wealthy and distributed the grain and money to the peasants. Naturally, the Taiping were regarded as saviors, and thousands of peasants enlisted in their army.

In January 1853, the Taiping army was again on the march. This time it captured Wuchang, the capital of Hubei Province; the city was considered too difficult to defend, so the army left it and moved eastward along the Yangtze River. Before the Taiping, the Qing forces collapsed, one after the other. In February the Taiping entered Nanjing and renamed it Tianjing ("Heavenly Capital"). Then came the complete breach: The Taiping declared a revolutionary government for all China.

In between the battles Hong was establishing a social system based on the redistribution of land. Everyone over 16 received a share of land, and each child received a half share. The land was divided into nine grades, according to fertility of the soil, and family units were given both fertile and infertile land to equalize the grants. The basic unit of land management and government was a village of twenty-five households; this block unit administered the law. Income from farm products and by-products was first devoted to the needs of the people. Any surplus was turned over to the local treasury to pay extra expenses of the village, such as wedding, funeral, and travel expenses. It was a communal society, dedicated to the proposition that "land, food, clothing and money should all be shared equally, and all under Heaven should be well fed and clad."

Almost immediately the land distribution system degenerated. The small size of its basic unit hampered the adequate production of crops. Even so, in the area controlled by the Taiping, the illusion of success remained, symbolized by the fall of the landlord and the refusal of most peasants to pay land rent.

One other precept of the Taiping was important in the history of China: Women had the same rights as men. The Qings regarded women as chattel, but not so the Taiping. Women walked in the streets like men, or they rode horseback, something that was not seen in Qing China. The Taiping prohibited prostitution and the buying and selling of women. Women were appointed to official posts, and they had the right to take examinations for higher office. In addition, a women's army was organized.

A new system of justice was established. Outside the *yamen*, the headquarters of government, hung two big drums. Anyone who had a complaint was free to strike a drum and demand justice from the magistrate. There were no lawyers; plaintiffs and defendants pleaded their own cases. And unlike Qing policies, there was no torture or cruel physical punishment for offenses.

One of the important facets of the Taiping Rebellion was its ability to draw on educated liberals who did not believe in the strictures of the Qings. Wei Changhui and Shi Dakai were members of the landowner class in China, but they cast their lot with the people. They were forerunners of the sort of intellectual who flourished in China in the early years of the twentieth century; among such people the Communist revolution would find many of its leaders.

In 1853 the Taiping sent an army on a northern expedition. It crossed Jiangsu, Anhui, Henan, and Shanxi provinces and threatened Tianjin, but here the Qings put up a stubborn defense, recognizing the very real threat to the capital at Beijing. The Taiping, who had begun their march in summer, without either grain supplies or winter clothing for the hard northern winter, withdrew to Shandong Province. In the spring they again attacked, but once more the Qings held, and once more when winter came the Taiping had to move south. So the great northern expedition, which held the key to Taiping success, failed after three years.

At the same time—1853—the Taiping sent an expedition west to guard the Anhui capital, Nanjing (Tianjing to the Taiping) from a flank attack. This expedition moved along the Yangtze River to Hankou and Hanyang and further into Hubei Province. But when the troops reached Hunan, they found themselves up against a determined and powerful Qing general, Zeng Guofan, who had organized the landlords of the province into a highly effective feudal army. The Qing forces drove the Taiping out of Hunan and then out of Hubei Province. But then Shi Dakai, the liberal general from the landlord class, brought up reinforcements who fought to a victory over the Qing army. By the middle of 1856 the Taiping were in control of most of Jiangxi and Anhui, and their position seemed quite secure.

In the wake of the successful Taiping Rebellion in the south, other regional leaders staged successful revolutions within the Qing empire in the 1850s. The Xiao Dao Hui ("Small Sword Society") of Shanghai took over the whole Shanghai region. But then the foreigners took a hand: British and French troops, siding openly with the Qing leaders, sent an expeditionary force to

Shanghai, defeated the Small Sword Society, and returned control to the Qing rulers. Thus western imperialism and Manchu imperialism worked hand in glove.

North China was the scene of the Nian revolt. The Nians were mostly bankrupt peasants and small landholders who had been impoverished by Qing policies. The final straw for many had been the flooding of the Huang He (Yellow River) in 1851; although millions of people were affected adversely, the Qings did virtually nothing to help them. But the northern expedition of the Taiping did help, and thus the Nians were able to put together a rebellion of their own. By 1855 they had established the Great Han regime, which combined several forces. This was the major element of anti-Manchu activity in north China, and it spread across eight provinces.

In the southwest, the Miao people rebelled in Guizhou Province in 1855. Soon the rebellion lost its racial overtones, and Han, Buyi, Dong, and Shui people joined up; they, in turn, were joined by the Hui people of Yunnan Province. The rebellion continued to spread through the southwest, where it persisted for many years.

The Taiping were taken seriously by western powers, and Britain, France, and the United States all sent ministers to Nanjing. Their purpose was to secure Taiping endorsement of the treaties already established by the western powers with the Qing rulers. The Taiping, however, refused to accept the import of opium, and they denied the extraterritoriality and other unequal provisions of the treaties with the west. The ministers went away empty-handed.

Only the British minister seemed to come to grips with the real problems. He visited Yang Xiuqing, the ruler of the eastern area of the kingdom, and asked for a statement of fundamental principles, which he received. Once the Taiping ruled all China, they would grant equal freedom of trade to all western nations and would negotiate the opening of treaty ports. But all obnoxious goods were to be banned, particularly opium, which was the lifeblood of western trade and the scourge of China.

The westerners decided to go to war. Stripped of all verbiage, this decision meant that the western powers were determined to enforce the misery of China for their own profit. It was as vile a policy as that of the slave trade, which Britain and other nations had not long ago abandoned with many professions of virtue. One might say that the specter of drug addiction which haunts the western world in the twentieth century is the western nations' comeuppance for what they did to China in the nineteenth century.

In the end, the very virtues of the Taiping Rebellion were the seeds of its downfall. Had the Taiping succumbed to the westerners' demands to continue the opium trade and the many concessions, the situation might have been just as bad. But perhaps in this way the Taiping could have bought time, dealing with the Europeans, until sufficient strength had been achieved and then denying them what they wanted.

The Taiping chose instead to stand on principle, and the western powers' representatives went home to tell their governments that the future of trade and western well-being in China depended on maintaining the Qing dynasty. The western powers then set about instigating the Second Opium War, which was a bald effort to secure more concessions from the Chinese government and thus to line the coffers of more European merchants. In 1854 the British, not satisfied with the millions of pounds they were already making in China, insisted that the Chinese legalize the opium trade, provide channels for regular direct contact with the Qing government (which meant the establishment of embassies in Beijing), and open more ports for foreign trade and influence. The Chinese government refused, and so, on the pretext that British rights had been violated, the British and the French sent fleets of warships to China.

On October 8, 1856, the Chinese navy captured the *Arrow* off Guangzhou. Although the *Arrow* was a Chinese vessel, it was, in fact, under charter to the British and was flying the British flag. So the British, with plenty of troops in the area, took a high and mighty attitude.

On October 13 the British marched to Beijing. As a result, more concessions were granted. The British annexed the Kowloon mainland area, across from Hong Kong island, to the Hong Kong colony. They secured the right to trade in Tianjin. They established the "coolie labor trade," by which indentured laborers were shipped abroad. One of the principal beneficiaries of this trade was the sugar industry of Hawaii, dominated by British and American growers. French missionaries were given the right to buy land and build churches in China. And the greedy western powers increased the Chinese indemnities to 8 million silver taels each year to Britain and 8 million to France, bringing the Qing government nearly to bankruptcy.

They bombarded Guangzhou and occupied the city. The fighting was brisk, the looting was brisker, until the local people joined forces with the troops and drove the westerners out.

The westerners, determined to open the door to China wider, used any pretext to justify the dispatch of warships and troops. The French discovered that the Chinese had killed a priest in Guangxi, an intolerable affront to the French flag. Soon foreign troops—British, French, Russian, and American—were moving around in China. In December 1857 a British-French force of 5000 attacked Guangzhou. This was Qing country, but the Qing forces in south China were extremely weak, since the Taiping held so much of the territory. So Guangzhou fell to the invaders with very little effort. The unrest was widespread. Peasants and villagers in Guangdong Province set out to fight the foreigners. In Hong Kong, workers in the British factories went on strike.

But the westerners were adamant. They sent their invasion force up toward Tianjin, and it reached the Dagu forts in May 1858. When the British announced that they were planning to move on Beijing, the Qing court sent emissaries and the Treaty of Tianjin was signed. This treaty gave the British more trade ports: Yingkou, Yantai, Tainan, Danshui, Hankou, and others. The next day, June 27, the French signed an almost identical treaty with the Chinese government of the Qings.

At the same time, the United States and Russia negotiated treaties which gave them more favorable rights in China. The Russians were after territory; their new treaty provided for a commission to study the "uncharted" border. Thus the Russians reinforced their claim to territory that had been Chinese for generations. The treaty, in effect, rationalized another accord that had been reached in May 1858. The Russian governor general of eastern Siberia, acting on his own, had forced General Yishan, in the northeastern Heilongjiang region, to sign the Treaty of Aihui, which gave the Russians another 600,000 square kilometers of Chinese territory, south of the Outer Xinan mountain range and north of the Heilongjiang River. Further, the Russians demanded that the Chinese admit that another 400,000 square kilometers, from the eastern side of the Wusuli River to the sea, was under "Sino-Russian joint control." This gave the Russians a river as large as the Danube. They had all the extraterritorial rights of the other countries. They secured trading posts in Kulun and Zhangjiakou, in Hebei Province, just a few miles from Beijing, and they established a consulate at Kashgar in Xinjiang.

So the Russians had taken a million square kilometers of Chinese territory, more than the combined area of France and Germany, and they had begun moving into large areas in the northwest. Thus was established a basic enmity which would affect Russian-Chinese relations for more than a century, even until the last quarter of the twentieth century. For once they had annexed this territory, the Russians began to believe it belonged to them.

In 1859 the westerners were back again. The United States has long claimed that it did not interfere in Chinese affairs in the nineteenth century, but the fact is that this "noninterference" was an illusion. The Americans lent their military presence to the British and French in 1859 when warships from those countries once again bombarded the Dagu forts. This time the Chinese forts acquitted themselves with honor, damaging many of the enemy ships and inflicting 500 casualties. The British and French sailed away, and the Americans, who had not actually participated, followed them. Yet the American protestations of innocent intent continued.

The British and French returned in the following year. The Americans were already on the verge of civil war, so they did not join in.

This foray of 1860 has gone down in history as one of the west's most vicious assaults on the east. Under the leadership of Gen. Charles George "Chinese" Gordon, the British expeditionary force landed at Dagu in July 1860 and marched to Beijing. Emperor Xian Feng fled to Chengde, Hebei Province. The British and French entered the Adningmen gate of Beijing and made their way through the city, looting as they went. They destroyed the Yuan Ming Yuan summer palace.

More concessions were made by Prince Gong, the Emperor's brother. More indignities were forced on the Chinese. More indemnities were paid, once again enriching the foreigners and threatening the livelihood of China.

By the end of 1860 China, in total disarray, was really a vassal state of the west. Seven coastal provinces were wide open to foreign trade on the most favorable conditions for the westerners. The customs service of China was under foreign control, which meant that the Qing government had lost control of its own power of taxation. Britain, France, and Russia maintained embassies at Beijing which developed enormous power through the Zongli Yamen, a body established by the Qings to deal with foreign affairs and presided over by Prince Gong.

In the summer of 1861 Emperor Xian Feng died of illness, and China went into yet another phase of dissolution. The new emperor, Zai Chun, was still a child, so his affairs were managed by Dowager Empress Ci Xi

(Tzuhsi). She had begun life as the daughter of a minor Manchu official cashiered during the Taiping Rebellion for failing his post before the enemy, but she later became a concubine of the fifth rank to Emperor Xian Feng. In April 1856 she gave birth to the emperor's only son, which made her his favorite concubine and a power within the palace. Soon after Xian Feng's death in 1861 she was conspiring with Prince Gong and planning a coup d'état which would give her power. With British and French support she parlayed this into a *tong zhi* ("joint reign") with the child emperor. Then, with foreign support, the throne set out to suppress the Taiping Rebellion, which was regarded by the foreigners as anathema. For years they had been searching for a way to destroy the Taiping, and now they had the willing assistance of the Qings, who certainly must have known the price.

Down in Nanjing, the Taiping were having their own problems. In 1856, after six years of military successes, the Taiping leadership had begun to unravel. Several of the generals demanded more honors, particularly Yang Xiuqing. A furious Hong Xiuquan ordered Yang killed; he was, along with about 20,000 of his followers. But this action created a reign of terror which had its own reaction. Shi Dakai, one of the most prominent generals, broke with the Taiping leadership over it. Although the damage was apparently repaired, in reality the effects lingered on. The Taiping leadership fell into disarray, and in 1857 the army suffered its first major defeat in actions against the Imperial troops at the Dadu River. Shi Dakai was killed in battle.

The Taiping, though in decline, had recently won several important battles, and in 1861 they occupied most of southern Jiangsu. Still, the foreigners were determined to help the Qing government overcome the Taiping. An American, Frederick T. Ward, recruited a foreign rifle detachment, while the Russians supplied the Qing government with 10,000 rifles and 50 cannon. The Taiping fought around Shanghai and for a time seemed to be winning, but in 1864 the Qing manpower, combined with foreign money and military supplies, finally triumphed. Hangzhou fell, then Zhenjiang, Suzhou, and Changzhou. More and more foreign mercenaries were employed by the Qing forces, and they were good fighters. In July 1864 the Taiping capital at Tianjing (Nanjing) fell to the Qing troops and the mercenaries. The Taiping remnants continued to fight until 1868 and other rebels carried on until 1873, but with the central core of the rebellion gone, they were defeated one by one.

*   *   *

Taiping had been the largest and most successful rebellion of the common people in China's history. It failed because its leaders were unable to deal with the problems of administration and management of the area they had conquered. By the time the Taiping had been defeated, the Qing empire was but a shell, riddled with intrigue and incapable of carrying on progressive government. China, in reality, was in the hands of the foreigners.

Years later, assessing the causes of the Taiping defeat, historians of the Chinese People's Republic attributed the decline to three factors:

1. The fall of the Taiping leaders into dissolute lives
2. Their loss of egalitarian ideals and revolutionary spirit. Once lost, that spirit was gone forever. During the Second Opium War they tried to recoup, but they could not regain the support of the people that had come so easily before.
3. The support of the foreign governments and foreign mercenaries. The foreigners supplied modern gunboats and cannon to the Qing forces. They sent western-trained officers to train the Qing troops. Two of the most effective of these were the American Frederick Townsend Ward and the British officer Charles George Gordon.

The Taiping Rebellion had been costly to China. The loss of life was estimated at more than 20 million people, making it the single most destructive civil war in the history of the world. So many peasants were killed in south China that large areas of farmland lay untilled for the next twenty years.

But theoretically, by the middle of the 1860s, the Qing dynasty was once again serene, in control of the Chinese empire, and ready to progress. The leaders of the Qing government had high hopes that out of the turmoil of the past could come a united China, which would grow strong and mold itself in the pattern of the modern industrial world. That was the face they adopted in the last quarter of the nineteenth century.

3

The Decline of the Manchus

Our empire is now labouring under great difficulties which are becoming daily more and more serious. The various powers cast upon us looks of tigerlike voracity, hustling each other in their endeavors to be the first to seize upon our innermost territories.

—Empress Ci Xi, November 11, 1899

By 1895 the devil's compact made by the Qing emperors with the western powers for aid in suppressing the Taiping Rebellion was ripe for collection. In the 1860s and 1870s the brightest of the men surrounding the Qing Imperial throne had had high hopes for a revival of Manchu spirit and Chinese power, but something happened on the way to the modern world.

The program as planned was to be administered by the throne and foreign office. It was termed *yangwu*—"foreign matters." The first phase was *ziqiang* ("self-strengthening"), and it involved the purchase and manufacture of weapons for China's arsenals. Foreign advisers were imported, and so was machinery. But the advisers soon found themselves more interested in self-enrichment, and the machinery was often antiquated or of poor quality. Nor was the military buildup accompanied by any general improvement in the economy. The result was the manufacture and purchase of weapons of very poor quality at very high cost.

The second stage of the Manchus' self-improvement program was *fuqiang* ("wealth and power"). Several joint enterprises—including shipping, trade, and mining—were established between the Qing government and private Chinese capital. But the inflexibility of the Qing system prevented the success of these capitalistic ventures. The investors were limited to 10 percent profit, and millions of dollars were stolen by the officials who were in control. So the enterprises languished.

The third phase of the Chinese improvement movement involved the creation of a navy and the establishment of modern steel mills. By 1894 the Chinese had a fleet of sixty-seven ships, divided into four squadrons.

17

The size of the navy was illusory, however, as it was badly manned and most of the ships were antiquated. For example, the steam gunboats built by the foreigners in China for the Chinese navy were so badly constructed that they could not be steered in a rough sea. At the same time, the westerners took unbridled advantage of all they learned in China. In the 1870s the French built a shipyard for the Chinese at Fuzhou. When war erupted between China and France in 1884, the first thing the French did was pull out the plans of the shipyard and then bombard it, destroying the fleet the Chinese had built and the shipyard installations.

Accompanying this three-part program came demands from within the Qing establishment for reforms to match. Opposition to the devil's compact made with the west was voiced by a number of prominent men, including Wang Tao of Suzhou, Xue Fucheng of Wuxi, and Zheng Guanying of Xiangshan. They opposed concessions to the foreigners, seeing them as dangerous to the empire. They asked for the abolition of the unequal treaties that had already made China an economic vassal of the west. They asked for abolition of the state capitalism that had evolved, in which officials actually controlled the enterprises and the investors had no say. They advocated the development of Chinese capitalism as the only way to avoid the colonization of their country by the west. They also called for the establishment of a constitutional monarchy in China to replace the feudal system of the Qings.

Unfortunately, these calls fell on deaf ears. The Qing rulers—especially the dowager empress—saw no reason to change their lives or their manner of rule. Thus, while China and Japan both recognized that change was needed to accommodate themselves to the western incursions, their methods and attitudes were entirely different. The followers of the Japanese emperor rose up in a rebellion that cast out the Tokugawa Shogunate, which had given indications of yielding to the foreigners. The Japanese Meiji emperor gathered around him the best minds in his kingdom; they brought in the foreigners, used them, and then cast them out. From the beginning of the Japanese modernization program, the Japanese were in charge. The concepts of extraterritoriality and trade concessions, although introduced into Japan, never stuck there and soon were abandoned. The Japanese state was too vigorous to be colonized.

The Chinese empire was not. Since the days of the Khans, five hundred years of Imperial rule had sapped the empire of its vigor. China's armies were mercenary in nature; Japan's new army was nationalistic. The Chinese revered the quiet arts, scholarship, painting, the sciences. "Good iron is not used for nails, and good men do not become soldiers" was the adage. So Japan grew strong, modeling its army on the Prussian army and its navy on the British navy, but always maintaining control of personnel and resources; while China allowed the foreigners to lead it down tortuous paths and its own officials to sink into new corruptions. Principal among the corrupt was the dowager empress herself, whose power was built on the corruption of the palace eunuchs and major scholars. She was the power behind the throne of Qing, for in 1861 when the Emperor Guang Xu came to the throne, he was only 5 years old. By scheming and even murder, the dowager empress held the reins of power for the next third of a century. Steadily the power of the empire declined. Steadily the best minds turned themselves inward or to rebellion. The relative positions of the two great eastern empires were displayed for the world in the Sino-Japanese war of 1894.

For a number of years various nations, including the United States, had landed troops on Taiwan island and held control for a time. But always the island had reverted to Qing rule.

In 1894 the Japanese and the Chinese staged a confrontation in Korea. It began with a call from the Korean kingdom to Beijing for help when a peasant uprising threatened the royal power. This uprising was actually indigenous, but the Japanese saw in it a way to help their own cause. The Japanese sent a military force in a hurry, without being asked.

The Chinese dallied. By the time the Qing force reached Seoul the uprising had ended and the Japanese were in charge, 18,000 strong. The Japanese military force outnumbered the Chinese 6 to 1—an indication of the different military philosophies of the two countries. Japan was bent on the conquest of Korea.

The Chinese soon learned that and proposed the evacuation of that country by both armies. The Japanese refused. Then came an incident or two, on land and on sea. War with China was formally declared on August 1, 1894, by the imperial Japanese government, but already Japan had followed the old samurai adage: "Win first, fight later."

From the beginning of the landings of the two military forces in Korea, the Chinese forces were outclassed by the Japanese. There was no mystery involved: The Japanese had been working steadily at building a modern army and navy. The old samurai system had been outlawed, and a conscript army—a people's army—had been put in its place. It was democratic in concept—a soldier could rise to become a general—quite unlike the Chinese concept, in which court rank was everything.

In July, at the start of the confrontation on land, the Japanese attacked the Chinese Yashan, and the Chinese retreated to Pyŏngyang. Chinese and Koreans resisted there, but by the end of September the Chinese had fled north and crossed the Yalu River into Manchuria.

At sea, operations had opened even before the formal declaration of war. Indeed, the Japanese naval pattern indicated precisely the huge difference between China and Japan just then.

When the Chinese government had received its call from the Korean kingdom for help, Beijing had replied in a letter which described Korea as "a tributary state of China." This statement infuriated Japanese Prime Minister Ito, who called together the chiefs of army and navy and asked how they felt about war. They, in turn, called together their senior officers. All were in favor of war—even, as seemed likely at the moment, if the Russians came in on the side of China. So determined was Japan's military establishment, just thirty years after the modernization had begun, that the leaders would risk anything to bring their country to the new standards of imperialism promulgated by the western powers. So on July 23, 1894, the Japanese fleet sailed from Sasebo on Kyushu with the admiral's message ringing in the men's ears: "Add to the fame of the Imperial navy," said Admiral Kakayama.

That was not a very hard task. Although the Imperial Japanese navy had so far not accomplished much of anything, this time the naval officers vowed that they would bring home a victory—even though they did not yet have a war. Outside land, the three armored cruisers *Yoshino, Akitsushima,* and *Naniwa* left the main fleet and headed for Yashan, where the Japanese were landing troops. They were really looking for Chinese ships bearing Chinese troops.

The three cruisers arrived at Yashan on the morning of July 25. It was misty but still fine weather, and a light breeze was blowing. Soon two ships were seen coming out of Yashan Strait: the 2300-ton steel Chinese cruiser *Ji Yuan* and the 1200-ton gunboat *Guang Yi.* For some reason the two Chinese ships headed directly toward the Japanese squadron, although it had to be apparent that the Japanese force was much stronger.

Then came a disputed action. Who fired the first shot? The Chinese say the Japanese did, and this seems most likely, for the commander of the cruiser *Naniwa* was Capt. Heihachiro Togo, a very ambitious and very able naval officer. After all, had not his admiral said that he was to seek new fame for the Imperial navy?

Anyhow, it did not matter who fired the first shot, because in a few moments the air was full of shells. All three Japanese cruisers were firing on the *Ji Yuan*, and soon the ship caught fire. Its secondary guns never did fire, but the *Ji Yuan* came on toward the Japanese bravely enough, as if ready to fire.

The mist settled in and became fog, and the two Chinese ships disappeared from view. Both had been hit. Then Captain Togo saw them come out of the mist, and he ran up a flag: "Request freedom to maneuver."

The request was granted, and Togo headed the *Naniwa* out after the *Ji Yuan*. Togo's ship was followed by the *Yoshino*. The Japanese were overhauling the Chinese vessel when suddenly the Chinese ran up a white flag.

Surrender!

Or was it?

The *Ji Yuan* did not slacken speed, but continued to try to escape. Once again it threatened to disappear in the fog.

Just then Togo's lookouts spotted two more ships coming up. One was a Chinese sloop called the *Cao Jiang*; the other was a British merchant ship, the *Gaosheng*. Togo steered toward this convoy, since the *Ji Yuan* seemed to be getting away.

The British merchant ship made no attempt to escape. It represented the most powerful naval nation in the world, and its captain believed his ship had nothing to fear from anyone. But Captain Togo stopped the *Gaosheng*, and when he boarded the vessel, he discovered that it was carrying 1100 Chinese soldiers.

In the discussions that followed, aboard ship and by flag signal, it was established that the Chinese officials aboard the British ship had seized power and that the British crew was no longer in charge. Two hours later the *Naniwa* opened fire on the British merchantman, and after a few rounds the *Gaosheng* began sinking. The situation ended with the Chinese shooting other Chinese aboard the ship, and the British crew escaped. Captain Galsworthy, the master of the vessel, was picked up by the *Naniwa*.

Later, the British captain testified in a Japanese court that he had been prevented from surrendering the ship by a Chinese general. Long after the event Togo, who was by that time an admiral, was reproached for his failure to rescue Chinese survivors and for attempts to kill them in the water (as was charged).

But the battle was over. The Chinese had failed to deliver their troops. The Japanese military occupation went ahead. And Heihachiro Togo became the first national Japanese hero in the Japanese war against China.

Then, on September 17, came the Battle of the Huang He. The Japanese fleet was cruising in the Bay of Korea, off Haiyang, when lookouts sighted smoke. It was the Chinese fleet. The two fleets approached one another. The Chinese fleet included five of the new ironclad cruisers, wooden ships with iron belts of armor to protect the hulls. The Chinese also had seven unarmored ships, four torpedo boats, and three gunboats. The Japanese had seven ironclads, one small unarmored cruiser, two old armored ships, a gunboat, and an auxiliary cruiser, which was nothing more than a renamed passenger steamer mounting a gun. Although the Chinese fleet had heavier armor, the Japanese ships carried bigger and more modern guns and the gunners knew how to use them.

Before noon the two fleets met. The Chinese fleet was manned by Chinese sailors, but there were many foreign officers aboard. This probably created confusion, because of language difficulties and the reluctance of Chinese sailors to take orders from foreigners. The Japanese fleet, on the other hand, was purely Japanese, and had no such problems.

The Japanese came up obliquely to the Chinese, firing on the horizontal line of Chinese ships that cut round the corner, thus making it possible to "cross the T" and fire on all the Chinese ships at once from various positions. (The Japanese said this was because the Chinese admiral had failed to remember "all" his instructions from the foreigners, and this may be correct.)

Soon the fleets opened fire—the Chinese first, from a distance too far to be effective. The Japanese were firing on and hitting the Chinese ships, and the battle cruiser *Yang Wei* was soon afire. Then the battle cruiser *Chao Yong* burned, and at 1 p.m. it sank. By midafternoon, Admiral Ding, the Chinese naval commander, had lost four ships, including two light cruisers. The rest of the Chinese fleet escaped to Port Arthur (Dalian), the Russian-held port on the Liaodong Peninsula, for repairs.

The Japanese milled about but did not accomplish anything more. The Chinese had not been inactive in the battle; even though their armament was not as strong as that of the Japanese, the Chinese gunnery was better than their guns. The Japanese had lost four ships to the exigencies of battle; they were out of the fight, although not destroyed. The flagship *Matsushima* was badly damaged, and fifty men had been killed by a Chinese shell.

By late afternoon the battle was really over, and the Japanese had won. At about dusk they decided to break off the action. The Chinese headed toward the port of Weihaiwei, the base on the northern side of the Shandong Peninsula.

Morning came, and the Japanese were off the Korean coast. The Chinese admiral arrived at Port Arthur and announced that he had won a victory, but the fact was that four Chinese ships had been lost and many others suffered serious damage. A thousand men had been killed.

The *Matsushima* had suffered most among the Japanese vessels. The *Akagi*, the *Saikyo Maru*, and the *Hiei* were also damaged badly. The Japanese casualties were 90 killed and 204 wounded. The really important matters were that the Japanese fleet was in command of the Huang He and the Russians had not intervened on the side of the Chinese, as the Japanese expected them to do.

For the next few months the Sino-Japanese war continued. Ultimately, the Chinese asked for peace, and a treaty was signed on April 17, 1895.

In the final naval fighting, Admiral Ito, the Japanese commander, addressed a frank letter to Admiral Ding, the Chinese naval commander.

> The present condition of your country is not due to the faults of a few leaders, but is beyond question the outcome of your system of government. You appoint a man to office in consideration, solely, of his literary eruditions, which is an immemorial custom. Those in power are all accomplished men of letters. I do not argue that this system is altogether bad, and no doubt it was good for just so long as your country remained in isolation; but it is now archaic. Moreover, in the present condition of the world, it is not possible for any country to live in isolation.

There was much more. The essence was that if Admiral Ding would surrender, he would live to fight another day. But Admiral Ding said he would die rather than surrender at Weihaiwei. So the Japanese attacked on February 5 and 6, and five Japanese torpedo boats sank first the *Ding Yuan* and then three other Chinese warships. On February 7 the main Japanese fleet attacked. The Chinese responded with an attack by twelve torpedo boats. It was a brave attempt, but the Japanese cruisers sank or captured ten of the torpedo craft. During the next four days the Japanese bombarded the Weihaiwei base incessantly, reducing the Chinese holdings to a single fort at the western end of the harbor. This fort, Huang Tao, was still fighting when the cruisers *Naniwa* and *Akitsushima* came in to attack again. This time they were met by a Chinese gunboat flying a flag of truce. The boat carried what purported to be a message from Admiral Ding to Admiral Ito; actually the message was forged.

It was my intention to fight to a finish, desisting only when all my ships were sunk and all my men dead. But I cannot bring myself to cause the death of thousands more. I surrender to your forces one warship, the island of Liugong, the forts and their armament. I ask you most earnestly to put an end to the fighting and to let soldiers, sailors and the local inhabitants return to their homes and live in peace.

After delivering the message, the two envoys from Admiral Ding collapsed and slept in the chairs of the Japanese flagship wardroom. They had not been to bed for ten days. The fact was that Admiral Ding was already dead. He had fought to the end, and then committed suicide.

Believing that Ding was still alive, Admiral Ito sent back a message:

I am agreeable to all your proposals. When all arms have been handed over, my ships will take you and yours under their protection, and will escort you to whatever destination suits you best. But as I suggested the other day, the best solution for the future well being of your country would be for you to come to mine and there await the end of the war. Nevertheless if such be not your wish, I have no desire to force such a decision.

This message was sent back to the Chinese admiral with a gift of a case of champagne and cakes. The next morning, the Chinese gunboat appeared once more, again flying its white flag but carrying only one of the Chinese envoys. He returned the champagne and cakes, and had a new message for Admiral Ito, purportedly from Admiral Ding:

I have received your message and, in the name of my men, thank you from the bottom of my heart. I regret my inability to accept the gift

you so kindly sent and I beg you to consent to receive it back with this
message and my thanks for your excellent intention.

And the Chinese envoy had a message of his own. This one was truthful.

Our admiral was grateful for your kindness and declared that he now
had nothing more to regret. He then turned toward Beijing and, having swallowed poison, died.

The body of Admiral Ding was placed aboard a Japanese transport and
carried toward China. The transport also carried the remaining senior officers of the Chinese fleet, left at liberty by Admiral Ito. As it steamed out
of Weihaiwei, the Japanese fleet gave the transport a funereal salute, the
guns booming out slowly and dramatically. Flags aboard the Japanese vessels were lowered to half-mast, as Admiral Ito saluted a gallant enemy.

But when the ship reached Tianjin, and the officers went ashore in China,
they were brought before the Imperial court and summarily beheaded for
losing the battle of Weihaiwei. Thus was the dowager empress avenged,
not on the Japanese enemy but on her own people.

The Sino-Japanese war went on, fought on land in Manchuria. The
Japanese invaded Taiwan with cruisers led by Heihachiro Togo, who had
been made a rear admiral, and they took the island. The war ended, and
the peace negotiations began.

The Chinese were very lucky in a way. In Japan a zealous nationalist
Japanese assassin fired a shot at Chinese peace negotiator Li Hongzhang
and wounded him. The Japanese were so embarrassed that they reduced
their demands in the peace treaty. Still, the treaty provided for the cession
of the Liaodong Peninsula and Taiwan, as well as the Pescadores Islands,
to Japan. Korea was to become "independent" of Chinese authority—which
meant the Japanese were to have a free hand there.

After the treaty was signed the Russians took a hand. They wanted the
Liaodong Peninsula, so they warned the Japanese against taking it. The
Japanese backed away, quietly promising themselves that this would not be
the last of it.

So the Sino-Japanese war established Japan's military force as a modern one, in many ways equal to those of the European nations. Japan had

learned its lessons well. In less than thirty years the country had risen from feudalism to a modern society capable of carrying on a modern war.

China, on the other hand, was now regarded by the European nations the way a falcon regards a wounded bird. As Lord Rosebery, the British Foreign Minister, summed it up, "There we have a sick man...as a commercial inheritance, priceless, beyond all the ivory and peacocks that ever came out of Africa."

The Europeans rushed in.

Russian and French banks put up the money for China to pay its war indemnity to Japan. In return, France got the right to run railroads from Indochina up to Nanjing and Kunming. Russia got the right to build the Trans-Siberian Railroad through northeast China to Vladivostok. Britain and Germany lent China money to pay the second installment of the Japan indemnity, so they too received concessions. Soon all the powers were vying to "help" China, in order to get more bites of territory and rights inside China.

In 1897, using the by then common excuse that missionaries had been murdered, the Germans seized Qingdao on the Shandong Peninsula. They extended its perimeters and called the colony Kiaouchao (Jiaozhou). The Russians countered by taking Lüshun and Dalian, which they called Port Arthur. They also got the right to build a railway into south Manchuria, which brought the whole northeast area of China under Russian control.

Seeing this, the British seized Weihaiwei and France seized Guanzhouwan on the south China coast, where Zhanjiang is now located. The French declared the provinces of Yunnan, Guangdong, and Guangxi under French "influence," which was a warning to all other foreigners not to try to exploit the resources there. Britain added another 1000 square kilometers to its Hong Kong colony at Chinese expense.

By 1898, then, China seemed in danger of being carved up completely by the European powers and Japan.

At this time the American government issued its "open-door" policy toward China, which said in effect that whatever other countries got, America wanted too.

———

In 1898 Emperor Guang Xu was persuaded by reformers to inaugurate what was called "the Hundred Days' Reform." It was a direct response to the German occupation of Qingdao, and the purpose was to secure public support for the government and thus forestall further foreign incursions. The emperor ordered the dissolution of many useless offices, the modernization of the army, and the establishment of new colleges and universities in the modern pattern. Beijing University was founded at this time. The Confucian classics were no longer to be the sole source of wisdom; foreign books were introduced.

But from the beginning the reforms were opposed by Dowager Empress Ci Xi. In fact, they became the focal point of the battle for power in the palace between the dowager empress and the young emperor. In the struggle that followed, half a dozen of the most prominent advocates of reforms were murdered by the order of the dowager empress and the reform movement collapsed. The only thing left was Beijing University, a solitary monument to a gallant attempt at change.

The dowager empress was now supreme in China, the young emperor having lost most of his influence. But she soon enough learned that even her powers were limited by public opinion. The response to the failure of the reform movement and the German colonization of part of Shandong Province was a series of uprisings. From this developed the movement of Yi He Quan ("Righteous and Harmonious Fists"), known in the west as the Boxer Rebellion.

The Boxers were a semireligious organization, practicing martial arts but believing in incantations and amulets that were supposed to defend them from the modern weapons of the westerners. Their protector was Governor Yuxian of Shandong Province, a protégé of the dowager empress, so one might say that they enjoyed from the beginning at least the left-handed support of the dowager empress. The reason for this was her own basic distrust of and dislike for the foreigners, who were snipping off bits of the empire year after year.

After two years the Boxer movement had spread through northern China and Manchuria. In the spring of 1900 a number of Boxers came to Beijing. They set up altars on the streets, where they practiced martial arts and made weapons out in the open. They began to attack Catholic and Protestant churches.

Nervously, the foreign embassies protested to the Forbidden City. They were informed by the dowager empress's spokesmen that she did not like the Boxers and would suppress them just as soon as they committed some overt actions. Privately, however, she approved of them. She saved face by ordering their reorganization into the Yi He Tuan ("Righteous and Harmonious Militia").

The foreigners did not entirely trust the old woman in the Imperial Palace. They pressed until she replaced her favorite in Shandong with a new governor, Yuan Shikai. He led a force of 7000 men to Shandong and suppressed the Boxers there. But the Boxers kept moving and kept infiltrating the local militia. They gained power swiftly. In Zili the movement grew very strong, and soon its flag was flying over many villages. Landlords and others began flocking to join this basically peasant movement. As it grew, it became more xenophobic. The Boxers rejected modernism in every way, and they demanded the ouster of the foreigners from China. They continued to attack the missionaries, but they attacked even more strongly the Chinese converts to Christianity.

By the end of 1899 the Boxer movement had seized the imagination of north China. The dowager empress decided to use it for her own reasons, because she was furious with Britain and Japan, which were opposing her plan to dethrone the emperor and seize total power for herself.

So the Boxer movement grew in Beijing and Tianjin. It also grew in Shandong, spreading to Shanxi, Shaanxi, Hunan, and Inner Mongolia. The north was aflame with emotion against the foreigners.

From the foreign embassies in Beijing, a steady stream of warnings went home to the European nations and to America. Something was going to have to be done about the Boxers, the warnings said. They were growing too powerful, and they seemed to have the support of the Qing governors, although no one could prove anything. A dreadful crisis was approaching.

The western European powers, the United States, and Japan decided to send troops. The British were first to arrive off Dagu Bar; they landed there, some 60 kilometers southeast of Tianjin. Soon there were Americans, Japanese, Russians, Germans, French, Italians, and Austrians involved. The military force of about 2000 men moved from Dagu to Tianjin, by rail, and then toward Beijing. The announced purpose was to "rescue" the foreign embassies, which were besieged by the Boxers behind the wall of the embassy quarter in Beijing. The Qing army seemed to be unable to protect them.

The Boxers came up to the rail line. Battles were fought at Luofa and Langfang. Many Boxers were shot down, still believing in the protective power of their prayers and amulets against bullets. But many Boxers got through with their knives and spears and swords, and attacked the foreign troops. The foreigners retreated along the rail line and back to Tianjin.

More troops were landed. Soon 2000 Russians arrived at Tianjin railroad station. The Boxers then combined forces with the Qing army and defeated the Russians. But the foreigners had more military power, and they showed that they were willing to use it.

In Beijing the dowager empress played a dangerous game. Appearing to support the Boxers, she declared war on the foreigners, but secretly she was negotiating with the British. Four days after her war declaration she lifted the siege of the legations by the official troops and called for truce talks.

The British-led military force of foreigners moved on, defeating the Boxers in Tianjin and taking the city on July 14. The foreigners continued to amass forces. On August 4, when the allied army began to march on Beijing, it numbered 20,000 men equipped with modern rifles and field guns. On August 14 the allied army broke through to Beijing, entered the city, and occupied the great wall around the embassies. The dowager empress fled to Xi'an, kidnapping Emperor Guang Xu and taking him along.

In Beijing, the allied troops looted for three days, after the dowager empress ordered the disbandment of the Yi He Tuan.

Meanwhile the disaster was growing. Under cover of this activity the Russians had sent 150,000 men into Heilongjiang, Jilin, and Liaoning provinces, supposedly to protect the Chinese Eastern Railway. By October the entire northeast was under Russian control, but the control was not effective. Some 200,000 local people formed into bands to fight the Russians, and they fought for weeks. The Russians held the towns and the roads by day, but by night they could not travel. They were besieged within their conquered towns.

Seeing what was happening in the northeast, the other Europeans and the Americans became aroused lest the Russians take over China. Once again, they decided it would be expedient to support Dowager Empress Ci Xi's rule, obnoxious as it was to them. They imposed a strict peace on the Qings, demanding a huge indemnity of 450 million taels of gold, tightened foreign control of the Chinese customs (so they could collect their indemnities), and the establishment of a legation quarter which would be manned by foreign troops to "protect the Embassies." Antiforeign movements were to be banned in the future, on pain of death, and the foreigners reserved the right to station troops in north China along the rail lines to Beijing.

===

For one reason alone the Boxer Rebellion was fatal to China's Qing dynasty: the enormous indemnity of 450 million taels of gold. The indemnity was to be paid over thirty-nine years, ending in 1940. Altogether, with interest, it came to nearly a billion taels of silver (there was not that much gold available), which was more than twelve times the total annual national revenue. In other words, the foreigners so impoverished China that no further hope could be held for economic development. China, in effect, belonged to the foreigners. From that point on the foreigners ran not only the customs but, in effect, the Qing government. If antiforeign sentiment had developed in China before, now it ran rampage; but it was the cold, seething sort of fervor that was hidden beneath silky exteriors. The foreigners were too powerful to be faced openly. China was still sleeping.

Examining these events of the last third of the nineteenth century, many Chinese began to realize that the Qing dynasty was the ruin of China and must be eliminated. Even Dr. Sun Yatsen turned to this point of view, although he had left China, studied abroad, and come home with western ideas and a distinct loyalty to the Qing rulers.

Always, Dr. Sun had considered the need for change. One of his heroes was Hong Xiuquan, the leader of the Taiping Rebellion, who came from a village near Dr. Sun's own birthplace. In 1892, after studying in Hawaii and Hong Kong, Dr. Sun returned to China to practice medicine in Guangzhou Province and in Macao. But soon his mind was filled with political problems. One of his first political acts was to write a memorial to Li Hongzhang, an intimate of the dowager empress and the most important figure at the Imperial court aside from the empress. The year was 1894. When Dr. Sun received no reply, he went north to Tianjin and Beijing to press for reforms in agriculture, industry, and education. But Li was not interested in this unknown young man from the south, and Sun Yatsen was ignored. While hanging around Beijing, he soon learned that the Qing dynasty was totally rotten and that the dowager empress was much more interested—even then, during the Sino-Japanese war—in the celebration of her sixtieth birthday at the summer palace than in the fortunes of China in the war.

This was the point at which Sun Yatsen became a true revolutionary. He had realized suddenly that there was no chance of reform of the Qing government: It must be overthrown, and a democratic republic substituted for it.

On his way back south, Sun Yatsen visited Wuhan and Shanghai, where he saw further evidence of the decline of China and the growing power of the foreigners. So he went to Hawaii again, seeking support and money. He got it from some two dozen Chinese who formed with him the Xing Zhong Hui, a revolutionary organization based on the ideals of the French and American revolutions. Their slogan was: "Regenerate China and maintain National independence."

In the spring of 1895 Sun Yatsen and some followers returned to Hong Kong and staged an armed uprising against the Qing dynasty in the fertile grounds of Guangzhou, cauldron of rebellion in years past. But the Qings were powerful and Sun Yatsen's people were weak; and the ideas of France and America, as the rebels expressed them, did not appeal to the broad spectrum of the peasantry whose support would have been needed for success. The rebellion failed. From the ashes, however, Sun Yatsen emerged as a full-fledged revolutionary leader with a price on his head. He fled to Japan to spread the doctrine and create new support. He traveled to the United States and to Europe to raise money. Everywhere, he went among the Chinese communities to spread his doctrine of revolution.

He became very well known both within China and outside the country. When he was in London in the fall of 1896, he was kidnapped by officials of the Qing legation there, who intended to take him secretly back to China for trial and execution. But through the assistance of English friends Sun Yatsen escaped this fate. He returned to Japan in June 1897 to plan for the coming revolution, which he knew he must bring to China.

The Boxer Rebellion brought Sun Yatsen to grips with insurrection once more. From Japan he directed an uprising in Huizhou which was to be supported by the Xing Zhong Hui. That group formed another secret society, the San He Hui, which had some sixty members. Sun Yatsen had planned a rebellion supported by foreign arms, to be shipped from Taiwan, but the Japanese government got wind of the rebel attempt. Knowing that it would interfere with their own exploitation of China, the Japanese stopped the shipment of arms. Thus the first big revolutionary attempt by Dr. Sun failed miserably. But Sun Yatsen did not give up.

"The Manchu rule is like a building about to collapse," he said. "Its structure is completely rotten. No outside force can save it from falling." By outside force, Dr. Sun meant the foreigners, who were trying to bolster the Qing government for their own purposes.

During this period Dr. Sun was working out his political theories. They were embodied in the tract San Min Zhu Yi, the three principles of the people: nationalism, which meant the creation of a new state; democracy, which meant a republic with a constitution that guaranteed democratic government; and the people's livelihood, which meant primarily land reform, since China was basically an agricultural nation. In this sense, from the beginning, Dr. Sun's philosophy went beyond that of the American and French revolutions, presupposing a government responsibility for the economic welfare of the people as well as their political independence.

Dr. Sun's book *Solution to China's Problems* was published in 1904. At that time the center of Sun's activity was Japan, for there he and others could see an oriental society, starting from the same feudal beginnings as China in the middle of the nineteenth century, which was succeeding in its program of modernization and independence. Thousands of Chinese were flocking to Japan in those days to enter universities and to observe the Japanese system, while trying to relate what they saw to their China. One group advocated revolution. Another group, led by Kang Youwei, still believed that it was possible to rescue the Qing empire and make of it a people's government.

When Dr. Sun arrived in Japan in 1905 from Europe, he called a meeting of the revolutionaries. He put forth his program, calling for unity if they wished to get anywhere. The result was the formation of the Tong Meng Hui ("China Revolutionary League"), which came into being on August 20, 1905.

During this period the problems of China's reformers and revolutionaries were exacerbated by events outside China itself. The Russians and the Japanese went to war in April 1904. While China was not involved in the war as a government, the war was fought in Chinese waters and on Chinese land. The Russian fleet, which was located at Lüshun, was attacked first. Land battles were fought at Shenyang, Lüshun, and Dalian. In the great battle of Shenyang, a quarter of a million men were engaged on each side.

The major naval battle was fought at Tsushima Strait in Japanese waters, and then in the Sea of Japan.

When the war was over, China was again the loser. The Liaodong Peninsula of Manchuria was transferred from Russia to Japan, without consulting the Chinese. Theoretically, Manchuria was recognized as part of China, but actually the Japanese had far-reaching designs on it. They secured control of the railroad from Lüshun to Changchun, and within a year they organized an enormous enterprise, the South Manchuria Railway Company. This was really an exploitation company backed by the Japanese government and operated by the *zaibatsu*, the increasingly powerful cartels of Japan. In its area, the South Manchurian Railway controlled electric supply, gas, water, hospitals, mines and factories, schools, hotels, steamship lines, and harbors. In fact, every part of life in the area of the South Manchurian Railway system depended on the railway and its Japanese administrators.

By 1905 even the bitter old dowager empress recognized the need for reform of Qing rule if the dynasty was to be maintained. But, in fact, she had already weakened the dynasty irreparably. Her measures—abolition of the Confucian examinations as the criteria for government office, reorganization and modernization of the universities, reform of the military, study of western political systems with an eye to adapting parts of them to China—all sounded excellent. But they were too few and too late. One result was the dispatch of thousands of Chinese students to foreign countries. Instead of saving the Qing dynasty, this step hastened its demise, for most of these students became revolutionaries. The majority went to Japan (in 1902 there were 275 Chinese students in Japan; in 1906, 15,000), where they were soon conscious of Dr. Sun's Tong Meng Hui.

Meanwhile, on the Chinese mainland, rebellious moves were afoot. Shanghai had its Guang Fu Hui, led by Cai Yuanpei. The women had their own revolutionary movement there, Gong Ai Hui ("Mutual Love Association"), whose leader was Qiu Jin, a young woman from the official class who had become indignant over the treatment of her country and her people and who now became an active revolutionary. Dr. Sun's groups staged a rebellion in 1906 in Hunan Province. In 1907 they tried another uprising in Anqing, the capital of Anhui Province, but Qing troops surrounded the area. Among those captured was Qiu Jin, who had gone to Datong to establish a revolutionary school. She was imprisoned, tortured, and finally executed; she was 33 years old. This sort of self-sacrifice, offered boldly and without fear, marked the revolutionaries of China in the period 1905–1910.

Although the dowager empress issued an edict in September 1906 announcing the preparation of a constitutional monarchy, nobody believed her. Yet she was determined to continue in control. Emperor Guang Xu never recovered from the kidnapping that had taken him to Xian: With no semblance of power remaining, he was completely the creature of the dowager empress. He was neglected (by 1903 his apartments were the only ones in the palace that were not lighted by electricity). He was reviled. He was ignored by the eunuchs, who pandered to the dowager empress's every whim. She celebrated her birthdays—she was now in her seventies—in splendid fashion, with orgies of ceremony and feastings.

Guang Xu was really quite ill, and would have been unable to govern even if he had the chance. In November 1908 the dowager empress appointed Pu Yi, son of Prince Chun, as emperor. He was 2 years old. Shortly after that time, under very mysterious circumstances, the ailing Guang Xu died; it was commonly believed that the empress had him poisoned. His death occurred on November 14, 1908. A few hours later, on November 15, the dowager empress also died. And with her death the fate of the Qing dynasty was sealed.

This end of empire was only a matter of time.

4
The Revolution of 1911

Those in China who urge the establishment of a National Assembly do not bother to ask whether we are sufficiently educated or not. Even if such a step were feasible, what good would be served by ignorant discussions?

—Yan Fu, Chinese reformer, 1910

For five years Dr. Sun's Tong Meng Hui had spread rebellion and resentment throughout China. Following the large uprising in Jiangxi and Hunan in 1906 six other uprisings were launched in 1907 and 1908, keeping the Qing forces off balance. Sun Yatsen personally took part in the fighting in Guangxi Province.

But none of these rebellions was powerful enough to succeed. The problem was that Dr. Sun had never achieved a large popular base for his rebellion. He was surrounded by ardent young intellectuals, many of whom gave their lives for the dream of freedom. But dreamers do not make a successful revolution; it takes organization, and Dr. Sun did not have the backing he needed. More planning was wanted.

Dr. Sun devoted himself to that planning until, in the spring of 1911, he was ready to start once more. This time he launched the Guangzhou rebellion. A force of about a hundred men under a rebel named Huang Xing attacked the yamen of the governor general and fought the Qing army forces there. The fighting lasted all night; the Qings were superior in power, and the majority of the revolutionaries were killed in the battle or captured and executed. The rest, including Huang Xing, escaped with their lives, nursing their wounds. The Qings announced that anyone helping the rebels would be dealt with just as summarily. It was a measure of the people's resentment against the Qings that a group collected the bodies of seventy-two of the revolutionaries and gave them a martyr's funeral at Huanghuagang in the outskirts of Guangzhou.

*   *   *

In Beijing, Zhang Zhidong and Yuan Shikai, two of the old dowager empress's most trusted sycophants in years gone by, hoped to achieve control of the Qing government. Yuan had been a star in the Qing galaxy for a long, long time. He first came to the Imperial attention in 1883 when, as a young officer, he went to Korea. The Japanese had begun attempts to take over Korea, and in 1875 they had sent a naval force. In 1882 the Americans interfered with China's position as lord of Korea by concluding a trade treaty which, in effect, denied China's special position as suzerain over Korea. By 1883 civil war in Korea was about to break out over the question of adherence to China, with the Japanese counseling a policy of independence and securing many adherents.

When, on the advice of Li Hongzhang, one of her most trusted advisers, the dowager empress sent a force into Korea, Yuan Shikai became chief of staff. In the arguments and activity that followed, Yuan distinguished himself by seizing the king of Korea and keeping him away from the Japanese. For this, at the age of 21, Yuan was appointed Chinese resident in Seoul. Korea had been saved from Japanese encroachment for the time being, because of his swift actions.

From 1903 on Yuan had led the movement for military modernization of the Qing army, and he built up six divisions in North China. He began as had the Japanese, using German instructors to establish discipline. Then he switched to the Japanese, who were cheaper because they were more eager to achieve influence in China.

By 1907 Yuan Shikai had lost the old dowager empress's affection. She subverted him with her choice of Pu Yi as the new emperor, with his family behind him as regents. But she meddled once too often, and after she died, the court began to divide into factions. In order to keep Zhang Zhidong and Yuan Shikai from seizing power, the court gave each the title of grand minister of the privy council—and nothing to do. Thus the regents hoped to pull the teeth of these powerful men.

Meanwhile, with much fanfare, the preparations for "constitutional government" continued. In August 1908 the court had issued an "Imperial Constitution" that set up a nine-year period during which the people were to be prepared for constitutional government. The fact was that for several years missions had been going around to various parts of the world, studying representative governments and assessing their values. The most popular government, in Qing circles, was that of Japan, for Emperor Meiji and his councillors had set up a constitutional government which was apparently very democratic. But on top of the whole pile sat the emperor, with total authority to act at any time. In other words, he could let the democratic processes go on, but if he found them distasteful, he could then throw out the whole kit and kaboodle. This idea appealed enormously to the Qings, who were completely afraid of the people. They were heeding the advice of men such as Yan Fu (see the epigram at the start of this chapter), who felt that time was needed to prepare the Chinese people for real freedom and responsibility.

In the Forbidden City the struggle for power continued. Pu Yi's Qing title was Emperor Xuan Tong. His father, Zi Feng, wielded the real power as regent. Yuan Shikai, who stirred around trying to seize power, was forced in 1908 to retire from public life.

Zi Feng then supervised the establishment of provincial consultative councils and a National Consultative Assembly which met in Beijing in 1910. Had these been made twenty-five years earlier, they might have preserved the Qing dynasty and begun the orderly transition to democratic government. But they were too late. The methods of the eunuchs and the government functionaries were too firmly established. Corruption could be cut out of government only with a sharp knife, and there was no one to wield it. Indeed, the more things changed, the more they appeared to be the same. A cabinet was appointed in the spring of 1911, but nine of the thirteen ministers were Manchu noblemen, and five of them were members of the Imperial family clan. Thus political and military power continued to be concentrated in the same old hands, Manchu hands.

By 1911 the political cauldron in China was seething. At that moment the government made a serious error, given the public feeling about foreign encroachments on China. The nation had been very slow to build railroads, although the Japanese had built some and the Russians and Japanese had built railroads in Manchuria. But by 1896 the Chinese had only 250 miles of railroad under their own control. In 1911 the government realized that it had to get control of its railroads if there was to be any order in transportation, and it tried to seize various lines. They were to be "nationalized" but actually would be turned over to foreigners to build and operate. The move affected four provinces immediately: Sichuan, Hunan, Hubei, and Guangdong. In the province of Sichuan the move was met by immediate and violent opposition which led to an uprising that attracted thousands of railroad workers and students. The revolutionary movement was gaining more popular support.

All of this occurred in the summer. In the fall of 1911 a very important uprising broke in Wuchang. It was fomented by the Tong Meng Hui and several other secret societies which had been organizing the army of Hubei Province. By this time the secret organizations had enlisted about a third of the Hubei army officers and men.

The surprise element of the uprising was botched; the government got information about it, arrested many people, and executed them summarily. But the revolutionaries decided to go ahead anyhow, and on the night of October 10 shots rang out in Wuchang. The struggle had begun. It would be commemorated as "Double Ten Day" (the tenth day of the tenth month). The revolutionary army, this time organized, seized Wuchang and the government offices, and also Hanyang and Hankou. So all of the big complex called Wuhan fell into the hands of the rebels.

On October 12, the Wuchang rebels set up a government. The name of the government was changed to Zhonghua Minguo ("Republic of China"). The real revolution was beginning.

There were many difficulties, largely because the rebels felt they had to depend on the old reformers for support and intellectual leadership. In fact the old officials retained most of the power. In Jiangsu the governor of the Qings, Cheng Dequan, simply changed his signboard to read "military government" instead of "civil government"; he retained all his old power. But some rebels did not accept this move, and soon they had captured Nanjing.

Sun Yatsen returned to China, where the provincial delegates were meeting in Nanjing. They elected him provisional president on December 29, 1911. On January 1, 1912, Sun took office as president and proclaimed the establishment of the Republic of China. Li Yuanhong was elected vice president. A republican regime was established.

The government set about modernizing China in its own way. It did not address the major problem of land reform, but it did address political, social; and economic questions. Opium traffic was prohibited, as was trade in Chinese indentured labor. Laws to protect Chinese investment were passed. The foreigners were to lose many of their privileges. These reforms indicated the deep respect the lawmakers had for democratic principles, but they reflected a failure to understand the source of power in China, which was and always had been the land.

The Republic of China was not popular with the foreign governments. They set out with the Qings to try to destroy it, as they had destroyed the Taiping Rebellion. A few days after the establishment of the new government a dozen British, American, Japanese, German, and French warships assembled on the Yangtze River, opposite Wuhan, implying a threat to the revolutionaries. The foreigners also hoped to bankrupt the new government by continuing to collect taxes and customs duties, sending them to the Qing treasury in Beijing. A four-power consortium of banks (British, American, French, and German) lent 3 million taels of silver to the Qings to carry on their affairs and put down the rebellion. Russia fished in these troubled waters by instigating several mongol princes to declare "independence," hoping in this way to saw off Outer Mongolia and part of Heilongjiang Province in the northeast.

It became apparent in Beijing that the Qing government was dissolving rapidly. So pressure was put on by the foreigners to appoint Yuan Shikai, a strong man, to an important job. He was made prime minister and commander in chief of the Qing forces.

Yuan marched troops down to Wuhan and captured the city of Hanyang, one of the three in the Wuhan complex. The foreign powers supported him completely, and they persuaded the Sun government to hold talks at Shanghai. Dr. Sun saw how the wind was blowing: The foreigners would support Yuan. Sun Yatsen was wise enough to know what was needed, and he soon negotiated with Yuan. If Yuan would become president of the republic, then he, Sun, would resign. Yuan, of course, was itching for power and he agreed.

Pu Yi, the emperor, was told to abdicate on February 12, which he did. Sun resigned as Republic of China president. Yuan was elected president at Nanjing and inaugurated as provisional president at Beijing. Thus, in a whirlwind of events, and before the eyes of the astonished foreigners, China's government turned around. It was a measure of the debility of the Qing empire that it collapsed so completely and so suddenly in favor of a republic.

But what sort of republic? The revolutionaries said that they had been betrayed, that Yuan was setting up a government of the landlord and business class.

The day after Yuan took office in Beijing, Dr. Sun proclaimed a provisional constitution which had been drawn up virtually overnight in Nan-jing by the provisional senate to stop Yuan from seizing outright power. On February 25 a delegation went up from Nanjing to Beijing to escort President Yuan south. The party was received with all the pomp left over from the Qing days. The gate from the Tartar city into the Chinese city was thrown open, as it had been done before only to admit passage of an Imperial cortege. All seemed serene. But on the night of February 29 a revolt broke out among the troops, and Yuan used it as an excuse to avoid leaving north China. On March 10 he assumed the presidency, but he remained in Beijing, his seat of power, rather than going south into the hands of the real revolutionaries.

So the legislative *yuan* ("legislature") moved up to Beijing and held its sessions there. Yuan made sure that the key ministries of power (army, navy, and interior) were run by men of his own choosing. By the summer of 1912 a parliament of two houses was in session, and all seemed to be going very well. In fact, however, the republic had the trappings but not the es-sence of a democratic government.

From the very beginning, Yuan Shikai proved to be an autocrat. And why not? He had been raised in an autocratic society, and his idea of a republic was not that of the reformers. Much more, the idea of a govern-ment like that of Japan, which had the accoutrements of democratic rule but the essential dictatorship of a monarch, appealed to Yuan.

To counter his autocracy, the members of Dr. Sun's Tong Meng Hui formed the Guomindang ("Nationalist") party in the summer of 1912. The platform called for political unity, development of local government au-tonomy, as opposed to central control, and—very important—basic atten-tion to the "people's livelihood." The Guomindang won the majority of seats in the national parliamentary elections held in 1912 and 1913. The leaders then hoped to be able to bridle Yuan Shikai.

One of the leaders of the Guomindang was Song Jiaoren, who has gone down in history as "China's first parliamentarian." His aim was to control Yuan, but Yuan formed a rival group, the Republican party, which drew its support from the old "liberal" element of the Manchu constitutional supporters.

After the Guomindang won the elections, Yuan's days in power seemed to be numbered. But Yuan was a master of the art of government by assassination, practiced so handily by the dowager empress in the Qing days. On March 20, 1913, Song Jiaoren was shot to death at the Shanghai railroad station. The assassin was arrested a few days later and identified; he was a soldier who said he had been hired by a local gangster to do the killing. The gangster would not talk, but it was generally assumed that he had been employed by Yuan Shikai's agents to do the deadly job. Before the investigation could bring a trial, the soldier assassin died mysteriously in his prison cell. Without evidence, the whole case was dropped. The gangster hung about for a time, bothered Yuan Shikai for money, and ended up dead himself, shot by two men in uniform who boarded the train he was riding.

Yuan Shikai continued in power. He negotiated with a five-power foreign consortium for a loan for China, and he got 25 million pounds sterling. It was all done without consulting the legislative body, which infuriated Dr. Sun and his followers. Sun wanted to rebel against the government, but he was persuaded to wait, to try to keep together the framework of parliamentary democracy.

Yuan Shikai was equally determined to destroy that framework. His first move was in the pattern of the old empire.

The sinews of Guomindang power lay in south China, that fertile field of rebellion over 200 years past. The military commanders of the Chinese Republic in the south were southern men with southern ties. In June 1913, Yuan Shikai set about replacing these southerners with northern generals. To reinforce his decisions, he sent units of the northern army, which was loyal to him, down south. This dispatch of northern troops angered the southerners, and in July the seven provinces of Jiangxi, Anhui, Jiangsu, Guangdong, Sichuan, Fujian, and Henan announced their secession from the Chinese Republic and declared war against the Yuan government. This was called the "Second Revolution." It came to nothing, ending in two months because there was no popular support for the movement, which was seen by the common people as nothing more than a quarrel among politicians.

Sun Yatsen did very little in this period. Seeing that his own safety was endangered, he escaped to Japan once more. In September 1913 Yuan's forces, led by Gen. Zhang Xun, captured Nanjing and subjected it to a bath of blood and looting. For three days the soldiers ran through the streets, raping, murdering, and stealing. By the end of 1913 Yuan Shikai's northern army controlled all the provinces south of the Yangtze, except Guizhou, Yunnan, and Sichuan.

Yuan then set out to legitimize his changed government. He pushed the parliament into electing him president again, and on the second anniversary of Double Ten (October 10, 1913) he was installed for a new term of five years. He held a military review at the Gate of Heavenly Peace in Beijing. Almost immediately virtually all the European nations recognized the Chinese government as legitimate.

By November 1913 Yuan had sufficient power to dissolve the Guomindang; a few months later he dissolved the parliament. The Republic of China, for which so many had had such high hopes, had become an autocracy. Yuan tried to hide it by appointing a political council consisting of sixty-nine members from the provinces, but they all represented Yuan's followers. They chose a constitutional council, and in May 1914 the council produced a "constitution." For all practical purposes Yuan Shikai was dictator. He could declare war, sign treaties, appoint officials, and issue emergency decrees without any restrictions. At the end of 1914 he appointed himself president for ten years, with the right to pick his own successor or succeed himself. That month, December 1914, he went formally to the Temple of Heaven, and in the fashion of the old emperors he made sacrificial offerings to the gods. The gesture was not lost on the people of China, who could see that Yuan was preparing to install a new Imperial dynasty over China.

A convention of "citizens representatives" was called, and oddly enough, the convention delegates outdid each other in their demands that Yuan Shikai declare himself emperor. The people of China, they said, were not ready for republicanism. The idea was planted in the press, and given credence by a number of learned professors and intellectual lights, including the correspondent of the London *Times*.

So the stage was set for another round of imperialism in China.

But in Japan, Dr. Sun Yatsen was conspiring again. In 1914 he founded the Revolutionary Party of China. He dusted off all the old secret societies of the past, all the old relationships with the *hua jiao* ("overseas Chinese") that he knew so well, and he secured support from abroad for what could not be supported in China proper at the moment: rebellion and democracy in favor of the people.

Within China, many of those who had supported Yuan Shikai now began to become disillusioned. One such was Yan Fu, who had once said that China was not ready for democracy. He had become Yuan's adviser on foreign affairs, casting his lot, seemingly irrevocably, with the last reminder of the Qings. But Yan Fu tired of the game. In 1914 he remarked that although Yuan was an outstanding man, he did not have the knowledge and experience needed to cope with the leaders of the foreign powers. "His obstinacy and his wrong choice of subordinates cause much dissatisfaction. To expect him to change society and lay the foundation of a stable regime is out of the question."

As matters developed, it was not erudition or polemics that decided the outcome.

In the winter of 1915 the provincial governor of Yunnan sent a message to Yuan telling him to abandon the idea of empire. It was not answered, so Yunnan seceded from the Beijing government. Guizhou followed. Suddenly, Yuan discovered that all his maneuvering had cost him the loyalty of his generals, who were now setting themselves up as independent warlords of the areas they controlled.

Guangxi also joined the rebellion. Yuan's generals there announced that he must give up the idea of empire and resign from public office. This bitter pill was the last. One by one the other provinces seceded from Yuan's government: Guangdong, Zhejiang, Sichuan, Henan. By June 1916 Yuan had lost the support of most of China. On June 6 he died, bitter in the realization that he had failed to realize his ambitions.

5

The Warlords

Our Sixth Army, however, was under the direct command of General Headquarters. We did not have a local territory from which we could tax the people. We depended entirely upon Headquarters for our daily maintenance. When General Headquarters was disbanded after the war [World War I] we were transferred to the command of the Military Governor of Guandong [Guangdong]. In those days, however, the Provincial Government of Guandong could hardly support itself. As a result of this financial hardship not only was our pay deferred from month to month, but even our daily maintenance could not be met.

—*The Reminiscences of Li Zongren*

Above, in a nutshell, is the story of the rise of warlordism in China in the second decade of the twentieth century. As Yuan Shikai lost the confidence of the provincial governors and the generals around China, they looked for methods by which to support themselves. As long as the northern army he had founded held together, all went fairly well. But with Yuan Shikai's death in 1916, the northern army began to break up. Soon it was every general for himself. Every general who could retain the loyalty of his troops, one way or another, became a warlord.

Within months the entire country was under the control of small military units. There were, in fact, hundreds of warlords. Two of the most important were Feng Guozhang and Duan Qirui. The first was a man from a family of landlords; he had failed the Imperial civil service examinations and had then turned to a military career. The second was a soldier from a family of soldiers. Both were intimates of Yuan Shikai until he fell from grace. They had, however, fallen out with him when he opted to become emperor. The reason was Yuan's son, Li Yuanhong, a completely arrogant young man who had little ability and much ambition. He expected to become the second emperor of China in the Yuan dynasty, and he bullied everyone around him until, by the time of his father's death, he had no support whatsoever within the military community.

When Yuan died, Vice President Li Yuanhong took over as president of China, but the republic was hollow. The real power was in the hands of generals Duan and Feng. Duan's followers were called the Anhui Clique, and Feng's were called the Zhili Clique. Both generals had held high office at one time or another; Duan was once prime minister, Feng once president. But at no time did they secure the adherence of more than a fraction of the governors and generals of China. In a sense, they fought each other into oblivion. By 1919 they had ceased to be important, as China wallowed in warlordism.

Two of the important northern warlords of the 1920s were Zhang Zuolin and Wu Peifu. Wu succeeded to the command of the Zhili Clique. After they defeated the Anhui warlords in the civil war of 1920, Wu's troops dominated the government in Beijing. He made an effort early in the 1920s to force national unification. In other words, he set out to take on the other warlords, one by one, and beat them, thus bringing ever-larger areas of China under his control. But he ran into the problem faced by every minor despot: With only limited resources, and an expanding army and area to control, he was more and more at the mercy of subordinates. And these subordinates had ambitions of their own. In 1924, Wu took on Zhang Zuolin, the formidable Manchurian general, but during the campaign Feng Yuxiang, one of Wu's generals, defected, bringing about the collapse of Wu's army. He managed to recover sufficiently enough to keep control of his army, but military adventures into other regions became a thing of the past. In 1928 he retired to Sichuan and undertook the age-old occupations of retired generals: studying Buddhism, practicing calligraphy, writing poetry, and drinking heavily.

Now the most important of the northern warlords was Zhang Zuolin, the Manchurian leader. He was a slender man, a peasant who had gone far since the day of his enlistment in the Chinese army during the Sino-Japanese war. After that war he had gone home to Fengtian in Manchuria, where he set up a small militia to defend the area. Ultimately, his militia was enlisted entirely in the regular Chinese northern army as a regiment. So in Yuan Shikai's heyday, Zhang Zuolin progressed up the military ladder through his own abilities and shrewdness. When Yuan Shikai announced that he wanted to be emperor, Zhang Zuolin demanded, and got, appointment as military governor of Fengtian in exchange for his support of Yuan.

By 1919 he had managed to install his protégés as governors of Jilin and Heilongjiang provinces in Manchuria, and he was himself inspector general of the three eastern provinces. Thus he was in control of Manchuria. During the 1920s he ruled the area as a kingdom of his own. When the Japanese began casting eyes on Manchuria, they knew that Zhang Zuolin was the man with whom they must deal in one way or another.

The warlord Chang Xun, the "pigtailed general," was notable for his attempt to restore the Manchu dynasty. He had always been loyal to the Manchu concept, and long after others in China had cut their queues in defiance of the Qings, he and his army retained theirs. They had engineered the terrible rape of Nanjing when Yuan ordered the south pacified. In 1917 Chang attempted to reestablish the Manchu dynasty in Beijing, coming to Li Yuanhong's rescue, but his attempt failed in two weeks and he went into oblivion.

Another northern warlord of notoriety was Zhang Zhongchang, "the dogmeat general," so called because of his fondness for dogmeat and his use of it as rations. One of the most brutal military leaders in modern China, he became governor of Shandong and was known there for his cruelties and particularly his greed. He once had a newspaper editor shot for criticizing him. His troops moved around the province, leaving a trail of "open melons" (split skulls) and strings of severed heads hanging from telegraph poles. Thus he maintained power in Shandong until 1928. He was supposed to have had between thirty and fifty concubines, most of them of different nationalities, who each had a washbowl marked with the flag of her nation.

From the south and west came other warlords.

Chen Jiongming began as a revolutionary. He had received a Confucian education, and he passed the first-degree examinations of the Qings in 1898. He enrolled in a school to learn about the western world, graduated, and became editor of a revolutionary newspaper. When the provincial assemblies were created in 1909 by the Manchus, he became a member of the Guangdong assembly. Soon he joined Sun Yatsen's revolutionary movement. When the 1911 revolution began, he raised a military force, and in 1920 he conquered Guangxi for Sun. But then, having gained some power, he decided that China would be best served by the establishment of a federation of autonomous provinces. It was rather the attitude of the southern American states as opposed to that of the northern American states in the 1850s. Ultimately, Chen was driven out of Guangzhou by Sun's forces.

Li Zongren was the son of a family that had fallen on evil days. He entered the Guangxi Military Elementary School, where he met a number of young men, all in more or less the same situation. They became schoolmates, and some of them became friends. They also became the "Guangxi military clique."

In 1916 Li joined the Guangxi army. When Chen Jiongming invaded Guangxi in 1921, Li and his unit escaped to the mountains. There he created a larger force, which became, in essence, a personal army. When Chen took his force out of Guangxi in 1922, provincial authority had been destroyed. The whole province was in confusion, with fifteen separate armies functioning—really as bandits—within the province. Li had about 2000 men then, and he dominated five districts of the province. From this base, he added power, and men, until by 1925 he controlled Guangxi Province.

Early in 1926 Li cast his lot with the Guomindang. His army was named the Seventh Army of the National Revolutionary Army, and Li Zongren became the commander. Thus, he fell into line with the forces of the republic.

Also from the north was the warlord Yan Xishan, who came from a family of bankers and merchants in Shanxi Province. He had gone to Japan to study during the last years of the Manchu program and graduated from the Japanese Imperial Military Academy in 1909. He went back to Shanxi and there established his little empire, for Shanxi is surrounded on three sides by mountains and on the fourth by the Huang He, which in that area is not navigable.

Another warlord was Feng Yuxiang, the son of an army officer of the old school. He had very little formal education but much knowledge, for he learned steadily by himself. He was also fortunate in marrying the niece of one of Yuan Shikai's lieutenants.

Feng had become a Christian in 1914. The religion appealed to his puritanical tendencies: he did not drink, smoke, take opium, gamble, or run around with women. He became known as "the Christian general." His Christianity was militant and extremely physical. He demanded that his troops train constantly. He would stand for no corruption. He prohibited drinking, gambling, the visiting of prostitutes, and even swearing in the ranks. The officers were supposed to be able to do anything they asked their men to do.

Feng was the general who defected from warlord Wu Peifu's ranks during Wu's abortive campaign to capture Manchuria. After that, Feng's star rose steadily.

The problem for each warlord was finding a source of support for his army. Therefore, command of territory, and the ability to levy taxes on that territory—as well as collect them—meant the difference between a warlord and a bandit.

By 1926 China was very well divided into warlord territories. Manchuria and Shandong Province were controlled by Zhang Zuolin. Qahar, Suiyuan, Gansu, Shaanxi, Henan, and parts of the west were controlled by Feng Yuxiang, while Yan Xishan held mountainous Shanxi. Sun Chuangfang held Jiangsu, Anhui, Jiangxi, Zhejiang, and Fujian. Wu Peifu was warlord over Hubei and Hunan. Tang Jiyao was the warlord of Yunnan and Guizhou. The Guangxi Clique held Guangxi, and the Kuomintang army held Guangdong. Sichuan Province was fragmented among several small warlords.

But while China had gone into warlordism, Pu Yi, the Manchu heir, was carefully let alone. He had an English tutor, and people were still talking about the day when he would ascend the Dragon Throne and make it powerful once more.

The war in Europe attracted China's attention in 1917, and the government joined in. The role of the Chinese was that of labor force—not fighting force—on the western front. The Japanese captured the German colony in Shandong and then, feeling very sure of themselves, made a big loan to the Chinese government in Beijing.

But in 1917, when all this was occurring, Sun Yatsen moved to Guangzhou, the seat of his power in China, and there established a new military government. He was supported by the various warlords of the Guangxi Clique.

China went this way and that until the early 1920s, with first one clique and then the other taking control, or seeming to. In truth, it was the era of warlordism, the triumph of a handful of fiefdoms.

The big psychological change came to China on May 4, 1919, when Beijing students rioted against the Treaty of Versailles, which had denied China all its legitimate demands for return of territory held by foreigners. Japan got the former German concessions. The great powers would not even discuss China's other demands for return of rights and power. So on May 4 some 3000 Chinese students marched on Tian An Men Square and protested. They wanted the return of Qingdao and the end of colonialism in China. They marched to the house of the minister who had acceded to many of the foreign demands, and they set his house on fire.

In June more students struck in Shanghai. So did workers from textile mills and shops and transportation companies. Because of such pressure, the Chinese delegation at the Versailles conference refused to sign the treaty.

The student unrest led to some new political movements in China. Principal among these was Marxism, which the Chinese had discovered in the Russian revolution of October 1917. "The salvoes of the October revolution brought us Marxism-Leninism," said Mao Zedong, at that time a very young student.

The leading intellectual concerned with Marxism in China was Li Dazhao, chief librarian of Beijing University, and Mao's mentor. In 1918 Li had begun writing in periodicals about the Russian revolution in highly laudatory terms. His work "The World of the Future Will Be That of the Red Flag" began to attract students and others, particularly since they were disillusioned with the great powers of the west, which had failed to ameliorate China's condition one bit.

These intellectuals thus found a theme that pointed toward unification of China under one banner. At the end of World War I, 10 percent of the people (the landlords) controlled 80 percent of the arable land of China. The poor peasants, who made up about 80 percent of the people, owned perhaps 20 percent of the land. Taxes were high—as much as 50 percent. The landlords had "piggybacked" the tax system so that in Sichuan Province, for example, taxes were being collected for thirty-five years in advance. In all these areas, everywhere in China, the warlords were exacting the prices they wished, and the peasants suffered.

Thus the vacuum of power created by the warlords in the areas beyond their immediate control, banditry, nihilism in the countryside, and the distrust of the western powers brought about the glad reception of communism by many Chinese intellectuals. Here was a discipline that promised to put power into the hands of the people and destroy the evils the intellectuals saw around them.

*   *   *

The warlords recognized the threat. The most active among them was Zhang Zuolin, the warlord of Manchuria, who saw what the Communists wanted and what it would do to his seat of power. He ordered the strangling of Li Dazhao. It was the age-old practice of killing the messenger who brought bad tidings. That, said Zhang Zuolin, ought to put an end to that.

Thus, for the time being, the warlords, who possessed the only major fighting forces in China, continued to dominate the scene from Siberia to Hong Kong. From 1919 until the mid-1920s there was almost always war somewhere inside China, as each warlord struggled to extend his power. As far as the people were concerned, life was abject misery. Press-gangs roamed the provinces, forcibly enlisting soldiers and laborers.

> Even in the treaty port of Chongqing gangs of men may be seen roped together with cords around their wrists, being carried off by soldiers to act as transport coolies. No soldier in Sichuan ever carries his own baggage on the march and sometimes not even his rifle. These commandeered baggage coolies receive no pay but sometimes are given a kind of certificate for labour done... and often they are snatched away in the streets and forced to accompany the troops to distant places at a moment's notice, from which journeys they may not return for weeks, if at all.

From long experience the Chinese had a way of describing the situation under warlordism: "Bandits and soldiers are breath from the same nostril."

After the sorting out of strong and weak, which had begun around 1920, there developed, basically speaking, two sorts of warlords. First was the disciplinarian, such as Zhang Fakui. After a defeat in 1922 he led his troops into the mountains. They stayed there for six months, surviving.

> Whenever we ran out of food, we would raid a little village to get a few chickens etcetera. A village was inhabited by ten families or less. My men would surround a village before dawn and fire several shots to intimidate the people. We told them to come out and give up. This was the classic method of raiding a village. Sometimes we killed and carried away little pigs... we took corn, rice, potatoes, taro. Did we take money? No. There was no money to be had.
>
> We had moral principles. We were a different kind of bandit. We never indulged in fornication or rape. We only robbed because we had nothing to eat. I maintained military discipline and organization among my men.

But there was another sort of warlord, exemplified by Zhang Jingyao of Hunan Province, whose visits were feared more than a plague of locusts. One day, Zhang's force entered the town of Youzhou.

The arrival of Zhang himself on June 13 was the signal for a general looting of the city. I have never seen more thorough work. Every shop, every house in this beautiful and prosperous city has been literally stripped. There is not a vestige of any usable commodity from one end of the city to the other, including the great old Yamen used by Zhang himself. . . . Troops . . . lie disconsolate, dirty, hungry and demoralized on the floors and the counters of the shops and on every flat surface that is shaded from the sun. Most of the population has fled, but some 10,000 remain, all crowded into the American Mission Hospital."

The warlord period lasted about twelve years, a time marked by constant warfare, the fragmentation of agriculture, and the dissolution of orderly government. Opium had been virtually eliminated as a crop in China by 1916, but under the warlords the land used for growing poppies jumped from 3 percent in 1919 to 20 percent in 1929. The opium crop profited the warlords but not the people. By 1929 famine stalked in the provinces in north and central China, and the warlords were the cause.

If there was a positive aspect to warlordism, it had to be the fostering of nationalism. A young soldier who had joined Feng Yuxiang's army recalled that he often heard Feng lecture the troops on patriotic themes. The central theme was that China belonged to the Chinese and that foreigners must be deprived of control. This theme fit well into each warlord's own plans, so it spread across the land. And in this way the Chinese peasants were exposed to patriotic fervor, just as the intellectuals and students were exposed to it in other ways.

6

Making Revolutionaries

Outside the little Chinese school where I was studying, we students noticed many bean merchants, coming back from Changsha. We asked them why they were all leaving. They told us about a big uprising in the city.

There had been a severe famine that year, and in Changsha thousands were without food. The starving sent a delegation to the civil governor to beg for relief, but he replied to them haughtily:

"Why haven't you food? There is plenty in the city. I always have enough."

When the people were told the governor's reply, they became very angry. They held mass meetings and organized a demonstration. They attacked the Manchu yamen, cut down the flagpole, the symbol of office, and drove out the governor. Following this the commissioner of Internal Affairs, a man named Zhuang, came out on his horse and told the people that the government would take measures to help them. Zhuang was evidently sincere in his promises, but the Emperor disliked him and accused him of having intimate connections with "the mob." He was removed. A new governor arrived, and at once ordered the arrest of the leaders of the uprising. Many of them were beheaded and their heads displayed on poles as a warning to future "rebels."

—Mao Zedong, reminiscence of his boyhood

If one sifts through the events of the First World War as it affected Asia, one can find the beginnings of mass rebellion in China, stirrings reminiscent of the days of the Taiping.

The Japanese saw in the war what Lord Hatta Masayoshi, a nobleman of the nineteenth century, had called to the attention of the Imperial Japanese throne in a memorial. "In establishing relations with foreign countries," wrote Lord Hatta, "the object should always be kept in view of laying the foundation for securing hegemony over all nations." Japan should arm itself, he said, and then wait until such time as the Europeans turned their backs. At that time, Japan could move to take power in Asia.

And so it was: In 1914 the nations of Europe, split into two armed camps, went to war with one another. In the chancelleries in Berlin, Paris, and London there was no time to consider the hitherto burning issue of colonial expansion. But in Tokyo quite the opposite was true. The Japanese government saw in the great European war a capital opportunity to seize power in Asia, and it set about to do just that.

In 1914 the point of focus was Shandong Province, where the Germans maintained their Jiaozhou colony, the port of Qingdao, with rail fingers extending back to Jinan, the provincial capital. Within the year the Japanese, in connection with the British, had seized Qingdao and seemed prepared to settle down for good.

Then, in January 1915, the Japanese submitted direct to President Yuan Shikai the infamous "Twenty-one Demands." These included the demands that Japan control Shandong Province, as well as south Manchuria as far as Mongolia, and that China accept Japan as a participant in China's government. Indeed, the Japanese demand for police power in China could be construed as nothing else. China was to take on Japanese military advisers, to buy Japanese weapons, and to have Japanese railroads south of the Yangtze River. There was no place in China that Japan's ambitions did not reach. The acceptance of the Twenty-one Demands would have made China a Japanese colony.

Fortunately for China, the Japanese went so far that the European powers and America were forced for the moment to concentrate attention on Asia. They warned off the Japanese, who were not powerful enough to take on the world. And yet...

Within a matter of months, Japan achieved most of its aims in China, as the big powers had turned their attention back to Europe. The demand for Japanese police power in China was too great for anyone to swallow, but it was the only aspect of the Twenty-one Demands left unaccomplished.

In 1917 the United States, about to enter the war on the side of the Allies against Germany, persuaded China that Chinese interests would be served by entering the war on the Allied side. By doing so, China would have a seat at the peace conference, said Washington, and would thus be well served.

*   *   *

The war proceeded. The Russian revolution occurred. In Beijing and other places in China the events in Russia assumed an importance not noted elsewhere, because many young Chinese saw in the Russian revolution some of the solutions to their own problems.

One of the first to sense in the Russian revolution an application for China was Chen Duxiu, dean of the faculty of literature at Beijing University. Another was Li Dazhao, the librarian. Among the young people drawn to these two figures and their ideas was a 25-year-old library assistant named Mao Zedong.

So were many other people, including the writer Hu Shi, who at the time made common cause with the advocates of a Marxist-Leninist revolution. His ideas, however, were more pragmatic; he believed in attacking problems, not in pursuing theories.

During 1918, as the Russian revolution turned that country upside down, the Chinese watched with growing interest. China was particularly interested when it learned that the Soviet government intended to abandon extraterritoriality and other privileges.

At first the Chinese thought this meant the Russians were now ready to give up all their concessions in China, but this was not so. The Soviets still insisted on controlling the Chinese Eastern Railroad, the shortcut across Siberia to Vladivostok. And when the Communist International Movement was established in 1919 the Russians prepared to send delegations to China to further the revolution there. But more interesting to the government and to most Chinese was the Versailles peace conference, which was being held in France. There was much talk, largely from Woodrow Wilson and the Americans, about self-determination for nations. The Chinese welcomed this.

But there was also trouble, at Versailles and elsewhere. The Chinese delegates to the peace conference warned that the Japanese were starting a whole new series of encroachments, being helped, as in the past, by Chinese businessmen who were more interested in enriching themselves than in their country's welfare. "We now hope that public opinion at home will rise up against these traitors so that we here at Versailles may have a chance of negotiating the annulment of the Japanese demands," said the men at the conference.

Several important Chinese officials had indicated their acceptance of the Japanese movement in Shandong Province.

On May 3, 1919, students and faculty members at Beijing University organized a demonstration to be held the next day at the Gate of Heavenly

Peace to demand that China reject the Versailles treaty. The next morning 3000 demonstrators moved from the legation section of Beijing toward the Japanese Legation. They were stopped by American marines at the American Legation. The crowd then moved toward the house of the minister of communications, one of the offending officials. Some of the demonstrators broke into the house, beat up the people they found there, and set the house on fire. The police came in and arrested thirty-two demonstrators.

The demonstration caused a furor throughout China. Sun Yatsen came to the support of the students, as did other leaders of rebel and even right-wing groups.

Versailles engendered a powerful negative response among Chinese students and intellectuals. In Shanghai on June 3, 1919, a mass meeting called for a boycott of Japanese goods. Thus began the use of a weapon which would hurt the Japanese enormously in years to come.

The crisis continued. Many factories shut down. A group of bankers told the government that unless the demands of the public were met, the country would be faced with economic chaos. And so, on June 28, came word that the Chinese delegation had been instructed to leave the Versailles peace conference without signing the treaty.

Thus, for the first time, a relatively unorganized series of popular meetings had forced a new way upon the Chinese government. In history the whole story goes down under the banner "Fourth of May Movement." It was a hallmark in the Chinese revolution.

It was also a parting of the ways between the revolutionaries and the reformers. Hu Shi, a reformer, now saw that the radicals were going to follow a radical policy, and he warned that people should talk less of ideology and more of practical problems. Some were listening to this reiteration. Many were not.

———

The Soviets had sent representatives down to China. Gregory Voitinsky went out in 1920 to organize a Chinese Communist party. He met Li Dazhao. He met Chen Duxiu. He met the young Mao Zedong, head of the Communist cell in Hunan. By July 1921 he had recruited about fifty members for the Communist party of China. Twelve delegates came to Shanghai, and there, in an obscure building on an obscure street in the French concession, they held the First Congress of the Chinese Communist party. Chen Duxiu was elected secretary general, and the first party constitution was adopted.

The group's platform was largely that of the student rebels of the past:

1. Secure the return of territory seized by the Russians.
2. Restore the sovereignty of China.
3. Abandon payment of Boxer Rebellion indemnities.
4. Abolish extraterritoriality and all it implied.
5. Invalidate all unfair agreements made with the old Russian government, which had seized most of Manchuria and larger areas along the northern border.

In 1988 this list of demands does not seem very great, but in the 1920s it seemed enormous. The manifesto was distributed throughout China and it attracted many sympathizers, particularly since it was already known that President Wilson's big talk about "self determination of nations" was not regarded by the United States or the other powers as applying to China. So one might say that the callousness of the western powers, meeting at Versailles and refusing to consider China's demands for freedom, brought Marxism to China to stay.

And there, slowly, it grew. China was a fertile field, the field of revolution, abandoned by the westerners. Chinese students abroad also began to take Marxism very seriously, men such as Zhou Enlai and Deng Xiaoping, who were then students.

Zhou, who rose to become one of the two most powerful men in the modern Chinese People's Republic, and who was the leading pragmatist of recent years, was a boy from Shaoxing, the great rice wine center of Zhejiang Province. His grandfather had been a magistrate there under the empire, but he later moved the family to Huainan, on the Grand Canal, which was Zhou's home when he grew up. Zhou's father, Zhou Shagang, was only a petty official, so the boy did not grow up rich. Rather, he grew up in an atmosphere of debt and moneylenders, which left a distinct impression on his character. In 1910 Zhou Enlai moved to Shenyang, where he went to school and lived with one of his uncles. In 1913 he went to Nankai Middle School in Tianjin, where he was inspired by various revolutionary ideas. In 1917 Zhou went to Japan as a poor student; he studied Japanese and learned to read the language. But when the October Revolution came to Russia, he was immensely intrigued.

In 1919 Zhou went home to become editor of the Tianjin student union newspaper, the *Tianjin Student*. "Democracy: Government for the people, by the people and of the people, our motto," in English, adorned the masthead of the paper. Thus was the rebellion of the Marxists exemplified by and joined with the rebellion of the Americans 200 years earlier. In the Chinese rebels' minds this presented no conflict: A government by the people for the people was what was wanted.

So far, Zhou's philosophy seemed more akin to that of Thomas Jefferson than that of Karl Marx. The theme of the *Tianjin Student* was nationalist. Constantly, it called on the Chinese to struggle to liquidate the feudal bureaucracy and the influence of foreigners. Zhou wrote many fiery articles under the pen name "Fei Fei."

Other newspaper articles and magazine articles, written under the name "Wu Hao," brought Zhou to the attention of the police. In January 1920 the authorities were aroused by the cacophony from the students, and they arrested twenty-eight people, including Zhou Enlai. He was jailed for six months and would have been executed except that students throughout China demanded the prisoners' release. Zhou and his friends kept attention focused on their case by starting a fast, which was reported in student newspapers and embarrassed the government. Finally, the agitators were tried; they further embarrassed the government in the trial, and ultimately they were released.

Shortly afterward, Zhou left China for Paris on a work-study program. There he almost immediately joined the Communist movement, but he was mainly interested in finding in communism a cure for China's ills.

Thus Zhou was in Paris when Mao and the other young radicals formed the Communist party of China on July 1, 1921. Soon enough, the Paris group became a branch of the Communist party and Zhou was made secretary.

In 1922, Chen Jiongming, the warlord, made a lightning coup and overthrew the government of Sun Yatsen in Guangzhou. Sun fled to Shanghai, where he encountered the Russians. The Chinese Communist party had set up headquarters in Shanghai. Secretary Chen Duxiu was organizing labor unions, and calling strikes in mining, railroad, and shipping industries. These strikes were quite successful in bringing public attention to the Communists. The party grew.

The party had more than 120 members when it held its general meeting in Shanghai in the summer of 1922. That year the party voted to join the Communist International. A manifesto was promulgated, calling for a Chinese revolution, with the Communists side by side with the workers, peasants, and bourgeoisie (there were 3 million "middle class" in China, out of a population of 500 million).

After the Shanghai meeting, which, as usual, was in constant danger from police surveillance and raids, the Communists reassembled at Hangzhou, the lake resort city. There Comrade Voitinsky, the Russian, and Comrade Maring, a Dutchman who had come over from Japan, pushed the Chinese into joining Sun Yatsen's Guomindang movement as individuals. This was, said the foreign revolutionaries, the strongest rebel movement in China and could be used to further the Communist cause. At first, the Chinese Communists rebelled, out of a sense of purity, but they were hushed by the practical internationalists. Hushed, but not convinced. It took something practical to convince them, and this happened in February 1923, when the Communists called a strike of workers on the Beijing-Hangkou railroad. The strike began, but the warlord Wu Peifu sent in troops and broke the strike. Thus the Communists learned the need for combined effort and a policy of practical alliance.

The Communist movement grew, and by the summer of 1923 the party numbered 432 members. The party met at Guangzhou that year. In the meetings it was finally agreed to encourage the Communist members to join the Guomindang.

Meanwhile, other Russians had been approaching Sun Yatsen. After his flight to Shanghai in 1922, Dr. Sun gave up hope of dealing with the warlords. Sun had met with Adolf Joffe, another Comintern agent, and they had made a joint statement that Moscow wanted Chinese national unity. So did the Guomindang.

So a marriage between Guomindang and Communists was arranged. Li Dazhao joined the Guomindang. So did other Communists, as well as some Marxists who were not Communists. Chief of these, historically speaking, was Wang Jingwei, a long-time follower of Sun's revolution, who had recently returned from exile in France.

In the summer of 1923, the Russians promised support of Sun Yatsen's revolutionary government, and he moved down to Guangzhou. The Guomindang was preparing to seize power from the warlords, unite China under a revolutionary banner, and create the republic that had for so long been promised.

7
The Rise of the Guomindang

My mission is full of danger but as long as the people understand me
I have no fear.

—Sun Yatsen

In the summer of 1922 the nationalist Republic of China was in shambles,
and the warlords were in control everywhere, subject only to the authority
of the foreigners, who ran the ports and sent warships up the Yangtze River
from time to time. The attitude of the United States, Britain, Japan, and,
indeed, all the principal powers save Russia toward China was very clearly
shown at the Washington armament conference of 1922. On February 6
the nine powers attending signed a treaty which guaranteed China's independence and territorial integrity and reiterated the American "open-door"
principle. Another treaty returned to China some control over its customs
service. Still another treaty provided that Japan would give back the Shandong Province territories which it had captured from the Germans. The
essence of the treaties, however, was the preservation of the status quo,
with the warlords in control of China.

After Sun Yatsen had been driven out of Guangzhou by the warlord
Chen Jiongming, Sun had fled to the international concession in Shanghai, where he was safe from the warlords. Then the Comintern took a hand.

The Soviets decided to play a dual role in China. On the one side,
they organized and supported the small Chinese Communist party. But on
the other hand, they backed Dr. Sun's Guomindang. Lenin's theory held
that the "bourgeois revolution" could achieve power, because it had much
stronger backing from the peasants than the Communists did, and then the
Communists could take over from within. The theory worked time and
again in later years in other countries (notably in Hungary and Czecho-
slovakia after World War II). But the China of the 1920s was quite a different matter. It soon became obvious that the small, but dedicated and
loyal, band of Communists was a long way from power.

In 1922 the agents of the Kremlin were trying to decide just what to do. Comintern representative Maring had gone to Wu Peifu, the strongest warlord in north China, with an eye toward working out some deal with him. But Maring came away disappointed. Wu Peifu was certainly powerful, but he was totally untrustworthy from the Communist point of view. He had no socialist leanings whatsoever, and it seemed most unlikely that his position could be undermined from within.

Gregory Voitinsky was in China, working with the infant Communist movement, teaching Chen and Da and Mao how to foment strikes and create agitation in the cities. The strength of the party had doubled by the summer of 1922 when the Communist party held its second convention in Shanghai. One delegate who was supposed to be there was Mao Zedong of Hunan Province, but Mao had forgotten the address. He wandered around looking for the place but was unable to find it, so he went back to Hunan.

Mao's real work at this point was labor organization, and he was very good at it. He organized a number of strikes. That year the governor of Hunan had ordered the execution of two workers for agitation. One of these men, Huang Ai, was an anti-Communist, a member of an industrial school group. But Mao was shrewd enough to know who the real enemy was, so the Communists supported Huang Ai, although it did not do much good: He was executed.

While some Soviet agents were talking to various elements in China, hoping to find a roosting place, other agents were talking to Dr. Sun. He was receptive. He had not been able to attract the sort of support from the western powers that meant guns and bullets. The Russians offered him these things; and he was so certain of his own strengths, in spite of the dangers, that he was sure he could use the Russians, and not have it the other way around.

In September 1922 Sun Yatsen called a meeting of the Guomindang members and some others to discuss the reorganization of the whole revolutionary movement and the government. He invited members of the Communist party to participate.

In January 1923 the Sun-Joffe Manifesto was issued in Shanghai. It skirted the issue of communism: China was not ready for communism, said the participants. It stated that China needed help to become unified and independent and that the Russians were prepared to help Dr. Sun. A few months later Michael Borodin arrived in China and became Dr. Sun's special political adviser. Russian military and economic help began to flow into China, and the effects appeared almost immediately.

Borodin was a shrewd and able revolutionary, a Latvian Jew who had joined the Bolshevik movement very early and had been exiled to America by the czar's government. He had sought the company of radicals in America and taught English to European immigrants at Jane Addams's Hull House in Chicago. After the October Revolution he returned to Russia; he was soon made an agent of the Comintern and entrusted with missions to several countries. Borodin was generally successful in these, so he was dispatched to China to bring about successful revolution there.

By the fall of 1923 Dr. Sun had returned to Guangzhou, and Borodin was with him. Soon a number of Russian advisers began drifting into China. Members of the Chinese Communist party began to join the Guomindang, although they retained their memberships in the Communist party and there was no question as to where their sympathies lay.

The third Congress of the Chinese Communist Party was held in Guangzhou that year. Afterward, Mao Zedong moved from Hunan to Shanghai to work in the Central Committee of the Communist party there. He was also a member of the Executive Bureau of the Guomindang, a three-man committee whose other members were Wang Jingwei and Hu Hanmin. Mao worked very hard but fell ill, so ill that he had to go home to Hunan for a rest. But soon he was up and about and spent his time organizing the peasants of Hunan. Peasant organization was a job that not many Communist leaders were undertaking, but Mao understood, as did few others, the basic route that a successful revolution in China had to follow: a revolution of the life of the poor peasants.

Borodin set about reorganizing the Guomindang. Wang Jingwei soon became Dr. Sun's principal Chinese political adviser.

Borodin had precisely the right idea. If the revolution was to succeed, where all Dr. Sun's previous efforts had failed, then it must have muscle. "Muscle" meant a military force that could overwhelm the warlords, and the Russians pledged to support that military force. Dr. Sun appointed a young officer named Chiang Kaishek to lead the army.

Chiang was the son of a merchant who lived near the treaty port of Ningbo. After studying in a Chinese middle school, Chiang went to Japan in 1906. There he became attracted to Dr. Sun's revolutionary movement. Deciding on a military career, he hurried back to China to study at the

Baoding Military Academy. Then he returned to Tokyo to enlist young Chinese students as potential officers of the revolutionary army while he studied at the Japanese military academy. In 1911, once again in China, he began working his way up in the republic's military organization. It was a tortuous path and many slipped, but not Chiang. Several times he returned to Japan, and he came to know Dr. Sun better and better. Meanwhile, he was establishing himself in Shanghai, where he was associated with T. V. Soong, a rising capitalist (Chiang later divorced his wife and married Soong's sister, Soong Meiling). Chiang gained political and economic power through T. V. Soong, and through the "Green Gang," the power in central China's underworld.

Chiang had worked for Sun in Guangzhou in the early 1920s, but as an officer for Chen Jiongming, the local warlord, who was then supporting Sun. When Chen suddenly turned on Sun in 1922, Chiang escaped with Sun on a gunboat which Chiang had provided. Thus he gained the confidence of the revolutionary and was chosen to head the Guomindang military organization in 1923. One of his first assignments was to take a military mission to the Soviet Union in the fall of 1923.

He studied Soviet military science and tactics there, and he came home with his head full of respect for the Russian dictatorship. Then he settled down to work as commander of the Huangpu Military Academy. In 1924 he supervised the training of 2000 cadets, in three classes. This group would later emerge as the Huangpu Clique, the backbone of the Chinese Nationalist military forces.

Chiang, then, was to the military what Wang Jingwei was to the political system. He gained a good knowledge of the politics of the revolution and the ways of the Soviets and the Chinese Communists. Down to south China came more Soviet instructors, including Vassily Blucher, who was known to the Chinese as General Galen.

Also to south China came a young but highly competent man from France, Zhou Enlai, who had been managing the Chinese Communist party's affairs in Paris. He became political director of the Huangpu Military Academy and also, more than incidentally, director of the Communist party's education and recruitment program in Guangdong and Guangxi provinces.

On the political front, Borodin supervised the reorganization of the Guomindang on the lines of the Soviet Communist party. The organization was pyramidal. At the top was Dr. Sun, who became "president for life." The constitution drafted by Borodin gave President Sun ultimate power over policy. In January 1924 the Guomindang held a new congress in Guangzhou. Very prominent in the discussions were the Communist-Guomindang members. The congress declared war on the warlords and the imperialist powers that supported them. The Guomindang announced that it would lead a united front, supporting peasants and workers and all revolutionary forces, to triumph over the warlords. At that time, Lenin died, and Dr. Sun sent a message of support to Moscow.

At the same time, a hot debate was raging in Soviet Communist party circles. Leon Trotzky, who aspired to be Lenin's successor, had no faith in the arrangement with the Guomindang. He did not believe in alliance with bourgeois elements, and he wanted to jettison the Guomindang and support the Chinese Communist party. Josef Stalin, who also aspired to be leader of the Soviet Union, backed Sun Yatsen.

The "three principles of the people" (*San Min Zhu Yi*) were reenunciated and changed somewhat. Nationalism had earlier been dedicated to the overthrow of the Manchus. Now it was turned against the warlords and the foreign imperialists who controlled so much of China. The principle of "people's rights," which had been a cornerstone of Guomindang policy, was revised. The people were to have their rights, but not just yet. A military dictatorship was needed to unify the country. When unification was achieved, then the Guomindang would take over and lead the people. Little by little the people would be encouraged to participate in government, and to elect the legislative, executive, and judicial yuans, or branches.

The third principle, which enunciated the government's responsibility for the people's economic welfare, was left vague. Land was to be reformed, but not by taking it from the landlords. The "state" would provide land for landless peasants.

Many of the more conservative members of the Guomindang objected to the revision of the three principles of the people and complained that Sun Yatsen was playing into the hands of the Communists. But Sun was obdurate. "If you don't want to cooperate with the Communists," he said, "I'll declare the Guomindang dissolved, and join the Communist party."

Or so he was quoted as saying. Certainly, Sun understood, as did few others, the sources of his own renewed power. Cooperation with the Communists and the retention of Soviet assistance were essential to his revolution at the moment. He, like the Russians, was complacent about the future, expecting that at the proper moment he could cement his power without the coalition. He had been careful: When the Communists proposed to join the Guomindang, he insisted that they do so as individuals, which meant that their influence in the party councils could not be exerted as a bloc. Thus the Communist party could not seize control of the Guomindang.

In 1924 there were a lot of doubts in south China about the Guomindang and its alliance with the Communists. The Communists continued with their labor organization and fomented many strikes. A group of merchants and landowners had organized a Volunteer Defense Corps—really a hired band of soldiers—to protect themselves from the incursions of warlords in the area. In 1924 the merchants and landowners began to worry more about the Guomindang. Encouragement for their views came from Hong Kong, and Sun Yatsen blamed the British for this. He was very watchful, and in the summer of 1924 he discovered that the merchants were having a shipment of weapons sent from Hong Kong. The Nationalist forces seized them. When the Volunteers protested and tried to threaten Sun, he ordered Chiang Kaishek to suppress the whole volunteer army, which Chiang did in short order. Thus, for the first time, the new government had used its military power in a small way.

That year, 1924, was the occasion for a serious breach in the warlord front. Four years earlier Wu Peifu, the most important warlord in the north, had made an alliance with Zhang Zuolin, the warlord of Manchuria and Shandong. But in 1922 Wu had turned on Zhang and expelled his forces from north China inside the Great Wall. In 1924 Wu decided to invade the northeastern provinces, Manchuria, Zhang's home ground. The plan was to march to Shanhaiguan, where the Great Wall comes down to the sea, and then move outside and to the northeast. To guard his flanks, Wu chose Feng Yuxiang, "the Christian general."

There was not much love lost between these two, although Feng was Wu's subordinate. But Feng was a puritan of a man, and Wu was a supreme hedonist who drank like a fish. One time, Feng sent Wu a bottle of water for his birthday. The hint was not appreciated.

When Wu was so unwise as to move his troops to the Great Wall, far from Beijing, General Feng acted with celerity. He occupied Beijing and then called on all the generals to stop fighting and join together for national unity. Wu Peifu had to abandon his pursuit of power in Manchuria, with his rear in danger, and moved down to the Yangtze valley. Warlords Duan Qirui and Zhang Zuolin made encouraging noises about unity of all the forces in China, and to that end Sun Yatsen was invited to come up to Beijing and talk about a national government of unity. Sun, a very practical man in some ways, was delighted with the prospect. Although he had openly declared war on the warlords, he privately did not regard them as posing any greater threat than the Communists. As he had said, his road was fraught with dangers; yet he continued.

In January 1925 Sun went to Beijing. The warlords were not very pleased with the tenor of the talks, which called for a convention of a provisional assembly that would include workers and peasants, students and professors— all the people who gave the warlords so much trouble. But the issue never came to a head, for on the journey, Sun Yatsen fell ill; the doctors diagnosed his ailment as an advanced case of cancer. Sun had, in fact, only three months to live. He was in Beijing in March 1925 when he died, leaving the people the heritage of the San Min Zhu Yi, and the advice that they must continue to cooperate with the Soviet Union in China's interest.

8
Gathering Unity

The theater was filled with soldiers and officers of the Peoples' Army [the first Guominchun]. The main topic was the shooting at Shanghai [May 30, 1925]. The author of the play came onto the stage in parade uniform. He explained to the audience that the play, written by him in obedience to [Marshall Feng Yuxiang's] orders, represented the Shanghai shooting and the events of recent days. He hoped the spectators would be tolerant of the literary quality of the play for he was not a writer. He was only a patriot, and he said he would be glad if the play stimulated their feelings of patriotism and their readiness to fight for China. He finished his speech with the words, uttered in the typical fashion of Chinese agitators:

—"Foreigners are shooting our brothers and plundering our country. Can it be that you do not think we should arm ourselves?"

This appeal called forth a storm of applause and approving voices. The author saluted and went into the wings.

—Notes of a volunteer, depicting events two days
after the May 30 incident in Shanghai

It was May 1925. President Sun Yatsen was scarcely cold in his grave. Shanghai was seriously troubled that spring by economic dislocation, most of it caused by the expansion of Japanese and other foreign industries, which were literally taking the rice from the mouths of China's workers. In half a dozen years, the number of spindles in Japanese-owned cotton mills in China had increased to two-thirds of the number in Chinese-owned mills. The Japanese owned twenty-seven mills in Shanghai alone. In every industry the foreigners were encroaching more on Chinese business. Chinese businessmen were nervous, and some were on the verge of bankruptcy.

A dispute at a Japanese cotton mill erupted in violence on May 15 when the Japanese objected to Chinese labor organizers moving in to talk to the workers. The Japanese supervisory personnel opened fire on the Chinese. One worker was killed and several others were wounded. The man killed happened to be a member of the Chinese Communist party, which aroused the party to more than its usual heights of emotional oratory. Two thousand students moved into the International Settlement distributing leaflets complaining about foreign encroachment. The police arrested several hundred and were brutal in their assaults on others.

In the next few days they marched. On May 30 thousands of people surrounded the police station, demanding that the arrested people be released. Soon a crowd estimated at 10,000 was milling about. The British police officer in charge of the station panicked and sent the police out in force; they fired on the crowd, killing ten people and injuring fifty. It happened outside the Nanjiang Road police station, so the incident was named the "Nanjiang Road incident."

News of the event spread immediately across China. In Shanghai the Communists formed an action committee. The Workers' General Union, with 200,000 members, was established in the wake of this action. On June 1 a strike began, supported by students and Shanghai shopkeepers. Activity in that big city stopped cold. Foreign goods were boycotted. Shops and banks closed. Students stayed away from school. Workers struck. Fifteen days later 150,000 people were on strike in Shanghai, and people were striking in a dozen other cities in China.

But the Shanghai strike ultimately failed because of the divergent interests of the participants. The working class and students wanted power for workers and peasants, but the Shanghai merchants and industrial leaders were frightened of such an approach, seeing in it the end of their own management and profits. A joint committee had been formed to direct policy, but soon the merchants and industrialists were quarreling with policy. The General Chamber of Commerce of Shanghai announced that it would mediate between the Chinese striking force and the foreigners of Shanghai who ran the city. The joint committee offered to call off the strike if seventeen demands were met, but the Chamber of Commerce ignored four of these. It did not pass along the demands for the right of workers to strike, their right to organize trade unions, the abolition of extraterritoriality, and the control of the International Settlement by the Chinese.

And as the strike continued, the Chinese businessmen were hurt. By June 25 the strike was in shambles, as businessmen defected and began doing business with the foreigners once more.

The final blow came when the foreigners cut off electric service to the people (and industries) within the city. The Shanghai power plant was located in the International Settlement and was managed by foreigners. During the strike the Chinese workers walked off the job, and supervisors took over. They managed to keep the plant going, but in the arguments over policy the management decided that service to Chinese factories outside the settlement would be discontinued on July 1. More and more Chinese businessmen and industrialists then turned against the strike. By August the warlords in the area were talking about "punishing" the strikers. The strike leaders had hoped to achieve political gains as well as economic ones, but by mid-August they had given up the political aspect, and in September they settled for pay raises and some amelioration of working conditions. So the strike was not a complete failure, nor was it a success. It was, however, a warning to the two sides that neither could really trust the other.

In Hunan Province, in the wake of the May 30 incident, Mao Zedong organized some twenty peasant unions in a few months. The landlords in the area became enraged and appealed to the local warlord, Zhao Hengti. He sent troops to capture Mao, but Mao fled ahead of them and reached Guangzhou safely. There he arrived just on the heels of news that Yang Ximin, the Yunnan warlord, had gone down to defeat and that Liu Zhen-huan, the Guangxi warlord, had also been deposed by people's uprisings. The Guomindang was moving ahead. Wang Jingwei had become chairman of the government following the death of Sun Yatsen, and Chiang Kaishek had taken over as commander of the First Army.

The Communists were very active in the Guomindang at this time. One might say it was the halcyon day of the coalition between Communists and "bourgeois revolutionaries." The Communists had important posts in the organizational area in particular: Tan Pingshan was chief of the worker department; Lin Boqu was chief of the peasant department.

Mao Zedong became editor of *Political Weekly*, the Guomindang's propaganda magazine. Soon he was also put in charge of training organizers for the peasant movement, based on his successful efforts in Hunan. He wrote two pamphlets which were at the time controversial, and both were suppressed by the Communist party leadership because they advocated a radical policy of land reform and organization of the peasantry. He set up a training course which was attended by students from twenty-one different provinces. And then he was made chief of the Agitprop department of the Guomindang. In that role Mao was responsible for propaganda.

*   *   *

While the Communists were steadily gaining important positions within the organizational structure of the Guomindang, there was a struggle for power at the top. After Sun Yatsen died, the struggle came out into the open.

Three candidates now sought the leadership of the Guomindang: Wang Jingwei, Hu Hanmin, and Liao Zhongkai. All had been associated with Sun Yatsen since 1905. Hu Hanmin was the apparent leader, having been elected first-ranking member of the Guomindang Central Executive Committee in 1924. He had consistently been close to Sun Yatsen, and he had led several of the abortive revolutionary attempts of the early years. But Wang Jingwei had been elected number 2 man on the party's Central Executive Committee at the Guomindang congress of 1924.

Liao Zhongkai was the Guomindang financial man. He was close to the Communists in theory and advocated the development of socialism in China. Indeed, he had been the man who persuaded Sun Yatsen that his course lay with the Russians, and he had worked out the agreement with Joffe that was announced in Shanghai in 1922. He was a member of the Central Executive Committee; he was in charge of worker and peasant affairs; and he had taken charge of political education at Huangpu Military Academy, where he brought in the young Zhou Enlai, a Communist, to direct political education. He was the leader of the left wing of the Guomindang and was responsible for the rise of the Communists within the organization.

Following Sun Yatsen's death, government of the Guomindang passed into the hands of a committee of sixteen. Wang Jingwei was elected chairman of the committee for the time being. Hu Hanmin became foreign minister. It was a nice title, but it did not mean much because the Guomindang was not recognized as a national government by any other countries. Liao Zhongkai became finance minister.

For two years the conservatives in the Guomindang had fretted under the alliance with the Communists. They saw their party moving further and further to the left as the Communists assumed many new posts. Although Wang Jingwei was chairman, Communists held the key organizational jobs. The right-wing members particularly objected to a passage in the party's manifesto of 1924 which denounced warlords. The only warlord who seemed to be a threat at the moment they said, was Wu Peifu.

The quarrel between right and left began to come to a head in the summer of 1925. The first sign of real friction was the assassination of Liao Zhongkai, who was killed on the railroad platform at Shanghai. A committee was appointed to investigate the murder, and the finger was pointed at Hu Hanmin. He retired then as foreign minister and stepped down from public life. The furor abated, and the mystery was never solved.

At the end of 1925 a group of conservatives who called themselves the "Western Hills Group," because they met in the western hills near Beijing, met at the Green Cloud Monastery, where Sun Yatsen's remains had been taken. There they passed a series of resolutions demanding the removal of Borodin as adviser to the party, a break with the Russians, and the expulsion of the Communists from the Guomindang.

Back in Guangzhou the left wing of the Guomindang party adopted Wang Jingwei as its favorite. This move angered the right wing. Amid the struggle that continued to grow in intensity, the Second National Congress of the Guomindang was called for January 1926.

From the viewpoint of the conservatives the congress was an unmitigated disaster. More leftists were elected to high posts, and that meant more Communists. In fact, half the high posts were in the hands of the Communists or their friends.

Borodin was delighted with the results of the congress. He felt that it would soon be time to amalgamate the gains of the Communists and to prepare to take control of the Guomindang. Buoyed by this turn of events, Borodin set out north for a visit to Feng Yuxiang, "the Christian general," whose friendship the Russians found worth cultivating.

———

Chiang Kaishek was shrewd, probably the shrewdest man in the Guomindang. He saw that cooperation with the Communists was important to the revolutionary movement as long as it was relatively weak, so he advocated biding time. That attitude, indeed, was responsible for his being chosen by Borodin as military leader of the party, a post in which he shared government responsibility with Wang Jingwei. In the fall of 1925 Chiang had shown his loyalty to the party and his ability as a leader by defeating the warlord of Guangdong Province, thus putting the province for the first time under complete control of the Guomindang.

While Borodin was up north, several matters came up. First was the emergence of a group in the military academy that was advocating a new interpretation of Sun Yatsen's San Min Zhu Yi principles of the people. Saying there was no necessary conflict between landlord and peasant, this group wanted to eliminate the claim that a class war was essential for the revolution. The Communists opposed this attitude vigorously, and a conflict developed within the academy.

Chiang was very much alive to possibilities of a coup within the party, which might have come from either side in those days of tension. One day in March 1926 the captain of a gunboat suddenly moved the boat from its mooring to a place near the Huangpu Military Academy. Chiang said this indicated an attempt to stage a coup, and he seized the gunboat. At the same time a strike was being supported in Guangzhou and Hong Kong, and Chiang said that within the headquarters of the strikers was another group ready to stage a coup. The Guomindang army surrounded the headquarters and disarmed the volunteer militia which had been formed to protect the strike headquarters. In the name of the party Chiang declared martial law in Guangzhou. Further, the Communist leaders of the strike were arrested and so were the Russian advisers of the group. Later, those Russians were sent back to the Soviet Union.

Chiang said that his actions had prevented attempts to seize control of the Guomindang. The Communists said that Chiang himself had staged the events as a means of cementing his military power. He was certainly capable of doing just that. Chiang's maneuverings in the future showed a tortuous path, as he pitted one army against another, one warlord against another, one political faction against another, and one man against another, usually with marked success. Chiang was certainly the Machiavelli of the east.

Further, he really did seize control of the Guomindang, and he accomplished this by taking tight control of the army. Recognizing what was happening, Wang Jingwei left Guangzhou and went to France. Chiang called a meeting of the Central Executive Committee for May.

When the returning Soviet advisers got to Moscow, they had sad stories to tell. But when Borodin came back down from Beijing, he looked around and reported that Chiang had been quite right: The Communists of the strike committee had gone too far, too fast, and had brought down the wrath of the Guomindang leader on their own heads. Chiang, having cemented his personal power, said that he had no quarrel with the Communists within the Guomindang.

"For us to kill Communists," he said at the meeting of the Guomindang

Central Committee in May 1926, "would be just plain suicide." (History shows that he was right, but his actions a few years later belied his belief in this philosophy.) Moreover, he said that he did not believe the Communist leaders had in fact been behind the strike committee that was planning the coup. He had nothing against Communists, he said, as long as they were loyal to the Guomindang revolutionary movement.

But out of that meeting came several directives that pointed the way to the future. The Communists must not criticize Sun Yatsen or his works. No Communist was to be chairman of the Central Executive Committee or director of any Guomindang department. The Communists must also submit to the Guomindang Central Executive Committee a list of all their members who were also members of the Guomindang. This was important because the Communist party had been growing rapidly—it now numbered several thousand—and not all the Communists in the Guomindang were known. Some had first joined the Guomindang and later joined the Communist party.

The Guomindang continued to be revolutionary in its approach to Chinese life. As the revolutionary leaders agreed, it was important to change the lives of the people on the land. The principal advocate of this position in the Guomindang party was Peng Pai, one of Mao Zedong's mentors and director of the peasant department of the Guomindang. He was the son of a landlord, but he had become a Communist. Early on, Peng had persuaded the peasants of his district of Haifeng in Guangdong Province to organize a union. By 1923 he had organized the Haifeng Federation of Peasant Associations, which worked to achieve a better life for peasants, to lower rents charged by landlords, and to bring public education, welfare, and public health measures to the villages. By 1924 he had been made secretary of the Guomindang peasant department, and he brought in Mao and other agitators. By the end of 1925 the association numbered 600,000 members in Guangdong, and it was beginning to worry some in the Guomindang because of its radical policies. In some areas the peasants were banding together and forcing the expropriation of the lands of landlords and the execution of some of those landlords. More and more these measures worried the leaders of the Guomindang, even as Chiang Kaishek announced his solidarity with the Communists.

The fact, of course, was that in limiting the roles the Communists could play in the Guomindang, Chiang was showing his basic distrust of them. The coalition had really already come unstuck, although for practical purposes Chiang was not yet ready to throw the Communists out of the Guomindang and to seek the destruction of the party by killing all its members.

*   *   *

At the same time, though, Chiang maneuvered the party leadership into a new position. Not only were the Communists eliminated from leadership of the various departments of the Guomindang, but now they were to have no more than one-third of the seats in the party's Central Committee. Mao Zedong, who had risen so far so fast, was suddenly deprived of his important posts in the national party structure and sent back to Shanghai. There he had nothing to do with Guomindang affairs but directed the peasant department of the Communist party. Soon he moved back up to Hunan as inspector of the party for the peasant movement.

Chiang then set out to confuse the Russians and the Communists with a whole series of conciliatory actions and statements. He apologized to the Russians for sending their advisers back to Moscow and said it had all been caused by a misunderstanding between his subordinates. Perhaps that was true, for Chiang also dismissed several ultra-conservative officials of the Guomindang and asserted once more that there was no reason that Communists and Guomindang members could not continue to cooperate. But the Russian advisers were not invited back to Guangzhou, and what went almost unnoticed at the time was the change that Chiang had wrought in the control of the Guomindang. For the first time the leading figure, Chiang, was a military man. Civilian control, always so carefully maintained by Sun Yatsen, was being eroded rapidly. And very soon it would be eroded even more, for Chiang thought it was now time to launch a military expedition to the north to unify China under Guomindang rule.

By careful manipulation, in just two years Chiang Kaishek had elevated himself from commander of the Guomindang military academy—an important but basically technical post—to top leadership of the Guomindang itself. He still did not have absolute authority, but in 1926 he was easily the most important man in the Guomindang. In June the Guomindang conferred on Chiang authority as supreme commander of the northern expedition that was planned to unify the country and eliminate the warlords. From that point on, for Chiang Kaishek, there was no looking back.

9

The Northern Expedition

Prior to the arrival of the Guomindang in the Wuhan center in the fall of 1926, the labor unions in that region were inactive and reactionary, because they had long been under the suppression of the military authorities, especially since the unsuccessful strike of the Beijing-Hankou railway workers in 1923. But within three months after the Guomindang government was established in September 1926, about two hundred unions sprang up in Hankou, Hanyang, and Wuchang, following a series of prolonged and uncompromising strikes in the principal trades and industries there.

—Zhang Guotao

For several years the military leaders of the Guomindang had been talking about a "northern expedition" by which the armies of the south would march to Beijing, wiping out the warlord control of central and north China.

This new Guomindang army was highly motivated, led by officers trained at the Huangpu Military Academy under Chiang Kaishek and indoctrinated in the politics of revolution by Zhou Enlai, the political director of the academy. The soldiers knew that they would be fighting for a cause: elimination of the warlords and of foreign control of China.

Twice before, the troops had set out, but each time they had been called back by some negative turn of events in Guangzhou. The Guomindang congress of 1924 had called for such an expedition to eliminate the warlords, but the Communists in the Guomindang had disagreed: The southern armies were not strong enough to take on such men as Feng Yuxiang and Zhang Zuolin, they said. Borodin, the Russian adviser, had at first sided with the Communist leaders, but Chiang got around him. In effect, Chiang traded continued support for the principle of Nationalist-Communist cooperation for Borodin's approval of the northern expedition. In the spring of 1926 Chiang Kaishek was ready. He had achieved single-handed leadership of the Guomindang in the absence of Wang Jingwei, who had gone to France. Chiang had 50,000 troops ready to march.

In May the Third National Workers' Congress was held in Guangzhou. Five hundred delegates attended, representing 1,250,000 workers. That same month a peasant congress was also held in Guangzhou, attended by delegates from eleven provinces who represented a million peasants. The Guomindang had gone a long way toward organizing the people for revolution, obviously. Peasants and workers were instructed that they must work together to overthrow their oppressors and bring unity to those areas taken out of warlord control.

In June 1926 Chiang was given dictatorial powers for the duration of the campaign, and the first operations began. Guangxi troops entered Hunan.

Chiang issued a proclamation:

The bandit Wu Peifu has for his slogan "Put down the Reds!" This is the watchword of the Imperialists against the oppressed peoples of the world and is aimed at destroying the united revolutionary front. What does "red" mean? It means the Red party and the Red Army of Soviet Russia, who use the Red Flag as the symbol of the red blood of the revolutionary masses, shed as the price of national independence and freedom. It means the release of mankind from misery, the guarantee of human rights, opposition to international imperialism, the abrogation of unequal treaties and the liberation of two thousand and fifty million people over the whole earth. If a government is a government of the masses and its army is an army of the masses, why should it be called "red"?

The western wing of the army was led by a regiment under Gen. Ye Ting, a Communist. His objectives were the provinces of Hunan and Hubei. Ahead of him were the worker and peasant organizations, spreading Guomindang propaganda against warlord Wu Peifu.

This propaganda caused the peasants and the workers to stage strikes and to impede the movement of Wu Peifu's soldiers. By the end of July Hunan was cleared of warlord troops. On August 12 the Guomindang army captured Changsha, the capital of Hunan. Wu Peifu retreated into Henan.

Other Nationalist forces had moved into Jiangxi, Fujian, and Zhejiang. By the end of August the revolutionary armies were outside the walls of the three cities that make up the Wuhan complex: Hankou, Wuchang, and Hanyang, in the Yangtze River valley.

In September the Central Committee of the Guomindang met to consider events. The left wing was enormously pleased with news from Hunan. Mao Zedong's campaign of organizing the peasantry had apparently been more successful than anyone had hoped, and it had paved the way for the Guomindang military successes. But Communist leader Chen Duxiu and adviser Borodin were aghast. The word had come that Mao Zedong was taking the land from the landlords and giving it to the peasants. This was suicidal, said the gloomy Russians. Such action at that time jeopardized the support of the "bourgeoisie," without which the revolution could not possibly succeed.

The second and third columns of the Northern Expeditionary Force, led by Chiang Kaishek's Guomindang troops, marched against warlord Sun Chuangfang. The central force, led by Chiang, reached Nanchang in November, and he stopped it there to set up for the winter and consolidate his control. The third column reached Fuzhou on December 2. Soon the Nationalist forces moved into Anhui Province, north of Jiangxi.

Where the armies moved, the workers and peasants were quick to organize and seize power. In Hunan Province the young Mao Zedong was in his element. When the army arrived, the peasants arrested the landlords, put paper hats on their heads, and paraded them through the villages. The landlords were put before "accusation meetings," and their crimes were detailed by their accusers. Many of them were shot. Many heads were cut off. The peasants demanded reduction of rents and interest rates. They invaded the landlords' compounds, slaughtered their pigs, and took their grain, which was then distributed among the peasants.

Mao Zedong was ecstatic:

> In a few months the peasants have accomplished what Dr. Sun Yatsen wanted, but failed to accomplish in the forty years he devoted to the Nationalist revolution. This is a marvelous feat never before achieved, not just in forty years but in thousands of years.

*   *   *

The leftists in Guangzhou were eager to move the government up to the site of their success in Wuhan, particularly after Wuchang fell on October 10. Chiang Kaishek opposed moving the government seat to central China: If the capital was to be moved anywhere, it should follow the commander in chief, himself. But at that time Chiang had not yet captured any important center, and Wuhan was sitting there, ripe. After Chiang captured Nanchang in November and settled down there for the winter, he demanded that the government seat be moved to that city if it was moved anywhere.

The Guomindang back in Guangzhou was in the hands of the leftists, now that Chiang had left the city. They ignored Chiang's demands, and went ahead with their plans to move the capital to Hankou, in the Wuhan complex.

Chiang was deprived of his political posts in the party, but he still commanded his army in the field, or two prongs of it at least. The third prong, centered in Wuhan, was Communist. The Nationalist revolution had already begun to come apart as the Communist faction exercised the sinews of power. From Nanchang, Chiang Kaishek watched with growing alarm. The activities in central China indicated that the Communists would soon move to take control of the Guomindang. In fact, they had already done so by November 1926.

Foreign observers in Shanghai also became alarmed with the Communist success. Here is the recollection of John B. Powell, editor of the American-owned *China Weekly Review* of Shanghai:

> I had received numerous intimations long before the Nationalist armies reached the Yangtze that all was not going well with the Guomindang-Communist partnership. The information I had received in the form of two confidential pamphlets addressed by General Chiang Kaishek to the party leaders, in which he charged that the Communists were secretly plotting to oust the Guomindang and seize control of the party organization and ultimately of the Government.

The Communists got what they wanted in a hurry.

With the leftists in control of the Guomindang Central Committee in Guangzhou, the Guomindang Nationalist government then moved up from Guangzhou to Wuhan. After the government reached Wuhan, adviser Borodin wanted Chiang to move north and join forces with Feng Yuxiang, who had declared his adherence to the Nationalist cause (and therefore was no longer considered to be a warlord), against Zhang Zuolin, the warlord of Manchuria. But Chiang Kaishek rejected Borodin's advice and turned toward Nanjing and Shanghai, the rich industrial region that was the source of foreign control of China. The local warlord was Sun Chuangfang, who dominated the five provinces of the lower river valley. In the face of Chiang's threat Sun called for help from Zhang Zuolin, and he got it. The campaign of Jiang's First Army in the Yangtze valley slowed down in heavy fighting.

In Wuhan, the victorious Guomindang, heavily charged with Communists, staged a victory celebration on January 3, 1927. Two warlord generals who had been captured at Wuchang were put on "trial." Thousands of workers thronged the streets in parades and demonstrations. They were addressed by Agitprop workers, who called for more action. Students and laborers carried banners:

"Support the World Revolution."

"Down with Capitalists and Imperialists."

"Workers of the World, Unite."

The same sort of activity was occurring in other cities newly captured by the Guomindang armies. At Nanjing, 400 miles down the Yangtze River, the crowds surged around the American concession and began attacking. American gunboats fired on the demonstrators.

The demonstrators in Hankou, eager for action, looked over the foreign concessions there. The Japanese concession, they noted, was bristling with machine guns and fierce-looking Japanese soldiers. But the British concession was a different matter; it was guarded by only a handful of Royal Marines, augmented by a small police force. The paraders marched on the British concession. The British marines resisted and fixed bayonets. The crowd surged forward. In the melee one man was killed and several demonstrators were wounded. As the crowd of thousands moved toward the buildings, British Consul General O'Malley ordered the British population to move to the British warships in the harbor. From there, Consul O'Malley negotiated an agreement with representatives of the Guomindang to return the British concession to Chinese control. The British Foreign Office in London approved, and it was done.

The Communists were as ecstatic as Mao had ever been. Not only had the revolution freed much of the countryside from landlord control, but for the first time since the First Opium War, the Chinese had scored a victory over the foreign imperialists. The British Foreign Office said O'Malley's action "accorded with Britain's long existing intention to return her Concessions to Chinese control." If that was so, it was the first the Guomindang had heard of it. The victory strengthened enormously the prestige of the Communists within the Guomindang.

The trouble with America along the Yangtze was settled. Eugene Chen, the foreign minister of the Guomindang, cabled the Department of State in Washington, disavowing Guomindang responsibility for the actions of the mob at Nanjing and offering reparations for damage caused by the demonstrators.

Once the cheering stopped at Hankou, the Wuhan area became an enormous problem to the foreigners and to businessmen of the region. Most of the industries of Wuhan (the Pittsburgh of China) closed down. These included the Japanese Han Yeh Ping coal and iron company, the British-American Tobacco Company, and the shipping industry of the river valley, whose influence extended up to Chongqing and beyond. Foreign cotton-spinning mills, weaving mills, and vegetable oil processing plants, as well as many scores of small Chinese industries, all shut their doors as the workers paraded.

When the Guomindang armies arrived, they found a Wuhan with a trade union membership of about 100,000. Three months later that membership had tripled, largely augmented through strikes. In those three months thirty-six strikes had been called.

━━━━━━━

As the Guomindang armies moved north, a steady stream of foreign refugees poured into Shanghai, the key to China's industrial basin. Missionaries, businessmen, families—all flocked to this business center for the protection of the foreign concessions and their soldiers.

As Chiang and the Communist leaders all knew, control of Shanghai was essential to the success of the revolution; and if the Communists seized control there, then Chiang was certainly finished. No one knew better than Zhou Enlai, who had moved up from Guangzhou to organize for the revolution in Shanghai.

The Agitprop campaign in Shanghai against the soldiers of warlord Sun's army was supremely successful. The morale of Sun's army was shattered; in the winter of 1927, as the Guomindang armies moved toward Shanghai, the warlord's troops evacuated the city when the Guomindang force was still more than 100 miles away. They left behind a vacuum in which every element—Nationalist, Communist, and gangster—sought control.

The January incidents in Nanjing and Hankou spread fear throughout the city. "Shanghai was in such a nervous state that the wildest rumors were constantly in circulation and most of them were believed," said editor Powell of the *China Weekly Review*.

The Communists were preparing to seize control, staging parades, demonstrations, and strikes. The walls of buildings were plastered with posters denouncing the "foreign imperialists." The term "running dog" designated any Chinese who helped foreigners. The *compradores*, the go-betweens who spoke English or French and Chinese, were particularly singled out for abuse.

Many foreign Communists came to Shanghai in those days. Some of them rode around in brand-new American automobiles, spending money so freely that when Earl Browder, the American Communist leader, arrived and was given a banquet, he refused to eat anything but black bread and water. He denounced the "big spenders" who were, he said, disgracing the revolution.

The foreign community of Shanghai was very worried. Journalists from the English-language newspapers and from foreign publications went upriver to Hankou and reported on the state of affairs there. The reports were disturbing in the extreme, particularly to the foreign business community: Inflation was destroying the whole economy. The shops were bare; and the price of food, which had tripled and quadrupled, was continuing to increase.

Panic neared in Shanghai. The English-language *North China Daily News* printed a special supplement designed, said the editors, to combat the "Communist menace." "How to Spot Communists in Moving Picture Shows and Other Public Gatherings" was the headline of one article. As a result of this panic propaganda, the foreign concessions went on a war footing. Thousands of coolies were put to work constructing trenches, barbed-wire barricades, and concrete bunkers. Some 40,000 foreign troops came into the city: American marines, British soldiers, Japanese soldiers, Italian marines, and French troops.

One of these soldiers was notable: Gen. Smedley Butler, an American veteran of the Boxer Rebellion. As a Quaker, he opposed force and the use of troops; he advocated the withdrawal of all American and other foreign forces from China. The British, the French, the Japanese, and the business community all thought Butler was insane. Lord Gort, the British military commander, left Shanghai in disgust and went back to England when he learned from the Foreign Office that the British government had no intention of starting a conquest of central China, as he wanted to do.

The business community of foreigners swiftly began turning to support of Chiang Kaishek. This was particularly true after a delegation of businessmen went to Hankou and Hunan Province and was seized by the Communists; the men were paraded through the villages and forced to wear placards denouncing them as "imperialist dogs." They returned to Shanghai with tales of horror, and the community immediately began raising money for Chiang Kaishek's support.

Down in Nanchang, Chiang Kaishek sat, waiting and watching. To Shanghai came the Nationalist generals Li Zongren and He Yingqin. They announced to the foreign community that they had come to "restore order to the native areas." The Communists were preparing for a confrontation, and rifles and other weapons had been issued to factory workers by the Communist leaders. At this point the Green Gang leader, Du Yusheng, announced that he would restore order to Shanghai.

Up country, the gunboats were on the Yangtze. Everyone, it seemed, was waiting for trouble.

In January Chiang was still arguing with the leaders at Wuhan about the location of the capital. He issued a denunciation of the aggressive activities of the Chinese Communist leaders. He had organized an anti-Bolshevik league in Jiangxi Province and was reorganizing the municipal governments of Nanchang and Jiujiang to remove the Communists.

In Wuhan the leftist leaders of the Guomindang government were preparing to do battle with Chiang. They announced that he would be removed from command of the military, which meant he would lose all those dictatorial powers they had given him. He would simply be a member of a committee of military control.

And Wang Jingwei was preparing to return to China—Wang, who had sympathized with the leftists and then had gone to France when Chiang had maneuvered his way into power the year before.

On February 19 one column of Nationalist troops reached Hangzhou, and that day in Shanghai a general strike was called by Zhou Enlai. The Communists were preparing to take charge in Shanghai as they had done in Hankou a few months earlier. In the leadership circles the handwriting was on the wall. Chiang Kaishek had served his purpose, said the cocky leftist leaders of Wuhan, and was now to be reduced to size.

10

Confrontation

Foreign troops began to pour in. I did not know what regiments they belonged to; the only ones I could distinguish were the Scottish Rifles in their tartan kilts with the bagpipes leading the way as they marched down Nanjing Road to their barracks, and the Coldstream Guards, busbies and all, marching in beautiful formation, disdaining to look at the crowds lining the two sides of the road. It was said that Britain alone had sent a force of twenty thousand.

The U.S. 4th Marines were a somewhat informal and easygoing troop. Some of them were chewing gum (I was not acquainted with this habit then, and could not understand why they felt it necessary to eat things whilst marching), whistling at street urchins, calling out O.K.s and generally earning for themselves the liking of young Shanghai.

The Japanese bluejackets, in white leggings with bayonets fixed to the rifles slung across their shoulders, looked fierce and very business-like.

—Sam Ginsburg's recollections of Shanghai in March 1927

The scene of action was now the Yangtze River valley. Virtually all the Guomindang had moved north from Guangzhou. Borodin had come north to stay at the end of 1926. Madame Sun Yatsen, who had been Soong Chingling, had come north with her brother T. V. Soong. Wuhan was the showplace of the Guomindang. But the show was run by the Communists, and this worried Chiang Kaishek as much as it did the foreign businessmen in the valley.

Shanghai was the key. Shanghai, the banking and commercial center of China, sixth-largest city in the world, with a population of 3½ million people. The Communists understood the importance of Shanghai, and under Zhou Enlai's able leadership they were busily organizing and arming the workers for the day when they would rise up and seize the city.

Chiang Kaishek knew the Communist plan, and two of his armies were converging slowly on the city.

*   *   *

The day of revolution seemed near when, in March, warlord Sun's troops suddenly vanished from the city. The first indication was a series of demonstrations, one of them at the corner of Nanjing Road and Zhejiang Road, where the big department stores of Sincere Company and Wing On were located. Firecrackers exploded, the red-and-blue flags of the Guomindang and the red flags of the Communists appeared, and leaflets came showering down on the street from the tall buildings.

"Down with British imperialism" was the cry, and "Down with the reactionaries." Police whistles began to sound, and Indian and Chinese policemen moved onto the scene, clubbing as they came.

Every day it was the same: demonstrations, street speeches, parades, and strikes. The Northern Expeditionary Army was coming. It had occupied Zhejiang and was moving into Anhui. And Zhou Enlai was organizing his strikers.

As the warlord's troops moved out, the vacuum was filled by Shanghai's gangsters. They had been brought into a new organization, amalgamating the old Blue and Green gangs, by Du Yusheng, a 43-year-old ruffian from a little fishing village near Shanghai, who had shown the organizational powers of a Napoleon. He controlled the opium trade, gambling, prostitution, and even the "night soil" business of Shanghai. When the warlord troops moved out, Du informed the international community from his house in the French concession that he would take responsibility for maintaining law and order until the Nationalist troops arrived in the city.

On March 20 Zhou's people struck. Zhou had organized 600,000 workers, and they were flexing their muscles. Shanghai stopped cold. The streetcars quit running. Mail clerks closed down the post offices. All public business and transportation were tied up. Some buses continued to operate, but the drivers had to be protected by armed policemen from the crowds that surged around the buses and threw rocks. The mills stopped spinning and weaving and cutting lumber. The tall smokestacks that belched black, greasy fumes most of the time were suddenly clean and clear.

But it was not so easy here as it had been in Wuhan. Du's gangsters intervened. Du had already made his arrangements with Chiang Kaishek, and now he kept his end of the bargain.

On the morning of March 21 the boundaries of the International Settlement were reinforced with barbed wire and sandbags. A steady stream of foreigners moved inside the settlement. Thousands of Chinese tried to get in for protection, but only those who had influence with the police and those who could prove some connection with the foreigners made it. Then the firing began, as Zhou's militia came up against Du's gangsters. The center of the action at first was the north railway station, where some of warlord Zhang Zhongchang's troops had been holding out. That day, Russian mercenary troops set fire to the Commercial Press, the largest publishing house in China, which was closely allied to the Guomindang.

More Chinese tried to make their way into the International Settlement for safety. Some were allowed in, some were not, as had been the case all week. All were searched for weapons. Red Marias, police wagons, sped up and down the streets, filled with armed policemen and Du's men.

On that same day the Northern Expeditionary Army entered Shanghai by way of Longhua, southwest of the city, a place famous for its 1000-year-old pagoda and for its grounds, which were used for public executions by warlord Sun Chuangfang. Chiang's troops captured the north railway station.

Also on March 21 Zhou Enlai called a general strike. The 600,000 workers of the Shanghai Labor Union Federation went into the streets. Some 5000 armed workers seized the police stations, the arsenal, and the old garrison of Sun's troops. Some 50,000 pickets maintained order among the strikers. Zhou seized City Hall and proclaimed a "people's government" for Shanghai.

All night long Shanghai was disturbed by the fire of small arms and automatic weapons. When morning came, Zhou seemed to have succeeded. The houses were decorated with flags. Men and women wearing red armbands patrolled the streets. One demonstration followed another; parade followed parade. By six o'clock on the evening of March 22 it seemed that Zhou had indeed captured Shanghai. The firing died down to an occasional clatter.

For two weeks the Communists governed Shanghai, except for the International Settlement, which was an armed camp guarded by foreign troops.

On March 26 Chiang Kaishek entered Shanghai by gunboat, and there he learned that he had become, literally, nobody. The Guomindang Central Committee, meeting at Hankou, had deprived him of the leadership of the Northern Expeditionary Army. At least, that is what the Shanghai newspapers said. But the Hankou committee did not have control of the troops— Chiang did.

Chiang began conferring with Du and Huang Jinrong, the other powerful gang leader in Shanghai.

On April 1 Wang Jingwei arrived in Shanghai by ship from France. He conferred with Chiang Kaishek. It may seem odd that this Guomindang leader should consult with a "nobody," but Wang knew where the seat of power lay. Afterward, Wang issued a statement denouncing as vile falsehood the story going about the streets that the Nationalist-Communist coalition in China had come unstuck.

But the rumor was true.

On April 12 the fight broke out again, as Du's "troops" attacked the Communist-led militia. The gangsters surrounded the headquarters of the Workers' General Union and disarmed the volunteer troops. Most of the strike leaders were shot that very day. Most of them were Communists.

At the same time Du's gangsters carried out a very carefully planned attack against the Communist organization. Squads of armed men stormed the lodgings of the known Communists and shot them down. A crowd assembled around Chiang's headquarters to protest. Soldiers began firing and continued until the crowd dispersed in panic. Before the day was out, the revolutionary administration of Shanghai was disbanded, and Zhou Enlai was fleeing with a price on his head. Chiang Kaishek controlled Shanghai.

On April 18 Chiang proclaimed a new government seat for the Guomindang, the river city of Nanjing. So China then had three governments: the old warlord regime in Beijing, which was still recognized by the foreign governments as the legitimate government of China; Chiang's government at Nanjing; and the Communist government at Hankou, which still flew the Guomindang flag and proclaimed itself the true government of the revolution.

Chiang also engineered a coup in Guangzhou. This left the government at Hankou out on a limb, cut off from the coast and the provinces of Jiangxi, Zhejiang, Anhui, Fujian, and Guangdong. Seeing how the wind blew, the European businessmen switched their allegiance to Chiang.

Chiang and the Europeans began an economic boycott of the Wuhan area. The Communist leadership controlled Hubei, Hunan, and Guangxi provinces. They could not count on the support of the north, for Zhang Zuolin, the Manchuria warlord, was the deadly enemy of the whole Guomindang, and Feng Yuxiang, the Beijing warlord, had no faith in the Communists. Mao Zedong's organizational efforts in Hunan were creating a Communist society there, another fact that disturbed many people. It might even be said that Mao's very successes endangered the whole revolution, which is what many did say, including Borodin and Chen Duxiu. They saw the continued cooperation with the Guomindang as essential to the success of the Chinese revolution. The Comintern Executive in Moscow had suggested that the left wing should go into action, struggling against the right and arming the peasants. This, of course, meant an open breach with Chiang, but that was how Stalin saw it.

But now Mao and Zhou had gone too far, and the fat was in the fire. The Indian Communist M. N. Roy was sent to Hankou, and he arrived just before Chiang's coup in Shanghai with the word that Stalin supported the Mao position. It was far too late. Searching desperately for some solution, Roy showed Wang Jingwei a telegram from Stalin. Wang was seriously upset; he realized how strong anti-Communist sentiment was in the Northern Expeditionary Army. This became apparent in June, when the garrison commander at Wuhan disarmed the militia of the local federation of unions.

Then came collateral evidence from Manchuria and London which indicated that the Soviets were seeking to create in China a state in their own image, a state controlled by Moscow. In Beijing Li Dazhao, the Beijing University librarian, was arrested and hanged. The lines were being clearly drawn.

Wang Jingwei deserted the Communist government of Hankou. Borodin and Chen Duxiu made new promises to Chiang Kaishek, hoping to continue the coalition, but Chiang was uncompromising. On July 15 the Communists were expelled from the Guomindang en masse, and also from the National Government and the National Revolutionary Army. Thirteen days later Borodin and Madame Sun Yatsen (Soong Chingling) were on their way to Moscow. The great experiment, the coalition between revolutionary forces, had ended in failure.

═══════

But the end of the experiment created a whole new set of problems for the Guomindang. With the Communists expelled, the party was now fragmented into right and left sections. Wang Jingwei's group had been close to the Communists. Chiang Kaishek's group had moved further away from them. Could these non-Communist segments of the Guomindang be reunited?

In the spring of 1927 an attempt was made. Three weeks after the purge of the Communists, a group of the Guomindang at Nanjing sent a telegram to Wang Jingwei, who was in charge in Hankou. They suggested that the two groups should reconcile.

Wang delayed. He replied that until Chiang Kaishek was divested of dictatorial powers there was no hope of reconciliation. Thereupon, Chiang announced that he was going to resign all his posts and return to his native Zhejiang Province "to tend my mother's grave." Chiang was well known for such protestations of filial piety, a sign of his respect for the Confucian tradition.

With Chiang temporarily out of the way, the unification of the Guomindang became a distinct possibility. In September 1927 the Hankou government stepped down and was amalgamated with the administration at Nanjing. Some young officers at Wuhan suspected, quite rightly, that Chiang Kaishek was planning to retain control of the armies, and they rebelled. But the rebellion was squelched by the Nanjing government without Chiang's open interference. By November it was all over.

Chiang, meanwhile, was moving in a different direction to prepare for his future. He had made arrangements with the Green Gang in Shanghai, which supplied him with funds. He had also grown very close to T. V. Soong, the son of Charlie Soong, an American-educated Chinese who had made a fortune as a compradore for the foreigners in Shanghai. T. V. Soong had three sisters: Ailing, who had married H. H. Kung, a banker in Shanghai and Guangzhou; Chingling, who had married Dr. Sun Yatsen, and had now gone to Moscow since she was very close to the Communists; and the baby of the family, Meiling, who had been educated in America and was now 34 years old. Chiang and T. V. Soong agreed that a marriage would be useful to all concerned. There was one problem: Chiang had a wife and son already. But the wife was discreetly removed from the picture, and after taking Christian instruction (Meiling was a Methodist), Chiang married Meiling in December 1927.

That November uprising of the young officers had apparently been engineered by Wang Jingwei, who was trying to reinstitute leftist control of the Guomindang. Or so it was said, and most loudly by Chiang Kaishek's supporters. It was said so loudly that Wang moved out of Nanjing and back down to the more salubrious climate of Guangzhou, where he had many friends and supporters. In December, after his arrival, came an attempt to revolutionize Guangzhou and establish the government as a commune. The effort was again put down by forces loyal to Nanjing. Wang Jingwei decided it was time for him to go back to Paris and rethink the problems of state. He left China again. On January 7, 1928, Chiang Kaishek announced that he had once more taken charge of the revolutionary armies and that they would resume their march on the north to unify China under the Guomindang red-and-blue banner.

The northern expedition resumed in April. This time, Chiang had two new important allies, Feng Yuxiang, "the Christian general," and Yan Xishan, who had decided to cast their lot with the Nanjing government. Only Zhang Zuolin, the warlord of the northeastern provinces of Manchuria, was outside the fold, and he was ready to parley with Chiang and come inside.

Then Chiang ran straight into the problem that would dog him for the next seventeen years: Japanese imperialism.

The Japanese army had been building strength ever since the end of the war against Germany. In defiance of the western powers, Japan had maintained its troops in Siberia until 1925, as much to affirm the strength of the army against the popular belief that it should be cut down to size as for any other reason. In the army thousands of poor young peasants had found careers, and they were not willing to give them up. Nor were the army generals willing to go out to pasture. Rather, the Japanese army was following the advice of Lord Hatta and gathering power for an attempt to dominate Asia.

In 1927 the Japanese had sent troops to Shandong Province, which they had once controlled and still coveted, under the pretext that Japanese lives and property were in danger in Jinan, the capital of the province. The real reason was a plan by the Guandong Army to take control of China. Advance knowledge of this plan had been gained by the Chinese in what came to be known as the "Tanaka Memorial." Months earlier Baron Tanaka, the prime minister of Japan, had gone to Shenyang (then called Mukden) to speak to the officers of the Guandong Army. He had there outlined a program for the conquest of China. This plan was never really put on paper by the Japanese, but the Chinese learned of it and a "plan" was drawn up (by Chinese propagandists in all probability) and published in a Shanghai newspaper as "The Tanaka Memorial." The Japanese government immediately denied the authenticity of the memorial, or any ambitions toward China. Technically that was right—there was no "memorial" as such—but the facts pointed the other way.

Chiang Kaishek had enormous respect for the Japanese army, for he had learned the military trade under that army in the Japanese military academy. In the period of his "retirement" Chiang had gone to Japan to seek Japanese aid in his drive to unify China. He had met Baron Tanaka, and there had been talk about Japan's "special interest" in the Manchurian area. So Chiang knew the Japanese goals and they knew his. But nothing had been decided.

Now, on the northern expedition, Chiang's troops were moving up the railroad that runs from Nanjing to Tianjin, and at Jinan they ran into the Japanese troops of the Guandong Army who had come down from Shenyang earlier. Late in April clashes began. One of Chiang's most important officers was brought into Japanese headquarters, tortured and killed. Shooting began. The Japanese charged that the Chinese soldiers looted Japanese shops in Jinan, and they began a drive to push the Chinese army out of the area. In May they succeeded. Chiang's march northward was stopped, although he commanded some 400,000 troops.

But while Chiang's First Army group was stalled, not all the Chinese troops were. Feng Yuxiang's army was fighting the army of Zhang Zuolin in north Henan. Feng's troops moved steadily northward into southern Hebei (Zili) Province, where they joined the troops of Yan Xishan. By mid-May they had taken Zhangjiakou (Kalgan). On June 1 Zhang Zuolin left Beijing for Manchuria.

But Zhang, also, ran afoul of the Japanese. The generals of the Guandong Army had decided that it was impossible to carry out their program of Manchurian conquest as long as Zhang Zuolin was in power. So they staged an "incident" at Shenyang: Zhang was retreating in his private car in his private train when the car was blown up on the orders of the Guandong Army. Of course, the Japanese blamed "Chinese bandits," but the proof later came out. Zhang was killed, and his son, Zhang Xueliang, took command of the Manchurian area. The Japanese had high hopes of dealing with him.

═══════

Yan Xishan's troops marched into Beijing, and suddenly the western powers were faced with a new entity, a Nationalist government of China that controlled the entire country except Manchuria. Chiang symbolized the change by renaming Beijing (northern capital); it became Beiping ("northern peace"). The seat of all authority was removed to Nanjing, and in time the foreign embassies moved down there as well.

On July 6, 1928, Chiang Kaishek visited the Green Cloud Temple outside Beiping, where Sun Yatsen's body still lay in state. In the presence of "the father of Nationalist China" Chiang announced that China was pacified and unified. Neither claim was precisely true. Sun's body was taken down to Nanjing, where it was buried in a tomb on the Purple Mountain. It seemed that a new era had begun for China.

11
The Road of the Communists

On August 1, 1927, the 20th Army, under He Long and Ye Ting, and in cooperation with Zhu De, led the historic Nanchang Uprising, and the beginning of what was to become the Red Army was organized. A week later, on August 7, an extraordinary meeting of the Central Committee of the Party deposed Chen Duxiu as secretary. I had been a member of the political bureau of the Party since the Third Conference at Guangzhou in 1924 and was active in this decision, and among the other members present at the meeting were Cai Hesen, Peng Gongda, and Qu Qiubai. A new line was adopted by the Party and all hope of cooperation with the Guomindang was given up for the present as it had already become hopelessly the tool of imperialism and could not carry out the responsibilities of a democratic revolution. The long open struggle for power now began.

—Mao Zedong

At Changsha in the spring of 1927 Gen. He Jian of the army of warlord Tang Shengzhi attacked all the organizations of peasants and labor unions.

At 11 p.m. [May 19, 1927] we started to move. Shortly afterwards more than twenty communist dominated organizations and schools, including the provincial headquarters of the General Labor Union and Peasant Association, were swept clean of communists.

The soldiers conducted mass shootings, not only in Changsha but throughout the province of Hunan.

The Communists had lost their bid for power, but in the countryside, particularly in Hunan, they were very strong. Their organization of the peasants brought them growing strength in this important area. Mao Zedong organized "The Autumn Crop Uprising," a show of power of the peasantry against high rents and high interest rates.

The decision to take this road was made in Moscow by the Comintern, but it was not made for the sake of China. Rather, it was a part of the struggle for power in Moscow between Stalin and Trotzky, both aspiring to succeed Lenin as the leader of the Soviet revolution.

Trotzky had argued that the fall of the Communists from control of the Guomindang left wing was the result of the policy of conciliation of the right. He wanted to organize soviets to carry the work of the revolution.

But Stalin argued that the Communists must continue to work with the revolutionary left wing of the Guomindang, still in local power at Wuhan. What Stalin did not realize was that the fate of the Wuhan government was already settled and that the left wing of the Guomindang would never again be of much importance. Mao was quite right. When Chiang Kaishek had made his arrangements with the Green Gang and the foreign business community of Shanghai, he had abandoned the revolution. Thereafter, the Guomindang would move steadily toward the bourgeoisie. But Stalin did not know his China.

Stalin called for the elimination of non-Communists from the Red military organization and for the establishment of a new army of 20,000 Communists and 50,000 workers and peasants. All this came from Moscow; it was so unrealistic that Borodin, who knew his China, said that there was no way of implementing Stalin's orders.

Thus, the Wuhan government fell apart. Into the vacuum stepped Mao Zedong. In Changsha he organized the Autumn Crop Uprising, and after that, Mao's programs got more respectful attention. His basic program, laid down by the Comintern, called for severance of the party from the Guomindang, organization of a peasant-worker revolutionary army, confiscation of the property of small as well as large landlords, and transfer of all power to the Communist party.

By September 1927 Mao had organized the uprising and established "the 1st Division of the 1st Peasants and Workers Army." One regiment was made up of Hanyang miners; another was organized among the peasant guards in several areas; and the third came from the garrison force in Wuhan.

At this time Mao Zedong had a narrow escape. He was captured by some militiamen who were part of the Guomindang force. He was to be

shot out of hand, and for that purpose he was taken to the militia headquarters; but when he was only 200 yards from death, he escaped and ran
into the fields.

> I reached a high place, above a pond, with some tall grass surrounding
> it, and there I hid until sunset. The soldiers pursued me, and forced
> some peasants to help them search for me. Many times they came very
> near, once or twice so close that I could almost have touched them,
> but somehow I escaped discovery, although half a dozen times I gave
> up hope, feeling certain that I would be recaptured. At last, when it
> was dusk, they abandoned the search. At once I set off across the moun-
> tains, travelling all night. I had no shoes and my feet were badly bruised.
> On the road I met a peasant who befriended me, gave me shelter and
> later guided me to the next district. I had seven dollars with me, and
> used this to buy some shoes, an umbrella and food. When at last I
> reached the peasant guards safely, I had only two coppers left in my
> pocket.

With the establishment of this army division, not sanctioned by the
party's Central Committee, Mao became chairman or political leader, of
the party's Front Committee. Yu Sadu was commander of the division,
but soon he deserted and went over to the Guomindang. So did two-thirds
of the troops. Mao held the army together. It moved south through Hunan.
Lu Deming was appointed commander of the remnants, about a regiment
of troops. Mao led them to Jinggangshan, an almost impenetrable mountain stronghold on the Hunan-Jiangxi border, where the army holed up
during the winter of 1927–1928. More desertions cut the force down to
about a thousand men.

The Central Committee repudiated Mao and the army. He was dismissed from his posts in the Politburo and on the Front Committee. His
army was called "the rifle movement" by cynical party leaders. So Mao
went out into the countryside to recruit, and soon he had brought the division back up to strength. Two bandit leaders, Wang Zuo and Yuan
Wencao, joined with their bandits. Wang and Yuan were made regimental
commanders. This time Mao became the division commander himself. In
May 1928 Zhu De arrived at Jinggangshan with more troops.

From the winter of 1927 until the fall of 1928 the army remained in
the mountains at Jinggangshan. It claimed to be the real leadership of the
Communist movement in China. The army devised three rules of conduct, which were to stand for many years:

1. Respond with prompt obedience to orders.
2. Do not confiscate goods from the poor peasants.
3. Deliver promptly to authority all goods confiscated from landlords.

The first soviet was set up in Chaling, in defiance of the Comintern's decision that there were to be no soviets in China just yet. Stalin was committed to a policy of working with the other leftist elements of China. The establishment of a soviet was a final act, an indication that the Communists would not share power.

At Jinggangshan Mao built a mobile army in the area known as Da Xiao Wu Jing, so known because it had five main water wells on its perimeter. It was 500 *li* around and a natural fort. There, in the winter of 1928, the army was reorganized; it became the Fourth Red Army. Zhu De was commander, and Mao Zedong was political commissar. Soon other troops came in, mostly from Nationalist desertions, and from these the Fifth Red Army was formed, under General Peng Dehuai. Peng was already famous in Communist circles as a leader of the Nanxian uprising. There, in September, the big landlord of the area, a man called "Living Satan" by the villagers, was paraded through the streets by soldiers of the Red Army. This brought about a strike backed by "white" forces, as Nationalists were called (the Chinese Communists in those days were aping their Russian comrades).

Peng Dehuai had been a soldier for ten years, but not a Communist. He became a Communist in 1927, indoctrinated by Duan Dechang, one of the early army members of the party. As everyone knew, said Duan, the "great revolution" had failed. It had been betrayed by the Guomindang and by "adventurism" within the party itself. What was needed were loyal followers of the Communist party, and Peng had shown himself to be one of these. So Peng became a party member and began communizing his own military unit.

Mao was not as radical as some other leaders. The radicals, whom he called "putschists," wanted to kill the landlords and burn their houses. Mao refused to use the army for that purpose.

In May, with Zhu De's forces augmenting the army, a plan was made to establish a large Soviet area in the Hunan-Jiangxi-Guangdong border region and then to expand. The Central Committee heard of this plan and tried to stop it. A representative meeting was called, at which some argued that the establishment of this area limited the future. But Mao carried the day.

In the winter of 1928 Moscow was the scene of the Sixth Congress of the Soviet Communist party. That organization changed the approach toward China, backing the establishment of communes and calling for a break with the other leftist organizations. This was right down Mao Zedong's alley; he and Zhu De had long held that the soviets should be established in various districts. A number of uprisings were staged in Nanchang and elsewhere. Red military units began surfacing in various parts of China, and several worker-peasant armies came into being. A Communist base was established on the northeast frontier of Jiangxi Province. When the Nanchang uprising failed, as it did, Peng Pai led the survivors to Hailufeng, where they formed a soviet. It did not last long; the members fell out among themselves. Part of the troops emerged to join Zhu De and Mao Zedong. This part later became the nucleus of the Eleventh Red Army.

In the spring of 1928 Communist partisans roamed Xingguo and Donggu, in Jiangxi Province. These partisans later became the base of the Third Red Army. In western Fujian Province several soviets were established.

At the end of 1928 the Nationalists surrounded the Jinggangshan area, but they could not break in. Conditions in the camp became almost intolerable, however. The troops had no winter uniforms and were short on rations. Finally, Zhu De led a breakout, and the Fourth Red Army crashed through the Nationalist line. It moved into southern Jiangxi Province, into Yongding, Shanghang, and Longnan. Where the army went, it established soviets and eliminated landlords. By 1930 most of southern Jiangxi was in Communist hands, and that February the Jiangxi provincial Soviet government was established.

The Red armies were becoming tightly disciplined units. Eight more rules were added following a party conference:

1. Replace all doors when you leave a house.
2. Return and coil up the straw matting on which you sleep.
3. Be courteous and polite to the people and help them when you can.
4. Return all borrowed articles.
5. Replace all damaged articles.

6. Be honest in all transactions with the peasants.

7. Pay for all articles purchased.

8. Be sanitary; in particular, establish latrines a safe distance from peoples' houses.

Those rules give an idea of the lifestyle of Chinese armies. The matters addressed were deemed important enough by the Communist leaders to require special rules, which gives an indication of the carelessness and brigandage practiced by warlord troops and even many of the troops of Chiang's Guomindang armies.

The eleven articles of the soldier's code soon became famous throughout the Red armies; they were even the subject of a song.

———

In 1929 the Red Army moved into northern Jiangxi, where it carried out many attacks on the Guomindang forces. The Communists attacked Changsha. Peng Dehuai's army moved into the Jiangxi-Hunan border, while Zhu De's First Army Corps moved into Fujian. In August 1930 the second attack on Changsha began.

In 1930 the Communists again gained strength. Peng Dehuai's Fifth Army numbered a thousand men. The First Army Corps was established, with Zhu De as commander and Mao Zedong as political commissar. It was composed of the Third Army; the Fourth Army, then commanded by Lin Biao; and the Twelfth Army, under Luo Binghui. The corps strength numbered 10,000 men, organized into ten divisions.

By 1930 the Chinese Red armies had devised a simple strategy to make maximum use of the army's strengths. The forces involved had to be small (they would always be exceeded from ten to twenty times by the Nationalists, and later by the Japanese). The Red armies were always short of weapons and supplies; thus they had to use guerilla tactics.

Their most important single tactic was the ability to concentrate their force and then to separate that force into small units. In other words, positional warfare had to be avoided at all costs. Thus was developed what the Chinese armies called "the short attack."

Mao Zedong devised a slogan for the process:

When the enemy advances, we retreat!
When the enemy halts and encamps, we trouble them!

When the enemy seeks to avoid battle, we attack!
When the enemy retreats, we pursue!

Not all the Communist leaders agreed with Mao's theories of warfare. The most vociferous opponent was Li Lisan, another of the original members of the party; a tall, gangling young man, he now had enormous experience, as had Mao. Li had also been born in Hunan. He had studied in France and joined the Communist party cell there with Zhou Enlai. When the revolution began in earnest, in conjunction with the Guomindang, Li Lisan had gone to Shanghai to organize and had also spent some time in Hankou. All agreed that he was perhaps the most brilliant of all the Chinese Communists, but he was considered by Mao to be erratic. Like Leon Trotzky, Li's counterpart in the Soviet Union, Li advocated the theory of total destruction of the old in pursuit of revolution on a world scale. It was more important, in this theory, to destroy than to create. From 1929 to 1931, when the Russian Central Committee and the Comintern advocated this course in China, Li's star was ascendant.

Mao advocated the "wave" theory of Communist expansion. The idea was to move into a territory and envelop it with troops, peasant militia, and partisans. Then, when the territory was safely consolidated and the lines of communication secured, land reform and other changes could be made safely, without fear that the changes would be overthrown by Nationalist incursions.

Li Lisan wanted to pursue a more radical course, one that to Mao's eye was far more dangerous. Li saw the Red Army as the only trustworthy agent of change. He wanted all weapons to be given to the Red Army and all partisan groups to be absorbed into that army and controlled directly. He wanted to attack the Nationalists everywhere, withdraw if necessary, and then attack again. But Mao said that this strategy left the workers and peasants in every area open to the revenge of the Nationalists. Assaults on big cities, temporary occupation, the encouragement of strikes and uprisings, and then abandonment to a more powerful Nationalist force could only mean disaster for the supporters of the Communists in the countryside.

During this period, the late 1920s and early 1930s, Li Lisan's theory prevailed within the Central Committee, which was following the Moscow line. Consequently, a major assault on Changsha took place in the autumn of 1929, a move Mao Zedong had resisted.

*   *   *

The results were as Mao had predicted. The Red Army, moving against Changsha, had failed to consolidate its power in Hunan. Therefore, the Nationalists moved into Xiangtan, Mao's hometown, and confiscated the lands he had inherited from his father. Mao, the landlord, had supported his own efforts in organizing the peasants in Hunan with the rents from his lands, but no more. His wife and his son, his cousin, and the wives of his two brothers were arrested by Gen. He Jian. Mao's wife and cousin were executed.

The Red Army's attack on Changsha was a failure. Chiang Kaishek sent thousands of reinforcements to the city, as well as a large army to surround it and destroy the Communist forces. The Communists fought valiantly and battered two brigades of Nationalist troops, but then they had to withdraw. Changsha remained in Nationalist hands, and the blow to the prestige of the Communists was enormous.

"The error was a strategic and tactical one, in attempting to make a base of Changsha while the Soviet power was still not consolidated behind it," said Mao Zedong. "This failure helped destroy the Li Lisan line and saved the Red Army from what would probably have been a catastrophic attack on Wuhan, which Li was demanding."

Despite the failure at Changsha, Li wanted to move ahead with violence. He had no faith in the people; control, he said, must rest entirely with the party. He proposed attacks on Nanchang as well as Wuhan. He demanded the terrorization of the villages as a means of demoralizing the landlords. He wanted "mighty offensives" to be staged by the workers, with uprisings and strikes—no matter the cost in lives. The people, said Li, were expendable. He proposed major attacks in the north, from Outer Mongolia and Manchuria, to be backed by the Soviet Union's Red Army.

But Li Lisan had overestimated the military and political strengths of the party and the Red Army at that time. As Mao kept saying, Li Lisan's program could bring nothing but disaster to the Chinese Communists.

Mao's position gained attention and support after the Changsha adventure ended in failure and the attempts to stage strikes and uprisings in other cities were put down by the Nationalists. The Central Committee reversed itself and ordered the recruitment of new troops, the Sovietization of new rural areas, and the consolidation of Communist control of all the areas held by the Red Army. There would be no more "adventures." Li Lisan was removed from the Politburo and dispatched to Moscow "for study." He did not return to China until the end of the anti-Japanese war in 1945.

Once Li was gone, his theories collapsed completely. It appeared that Mao was rising swiftly in the party. But there is many a slip twixt cup and lip in Communist circles as elsewhere, and Mao's apparent triumph did not last. A new element soon came into the China picture.

12
Chiang Consolidates His Power

Li Lisan overestimated both the military strength of the Red Army at that time and the revolutionary factors in the national political scene. He believed that the revolution was nearing success, and would shortly have power over the entire country. This belief was encouraged by the long and exhausting civil war then proceeding between Feng Yuxiang and Chiang Kaishek, which made the outlook seem highly favorable to Li Lisan. But in the opinion of the Red Army, the enemy was making preparations for a great drive against the Soviets as soon as the civil war was concluded, and it was no time for possibly disastrous putschism and adventures. This estimate proved to be entirely correct.

—Mao Zedong

Chiang Kaishek is popularly believed to have consolidated the power of the Guomindang over China with the northern expedition. He declared, himself, that the country had been unified.

But this was true only in the most limited sense in 1930. Chiang had brought the warlords under Nationalist control, but in effect he had created a government that was, and would be, dominated by the military.

In the old days of Sun Yatsen the revolution had depended largely on the support of workers and peasants. The strikes and uprisings around the country had been major factors in breaking the warlords' control and the old "republic" of the north. But in rooting out the Communists, Chiang had destroyed the Guomindang labor unions and peasants' organizations. The military, which had control, was not really committed to the old·San Min Zhu Yi—the three principles of the people—and least of all to the principle that the government was responsible for the economic welfare of the people.

The principal leaders under Chiang's "control" were Feng Yuxiang and Yan Xishan. Their armies were intact, and so were their ambitions.

At the end of the northern expedition, in the moment of triumph, the country was divided into five major areas. Chiang claimed authority over all China, but he actually held only Jiangsu, Jiangxi, Zhejiang, Anhui, and Fujian provinces; and, as can be seen in the accounts of Communist activity in the previous pages, Nationalist control of Jiangxi was far from complete.

The four provinces of Guangdong, Guangxi, Hunan, and Hubei were controlled by the Guangxi faction: the warlords Li Zongren, Li Jishen, and Bai Zongxi. Feng Yuxiang held Gansu, Shaanxi, and Henan. He also claimed Shandong, but that was really Japanese territory. The Guandong Army was in control there. Yan Xishan held Xili and Suiyuan provinces, as well as Shanxi. The three provinces of Manchuria were held by Zhang Xueliang, son of the old marshal Zhang Zuolin. In all the other provinces of China control was confused.

Chiang had then tried to cement his power by a political reorganization of the Guomindang. To ensure his loyalty, Feng Yuxiang was made minister of war and vice chairman of the executive yuan. Other important generals were given other important posts in the national governments, and their trusted subordinates remained in control of their regional armies. The military was the most important branch of the government, and the military organizations were still responsible to their warlord generals, although all now wore the "Nationalist" uniform and proforma took orders from Nanjing.

Here is the distribution of forces, as reported by Ernest B. Price, the American consul at Nanjing:

Chiang Kaishek	240,000
Feng Yuxiang	220,000
Yan Xishan	200,000
Guangxi faction	230,000
Zhang Xueliang	160,000
Long Yun (Yunnan warlord)	30,000
Divided control in Sichuan, Guizhou, and elsewhere	540,000

To an outsider, the union seemed secure. Actually, it was like a top-heavy pyramid, with the warlord armies resting nervously at the apex. Chiang knew all this. His strategy was to hold the country together while he suppressed and brought into line one area after another.

In early 1929 the Guangxi faction rebelled against Chiang. At issue were the revenues of the central city of Wuhan. Into that city came the monies collected in Hunan and Hubei provinces, monies that were vital to the operations of the Nanjing government.

Generals Li Zongren, Li Jishen, and Bai Zongxi controlled the Wuhan Branch Political Council of the Guomindang. But Chiang had brought down Lu Diping, who was loyal to Chiang, to be head of the Hunan provincial government. He collected the taxes and sent the money to Nanjing.

The military leaders were finding it hard to pay their soldiers. In February 1929 they formally asked the Nanjing government to permit the Wuhan Political Council to supervise tax collection and disbursement of funds in Hubei and Hunan provinces. Chiang refused. The generals then dismissed Lu Diping on February 19. Two days later the generals sent an army to attack Lu's government headquarters at Changsha. Lu fled, and the generals appointed their own man, He Jian, as chairman of the Hunan government.

This move was an outright defiance of Nanjing. Chiang was not slow to act.

It was a complicated matter. If Chiang was to put down the central China rebellion, he needed to be sure that his rear was protected. To the north stood Feng Yuxiang, so Chiang first of all made a deal with him: He gave Feng $2 million and promised him that once he, Chiang, completed negotiations to get the Japanese Guandong Army out of Shandong, Feng would have control of the province outright. All this was done through Chiang's personal representative, Shao Luzi. Feng promised to support Chiang, and Shao went back to Nanjing.

Feng exceeded his promises. He immediately ordered Gen. Han Fuju to go to Wuhan at the head of a large force and defeat the Guangxi troops. When Chiang learned of this, he rushed troops down from Nanjing and occupied the three cities before Feng's men could get there. The Guangxi troops, seeing that they faced both Chiang's and Feng's men, evacuated Wuhan and the rebellion was over. Feng's troops, seeing that Chiang was in control of the cities, left without trouble. Thus had Chiang's swift actions saved the day.

That rebellion had scarcely ended, and Nationalist control had barely been established, when Feng Yuxiang rebelled against Chiang's orders concerning Shandong Province.

Chiang had given Feng control of Shandong, with its important port Qingdao and its coal mines and railroads. Feng's man, Sun Liangcheng, was chairman of the provincial government. But since the spring of 1928 Japanese troops of the Guandong Army had controlled Jinan and the rail line that led from that city to Qingdao.

Feng waited for Chiang to complete negotiations that would return control of Shandong to the Chinese government. In the meantime, to show the Japanese how friendly he was, Feng took a trip to Japan. It did not change matters.

In the spring of 1929 the Japanese made plans to leave Shandong and turn the area over to Chinese troops. They expected to be gone by May 4. Feng had planned to send his troops to supplant the Japanese, but Chiang interfered and sent Nationalist troops down. As a result Sun Liangcheng, Feng Yuxiang's man, found himself with only 40,000 men, facing 60,000 men controlled by Chiang Kaishek.

Feng Yuxiang then withdrew his armies from Shandong Province. He charged publicly that Chiang was trying to make the Guomindang into a personal government. Chiang had packed the Third National Congress, he said, and favored his own First Army group with distribution of military funds over all other armies.

Chiang played a pious role. He said he had no intention of seizing personal power, and he invited Feng to come to Nanjing to talk things over. But Feng remembered that a few months earlier Li Jishen, one of the leaders of the Guangxi faction, had gone to Nanjing at Chiang's invitation and, immediately on arrival, had been arrested by Guomindang troops. Feng declined the invitation.

It was apparent that Feng and Chiang were heading for open warfare. Feng notified the various foreign legations in China that he was now commander in chief of the Northwestern Route Army of the Party-Safeguarding and National Salvation Forces. In short, he was setting up an army to fight Chiang. He asked the foreign powers to remain neutral, and he warned them not to make loans to Nanjing, because his new revolutionary government would not honor them.

The wordy struggle continued. Before the end of June Feng had been formally dismissed by Chiang from all government and party offices, and the Central Executive Committee of the Guomindang had authorized a punitive expedition against Feng.

Moreover, through promises of more power, Chiang cleverly engineered the defection of some of Feng's key generals. These defections seriously weakened Feng's power, so much so that Chiang felt confident enough to send Feng a telegram urging him to "go abroad" and thus avoid confrontation.

But Feng then concluded a secret alliance with Yan Xishan. Chiang soon learned of it and called for a meeting to resolve the problems of power in Northern China. The meeting was held in June, and by July agreement had been reached. Feng would keep control of Shaanxi, Gansu, and Ningxia (a new province, carved out of Gansu). His armies would receive $3 million, and other concessions would be made.

Secretly, however, Feng and Yan Xishan were trying to force Chiang's resignation as head of the Nationalist government. They were dealing with the left wing of the party, the Reorganizationists, who opposed Chiang all the way. They, too, now claimed that Chiang had packed the Third Congress of the Guomindang. Feng and Yan's people met with the Reorganizationists in the fall of 1929, but nothing came of these meetings. Feng Yuxian and Yan Xishan used the meetings, however, as a new excuse to begin an expedition against Nanjing. Their combined forces were called the Guominjun.

Once more Chiang proved equal to the task. He sent his armies to fight the combined forces. Most of the war was fought in western Henan, in a semicircle south and east of Luoyang. Late in November Feng's forces suddenly retreated.

Even so, in February 1930 Yan Xishan demanded Chiang's retirement and disarmed all the Nationalist government units in his territory. The Guomindang newspapers were closed, and the post and telegraph systems of Beijing were taken over. The poles of power had changed. Now Yan was commander of the anti-Chiang forces, and Feng became vice commander. They formed a "new government" on September 9, 1930. But in the field the Nationalists had begun an offensive in July on the Tianjin-Pukou railroad. By September Shandong was in Nationalist hands completely. In the north the fighting continued.

Then came a startling military and political event. Zhang Xueliang, the ruler of the three provinces of the northeast, cast his lot with Chiang Kaishek. His troops marched south and occupied Beijing. Yan Xishan fled. Chiang's troops occupied most of Henan. In October the war was over and Chiang was victorious. He really had unified most of China.

This long struggle had been seen by Li Lisan as the dissolution of the Nationalist regime and the opportunity for the Communists to seize power. But Li Lisan had underestimated Chiang's political sagacity and military strength. And now the Communists would pay the price for it.

13

The Collapse of the Red Army

In October 1930 the war between the warlords [Chiang versus Feng and Yan] came to an end, and the enemy began making preparations to attack the Red Army on a large scale. At the same time our General Front Committee obtained reliable information that the Li Lisan line had been dropped.

After the First Army Group took Jian, the General Front Committee changed the plan for waging a mobile war between the Xiangjiang and Ganjiang rivers to one for creating base areas in the vast expanse stretching from the Ganjiang River eastward to the seacoast. The new plan envisaged a strategy of luring the enemy deep into the base areas, taking careful measures to frustrate his first "encirclement and suppression" campaign, and preparing for a protracted struggle. Strategically it was more comprehensive and correct than the old plan. I supported it wholeheartedly without any hesitation.

—Marshal Peng Dehuai

The secret of the success of the Communists in central China in the late 1920s lay in the nature of the land and the people. The China of that day was still a feudal society. Chiang Kaishek may have claimed control, but control still rested in the landlord system.

Within that system the peasants worked the fields. They gave at least half their crops to the landlord, who in turn was heavily taxed by the agents of the central government. From the top it was a relatively simple system: the landlord could not escape the taxation and neither could the peasant.

The central Guomindang government lived off taxes on trade and in the city complexes, leaving the land taxes to the provincial governments. Naturally, they found it easiest to continue the old landlord system. Therefore, in the Nationalist-held rural areas of China very little had changed since the days of the Manchus.

The peasant's salvation lay in his or her personal labor. The father worked the fields; the rest of the family helped in the fields and also wove cloth, raised domestic animals for food and clothing, and worked in handicrafts, making baskets and rugs and mats. They sold or bartered their goods at local markets, and they bought what others offered. Virtually every rural area was self-sufficient economically.

Communications were anything but nationwide. Water communication had broken down in the interior; the Grand Canal system no longer served. Ships and boats plied the Yangtze and other major rivers, and moved up and down the long coast, but they served only the cities. The railroad network connected only the major cities, too. There was no real road network, and the airplane was yet to come. The roads between villages were (and still are in many areas) nothing but dirt tracks that bogged down in mud in the rains. Telephone systems existed only in the cities, and telegraph systems ran only along the railroads. Radio was not yet developed well enough to be a major means of communication.

Consequently, such strongholds as Jinggangshan, protected in its mountain ruggedness, could hold out for months or even years against attack. The Communists capitalized on this geographic advantage; and by befriending the peasants and observing the rules of conduct of the Red Army, they gained peasant support. Other Communist strongholds were established at Ruijin in the hills of Jiangxi Province and in the Dabie Mountains northeast of Wuhan.

In these areas the peasants appreciated the Communist policy. Wherever the Communists took control, and built a broad base as advocated by Mao Zedong, they eliminated landlord control and distributed land to the people who worked it. Because each locality was primarily self-sufficient, the policy was almost always successful; thus in this independence lay the strength not only of the peasants but also of the Communists. They won the hearts of the peasants and laborers, who had previously had nothing but suddenly found themselves relieved of misery. Further, Communist taxation was much less onerous than that of the old warlords or even the Nationalists. In the Communist areas land taxes were limited to 20 percent of the crops at the most, and they were often less. In areas such as Gansu Province, which had been repeatedly swept by famine and by the tax agents of Feng Yuxiang, who were more rapacious than the locusts, there was no tax at all. It was an enormous change from the days of Feng Yuxiang's control of these areas. And Feng's reputation as a voracious tax eater applied to many of the Nationalist officials of later days.

It was possible for the Communists to keep costs down because the Red

Army lived spartanly. Mao had established the pattern at Jinggangshan in 1928:

> In addition to grain, each man receives only five cents a day for cooking oil, salt, firewood and vegetables, and even this is hard to keep up [because the Communists had no base of taxation]. Cold as the weather is [down below freezing most of the winter], many of our men are still wearing only two layers of thin clothing. Fortunately we are inured to hardships. What is more, all of us share the same hardships, from the commander of the army to the cook, everyone lives on the daily food allowance of five cents, apart from grain. Consequently the soldiers have no complaints about anyone.

The confusion within the Communist party in the late 1920s arose because the leaders of the Central Committee were trying to ape the Russian revolution. Both Mao Zedong and Li Lisan believed that China had its own road to revolution, but their strategies were entirely different. Li Lisan's strategy of attacking the cities failed miserably. After his disgrace, Mao's philosophy predominated because the Communists had no other course to follow. Chiang Kaishek had consolidated his power in the cities; when he had finally eliminated Feng Yuxiang and Yan Xishan as rivals for power, only a handful of local warlords remained, as in Yunnan Province. By paying lip service to the Guomindang, they managed to retain their local power, simply because Chiang had too much to do to suppress each area individually.

In 1930 the Communist party was still badly fragmented; the seat of its power was apparently in Shanghai, where the Central Committee operated more or less secretly. One reason for Li Lisan's disgrace and expulsion to Moscow was the return to China of twenty-eight ardent young Bolsheviks who had been studying the Russian ways in Moscow; they came back before the Changsha debacle. Although they did not offer any positive programs, they criticized Li's leadership. When the attack on Changsha failed, the twenty-eight emerged to place the blame squarely on Li and to force their wishes on the party by sheer enthusiasm. Li was disgraced, as noted, and moved to Moscow, where he settled in. He even married a Russian woman. The twenty-eight from Moscow brought with them the newest Kremlin line, which they now began to impose on the Chinese Communist party. It was more radical than anything Li had suggested. The twenty-eight said they knew what to do: Prepare the urban proletariat for uprising.

In the leadership of the Chinese Communist Party the single survivor from the past was Zhou Enlai, whose friendly manner and superb diplomacy saved his position in the Central Committee. But to survive he had to be very careful.

In the failure of Li Lisan's radical policy, Mao Zedong's gradualism had gained support within the city centers. The twenty-eight Bolsheviks set out to undo all that and return the party to the Russian pattern, with emphasis on urban action. Their first move was to "clean up" the Communist Central Committee, which they did by the simple expedient of betraying a meeting to the Guomindang secret police. The Guomindang attacked the meeting and arrested twenty-four people, who, in the Guomindang tradition of dealing with Communists, were shot out of hand. The Guomindang made much of the death of five young writers (The Five Young Martyrs), who, safely dead, could now be lionized. The twenty-eight Bolsheviks then *became* the party's Central Committee.

As in the past, though, the urban revolution failed miserably. The Communists had to live underground, hounded by the efficient Guomindang police. They talked of bringing revolution to the cities, but the Nationalist government controlled those cities; and in the cities the bourgeoisie, and some workers, still believed that the Guomindang was proceeding with the revolution and the modernization of the country. It was impossible for the Communists to find a base of support, as the Guomindang had found before 1925 in the excesses of first the Qing rulers and then the failed republic of Yuan Shikai.

Chiang was doing well in building up the Guomindang in the cities. Shanghai prospered once again, and by 1933 the Communists had so little support there that they felt impelled to move back to the central base at Ruijin in Jiangxi. There they found themselves in Mao territory. He was chairman of the Jiangxi Soviet Republic.

The move back to the countryside was an admission of the failure of the Central Committee's policies, of course, although the committee did not verbally admit it. The strength of the Communist party in 1930 had risen, but only in the countryside. The Red Army numbered 100,000 men, scattered in fifteen revolutionary bases, each carefully selected for its defensive capabilities. By 1931 the Communist-controlled areas of Jiangxi and the adjoining mountain regions had grown to twenty-one counties, with 2.5 million people.

*   *   *

The morale of the Red Army in 1930 was very high, despite past military debacles. The reason was the introduction of military democracy. Officers were not permitted to torture or abuse their men, let alone to kill them (as had been the practice of the past against almost any breach of discipline). The soldiers could hold meetings and could address their officers on matters they considered to be important. In the Guomindang army the generals cheated their soldiers of their pay and allowances. Not so in the Red Army—the military accounts were open for any soldier to see.

Recruitment for the army was much easier for the Communists than it had been. As Mao ordained, prisoners of war were gently treated. The policy paid off; many of those prisoners enlisted in the Red Army ranks, and some became important figures. Prisoners who did not want to join the Communists were given money to go home.

At first, it seemed that the Central Committee was simply transferring its power base and would take control, but it did not work out that way. The Moscow-Shanghai people did not understand the peasantry's relationship to Communist power, an understanding that was Mao's strength. So, gradually, instead of the Central Committee taking over, the committee itself became absorbed.

But not without a fight. The twenty-eight Bolsheviks came in like a storm, intent on reorganizing the rural areas in the urban image. Mao had carefully drawn a line between rich landlords and well-to-do peasants; the major difference was that the well-to-do peasants worked their land. But the Central Committee could not see the difference. While Mao knew that the rich peasants served as examples to those poorer, and were thus valuable to the revolution, the Central Committee insisted that these rich peasants be deprived of their land and killed if they resisted. The policy was criticized by Mao's followers. More important, the policy failed.

———

Meanwhile, the major reason for the flight of the Communist Central Committee from Shanghai was causing increasing concern in the Communist-held countryside.

Chiang Kaishek, having defeated his major enemies within the Nationalist sphere, set out to eradicate the Communists completely. At this point there were about 40,000 Red Army troops in the Jiangxi stronghold. Chiang sent 100,000 men against them, with instructions to wipe out the Red Army. "Rather kill a hundred innocent people by mistake than let a single Communist get away" was a slogan of the Nationalist army.

The first foray against the Communists was not very successful for Chiang. His commander, Gen. Lu Diping, decided on a frontal attack on the Jiangxi stronghold and sent his troops forward in columns. This was precisely what the Red Army defenders wanted him to do, for they had followed Mao Zedong's program of establishing powerful defenses deep within their base. They let the Nationalist troops come in, and they depended on the terrain and the support of the peasantry (as eyes and ears and guerillas). The result was a five-day running battle deep in Communist territory.

Mao's strategy was to lure the Nationalists back across the Ganjiang River, between Xiajiang and Zhangzhou. The Red Army troops moved back steadily, followed by the point force of Gen. Zhang Huizan, who advanced to Longgang. The Red Army stopped the Nationalists completely, seized many weapons, including 13,000 rifles they needed badly, and captured General Zhang, one of the commanders of the army.

This Communist tactic was totally new to China, just now being tried by Peng Dehuai, commander of the Third Army. There was considerable opposition to the movement, particularly by followers of the twenty-eight Bolsheviks within the party. Indeed, the General Action Committee of Jiangxi Province objected so strenuously that members forged a letter to Peng and other commanders, purportedly written by Mao Zedong, which suggested that General Peng be disgraced. The letter indicated a plot by Mao to eliminate a potential rival, and the committee suggested that Mao had turned traitor.

But the letter was denounced by Peng as a forgery, and the battle had been fought as Mao wished. The positive results proved once and for all the validity of Mao's approach to warfare.

That offensive ended in January 1931. But Chiang was not to be easily foiled in his attempt to smash the Communists. Immediately he launched a second offensive.

In April 200,000 troops were instructed to carry out the "encirclement and suppression" of the Communist area. New tactics were to be used by

Gen. He Yingqin: "Advance abreast, consolidate at every step, and strike sure blows." This was a direct reversal of the previous Guomindang army tactics. It involved building blockhouses and advancing slowly and steadily along a broad front. The camps extended 125 miles from the Ganjiang River east into Fujian Province.

The main fighting took place around Donggu, deep in the mountains, and involved the Communist First Army group and Third Army group. The First Army group set up an ambush, and the Third Army group went around the Nationalist right flank and rear.

The movements were rapid: the short strike. The results were formidable: The First Army Group routed the enemy after two hours, and only because the Third Army group did not move quickly enough did even part of the Nationalist penetrating force escape. In fifteen days the 40,000 troops of the Red Army moved 125 miles from west to east and smashed the Nationalist effort. The whole Liu Heding division was wiped out in Jianning.

It was Mao's victory from beginning to end. He had devised a new strategy of cutting off bits and pieces of the enemy, wiping out a division here and one there, never attacking unless he could mass a superior force. "Cut off one finger of the enemy rather than wound all ten fingers" was his slogan for the plan. The results helped to destroy the enemy's morale.

This second defeat of the great pacification campaign was troublesome in the extreme to Chiang Kaishek, and he decided to use a new strategy to defeat the Red Army: divide and conquer.

First, he appointed Huang Hanxiang as pacification commissioner, with his offices in Nanchang. The appointment was given great publicity, because Chiang wanted to be sure that the word went to Huang Gonglue, a major Communist army commander, who was Huang Hanxiang's nephew.

A few days after the appointment, another nephew, Huang Meizhuang, arrived at the Communist army headquarters at Lichun, accompanied by a "friend" who was a "student." (The friend was actually a Guomindang special agent.) Gen. Peng Dehuai sensed that this was an attempt to suborn General Huang Gonglue, and he set out to trap the general's brother. Huang Meizhuang was taken to Gen. Peng Dehuai, and they had lunch. Huang wanted to drink, and he suggested that he would drink two cups of wine to every one of General Peng's. It was obviously an attempt to get General Peng drunk and thus obtain information from him. But General Peng had a great capacity for liquor, so he accepted the challenge.

After several cups the talk became intimate.

"You have won victory after victory," said Huang, drinking. "Your force has grown very fast."

"It's not so strong," Peng lied, quaffing another cup of wine. "Huang Gonglue's army is only 30,000. Mine is only 50,000." (Actually, after the second campaign, the whole Red Army was about 30,000.)

Huang Meizhuang proposed that Peng and Huang Gonglue desert the Communists and come over to the Nationalist side. He cut open the bottom of his suitcase and produced two letters from Chiang Kaishek, promising immunity and employment in the Nationalist army.

By this time Huang Meizhuang was quite drunk. Soon he went to sleep. Peng Dehuai called in three comrades, Teng Daiyuan, Yuan Guoping, and Deng Ping.

"Cut his head off," said Yuan Guoping. "Wrap it up and lock it in a leather case. Then let the special agent who came with him carry it to Nanchang city at night. Tell the agent that Huang has gone to Huang Gonglue's place in secret, and ask him to come back for him in a few days."

General Peng agreed. It would be a nice gesture to send the Guomindang agent back to Chiang not knowing the nature of the gift he carried with him. The matter was handled by the chief of the security section of the political department of the army. Deng Ping wrote a letter to Chiang Kaishek which was attached to the severed head:

You are a traitor who kills workers and peasants and you should be executed. . . . Huang Hanxiang, who sings your tune, should be condemned to death. Huang Meizhuang, your pawn, has been executed and here is the evidence. Let his head be a warning to others.

The messenger, all serene with his gift in hand, took the package back to Nanchang. A few days later Chiang Kaishek abolished the office of pacification commissioner. The strategy of deception had failed. Chiang returned to open warfare against the Communists.

━━━━━

Two months after the incident of Lichun, Chiang Kaishek launched his third pacification campaign against the Communists. This time he led the armies himself, and he employed 300,000 troops. Advancing on a broad front, he soon held all the major towns in the Communist area, but not the countryside.

The Communist army, now numbering about 30,000, moved fast and often. The troops broke through the Nationalist line at Liangcun, destroyed three divisions, and captured Huangpo. The Nationalists then sent more troops to Huangpo, but the Communists, slippery as eels, were gone. They had marched to Xingguo. The enemy came after them, but again the Red Army was gone. The march through the Communist countryside, where the peasants hid their produce and disappeared, was hard on the Nationalist army. The burnt-earth policy worked well. The Nationalist soldiers lost confidence. Many became sick with fatigue and hunger. Many died. In one month the Nationalist force in this area lost a third of its strength, without a battle.

The Nationalists retreated. The Communists followed Mao's dictum: "The enemy retreats, we harass him." The Red Army struck a brigade and then a division, shattering them; then it withdrew. But that was the end of the third pacification campaign. In three months of fighting the Nationalists had suffered one debacle after another.

In November 1931 the Red Army moved into the Huichang and Anyuan area. That January the army launched a campaign to destroy local landlord forces that had been built up to combat the Communists in the absence of any effective Nationalist army assistance. The Red Army did defeat the landlord forces, and it built up a new Soviet area, called the Independent Division of Southern Jiangxi. The Third Army recruited and brought its strength back up to about 15,000 men.

The defeat of the Nationalists in three encirclement campaigns had made the Communists cocky. At the end of 1931 they had convened the First Soviet Congress, at which it was decided that the Red Army should extend its activities and begin to capture cities. The first city chosen was Ganzhou, the marketplace of southern Jiangxi Province, located at the confluence of the Zhang and Gong rivers. The city, according to reports reaching General Peng, was garrisoned by about 8000 men. Although it was fortified, its capture by the superior Red Army ought to be easy.

But the attack failed miserably. General Peng had been misinformed: The Nationalist force was 18,000 men, not 8000.

Once more the Red Army retreated from its attempts to take cities and moved back into the open country. At Jiangkou a meeting of the Central

Committee military bureau fell into argument. Mao advocated a move into northeast Jiangxi to consolidate the area, but others wanted to move south. Beneath the argument was the struggle for power between Mao and the twenty-eight Bolsheviks, who had forced that second city attack which had failed so badly.

The Central Committee had ways of resolving such disputes without embarrassing anyone too much: The two major army groups were reorganized. Mao left the command of the First Army group, but Zhu De still commanded the overall army. Zhou Enlai became political commissar, while Liu Bocheng was the chief of staff.

Following this new political line, which Peng Dehuai later termed nothing but a continuation of the Li Lisan policy, the Third Army group was ordered in the early weeks of 1933 to capture Nanfeng, a Nationalist stronghold in eastern Jiangxi Province and a base for Chiang's pacification campaign. The city was garrisoned by six Nationalist regiments.

For two days the Communist army attacked. Chiang sent reinforcements up along the Communist border area through Yongfeng and Yihuang. From the peasants the Communists learned of the movements of the reinforcing unit, thus proving another of Mao's theories: The peasantry comprised the center of intelligence for the Communist armies. Armed with this information, the Third Army group then made a feint attack against Nanfeng, but its main force slipped around and attacked the two reinforcing divisions on their flank. They were both wiped out. The Yihuang garrison moved out to help, and the Communists destroyed it, too, capturing the commander, Gen. Chen Shiji. The Nationalists, who lost nearly 30,000 men, abandoned the fourth Communist suppression campaign.

This time Chiang could see that some basic change would have to be made in his tactics if he was to destroy Communist power in central China. He adopted a new system advocated by his German military advisers. It involved the building of fortifications as the Nationalist armies moved, making sure that the blockhouses had interlocking fields of fire.

The Communists now made a serious political mistake that shook the Red Army from top to bottom. The Central Committee was following the "Wang Ming line," a policy aping the Russians—indeed, a policy ordered by the Communist International. It was much like the old Li Lisan line: Concentrate on the urban revolution and ignore the peasants. The Central Committee ordered the army to abandon the committee system and depend on a single leader, the political commissar. A campaign was ordered to find and destroy "counterrevolutionaries." But who was a counterrevolutionary? Anyone who objected to the new party line. As Gen. Peng Dehuai put it, "Everybody in the army was worried about his own safety, and there was not much democracy." The "Section for Eliminating Traitors" became a security bureau with the same power as the political department. The army was actually in bondage to terrorists, and the demands on the troops became overwhelming. No time was given for rest or recruitment. The army was ordered to attack and defeat superior Nationalist forces. "Pit one against ten," said the commissars, "and ten against a hundred."

This was the exact opposite of Mao Zedong's philosophy. Mao recognized that while the Guomindang armies outnumbered his in strength, at any particular point he might be able to mass a superior force. That was the moment for a strike, then and only then.

The Third Army group was ordered to capture Liancheng, although it was garrisoned by three regiments of the strong Nationalist Nineteenth Route Army. The Red Army did capture the town, but the cost was very high.

Then the Third Army made a basic error. According to General Peng:

> By now we had occupied a large area of Fujian province, covering eight or nine counties. But we acted just like a monkey picking corncobs, grabbing one and dropping the other. We did nothing to consolidate the gains. The civilians were not warm to us, only a few attended the mass meetings. I felt there was something wrong with our land policy in these areas. No land was given to the landlords, who fled to White areas. Rich peasants were given poor land, and many fled too. Under the slogan of hitting hard at the rich peasants a few of the better off middle peasants were penalized, and some of them ran away. Those who fled helped spread all sorts of rumors so that it was very difficult to carry on our work in the border areas. The White areas imposed a strict economic blockade on the Red areas. Things got worse and worse.

The Third Army group fought several battles quite successfully, including the battle of Tuancun, in which a Communist force of 12,000 routed a Nationalist force of 40,000. But because of orders from on high, the First Army group did not join in what might have been a decisive battle. General Peng memorialized the error in a poem:

It's like a tiger after a flock of sheep.
Under a blanket of smoke and fire.
Our army surges forward;
The cries of battle reach the sky,
The earth and mountains shake,
My malaria disappears;
The enemy runs helter skelter,
Kicking up dust to the sky;
Our brother army has not come,
And so you live another day.

Steadily, the position of the Red Army grew more perilous. Soon Chiang had 500,000 men in the field, attempting to surround and eliminate the 50,000-man Communist army.

The Nationalist military superiority began to tell. At the Battle of Guangchang seven Nationalist divisions attacked, with the support of artillery and aircraft. Between eight in the morning and four o'clock in the afternoon the bombers and artillery razed the Communist fortifications. Every man of the battalion defending was killed, and altogether the Communists suffered 1000 casualties.

The Nationalists were hot on the trail of the moving Communists. The new Nationalist military policy, devised by German military adviser Hans von Seekt, with its pillboxes and fields of fire, was working for Chiang Kaishek. By January 1934 the Nationalists had the Jiangxi bases almost surrounded by such installations. By spring the Red Army had been squeezed into an area of about five counties and was in danger of annihilation.

So in October 1934 the Communist party's Central Committee ordered the Red Army to move north, leaving 30,000 men behind to fight guerilla warfare. The main force evacuated southern Jiangxi and sought a new base in central Hunan Province, as Mao, a Hunan man, had advocated for some time. But no one seemed to know quite what he was doing, and the army moved slowly, ponderously, loaded down with heavy equipment, including printing presses and sewing machines. Chiang Kaishek pursued them relentlessly. In three months the Red Army lost half its men.

Obviously something was drastically wrong. In the first three Nationalist pacification campaigns, the Communist forces had been under the generalship of Mao Zedong. After he was removed from command, the army began to falter. A meeting was held at Zunyi in Guizhou Province, and there the opposing factions had it out. The result was abandonment of the Wang Ming line. Mao Zedong became chairman of the party's Central Committee.

At a meeting of the Political Bureau of the party, Mao criticized the military maneuvers of the past. Zhou Enlai and Zhu De agreed with him. And so into command of the party came Mao, Zhou, and Zhu De. They decided on a drastic measure: The Red Army would move, but no one knew quite where. The object was to find some area of China where the troops could not be pursued and entrapped by Chiang's relentless and murderous campaign. Thus was set the stage for the series of movements that would go down in history as "the Long March."

14
Enter the Japanese

My memory, which is so clear on things quite trivial, fails me on the crucial events of September 18, 1931, and the days that followed. All I seem to remember is the excited yells of newsboys in the morning of the 19th:

"*Haowai! Haowai!*

Read all about the Chinese bombing of the South Manchuria Railway..."

I remember also the photographs in the English language newspapers showing the derailed carriages, wrecked by the bomb and the corpses of Japanese soldiers killed in the explosion.

The next thing my memory has retained, though very vaguely, was hearing someone say—that may have been much later—that the bomb had been planted by Japanese soldiers, that the Japanese had cooked up the whole thing to create a pretext for taking over the whole of Manchuria.

—Sam Ginsburg in Shanghai

It was true, almost every word of what Sam Ginsburg remembered, although it did not all come out in the beginning. (He was wrong about the corpses of Japanese. Only one Japanese soldier was killed in the bombing.)

There was a plot. It had started back in 1928 when the young officers of the Guandong Army, so far away from Tokyo, and thus removed from its control, began to think about the extension of the Japanese empire.

There was precedent in the army for such thought. The Meiji restoration had created a new "citizens' army" to replace the old system of warlord (*daimyo*) and professional soldier (*samurai*). This new army offered careers and advancement to Japanese farmboys who might otherwise have nearly starved, particularly in the bad years of the early 1920s when the glut of goods produced in World War I overwhelmed the world. Baron Tanaka had pinpointed Manchuria for the army. The army had made an alliance with the South Manchurian Railway, a major development firm, and the alliance included a sharing of power and prestige in Manchuria.

The murder of Marshal Zhang Zuolin in June 1928 was supposed to pave the way for Japanese hegemony, but something had gone wrong. The old marshal's son, Zhang Xueliang had been a playboy and an opium addict, a sick pussycat. Suddenly he pulled up his socks and became a tiger. He took over his father's domain, the three eastern Chinese provinces that comprise Manchuria, and recemented all the old alliances. The Japanese found themselves facing a young man who suddenly blossomed forth with Chinese Nationalist spirit and proved most recalcitrant to Japanese demands for further economic and political influence in Manchuria. Zhang's announcement that he would adhere to the new Nationalist government at Nanjing was a serious blow.

The Guandong Army, then, was just waiting for an opportunity to create an incident.

The opportunity came in July 1931. In June Capt. Nakamura Shintaro of the Japanese army set out from his base at Harbin on a mysterious mission to Inner Mongolia. He was apparently on a trip to suborn various local political factions in favor of Japan, for he carried a quantity of opium, a large sum of money, and a number of army weapons. With a Japanese assistant, and Russian and Mongolian interpreters, he traveled under a false name, telling the Chinese authorities that he was making an "agricultural survey." On June 27 the party arrived at an eating house along the Chinese Eastern Railway near Suolun, in the Xinanling Mountains. There they were questioned by a band of Chinese soldiers, who discovered in the process that the captain was using Japanese army maps. The soldiers investigated further and searched the men and their belongings. They found Japanese army weapons and surveying instruments, as well as the large supply of money and narcotics.

The Chinese soldiers took Captain Nakamura and his assistants to their barracks and held them there for several days while they decided what to do with them. Finally, the four were taken out to a hill in back of the barracks and shot. Their bodies were cremated in the Japanese fashion.

Word of the killings reached Tokyo and aroused a storm of nationalist fervor. In Manchuria Zhang Xueliang saw that a mistake had been made and tried to rectify it. He sent a special envoy to Tokyo to see Foreign Minister Shidehara and War Minister Minami Jiro, offering reparations.

But the Japanese army saw its chance. The talks got nowhere. All offers were refused. Meanwhile, the Japanese press had a field day with the story of the murders, and Japanese public reaction was very powerful, backing the army's announced sense of injury.

The real fact, of course, was that the army was building up a case for the invasion of Manchuria and its annexation to Japan as a part of the empire. There was nothing new about the plan: the Guandong Army had been moving in that direction for ten years. Following the Nakamura affair the army became unusually brutal, beating up and killing Chinese civilians without provocation. It was apparent that the Guandong Army was trying to create any sort of incident to justify action.

At home in Japan various officials tried to control the army, but all failed. By 1931 the Japanese army had become the single most important factor in Japanese politics. If the army minister resigned, he could force the collapse of a government, and everyone knew it. All the army had to do was refuse to name a successor. Under Japanese law the war minister had to be an officer of the army on active duty.

Early in September it became apparent in Shenyang (Mukden) that something was about to happen. Young officers were stockpiling military supplies in strange places. One of the directors of the South Manchurian Railway, who apparently was not in on the secret relationships that existed between the railroad management and the army, protested that the Guandong Army was going too far. Lt. Gen. Honjo Shigeru, the commander of the Guandong Army, turned a deaf ear to the plaint.

So serious was the trouble that Emperor Hirohito heard of it, and he called War Minister Minami into the palace and indicated his displeasure. War Minister Minami listened, but went back to his office and did nothing.

For the plot was already in motion. In Manchuria junior officers were talking openly about an incident that would occur within the month. At the War Ministry generals discussed the matter, but most of them believed the Guandong Army would never go so far as to defy the emperor—and the emperor had warned Minami that there was to be no incident.

———

The army thought otherwise. Army Chief of Staff Sakanaya wrote a letter to General Honjo, warning him. He sent it to Shenyang in the hands of

General Tatekawa. But on the same day that Tatekawa left Tokyo so did a message from one of the "young lions" of the army Military Affairs Bureau:

> Tatèkawa is expected to arrive Mukden [Shenyang] tomorrow. Hospitable treatment will be appreciated. His mission is to prevent the incident.

The plotters in Shenyang were a group of young colonels. They knew what "hospitable treatment" meant: Get the general off in a geisha house with half a dozen beautiful girls and a barrel of sake and let matters take their course. So when General Tatekawa arrived at Shenyang railroad station, he was whisked away to the finest geisha house in the city and virtually imprisoned there by his fair captors, with a guard outside to be sure that he was not disturbed.

On the evening of September 18 the young colonels of the Guandong Army staged their plot. Wearing Chinese uniforms, a group of Japanese soldiers dynamited the South Manchurian Railway and tore up some track. Then they fired on the Japanese army barracks northwest of Shenyang, killing one soldier. The Japanese force was roused and came out to attack the regiment of the "Northeastern Frontier Defense Army of the Republic of China," and the incident was complete.

By prearrangement, Japanese army troops from Korea began hurrying toward the Manchurian border to "reinforce" the Guandong Army. A detachment of army air force planes took off from Pyŏngyang for Shenyang. Although officials in Tokyo tried to stop the Guandong Army's movements, Emperor Hirohito let his greater displeasure be known. But so committed were the generals, and so mindless of public opinion, that they pressed on. The civilians tried to stop it, but the army ran roughshod over them. By the end of September 20 a military dictatorship had been put in power over the army, and it was heading for control of the nation.

All this furor was caused by a military unit—the Guandong Army—which was not an army at all, but the equivalent of two weak divisions: 12,000 men. With adequate power, the Chinese might have moved swiftly against the Guandong Army and stopped the incident then and there. But Chiang Kaishek was in the south, deeply involved in his murderous "pacification" campaign against the Chinese Communists, which was not going well. Zhang Xueliang, who was then in Beijing, asked Chiang what he should do.

Chiang replied:

In order to avoid any enlargement of the incident, it is necessary to resolutely maintain the principle of non-resistance.

Thus did the Japanese win control of south Manchuria with very little effort. Manchuria was sacrificed to Chiang's ambition to destroy the Communists.

A few days after the incident, Chiang did appeal to the League of Nations in Geneva. The League had been established to preserve peace in the world, but no hardheaded politician really believed it would be able to do so, since one of the largest world powers, the United States, had refused to join. The League sent a mission to Manchuria and demanded the withdrawal of the Japanese troops from the area. The Japanese listened and did nothing. The mission, called the Lytton Commission, fiddled and faddled over a report, and meanwhile Japanese power in Manchuria was consolidated. When the Lytton Commission report was read in the League of Nations, and the members solemnly condemned Japan, the Japanese withdrew from the League, thus establishing a precedent and destroying whatever influence the League of Nations had.

The next step, a few months later, was the establishment of the puppet Republic of Manzhouguo under Pu Yi, the last of the Qings, the emperor who had abdicated from the Qing throne in 1911. Pu Yi, by this time a grown man, had been living for several years in the Japanese concession in Tianjin. Now he became chief executive of the Republic of Manzhouguo.

The course of history is full of might-have-beens and Manchuria is a prime example, since it really marked the beginning of World War II. If Chiang Kaishek had seen the future clearly and if America and Britain had known what was going to happen, then Japan could have been stopped at Shenyang and the Japanese army might have been cut down to size, saving the world from general war.

Or would it have happened that way? It seems unlikely, given the activities of Adolf Hitler and Benito Mussolini in Europe. Such speculation is for novelists.

*　　　*　　　*

America and Britain, the two powers capable of stopping the Japanese aggression against China, were not sufficiently aroused by the dangers to act. Indeed, there were factions in both countries that saw in Japanese penetration of Manchuria a boon, rather than a liability. And, of course, both countries were suffering just then from the worst economic depression they had ever known.

The Japanese, sensing the western indifference, were quick to act. They were now ready to complete their economic penetration of the vast, rich resources of Manchuria.

The next Japanese step, in October, was the dispatch of troops westward, toward Rehe Province (now divided among Inner Mongolia, Hubei, and Liaoning), toward the towns of Jinzhou and Shanhaiguan at the eastern end of the Great Wall. A sort of test was made in the bombing of Jinzhou, the headquarters of Zhang Xueliang's army. At first the Japanese army denied that its planes had bombed, but proof—fragments of bombs clearly shown to have been made in Japan—was obtained and was offered to the world public. When nothing happened, the Japanese sent a military force to occupy Jinzhou. Then the sleeping Americans seemed to awaken, and President Herbert Hoover told a White House press conference that the Japanese army had "run amok."

Those strong words might have been followed by strong action, so the Japanese nervously called the invading force back. But the Americans did nothing, so the Japanese turned again to their task of conquering not just Manchuria but all of China.

They now turned their eyes toward north China, particularly the province of Rehe. Soon more Japanese troops were marching into Rehe, which had been declared by Japan to be part of Manzhouguo. Within two weeks they had driven Zhang Xueliang's troops from the province. In April, marching south, they crossed the Great Wall. Chiang Kaishek, still bemused by the Communists, signed a new accord with the Japanese. Rehe Province was abandoned to Japanese might, and 5000 square miles of territory south of the Great Wall was demilitarized. Chiang had accepted Japan's conquest of Manchuria and paved the way for the Japanese drive to capture north China.

From Chiang Kaishek's point of view, of course, he was faced by two tigers. He knew that the Chinese Communists were determined to make the Chinese revolution a Communist revolution. In this matter Chiang was remarkably prescient. He hoped to wipe out the Communists first and then, after consolidating his power and the support of the Chinese people, to force the Japanese out of China. But from the beginning Chiang made one basic error. Having driven the Communists out of the revolutionary Guomindang party, he had an obligation to replace their efforts in organizing workers and peasants if the revolution was to be a real people's revolution. In this, Chiang abandoned the people. It began in Shanghai when he made his arrangements with the Green Gang and the foreigners. From that point on the Guomindang revolution was lost.

15

The Blood of China

My home is in the northeast, on the banks of the Songhua Jiang,
A land of dense forests and deep coal mines,
Of high mountains and endless bean and sorghum fields.

My home is in the northeast on the banks of the Songhua Jiang.
My fellow countrymen live there,
My old and feeble parents live there.

In the tragic days of September 18th,
I left my native places,
Gave up the boundless hidden treasures,
To rove, to rove, all day long to rove south of the Pass.

When, oh when can I
Return to my beloved native land?
When, oh when can I
Recover the boundless hidden treasure?

Oh my compatriots, my compatriots,
When, oh when can we recover our native land?

—Song by Zhang Hanhui, a Chinese patriot, 1932

The Japanese invasion of Manchuria aroused the people of China far more than it aroused the Nationalist government. Chiang Kaishek was still deeply immersed in his campaign against the Communists, still hopeful that he could destroy them as a force in Chinese political life. And although his first efforts were failing in 1932, he continued to devote his greatest atten tion to this one effort. No government attempt was made to stop Japanese penetration.

But the people of China responded quite differently. In Shanghai, foreigners noticed suddenly that small groups of unarmed workers and students were patrolling the shops of Shanghai, talking to proprietors, occasionally bringing out bales of goods and burning them in the streets. These patrols were on the lookout for Japanese goods. Not only were the goods burned, but the patrols would then plaster the shop with posters announcing that this person collaborated with the Japanese. A boycott of Japan was declared by public consent, and it spread up the Yangtze River.

Such boycotts by the Chinese were extremely effective. American Secretary of State Henry L. Stimson had seen one in Hong Kong, and he pronounced the effect "catastrophic" to British business there. The boycott was a sort of passive resistance at which the Chinese were peculiarly adept, it seemed.

Sam Ginsburg, a Russian refugee from the Bolshevik revolution, watched:

I saw a group of students collecting subscriptions in the street. People would come up and drop a note or coins into a box. It was a moving sight: the donors were not only well dressed people or adults—among them were coolies, beggars, school children. I saw a rickshaw puller stop at the curb, put the shafts of the vehicle down, fumble in the broad sash that did him for a belt, take out a few coppers and drop them into the box. A couple of schoolgirls put in a coin. A foreigner, an American possibly, stood by for a moment, watching what was happening. Then he leisurely took out a fat wallet, selected a note and handed it to the girl student with the box. He gravely watched as the student shoved the note into the box, said something that sounded like "Thank you" and went on his way. I ran after him and asked him in English what it was all about. He said that they were collecting donations to support Ma Zhanshan. Then, noticing by my expression that the name did not mean much to me, he explained that Ma was a heroic Chinese general who had defied the Japanese in the Northeast. A soldier of fortune in his youth, he had risen rapidly, holding the post of commander of a cavalry division by 1931. After the September 18th incident, he was acting chairman of the Provincial government of Heilongjiang Province. In February he capitulated for a brief while to the Japanese invaders, but in April of the same year he announced that he had come over from the enemy's side. Ma fought bravely against the Japanese. Later, attacked by the invaders, he left the Northeast and began to wage guerilla warfare in Inner Mongolia.

The split within China became even more pronounced than it had been. Not only was there the struggle between the Guomindang and the Communists, but there was another sort of struggle dividing those who would fight the Japanese and those who would collaborate with them.

In 1931 the center of resistance was certainly Shanghai. Guomindang students and workers organized frequent demonstrations. *"Shou Fu Shi Di"* was the slogan: "Recover lost territory."

Strikes were not infrequent: Zhou Enlai had taught these people well in the old days of the united front. Occasionally, the whole city of Shanghai would break down as the students and workers called a general strike. It would last only a few hours, the police would come, and the strikers would disperse. But then they would do it again.

The losses to Japanese business were enormous. After all, the Japanese had established cotton spinning and weaving factories in Shanghai, and they were geared to the Chinese market. Suddenly, that market dried up; the goods piled up in the warehouses, and when they were shipped, they were usually destroyed on the docks or in the streets. From Tokyo's point of view, drastic action had to be taken.

It came on January 18, 1932. The place was a road off the big Ward Road in the Yangshupu district. The area was patrolled by Chinese pickets who were protecting a Chinese cotton factory from "incidents."

The pickets saw five monks loitering around the factory. They noticed the monks because there were no Buddhist temples in the area, and it was strange for a monk to be outside his own district. The pickets asked the monks what they were looking for. One monk answered them quite civilly, but then the pickets noticed that beneath their long robes the monks were wearing western-style trousers. When the pickets made the monks take off their shoes and socks, they saw that the monks' first and second toes were cleft, the result of wearing thong sandals. To them this proved that the men were neither monks nor Chinese. They were right on the second count, but wrong on the first. The five were Japanese monks, of the Nichiren Buddhist sect; they had come over to Shanghai through the connivance of the generals of the Japanese army to create an incident.

The furious factory pickets began assaulting the Japanese, beating one of them so badly that he died. Two escaped and ran away into a Japanese factory, where they told their story. The word was flashed to Tokyo.

The next day a large group of Japanese—whether more monks or civilians or soldiers in mufti was never quite established—descended on the Chinese towel factory where all this had occurred. They set fire to the building and then ran around the edges, beating the Chinese workers who tried to escape the flames and driving them back inside the burning compound. A number of armored cars bearing the rising-sun insignia of the Japanese army appeared from the Japanese concession. The Chinese inside the factory seemed to be putting out the fire. Then from behind the factory emerged a group of Chinese policemen, and the confrontation began. Shots were fired, and soon the dead and wounded were being picked up and moved away by both sides.

Two days later a thousand Japanese in Shanghai held a mass meeting at the Japanese Club to protest "Chinese provocations." Orators demanded that Japanese troops be sent to Shanghai to protect Japanese citizens' lives and property. The meeting broke up into a demonstration, which headed for the Japanese consulate. There the Japanese were greeted by the consul general, who tried to pacify them. (At this point the Japanese Foreign Office was not in sympathy with the Japanese army's ambitions and was not cooperating with the army.) The demonstrators did not like what the consul said, so they headed next toward the Japanese Naval Landing Party headquarters outside Hongkou Park. As the crowd marched, small groups broke off and stopped to hurl stones and bricks at the windows of Chinese shops. Some Chinese pedestrians were beaten up.

Even Chiang Kaishek's preoccupation with the Communists could not withstand such provocation. He sent one of his best military units, the Nineteenth Route Army, to strengthen the Chinese presence in Shanghai. Meanwhile, the army and navy in Tokyo had also responded. Every day the number of Japanese warships on the Huangpu River increased. More and more Japanese sailors were seen in the streets of Hongkou district. Violence broke out every day: Japanese were beaten up by Chinese, five Chinese girl students were raped, a Chinese boy was bayonetted to death by a Japanese sailor. Mobs roamed the streets, particularly the "Japanese ronin," the plug-uglies of the Japanese community of Shanghai, who had organized themselves for "defense."

At the end of January the Japanese civilian families of Shanghai were evacuated by the military authorities. So, too, were the Chinese evacuating the Chinese districts nearby, heading south of Suzhou Creek. By some sixth sense, the Chinese knew that the violence was about to erupt into actual war.

The Chinese Chamber of Commerce tried to take a hand; it began negotiations with the Japanese. Reparations were offered. Apologies were given by the Shanghai government. Promises were made. But the Japanese turned a stony face to all this. The army had seen its chance, and it was now going to take it. Shanghai was to be invaded, and the Japanese military was to establish its presence there. The second step in the paci-

fication of China, and the creation of a new colony for Japan, was about
to begin.

The Nineteenth Route Army had moved into the Zhabei district of Shanghai and had dug in for defense. On January 28 Adm. Kichisaburo Nomura
of the Imperial Japanese Navy announced that unless the Chinese troops
moved out of the district, he would send ashore parties of sailors and Japanese
landing troops to occupy Zhabei.

It was noon before the "proclamation" reached the office of Mayor Wu
Tiecheng. He telephoned Nanjing and received personal orders from Chiang
Kaishek to temporize. He offered more concessions, but the offer reached
more deaf ears. The "proclamation" had been issued only as window dress-
ing for the outside world. The Japanese military had already decided on
the occupation of Shanghai, no matter what. Even as the mayor spoke to
Nanjing, thousands of Japanese troops were moving against Zhabei district.

The fighting began. The Japanese attacked with aircraft from the car-
riers in the harbor. They used armored cars and field guns. Twenty warships supported the Japanese.

Although Gen. Cai Tingkai's Nineteenth Route Army was all alone,
Chiang Kaishek did not send reinforcements. Chiang, still preoccupied with
the Chinese Communists, did not want to enlarge the area of struggle.

The Japanese expected an easy victory, but they did not get it. The
Nineteenth Route Army fought stubbornly for a solid month, house by
house, road by road. After the first week the Japanese military commander
was relieved for incompetence. Two more military command changes were
made by the Japanese before the end of the battle for Shanghai. On March
3, 1932, the Japanese landed several thousand more troops at Liuhe, northwest of Shanghai, and they began moving on the city. Outflanked, the Nineteenth Route Army had to withdraw. When the Chinese army was finally
forced to retreat from Zhabei, 85 percent of the buildings had been destroyed and 10,000 civilians had been killed. It was the beginning of the
long, bloody war between Japan and China, a war that would last for more
than thirteen years and would cause the deaths of millions of Chinese and
Japanese.

During this time of bloody battle, 60,000 Chinese workers in the Japanese-
owned factories went on strike. The Japanese factories came to a standstill.

Chinese employees in all Japanese establishments quit their jobs, and the Japanese had to import workers from Japan. The whole Chinese population of Shanghai turned out to help the Nineteenth Route Army. Students cared for the wounded, and some fought as irregulars. Women and children collected food and medical supplies. The wholehearted struggle of Shanghai should have been an indication to Chiang Kaishek of where the sympathies of the Chinese people really lay. Perhaps it was. Perhaps he knew. His connections in Shanghai were deep and strong. But, as noted, Chiang also sensed that the Wuhan incidents had shown the determination of the Chinese Communists to conquer China for communism. His priorities were set: First eliminate the Communists, and then turn to dealing with the Japanese. Such reasoning betrayed a fatal character flaw: the failure to realize that times had changed and that priorities had to be rearranged.

When Chiang failed to send reinforcements to help the Nineteenth Route Army, he lost some of the old adherents to the Guomindang. He Xiangning, wife of one of Dr. Sun Yatsen's friends, sent Chiang a set of women's clothing. Soon defections from the rank and file of the Guomindang began.

There was a sequel, however, which proved that the Chinese Communists of 1932 were as blind as Chiang Kaishek to the realities of China. Gen. Cai Tingkai was ordered down to Jiangxi Province to participate in the elimination of the Communist bases there. Soon enough, disenchanted with Chiang's policies, he rebelled and established a people's revolutionary government in Fujian Province. At that time, November 1933, the Wang Ming line was the policy of the Chinese Communists. The party was interested only in securing control of the cities, and thus carrying the Communist revolution. Gone were all the old thoughts of coalition government. So when Cai's representatives approached the Communists for support of his revolutionary government, in the hopes that they might help him depose Chiang and fight the Japanese, the Communist Central Committee called Cai a right-wing opportunist who was attempting to set up a "third road." The Communists refused to help Cai, and the revolutionary government collapsed.

Thus was the way established: the struggle in China would be a fight between the Guomindang and the Communist party all the way through. No third force would ever be able to emerge to challenge successfully the claims of the two main gladiatorial groups. It was to be a battle to the finish, and from 1927 on both sides knew it. In a sense even the Japanese and the Russians were irrelevant in this struggle.

*   *   *

Early on, Mao Zedong saw the usefulness in operating a carefully managed "united front" against the Japanese military incursions. In January 1933
his government in Jiangxi Province announced that it would cooperate with
anyone who was willing to fight the Japanese. There were three conditions:

1. There must be no attacks on the Communist areas (which eliminated Chiang Kaishek as an ally).
2. There must be a guarantee of democratic rights—freedom of speech,
   press, assembly, etc.—for the people (which eliminated the remaining warlords).
3. The masses must be armed and volunteer units created (which eliminated just about everybody else).

At least, however, Mao recognized very early in the period that the
Japanese constituted a major threat which must be met if China was to
survive as an independent country.

In 1933 several units were organized in the northeast to resist the Japanese.
One was the Communist guerilla force of Gen. Yang Jingyu. He started
with a few hundred men, operating behind the Japanese lines; but the force
soon grew to number 10,000 men, and it then operated as an irregular
army. Yang's troops fought largely in the area around the Changbai Mountains in southern Manchuria, where they conducted a harassing campaign
against the Japanese for years.

In July 1934, after Mao had wrested control of the party from the Wang
Ming faction, the Tenth Army Corps of the Red Army was sent north under Gen. Fang Zhimin to fight against the Japanese. This force of about
10,000 men broke through the Guomindang lines in northeastern Jiangxi
Province and reached southern Anhui Province. But then the unit was surrounded by the Guomindang, and it suffered very heavy losses. Fang was
captured, exhibited in a cage, and executed when he refused to join Chiang's
armies. Thus did one of the earliest of the anti-Japanese military units go
to its end, destroyed by the Guomindang.

In 1934 the most effective force fighting against the Japanese was the
army of Feng Yuxiang. When the Japanese occupied eastern Qahar Prov-

ince in 1933, Feng came out of "retirement" and organized the People's Federated Anti-Japanese Army. By July of that year he had cleared the Japanese from Qahar and controlled that province. But Chiang was afraid of Feng. He tarred Feng with the Communist brush and forced his retirement into the Taishan Mountains by refusing to supply the Feng army. The Japanese reoccupied Qahar, and thus held the gateway to inner Mongolia.

In 1933 and 1934 Chiang was dividing his time between trying to eliminate the Communists and consolidating his power in the Nationalist areas of China. In 1931 a group of Huangpu Academy officers had formed the Blue Shirt Society, a tightly controlled secret organization which was very much like Mussolini's Fascist organization. The Blue Shirts supported Chiang as the "supreme" leader. Anyone who opposed him, the party, or the San Min Zhu Yi of Sun Yatsen (as interpreted by Chiang) was a danger to the nation and was to be eliminated. The Blue Shirts began a reign of terror, imprisoning and executing many dissenters.

But one must not get the idea that all China was seized by that reign of terror. Throughout this period the intellectual novelist Lu Xun, a highly political figure, lived in Shanghai and moved about in the foreign community without fear, although his views were known as not being in very much accord with those of the Guomindang. So there was a certain freedom in the Nationalist areas, as long as one did not espouse the cause of communism, or appear to do so. The greatest problem of the Nationalists during this period was the growing concentration of economic power in a few hands; as it turned out, the fatal error had already been made.

Theoretically, the government of the Nationalists consisted of five bases of power: the executive yuan, legislative yuan, judicial yuan, examination yuan, and censurate yuan. Actually, laws did not mean much. The government suffered from what historian James Sheridan called "the old principles of squeeze, bureaucratism, land nepotism"—and from Chiang Kaishek's drive for dictatorial power.

Chiang attempted to exert control over the country by reestablishing the old *baojia* system, which went back to the Song dynasty. Ten households formed a jia, and each household was responsible for the activity of all. Ten jia constituted a bao. The bao became extensions of the bureaucracy; the leaders had to be approved by the Guomindang. The real reason for the organizational structure was to wipe out communism; if a Communist were found in any jia, all members of the jia were held responsible and might be imprisoned or shot.

But from the beginning, the new Chiang Kaishek Guomindang failed to attract the support of the *laobaixing*, the common people. Social scientist C. K. Yang explained it this way:

Our conclusion is that the national government failed to substantially alter the traditional centralized pattern of local government in which the village political life operated largely by its own power structure and was but weakly integrated into the system of central authority.

The formal laws passed by the KMT [Guomindang] had very little relationship to local mores, and so in the villages the laws were disregarded.

The heads of the jia and the bao were given responsibility, but no compensation or sense of belonging to a great organization. Many of them were illiterate peasants who could not read the documents sent to them by the authorities.

After 1932 the government also embarked on a campaign of repression. Many people were arrested for their political views. "Communist" was a word thrown about with abandon. Hundreds of literary works were banned or burned. A group of liberals established the Chinese League for Protection of Civil Rights in 1933. Within a few months the government had assassinated the secretary. The league fell apart.

Theoretically, the Guomindang was still a political organization of different views. Wang Jingwei was working with Chiang Kaishek until 1935, but always Chiang was the central figure, for he controlled the army. And the army was what the Guomindang was all about in those postrevolutionary years.

By 1935, years after the end of the northern expedition, there were still only about a half million Guomindang members in China. Fewer than half the provinces had regular party committees. Most of the party strength lay in the Yangtze River valley. So the real China, the whole agrarian community, lay outside the purview of the Guomindang, where it was ripe for picking by the Communists.

Meanwhile Chiang was already moving toward "generalissimo" control. In September 1933, in a speech, he said:

The most important point of fascism is absolute trust in a sagely able leader. Aside from complete trust in one person, there is no other leader or ism. Therefore, with the organization, although there are cadre, council members, and executives, there is no conflict among them, there is only the trust in the one leader. The leader has final decision in all matters.

One element of this new fascism was the New Life Movement, an amalgam of fascism and Confucianism. As Chiang said, its purpose was to "thoroughly militarize the lives of the citizens of the entire nation so that they can cultivate courage and swiftness, the endurance of suffering and a tolerance for hard work, and especially the habit and ability of unified action, so that they will at any time sacrifice for the nation." It was a philosophy he could have picked up in Japan in the days when he was studying militarism under the men who led Japan onto "the Imperial way."

By 1935 all these elements were in place, and Chiang was moving rapidly toward becoming the sole authority in Nationalist China.

16

The Long March

High mountains, dangerous passes, deep ravines.
The enemy cavalry sweep the length and breadth at will.
Who dares stop them, astride a horse, gun at the ready?
Only our general Peng Dehuai."

—Poem by Mao Zedong during the Long March

The Long March of the Chinese Communist party actually began in October 1934. The Wang Ming faction leaders (who were still in control then) realized that they must either break out of the encirclement by the Nationalists or die. So for several weeks rations and supplies were accumulated. A rear guard of about 6000 troops was designated to carry on guerilla warfare, with Xiang Ying and Chen Yi in command. Ten thousand wounded were to be left behind.

The Communists were ready to go. One October evening an army group under Gen. Lin Biao and another under Gen. Peng Dehuai moved out of the Communist camp. Soon some 80,000 people, spreading out along 60 miles of road, were on the march.

Where were they going?

They were going to get out of the trap. That was all they knew.

Most of the marchers were men in their twenties. Many were experienced guerilla fighters. There were a number of women, but all children had been left behind with villagers, including the children of Mao Zedong.

The average soldier carried a rifle, if he had one, and 5 pounds of rice. He also carried a shoulder pole, supporting two boxes of ammunition, or old kerosene cans filled with tools and parts. His pack held a blanket and perhaps a winter uniform. He might have extra shoes or straw sandals, if he was lucky.

As the march continued the shoes wore out. The sandals disappeared. Some men went barefoot.

The Communists broke out of the Jiangxi stronghold toward the southwest. At first the Guangdong provincial forces seemed ready to fight to prevent the invaders from coming in, but Zhou Enlai was sent to talk to them.
He convinced the leaders that the Communists wanted only to cross their
territory, not despoil it; so the Guangdong army let them through, offering
only enough resistance to fool Chiang Kaishek and prevent reprisals. In
three weeks the Communists had made their way northwest, through three
lines of Nationalist forces, and crossed the Guangzhou-Hankou rail line.
Most of the marching was done at night to confuse and avoid the Guomindang soldiers. One soldier described the march:

> Night marching is wonderful, if there is a moon and a gentle wind
> blowing. When no enemy troops were near, whole companies would
> sing and others would answer. We made torches from pine branches
> or frayed bamboo. When at the foot of a mountain we could look up
> and see a long column of lights coiling like a fiery dragon up the
> mountainside. From the summit we would look in both directions and
> see miles of torches.

But Chiang's pursuit was unrelenting, and the Communists also had to
march by day. They were raided frequently by Nationalist bombing and
fighter planes, and their losses were very heavy.

The first big problem arose at the Xiang River, outside Guilin. They
were crossing the Xiang, a wide, shallow stream, when they were attacked
by local troops. Guomindang troops joined the attack from the flanks, and
the Communist army was split by the river. The baggage train was in the
rear, and it moved very slowly. The battle lasted five days and cost the Red
Army thousands of men.

The battered army moved along the northern border of Guangxi Province, crossing steep Laoshan and heading northwest. Chiang Kaishek had
guessed the Communists would go that way to try to link up with He Long's
army, and he had sent several divisions to bar the track. Mao argued that
they should go due west and avoid the trap; his view won out. Thus the
Red Army was committed to moving 1000 miles farther west than it had
expected. Then the army would go north. The new soviet would be established in the most remote country.

The Communists moved into Guizhou, one of the poorest of China's
provinces.

Because of the battle of the Xiang, and the attrition caused by Chiang's bombers, by the end of the first month the Red Army had been reduced to about 40,000, half its starting number. Some deserted—but not many, for it was known that the Guomindang troops took no prisoners. Even the sick gave up only when they could not move another step. If they stopped and were discovered by Guomindang troops, they were killed.

Stealing from the common people was forbidden, but landlords were the prey of the Red Army. A landlord was anyone who employed servants or farm laborers. The soldiers robbed the landlords' houses unashamedly, and they used everything they could find, including cloth and straw, from which they made footwear. Leather shoes were almost unheard of.

In that winter of 1934, as the cold came, the Red Army was moving west through Guizhou Province. By that time most of the heavy baggage and equipment had been abandoned. The marchers learned how to avoid air raids by splitting into four columns, following independent routes to a prearranged destination, and joining up again.

Then, in December, the Red Army captured Liping in eastern Guizhou and soon thereafter came to Zunyi.

In the conference held at Zunyi in January 1935, the Communist leadership assessed a desperate situation. Their army of 85,000 had been reduced to 35,000. This attrition rate was too high, and it was blamed on bad leadership. So new leadership came to power: Mao, Zhou Enlai, Zhu De, and some other hitherto-unknown figures such as Deng Xiaoping, chief secretary of the party's Central Committee.

It was at Zunyi that the paths of the Chinese and Soviet Russian Communist parties began to diverge. It had become apparent that what was good for Moscow was not necessarily good for China. The Moscow policies followed for the previous two years had been disastrous to the Chinese Communist party. What was needed were Chinese policies, designed to meet the conditions the Communists faced: total loss of the cities and total loss of their Jiangxi base, which was already being overrun by the Nationalist armies, who were returning the landlords to power and prestige. If the Communists were to survive, they would have to build a new base, and the base would have to depend on the common people, which in China meant the peasants. This much was seen by Mao at Zunyi. In fact, he had never wavered from his view that before the revolution could be completed, the people had to be drawn into the revolutionary force, not led from above in the manner that Moscow had demanded.

Lip service was paid to adherence to Moscow and the Communist International. Representatives were sent to Moscow to carry the word of the results of the Zunyi meeting. But no approval was asked, nor was any wanted. Zunyi represented the emergence of Maoism as the controlling factor in Chinese Communist politics.

Moscow having been advised, the Chinese Communists set out again on their trek, deep into the hinterland, where they would have very little contact with the Communist International.

Chinese communism was on its own.

One slogan adopted at Zunyi was: "Go North and fight the Japanese aggressor." Following the Shenyang incident and the seizure of Manchuria, the Japanese had continued to expand into Rehe Province and Inner Mongolia. Chiang Kaishek did nothing to stop this, so busy was he in his campaign to extirpate the Communists. Mao Zedong saw, where Chiang did not, that the people of China wanted to fight the Japanese. It was then that the first Communist troops were dispatched to harry the Japanese.

The Zunyi conference meant the end of power of Bo Gu, the Moscow-trained radical, and Li De, the German Communist adviser whose influence had been so strong and so wrong. Mao took over. Zhou Enlai, who had served the Wang Ming faction faithfully, managed to survive, largely because of one of communism's graces, the process of recantation and self-criticism that expunges error. Zhou admitted his past mistakes readily. He said he was now convinced that the Mao line was the right one, and so he became senior adviser to Mao, a post he would retain forever. He was chief political officer for Zhu De, the commander chosen by Mao to lead the Red Army.

At Zunyi Mao decided that the marchers' route would lead northward to make a linkup with Zhang Guotao's Communist force, somewhere in northern Sichuan. On they went. Four times they crossed the Chishui, a tributary of the Yangtze River. On the second crossing they captured the town of Zunyi again, winning their first military victory since the Long March had begun. But they still had to cross the Yangtze, and Chiang Kaishek's troops were waiting there. It was April 1935.

Mao decided on a simple strategy. Chiang Kaishek's headquarters was located at Guiyang. Mao made a feint at Guiyang, as if he were bent on attacking the town. Chiang moved many of his troops from the banks of the Yangtze to reinforce Guiyang. Mao's policy of befriending the peasants now paid off, for they informed the Communists of the movement of Nationalist troops. The Red Army moved swiftly west along the borders of Guizhou and Sichuan provinces, making forced marches to escape the Nationalist encirclement.

Mao then learned that Zhang Guotao's Fourth Front Army had been driven into the northwest corner of Sichuan Province, where it had established a base at Songpan, too far away to be of any help to the Red Army. Mao's troops were on their own, with the Yangtze still ahead.

Mao chose to cross around the town of Jiaochedu, on the upper Yangtze, known there as the "River of the Golden Sands." In that area the river streaked through deep gorges and there were no bridges, only ferries. Chiang was confident that the Communists could never make it across, so he made no special effort to stop them at that point.

But the Communists fooled him. After marching 85 miles in one day and one night, a battalion reached the ferry town of Jiaochedu. They entered the town in darkness and disarmed the garrison. All the ferryboats had been drawn across to the far bank. What to do? The Communist leader took the mayor down to the river and made him call out to the other side that a Nationalist unit had arrived and had to be ferried across immediately. A boat was sent across. The Communists captured it and took it back, manned with soldiers, to the far side of the river. They landed and surprised the defenders, who were so deeply engrossed in playing mahjong that they did not look up in time to escape.

Behind this advance party came the main Red Army. The troops arrived at the ferry town on May 17, and for the next nine days groups were ferried across the river in the six boats they found there: They managed the crossing without losing a man; then they resumed the march. The Nationalists came up four days later and found only a few rotted sandals and the debris of a 30,000-man army.

Chiang hoped to stop the Communists at the Dadu River. He sent messages to his warlord allies in Sichuan Province and to his own generals.

Once again there came a crisis in the ranks of the Red Army. The men and women were tired; several generals said their men must have rest. But no, said Mao, they must press on. If they did not move fast, the Nationalists might well catch them at the Dadu and destroy them all. Those who fell out must take their chances. A meeting of the Politburo was called at Huili, and the Mao Zedong view prevailed.

The Red Army passed through the wild country of the Yi tribesmen. The Communists made friends with the Yis, a part of their policy of treating all minority groups with care and caution. The Yi tribesmen guided them to the Dadu, which they reached at Anshunchang. There the Communists found a single ferry. For three days and nights they employed that ferry, but the boat was small and only a division of troops had crossed over in that time.

The bulk of the Red Army was coming up fast, pursued by Chiang Kaishek's bombers. The situation seemed desperate. To cross a whole army would take days, weeks. Chiang's forces were in pursuit. The Red Army was on the verge of disaster, it seemed.

But 100 miles upriver was the Luding bridge, a swinging bridge made of thirteen iron chains, two on the sides for railings and nine underfoot. The bottom chains were covered with planks. So troops went up both shores; the vanguard was to seize the bridge, while the main army hurried to arrive there and cross. On the second day the guard on the north shore met Nationalist resistance and stopped to fight. The main army kept moving, through mud, across mountains, in deep forest.

In a day and a night the main army covered 80 miles. The troops reached the Luding bridge at dawn on May 30, 1935, and held a meeting in an abandoned Christian church. The sound of mortar fire told them the Nationalists were there with them, on the other side of the river.

The Nationalists had not destroyed the bridge, but they had stripped the plank covering off all but the last 40 yards of it on their side. The Red Army would have to cross on the bare chains. There was no time to fell trees and make planks; the Nationalists would all too soon be upon the Communist troops. Doors were stripped from houses. Houses were pulled down. Any planks that could be found were found. And volunteers were called for to make the first crossing and fight the Nationalist soldiers on the other side.

Many volunteered. Twenty-two were chosen, led by Liao Dazhu. They strapped guns and swords to their backs and grenades to their belts. Liao Dazhu straddled one of the chains and began working his way to the other side. Machine guns covered the volunteers. Behind them came other Red Army soldiers, bringing up wood to make a plank floor for the bridge once again.

Liao Dazhu was hit by enemy machine-gun fire and fell into the river. Another man fell, and another. But the rest moved on. As they neared the far side, they saw Nationalist soldiers dumping kerosene on what was left of

the original planking and setting it afire. By the time they reached the planking, it was ablaze. But they climbed onto it, grasped their swords and rifles,
and rushed into the smoke, hurling grenades. Behind them, the new planking was being put into place on the chains. Soon the other Red troops were
moving. Then the men crossing heard firing from the far side of the bridge,
and they knew that the Red Army force sent up the north bank had arrived
and engaged the enemy. The troops continued to move, the planking was
totally restored, and the army crossed over.

In the afternoon Nationalist bombers and fighter planes appeared, bombing and strafing the town and the far side of the river. They tried to destroy
the chain bridge, but they did not hit it. The crisis was past. The Red Army
had crossed the Dadu.

That night Zhu De led a memorial meeting to honor the dead. He
said: "Our difficulties are great and our enemies many, but there is no mountain and no river we cannot cross, no fort we cannot conquer."

The Red Army surged on.

Western Sichuan is fierce country, mountainous and rugged, where strong
winds sweep like fiery ice across the land. Cold, fog, sleet, and snow were
the enemies. To be sure, the Guomindang sent planes to bomb, but there
were not so many of them now. The distances were great. So, after the
crossing of the great river, the major enemy was nature.

The Red Army still hoped to link up with the Fourth Front Army in
the northwest corner of Sichuan. The distance was about 100 miles; but as
the troops would go, up mountain and down valley, it was even farther.
The army spent ten days preparing to cross the Great Snowy Mountains
and during that time it fought the troops of the Sichuan warlords.

One warlord called for reinforcements from Tibet, and a regiment of
Tibetan soldiers came down. The Communists captured them and took
their magnificent uniforms, sheepskin coats for the soldiers and fur-lined
uniforms for the officers. There were not nearly enough to go around, but
any assistance was welcomed. The jewels and silver the Tibetan troops and
their concubines carried gave the Red Army something to trade to the villagers for supplies.

As they prepared for their rugged march, every man was told to carry
enough food for ten days. Mao and Zhu De decided they would move only
six or seven hours each day to conserve energy. They would be traveling at
high altitude: One pass was 16,000 feet high, and the mountains on its

sides were much higher. The Communists would make no frontal attacks on enemy troops unless ordered to do so by General Zhu.

The Red Army did not know the way, but the troops headed straight into the Jiajin mountain range, toward a pass they could see in the distance. They started one day at dawn, but soon the men were enveloped in fog. The fog became rain. As they climbed, the rain became hail. One officer remembered:

> Our breath froze and hands and lips turned blue. Men and animals staggered and fell into chasms and disappeared. Those who sat down to rest or relieve themselves froze to death on the spot.

They crossed the pass and started down the other side. Enemy bombers appeared, so they did not move during the day, but switched to night marches.

Hundreds died on the route. Most of the dead were southerners, who suffered from the cold in their thin uniforms and from the diet of mountain barley because they had no rice. Some ate the barley raw and fell ill with dysentery. Others suffered from malaria. Zhou Enlai had malaria so badly that he had to be carried on a stretcher across the mountains.

The journey seemed endless. At the end of June 1935 the Red Army reached a broad valley dotted with villages, and there the main body stopped, exhausted. Peng Dehuai led one regiment on ahead to make contact with the Fourth Front Army. The men marched for two days before they met their friends.

Soon, the armies were reunited, the handful of survivors of the march across the mountains and the 80,000 men of the Fourth Front Army. At first joy reigned, but old enmities were quickly revived. The most serious contest was that between Mao Zedong and Zhang Guotao, leader of the Fourth Front Army. Zhang had been supreme commander of his own army for so long that he refused to accept party discipline. An old competition that went back to their student days at Beijing University was rekindled.

Mao proposed that they now move north to establish a base in Sichuan, Gansu, and Shaanxi provinces. Zhang wanted to go farther west, to the grasslands near the Soviet Union, where there was even less chance of Guomindang encirclement. They argued, and they reached an impasse.

The stalemate was resolved when Zhu De suggested that they march into Gansu Province, establish a base there, and strengthen the army to be able to meet any Guomindang threat. He would be in command; Zhang would become political commissar. Mao did not like it, but he was resilient enough to accept the solution and bide his time. The breach was healed, on the surface, and the combined armies moved on.

To prevent trouble, Zhu De assigned Mao to command the forces on the right and Zhang to lead those on the left. Some units of the First Front Army now were assigned to Zhang, and some from the Fourth Front Army were assigned to Mao, to prevent new difficulties from arising out of personal loyalties. The march continued.

Now the Red Army faced an entirely new challenge: the steppe's broad grasslands. This 100-mile-wide expanse at 10,000 feet above sea level turned to swamp in the rainy season. The inhabitants were Tibetan tribesmen who hated the Han Chinese. They retreated everywhere, taking their animals and destroying anything left behind. War parties came down to raid the Red Army.

Their chief was a woman, and she threatened to boil alive anyone who helped the Red Army. So it was open enmity, the Communists taking turnips and upland barley, and killing sheep when they could find them, and the Tibetans lying in wait and killing Chinese stragglers all along the route. It was the first time the Communists had been unable to make friends with the local people of a region. Mao would not forget the Tibetans.

The rains came in August, and the land beneath their feet turned to mush. Food was short and so was water. The soldiers ate berries and roots, but some of the plants turned out to be poisonous, so more men died. When they came to villages, they ate everything, including the rats they found. And still more died. Mao's column of 40,000 men was reduced to 30,000 before they emerged from the marshlands.

It was September when Mao's ragged army reached the Gansu border and people of the Han race. And there another crisis developed. Secretly, Zhang Guotao had been sending messages to his Fourth Front Army men under Mao's control, telling them that he was going to head back southwest as he had planned. The Fourth Front Army commanders with Mao began to argue for that plan, trying to force Mao to accept Zhang's leadership. But Mao would not. One day he set out for the north, taking with him his First Front Army men and leaving the Fourth Front Army men behind to do as they pleased. Immediately, the Fourth Front Army men headed south to join Zhang. He took them down to Ganzio in far western Sichuan, and there he established his own base and his own political organization. Thus was the Communist party split.

There was trouble ahead for the First Front Army. The Guomindang had fortified Lazikou Pass, which led up out of the grasslands. It seemed impenetrable, but there was no other way to go, so Mao sent troops up the steep sides of the pass. When they reached the summit, they signaled their arrival by flare. Mao launched a frontal attack into the pass, and with the flankers moving too, he captured the pass. Mao's troops marched on to the Bailong River and the Liupan Mountains. They were marching toward Shaanxi Province.

Mao was talking more often about fighting the Japanese, who had strengthened their control in North China and had moved the enlarged Guandong Army into the three northeastern provinces of Manchuria. The Republic of Manchukuo had become an empire, and President Pu Yi had become emperor. Of course, it was all sham. The man behind the throne was the commander of the Guandong Army, and Emperor Pu Yi did precisely as he was told.

So Mao wanted to find a base from which he could begin fighting the Japanese, whom he referred to in a poem as "the grey dragon."

> If we do not reach
> The Great Wall, we are not true men.
> High on the crest
> of Lupan mountain
> Our banners billow
> in the west wind.
> Today we hold
> the tasseled standard in our hands.
> When shall we put bonds
> Upon the grey dragon?

They moved on, the men of the First Front Army, and indeed they were approaching the Great Wall and the territory into which Japan had moved. The Red Army reached Hadapu in Gansu, and Mao learned of the existence of a Communist soviet in Shaanxi. The army went that way, and at Wuqi Mao linked up with forces led by Xu Hiadong and Liu Zhidan, who had fought their way north from the Yangtze some time earlier. There, at Wuqi, the Long March ended after 368 days. A few thousand survivors had made the journey; some 80,000 had fallen by the wayside or had given up.

Among those who did not appear was the Fourth Front Army of Zhang Guotao, which remained in Sichuan. Forty thousand troops spent a terrible cold winter because of Zhang's continued belief that he, and not Mao, should be the leader of Red China. Zhang was joined in the summer of 1936 by the Second Front Army, under Gen. He Long, which had fought its way north from Guizhou.

In 1936 the Communist International proved invaluable to the Chinese Communists. Lin Yuying, a representative of the Comintern, arrived in Shaanxi Province, bearing word from Moscow that the Soviet Union would support a united front against the Japanese. But first, as everyone agreed in Shaanxi, the breach within the Communist party must be healed. From Moscow came the word: Zhang Guotao was to disband his Central Committee. He would be allowed to maintain a southwestern bureau of the party's Central Committee. So Moscow had spoken, and Mao was glad to listen. The decision made him undisputed leader of the Communist revolution in China.

The two southern armies, the Fourth Front and the Second Front, were soon marching north toward Shaanxi under Gen. Zhu De, who had gone south to make sure the generals followed orders. In October 1936 the forces met Mao at Huining. Mao Zedong and Zhang Guotao shared the platform for the celebration, symbolizing the healing of the breach.

Zhang Guotao still wanted to set up a soviet in the northwest, near the Soviet border. Mao was glad to get rid of him, and the Soviets welcomed the move. So Zhang set forth with his Fourth Front Army, including a regiment of 2000 women soldiers, who had proved themselves as sturdy fighters.

But on the way to the northwest, crossing the Huang He and marching across the grasslands, Zhang's forces were beset by Moslem tribesmen who wanted no one to invade their territory. They harried the army and literally cut it to pieces, wiping out whole companies. The women's regiment was attacked and scattered; the women were either killed or captured, raped, and sent to the slave markets of the south. Zhang's plan failed, and ultimately what was left of his scattered force made its weary way back to the Shaanxi headquarters of the Red Army.

Zhang Guotao lost all his influence. He was criticized by the party's Central Committee for his refusal to accept Mao's leadership. A year later he went south and joined Chiang Kaishek's Guomindang.

The Long March had been a long disaster for the Communist Red Army. Although the army had recruited all along its path, its recruiting could not make up for the losses. Altogether, about 170,000 people were lost on the march. Membership in the Communist party had shrunk to 40,000, and the Communists controlled only scattered bits of territory in China. According to Zhou Enlai:

> The darkest time in our history was the Long March, especially when we crossed the Great Grasslands. Our condition was desperate. We not only had nothing to eat, we had nothing to drink. Yet we survived.

And so they did. Soon the Red Army was ensconced in the caves of Yanan, far north in Shaanxi, in territory so rugged that the Nationalist armies left it alone. There, the Communist party would survive and plan its strategy: to fight the Japanese, gain strength, and bring the people of China to the side of the Communists and then to complete the revolution begun by Sun Yatsen.

17
Incident at Xi'an

So long as hope of peace is not altogether lost, we shall never abandon peace. We are determined to make even the ultimate sacrifice in
our efforts for peace.

—Chiang Kaishek, 1935, discussing Chinese-Japanese relations

Like bees, the Japanese swarmed through Manchuria and beyond, spreading over into China. From Manchuria they moved into Mongolia and north
China, establishing industries, often with Chinese front men manipulated
like puppets by the Japanese Guandong Army, the South Manchurian Railway interests, and the *zaibatsu*, or economic combines, back in Japan.

So bemused was Chiang Kaishek with the Communists in the early
1930s that he did nothing to stop Japanese expansion in north China. In
June 1935 he bent his knee to the Japanese, signing the He-Umezu agreement which promised the withdrawal of Chinese troops from north China.
Imagine, Chinese troops withdrawing from China in favor of Japanese
troops! The shock was felt around the world.

The He-Umezu agreement contained even more disgraceful provisions
for China. It promised the disbanding of Chinese patriotic societies in the
north and the banning of all anti-Japanese activity. That meant no more
parades, no more demonstrations, no more recognized strikes against Japanese military and economic aggression against China. But as was usual
with dragons, this rich food only whetted the grey dragon's appetite. In
October the Japanese government demanded more.

The five northern provinces—Hebei, Shandong, Shaanxi, Qahar, and
Suiyuan—were to become completely independent of the Chinese government. The Japanese planned to make each of these provinces a separate
"independent" government—independent of Chinese authority and subject to Japanese authority. They would, in effect, become small, important, highly specialized colonies of Japan.

The second Japanese demand that fall was for demilitarization of all

Leaders of the Hundred Days' Reform in 1898: Kang Youwei (upper left), Liang Qichao (upper right), and Tan Sitong (below).

Sun Yatsen (second from left) spreads revolutionary ideas among his Hong Kong schoolmates in 1888.

Yellow Flower Park in Guangzhou, where seventy-two revolutionary martyrs killed in April 1911 were buried.

Qiu Jin, woman revolutionary, executed at the age of 31.

Dr. Sun Yatsen in 1912, when he assumed office as provisional president of the Republic of China.

Zhou Enlai in Tianjin, 1919.

As chief political instructor at Huangpu Military Academy in 1924.

一九二四年攝於巴黎

Picture taken just before Zhou's departure for Guangzhou in 1924. He is sixth from right, first row, and Deng Xiaoping is third from right, fourth row.

Zhou reaching northern Shaanxi after the Long March, 1935.

hou with Liu Shaoqi
Yanan.

Mao Zedong and
Zhou in Yanan.

Zhou at the Yanan airport in 1936, after holding tripartite talks in Xi'an with Chiang Kaishek and his captors, Generals Zhang Xueliang and Yang Hucheng.

The Lugouqiao (Marco Polo) Bridge, southwest of Beijing. The China-Japan war started here in July 1937, when a column of Japanese troops attacked a column of Chinese soldiers.

Chinese militia units wreck a Japanese-held railway.

United front: Bishop Logan H. Roots, Anna Louise Strong, Peng Dehuai, Frances Roots, and Agnes Smedley at Wuhan in 1938.

Zhou Enlai (fourth from left) visits the New Fourth Army in central China in 1939. The officers include Chen Yi (first left) and Ye Ting (first right).

U.S. Ambassador Patrick J. Hurley with Mao Zedong and Zhou Enlai in August 1945, before their flight to Chongqing.

Zhou at his desk in Nanjing, 1946.

Chairman Mao Zedong proclaims the birth of the People's Republic of China, October 1, 1949.

Chairman Mao chatting with peasants during his cross-country tour in 1958. (*China Pictorial*, September 1958)

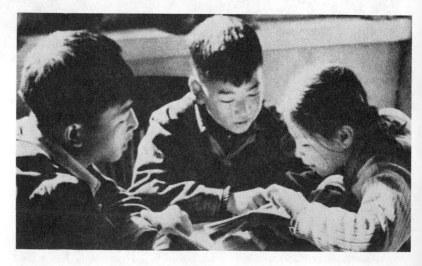

Children learn the ideology of collectivism in a small study group. (*Ren Min Ri Bao*, no. 6, 1966)

Mao in Jiangxi, 1961.

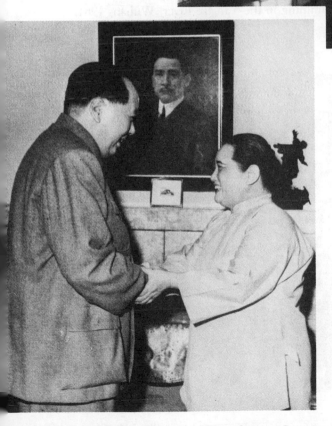

With Soong Chingling, Sun Yatsen's widow, at Sun
Yatsen's former residence in Shanghai, May 1961.

Mao swimming in the Yangtze River, Wuhan, 1961.

With Mao Anqing (first from left), his second son, Shao Hua (second from right), his daughter-in-law, and others in 1962.

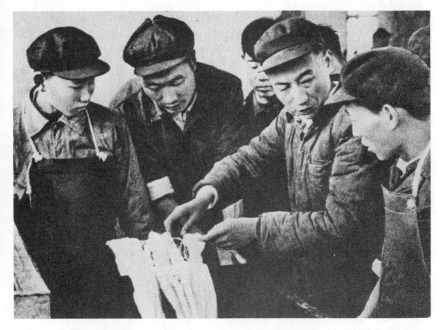

Factory director Yuan Yishen discusses cotton production with workers. (*Ren Min Ri Bao*, no. 6, 1966)

Commune members holding a small-group discussion to criticize antiparty, antisocialism thinking and behavior. (*Ren Min Ri Bao*, no. 10, 1966)

A mass criticism meeting in Qingdao. (*Ren Min Ri Bao*, no. 11, 1967)

Students at Beijing University posting *tatzepao*. (*Ren Min Ri Bao*, no. 11, 1967)

Mao with Edgar Snow and his wife on the Tian An Men rostrum, National Day, 1970.

Shaking hands with Kim Il Sung, general secretary of the Central Committee of the Korean Workers' Party and president of the Democratic People's Republic of Korea.

Premier Zhou Enlai at the Great Hall of the People on January 9, 1973.

Mao greeting President Richard Nixon in Zhongnanhai, February 21, 1972.

the coastal provinces of China. This too was part of the Japanese plan to secure control of eastern China.

The third demand was for Chinese withdrawal from the League of Nations and cooperation with Japan and Manchukuo in establishing a far eastern economic bloc. For years the Japanese had been planning for *Hakko Ichiu*, "the four corners of the world under one roof," and this was proof positive that it would be a Japanese roof. Out of this demand ultimately arose the Japanese plan for the Greater East Asia Co-Prosperity Sphere.

Having made these demands, the Japanese lost no time in implementing them, even though they were not accepted in north China. They secured the cooperation of Yin Rugeng, a north China leader, and set him up as head of the East Hebei Anti-Communist Autonomous Government near Beijing. The fact that the government was "anti-Communist" was a sop to Chiang Kaishek. But not many people were fooled. Most Chinese saw in the move an attempt by the grey dragon to swallow China piece by piece.

While still on the Long March, in the summer of 1935, Mao Zedong had issued an appeal to all Chinese people to join with the Communists in resisting Japanese aggression. The Red Army called for an end to Chiang's persecution of the Communists and for a united front against Japan. The Communists wanted a coalition government and a united army, with the Red Army fighting alongside Chiang's forces.

As time went on, the Communists issued more calls. They wanted the confiscation of all Japanese property in China. Again they called for unity of the Chinese people in the fight against the single enemy: Japan.

The call fell on friendly ears. In Beijing on December 9, 1935, thousands of students turned out to demonstrate. It was total defiance of the He-Umezu agreement, and the Guomindang police took to the streets to quell the demonstrations.

"Down with Japanese imperialism," shouted the students. "Stop all civil war and unite against Japanese aggression."

The police charged in. A hundred students were wounded in the fighting, and several score were arrested by the authorities. But the demonstrations continued and wall posters began to appear, calling for Chinese unity against Japan.

December 16 was the date set for the establishment of the Hebei-Qahar Political Affairs Council, a Japanese organization which would take over political control of those provinces. On that day some 30,000 Beijing students marched through the streets and rallied in the open air. Many other thousands of citizens joined them. When the Guomindang brought up its police forces and two regiments of troops, the demonstration erupted into violence. All day long the students ran back and forth throwing rocks, while the police and soldiers chased them, sometimes firing on the students. Clubs, bayonets, and water hoses failed to quell the rioting students, and the fighting lasted well into the night.

The Hebei-Qahar Political Affairs Council was not established that day after all.

Collectively, this whole series of demonstrations was called the December 9 Movement. Word of its success and violence spread throughout China and beyond.

Yet Chiang Kaishek still refused to come out against the Japanese.

However, other forces were at work in China during this tortured period.

In the summer of 1935 the Northeastern Army headed by Zhang Xueliang, the son of the assassinated "old marshal" of Manchuria, moved to the northwest, where it came up nervously with the Seventeenth Route Army of Gen. Yang Hucheng. Yang, the former governor of Shaanxi Province, had been rudely dismissed by Chiang Kaishek as part of Chiang's power play to achieve personal control of north China. Using the old philosophy of divide and conquer, Chiang did his best to keep these two generals at swords' points.

Both armies had been ordered by Chiang to "suppress bandits," which meant fight the Communist Red Army. Both armies did, usually with results disastrous to themselves.

In the spring of 1936 Yang Hucheng sought a conversation with Zhang Xueliang. What he wanted to find out was how Zhang felt about resisting the Japanese and how he felt about Chiang Kaishek's refusal to do so. In their long talk Zhang became very emotional, because until this point Chiang had alleged that the reason for the collapse of Manchuria into Japanese hands was the refusal of Zhang Xueliang to fight. This was patently untrue, but it had been a central pillar of Guomindang propaganda in the north for years. Zhang Xueliang resented the charge and was angry with Chiang for perpetuating it.

So General Yang learned that Zhang Xueliang was not a puppet of Chiang Kaishek, as he had believed Zhang to be, and that he could count on Zhang to help resist the Japanese.

Zhang and Yang, and the Chinese Communist forces, were soon in close contact, all agreeing that their major aim at the moment was to resist Japanese aggression. From mid-1936 onward the three groups worked together. The problem was: How could they force Chiang Kaishek to accept this position and stop creating trouble?

In June 1936 several uprisings flared up against Guomindang rule in Guangdong and Guangxi provinces, always centers of radicalism. The trouble in those areas was that Guangdong was under the control of warlord Chen Jitang and Guangxi was controlled by warlord Li Zongren. Unrest was the word for the situation in the whole area. As it continued, all China fretted under the growing Japanese incursions.

Chiang was now planning another set of military actions against the Chinese Communists.

On October 31, 1936, he celebrated his fiftieth birthday with pious incantations. He published an article entitled "Thinking of My Parents and Dedicating Myself to the Nation"; the title indicated that Chiang was consumed by filial piety, a stance he often adopted and one popular with the followers of Confucius. The Guomindang sought donations throughout China to finance the building of airplanes and commemorative schools in celebration of the generalissimo's birthday. The occasion marked the height of Chiang's effort to rule China by personality.

On November 17 Chiang flew to Taiyuan to see Gen. Yan Xishan, who was really a warlord but was masked under Nationalist banners. He then flew to Jinan, carrying word of his new plan to suppress the Communists. On November 23 Chiang caused the arrest, in Shanghai, of seven members of the All China Association for National Salvation.

On November 28 Chiang sent a representative to Suiyuan to see Gen. Fu Zuoyi, another warlord masked as a Nationalist, and to persuade him to join the "bandit suppression" campaign.

All this time Chinese and Japanese officials were meeting in Tokyo and Nanjing to arrange affairs so that Chiang could continue with his sixth campaign to suppress the Communists. He had high hopes now that he would be able to turn all his armies against the Reds and wipe them out. He had never faltered in his drive—the Japanese threat meant nothing to him. The Communist threat meant everything.

Chiang was mustering twenty-six regiments, numbering 300,000 men, for his new "antibandit campaign." He had imported 100 aircraft with the money donated by schoolchildren and others for his birthday. The planes were to be sent to Xi'an for operations. Chiang was talking about wiping out the Communists in one month and returning to Nanjing by the end of 1936.

On December 4 Chiang arrived in Xi'an, ready to start his campaign. He summoned Zhang Xueliang and Yang Hucheng to his presence and reprimanded the two generals for disloyalty. Then he began talking about rewards if they would do as he ordered. It was a tactic so familiar that no one in the room was impressed.

Zhang Xueliang and Yang Hucheng had already agreed that it was almost impossible to talk to Chiang Kaishek, as he never listened to anyone. They had also agreed that in order to make him perhaps listen to reason, they would have to have him arrested and held somewhere.

On December 9, 1936, the first anniversary of the December 9 Beijing student uprising, students of Xi'an, with the support of Generals Zhang and Yang, marched around the town, visiting various military and government organizations and calling for a united front against Japan. "Stop the civil war and unite to fight Japan" and "Support Generalissimo Chiang Kaishek's leadership in resisting Japan" were the slogans.

The two Xi'an generals cautioned their officers not to disturb the students but to protect them, which was in direct contradistinction to the activities of Chiang Kaishek's forces. The Second Regiment of the Central Gendarmerie and the Xi'an Public Security Bureau's police tried to break up the demonstrations, but when the two generals warned them not to interfere, they backed away from a confrontation.

Chiang Kaishek was not far away. He was staying at Lintong, just outside Xi'an. The students learned of his coming, and deciding to petition him, they headed for his villa. Chiang threatened to have them all executed. General Zhang went out to see the student leaders and warned them of this threat. He took their petition, promising to present it to Chiang and to report to the students. So the students disbanded their rally, and another confrontation was avoided.

Chiang was furious when Zhang visited him on December 10 to warn that the Chinese people were unalterably on the side of resistance against the

Japanese and that most of them in north China favored a Nationalist-Communist coalition to offer that resistance. All this was nonsense, Chiang said. There was only one way to deal with people like those students, and that was to open fire on their illegal rallies. Zhang was not serving China's cause by pleading for a united front, he said. With that, Chiang swept off to his bedroom, and the interview was over.

Zhang went back to his headquarters, and on that same day he saw General Yang again and asked him to try to reason with Chiang Kaishek. Yang went to Chiang's headquarters, but he found Chiang as impossible as ever when it came to talking about the united front.

So Zhang and Yang met again, and this time they decided there was only one solution. They must arrest Chiang, kidnap him, and force him to listen to reason. If he would not listen, they would kill him.

The two generals then made their plan: Chiang's main force in Xi'an consisted of the Second Gendarme Regiment of 1000 men, stationed inside the city; the Public Security column of 2000 men, both inside the city and outside the west gate; the Shaanxi Provincial Peace Preservation Corps of 1000 men; and Chiang's Guomindang agents, about 1000 strong; plus miscellaneous units. The whole force totaled around 7000 men.

Kong Congzhou, commander of the Seventeenth Route Army's Shaanxi garrison brigade, was put in charge. He assigned various roles to his officers. They stationed troops at the bell tower and the drum tower and on the city wall.

Zhang Xueliang's Northeastern Army would surround the Huaqingchi villa at Lintong and arrest Chiang. They would also guard the Xi'an-Lintong highway to prevent Chiang's personal troops from causing trouble.

Yang's Seventeenth Route Army would guard Xi'an city; blockade its railroad station and airport; disarm the Central Gendarmerie, who were loyal to Chiang; disarm the Guomindang special agents, the police, and the central army units in Xi'an; and arrest all Guomindang officials in the city.

By midnight on December 11 Zhang and Yang had done their jobs. The troops were all in position. The two generals went to Yang's Xi'an pacification headquarters, on the site of an old Ming palace. From there they would direct operations.

At midnight on December 11 the Seventeenth Route Army attacked Chiang's men. The Guomindang forces were all surprised, and they offered relatively little resistance. About 200 were killed, as were about 70 of

Yang's men. All the Guomindang officials were rounded up, including Vice Minister of War Chen Cheng, who was found hiding in a barrel in the basement of the Xijing Guest House.

Gen. Sun Mingjiu's Guards Regiment of the Northeastern Army was given the job of arresting Chiang Kaishek. Liu Duoquan and Bai Fengxiang had looked over the villa and knew where Chiang slept and where the various guards and officers were posted. They knew the roads and the buildings of the compound.

Before dawn, on December 12, General Sun and his men moved into Chiang's villa. They were discovered, and Chiang's guards opened fire on them with machine guns. The invaders shot back with automatic weapons and wiped out nearly all the guards. Chiang's aide, Qian Dajun, was wounded in the foot.

When Chiang Kaishek heard the shooting, he got out of bed, put on his shoes and a robe over his nightshirt, and ran outside. With the help of a guard he jumped over the compound wall. He fell into a gulley full of brush and lost a shoe, but he picked himself up and began to run. One of his officers saw him and offered to carry him on his back. Chiang accepted the offer and was carried up a hillside. After covering about a quarter of a mile, they hid behind a large rock.

When Zhang Xueliang's men entered Chiang's bedroom, they saw that their bird had flown. But he had left behind his false teeth and his clothing, so they knew he could not be far away. His bed was still warm.

Sun reported to Zhang and Yang. The two generals were shocked. How could their plan have miscarried? It could not have been leaked out.

For a moment they thought that Chiang might have drowned himself in the big pond outside the villa, but they soon gave up that idea. Chiang was not that sort of man.

Zhang suggested that Sun's men check all the automobiles to see if any were missing. None was. So they decided that Chiang must still be on the villa's premises somewhere. They ordered a foot-by-foot search of the grounds.

In the search the soldiers first found Qian Dajun with his injured foot, hiding outside. When they came to the big rock, the officer who had carried Chiang up the hill raised his head and a soldier shot him dead. Chiang was found behind the rock, lying curled up on the ground. He raised his hands.

"Here I am," he said.

Sun Mingjiu and Bai Fengxiang saw a skinny little man without any teeth dressed in a nightshirt, with only one shoe, looking as pale as death. His body was trembling.

"Get up and come with us."

"Whose troops are you?"

"Northeast Army," they said.

Chiang immediately began reviling them and demanding that they submit to his authority as commander in chief of the Nationalists. He refused to move. Sun carried him down the hill, and Bai put an overcoat over Chiang's shaking body. When they came to the car that was waiting for them, Chiang refused to get inside. He argued, until finally they forced him inside.

"Where is General Zhang?" Chiang asked.

"We're taking you to him now," said General Sun.

And so they were.

18

The United Front

It is now over five years since Japan occupied China. National sovereignty has been infringed upon and more and more of our territory lost to the enemy. The humiliating Shanghai Armistice Agreement of early 1932 was followed by the signing of the Tanggu and He-Umezu agreements. All our fellow countrymen feel distressed at these events. Recently a great change has taken place in the international situation, with some forces working hand in glove to make a sacrifice of our country and people. The start of fighting in East Suiyuan has thrown the whole country into a ferment, and the morale of our troops has never been so high.

At this very moment the central authorities should do their utmost to encourage the army and people to launch nationwide resistance against Japan. But while our officers and men are engaged in bloody fighting against the enemy at the front, our diplomats have been doing their best to reach a compromise with alien invaders. The imprisonment of the Shanghai patriots has shocked the whole world besides paining the Chinese nation. It distresses everyone to see patriots tried as criminals. Generalissimo Chiang, misled by mean officials and divorced from the masses of people, has made our nation suffer greatly. We—Zhang Xueliang and Yang Hucheng—have repeatedly offered him our earnest remonstrances only to be harshly reproached. When the students in Xi'an demonstrated for national salvation, police were ordered to open fire at these patriotic youths. Anyone with a conscience could not have let things go so far! Having for long years been colleagues of the Generalissimo, we could hardly sit by idly. So we offered him our last remonstrance for the sake of his personal safety and in order to stimulate his awakening.

> —Part of a telegram sent out to the world by Zhang Xueliang and
> Yang Hucheng following the arrest of Chiang Kaishek
> on December 12, 1936.

After Zhang Xueliang and Yang Hucheng had arrested Chiang Kaishek and imprisoned him in Yang's headquarters in the Xincheng building, they dispatched the above telegram to the nation and the world. They also sent a special message to Mao Zedong up in Yanan, asking him to send a delegation to Xi'an to talk about the future of China.

The messages included the generals' eight-point program for "national salvation":

1. Reorganize the Nanjing government to admit representatives of all parties and groups to jointly share the responsibility of saving the nation.

2. End all civil war.

3. Immediately release all the imprisoned leaders of the patriotic movements in Shanghai.

4. Release all political prisoners in the country.

5. Give a free hand to the patriotic mass movement.

6. Safeguard the political freedom of the people, including the freedom of assembly.

7. Earnestly carry out Dr. Sun Yatsen's will.

8. Immediately convene a conference on national salvation.

Meanwhile, in Xi'an, the generals took action. Martial law was declared in the city. The Guomindang officials had all fled the area, so their offices were given to mass organizations formed on the spot, groups such as the Anti-Japanese Fellowship and the All Circle National Salvation Association of Northwest China. The newspaper *Xijing Daily* was reorganized, renamed *Liberation Daily*, and given a new editor. Political prisoners were all released.

It did not take Mao Zedong long to send a delegation down to Xi'an; the group opened offices there. The Northwest Bandit Suppression headquarters was shut down on December 14. The Shaanxi provincial government was reorganized, and Guomindang control of Shaanxi was wiped out completely.

When Chiang Kaishek was brought to Yang's headquarters and locked in a room, he asked for a brush and paper so that he could write his will. He expected to be executed. Zhang Xueliang came to see him. Chiang, hoping there was some rift between Zhang and Yang, tried to play on this, but he was rebuffed quickly enough.

Zhang and Yang decided that Chiang should be moved to the Gao mansion. When two officers were sent to tell him, he looked at the pistols in their belts, climbed up on the bed, slid back against the wall, and said he would not go. He wanted to die right there, he said. He refused to move. Zhang and Yang had to come and convince him that he would not be killed.

There was reason for Chiang's concern. When the people of Xi'an learned that he had been arrested, demonstrations began and the newspapers all put out extra editions.

"Down with Chiang Kaishek" was the cry. "Down with the Nanjing government." "Down with Japanese imperialism." "Try Chiang Kaishek. Execute Chiang Kaishek." These slogans were affixed to banners and placards and carried through the streets by paraders all day long.

In Nanjing the Guomindang's ruling bodies held a joint meeting on the night of December 12 and decided to send a large army to Xi'an under He Yingqin. It was to be a "punish the rebel army" expedition. The next day Zhang Xueliang was removed from all his Nationalist posts. On December 16 Nationalist planes began bombing in Shaanxi Province. They killed hundreds of people, mostly civilians.

He Yingqin cabled Wang Jingwei, the Guomindang founding leader and at one time Dr. Sun's assistant, who was traveling abroad. Wang had recently turned very pro-Japanese. He had just been visiting Hitler, and he approved of the German-Japanese anti-Comintern pact. It seemed that He Yingqin and Wang were planning a coup, now that Chiang was out of the way, and the subsequent alignment of China with Japan.

Chiang's major supporters, including the Soong family (his wife was Soong Meiling) began efforts to get Chiang freed. Soong Meiling arranged a confrontation with He Yingqin to chide him for using military efforts, which would probably only cause Chiang's death. He called her "an ignorant woman." She called him "Franco of the east."

He Yingqin prepared to march. The Communists did march, moving the Fifteenth Army Corps down near Xi'an to help Zhang's and Yang's armies if the Nationalist forces attacked.

At 4 p.m. on the afternoon of December 14 a plane from Nanjing brought an Australian named W. H. Donald to Xi'an. The plane circled the airport and dropped a message: If the people below wanted to let Donald land and discuss Chiang Kaishek, they should light a bonfire. Donald said he represented Madame Chiang.

Zhang Xueliang knew Donald well; the Australian had once been his economic adviser in the northeast. Donald was allowed to land, and he brought with him two letters from Madame Chiang. One was to Zhang Xueliang; Madame Chiang said she hoped Zhang would keep the interests of the nation at heart in dealing with Chiang. The other letter was to Chiang:

> Your temper is no good. You never patiently explain things to your subordinates. Also you never listen to their opinions. I'm much worried because of all this. So, I've made it a point to accompany you each time you go out. This time, however, I could not go to Xi'an with you because I had to attend a meeting in Shanghai. Little did I expect that something would go wrong with you in the Shaanxi provincial capital.
>
> The officers and men of the Northeastern Army have been driven out of their homeland by the Japanese, and it is only natural that they demand resistance to Japan. You should have told them what is in your mind and never hurt their anti-Japanese feelings. But you acted otherwise, and that's why things have come to such a pass.

After reading both letters, the generals agreed to talk to envoy Donald. In their talks Zhang explained why he and Yang had kidnapped Chiang, and Donald agreed that it was all they could have done.

Zhang and Donald went to see Chiang. Donald explained that Chiang's life was in no danger but said the two generals were demanding that Chiang resist the Japanese. If he would do this, the country would unite behind him. When Chiang learned that he was not to be killed, he smiled.

In the next few days there was much talk. Chiang was persuaded to send a message to He Yingqin, telling him to call off the attack on Xi'an. On December 17 he ordered He to stop the bombing of Shaanxi Province.

On December 20 T. V. Soong arrived in Xi'an. He was one of Chiang Kaishek's intimates and the brother of Soong Meiling. Soon there was a whole parade of people coming and going to Xi'an, including Dai Li, the chief of China's infamous secret service.

With all the activity, Chiang regained his confidence and set down conditions. First, the Soongs would take part in the talks. Second, the results would be kept secret until Chiang released them from Nanjing later.

At this point the Communists entered the talks, which lasted until December 23. On December 24 agreement was reached on six points:

1. The national government would be reorganized and anti-Japanese elements (the Communists) would be admitted.
2. The Shanghai leaders would be released.
3. The policy of suppressing the Communists would stop and the Red Army would be allied with the Nationalists to resist Japan.
4. A national conference would be convened to decide on the policy of resisting Japan.
5. China would cooperate with all nations that were sympathetic to China's resistance against Japanese aggression.
6. The central army units would withdraw from Shaanxi and Zhang's and Yang's armies would control military and civil affairs.

Chiang accepted the "six promises," and Zhang Xueliang agreed for the national interest to escort Chiang Kaishek back to Nanjing so that it would not appear that Chiang had been simply dismissed. He and Yang knew that Chiang had suffered a severe loss of face in the kidnapping and that this gesture would restore some of Chiang's prestige. Zhang felt this was in the interest of national unity and fighting the Japanese, though he knew that Chiang's promises were not always to be trusted.

Yang did not entirely agree. He knew Chiang Kaishek better than Zhang did:

There are no other warlords in China capable of outwitting Chiang Kaishek, the scoundrel. I'm no match for him either. Only the Communist Party can cope with him.

Yang was most distrustful of the whole arrangement.

On the afternoon of Christmas day, 1936, Chiang left for Nanjing with Zhang Xueliang. Yang Hucheng objected one last time. He knew how important Zhang was to the Northeastern Army—no one could replace him in holding that army together. As long as Zhang stayed clear, three elements opposed to Chiang Kaishek could operate together: Zhang, the Seventeenth Route Army, and the Communist Red Army. That would keep Chiang under control; he would have to live up to his six promises.

Actually none of the three men opposed to Chiang really expected him to live up to his promises once he got away from Xi'an. For that reason some leaders of the three elements objected to letting him go. Others wanted him to be forced to make a broadcast to the nation, putting forth the promises. Others wanted him to put them in writing.

But Zhang forestalled all this, in his own naive fashion, by promising to go with Chiang to Nanjing.

Zhang Xueliang knew that his friend Yang Hucheng objected to his trip south. He knew that Zhou Enlai would object too, so he did not tell Zhou that he was going. When Zhou learned of the departure from one of Zhang's officers, Sun Mingjiu, Zhou was visibly upset.

"How long has he been gone?" he asked.

"About ten minutes or so."

"But why didn't you tell me earlier?"

"I just learned of it."

The two got into a car and sped to the airport. But Chiang's plane, and Zhang Xueliang, had just taken off.

The plane took off at 4 p.m. and arrived at Luoyang an hour and a half later. By that time Chiang had recovered his aplomb and was trying to re-establish the prestige he had lost in the kidnapping incident. At Luoyang Chiang issued a statement, "Admonition to Zhang Xueliang and Yang Hucheng," in which he tried to make it appear as though he had voluntarily chosen to fight the Japanese. When Mao Zedong saw this bit of work, he answered it, indicating that Chiang had responded only when forced by public indignation. If Chiang failed to keep his promises, said Mao, "if he wavers on the issue of resisting Japan or delays in fulfilling his pledges, then the nationwide revolutionary tide will sweep him away."

By the time the plane reached Luoyang, Chiang had decided that he would have Zhang Xueliang detained as a prisoner. Before he did so, he persuaded the impetuous Zhang to telegraph General Yang, asking for the release of Chen Cheng, Wei Lihuang, and several other Guomindang officials. Zhang did so. Immediately after the men were released, Chiang clapped Zhang under house arrest, as perfidious an act as he had ever carried out. Zhang was first housed with Chiang's friend T. V. Soong. Then he was moved to H. H. Kung's villa at Lingyuan, where he was guarded by Guomindang secret police agents. Chiang added one other touch: Zhang in his youth had been an opium addict, a habit he had shucked when he decided to fight the Japanese. Chiang made sure that Zhang was reintroduced to opium.

Meanwhile, Chiang was trying to make up for lost time and prestige. He pulled his usual trick: He said he was going to resign from the government to go south and tend his mother's grave. The Guomindang leaders refused his resignation, as he knew they would. He resigned again. Again it was refused. Finally, he insisted on leave and was granted a month. As was his habit, he went to his home in Zhejiang Province, to pull strings while pretending great piety.

By this time Zhang Xueliang, once more a slave to opium, was putty in Chiang Kaishek's hands. Chiang insisted that Zhang make a confession of his crimes ("organizing followers to coerce one's superior by force"), and Zhang signed the confession. He was tried, by Nationalist judges, and sentenced to ten years imprisonment. On the same afternoon Chiang Kaishek grandly requested "clemency," so Zhang was given amnesty. But he was placed under the close surveillance of the National Military Council and kept in slavery to opium, so he passed out of the life of the revolution. Zhang Xueliang played no further role in the history of China.

As these events occurred, Chiang was still planning a military excursion against Xi'an to punish Yang and the officers of the Northeastern Army and to deal with the Communists. Yang demanded Zhang's return to Xi'an. Chiang answered from Zhejiang that he was at home and in no position to act. It was a convenient ploy. He had no intention of letting Zhang go, and he never did.*

Chiang then set out to restore control of the armies to himself. He ordered the Northeastern Army transferred to northern Jiangsu and Anhui. The pill was sweetened by giving the army the power to appoint the governor of Anhui.

He ordered the Seventeenth Route Army transferred to Gansu Province, giving it the same right to choose the governor. But once the armies had marched, Chiang went back on his promise. After his return to Nanjing,

---

*Zhang Xueliang was kept under constant house arrest until the Guomindang leaders fled to Taiwan in 1949, taking him with them. In Taiwan he was kept under arrest as long as Chiang Kaishek lived. As of 1988 he has never returned to mainland China.

Chiang began going back on all his promises, as General Yang had expected he would. The Guomindang's Executive Committee rejected everything that he had promised to do—naturally enough, because Chiang controlled the Executive Committee. To the proposals submitted by the Xi'an Committee for the reorganization of the government, the Guomindang said this:

> Whatever its contents, since it is motivated by rebellious intentions and put forward in a threatening manner, the proposal is obviously a pretext for creating confusion in the country. It runs counter to law and military discipline. The plenum, therefore, resolves to ignore said proposal so as to prevent similar ones from being put forward in the future.

So, by the sort of political and military sleight of hand at which Chiang was so clever, he managed to force the Seventeenth Route Army and the Northeastern Army out of their strong positions at Xi'an and into new areas where they could be more easily controlled. By direction of the Nationalist government, Gen. Yang Hucheng was deprived of all his military posts and was later sent abroad, where he remained for some time.*

So what General Yang had said about Chiang Kaishek was true. No one could deal with this slippery figure except the Chinese Communists. Chiang had made many promises, and he had gone back on all but one of them. The one promise he dare not go back on was the promise to fight the Japanese, because even he finally sensed that the people of China were squarely behind Zhang Xueliang, Yang Hucheng, and Mao Zedong's demands that the Japanese be driven out of China. Chiang had to fight, or at least pretend to fight, the common enemy.

Chiang had emerged from the Xi'an confrontation alive and without apparent harm. Only the Communist party remained in determined, distrustful opposition to him.

---

*Chiang got rid of General Yang by making him commissioner of the National Military Council to study military affairs in Europe and America. Yang went abroad on June 29, 1937, aboard the liner *President Hoover*. He returned to China on November 30, 1937, and was immediately imprisoned on Chiang's orders. He was held prisoner for the next twelve years. Just before Chiang Kaishek fled to Taiwan, he ordered that General Yang be killed by Guomindang secret police and that his body be buried in a secret grave at Chongqing. After the Communists captured Chongqing, the secret policemen were interrogated, tortured, and forced to tell where Yang's body was buried. It was dug up, taken to Beijing with great ceremony, and reburied at Xi'an.

In 1935 the Comintern had lost its power over the Chinese Communists. They still paid lip service, but Mao had discovered that the key to the success of communism in China lay with the common people. Only by securing their trust and cooperation could he succeed in uniting the countryside. The people were willing to fight and sacrifice to deal with the Japanese, but only if they were taken in as partners. And that is what Mao did, despite the demands of the Comintern. Liu Shaoqi, one of the hardline Comintern followers, had been spending his time doing the old thing: trying to organize labor unions in the cities and stage uprisings. The policy was a total failure. In 1937 Liu gave up and joined Mao Zedong at Yanan. Moscow had been calling for a united front against Japan for a long time, and now it was coming into being, in spite of Chiang's reluctance.

Mao, however, would not put himself into Chiang's hands. He decided to maintain a double front: fight the Japanese, but maintain and strengthen the soviets in the north, waiting for the day when the great confrontation with the Guomindang would come. For the time being, in 1937, the two-line policy had to be carried out. The Communists began attacking the Japanese in Shaanxi Province. In April the united front was a reality, or as much of a reality as it would ever be. Mao was fighting the Japanese. He was also winning the struggle against the remaining Bolsheviks of the old twenty-eight-man Central Committee from Moscow and Shanghai. The armed forces of the Chinese Communist party were setting up bases, working with the people, and establishing the social revolution for China even as the military fought the Japanese enemy.

For the next eight years the war against Japan would take precedence over all else, but never, in that time, did Mao's Communists lose sight of their final goal: control of the revolution that would change all China.

19

United Front against Japan— but Not Very

The aim of the Nationalist Revolution is to seek freedom and equality for China. Dr. Sun Yatsen said that the San Min Zhu Yi are fundamental principles of national salvation. He earnestly hoped that all our people would strive with one heart to save the state from its perils. Unfortunately, during the past ten years not all of our countrymen have had a sincere and unwavering faith in the Three Principles of the People, nor have they fully realized the magnitude of the crisis confronting our country. The course of the Revolution in its efforts at national reconstruction has been blocked by many obstacles. The result has been waste in our national resources, widespread suffering among the people, increasing humiliations from outside, and growing dangers to the state.

—Chiang Kaishek, 1937, in connection with the united front against Japan promised by Chiang at Xi'an.

The Chinese Communist party followed up the agreement reached at Xi'an with a telegram to the Guomindang Central Executive Committee. The Communists pledged to stop trying to overthrow the Guomindang government, to convert the Red Army to an element of the National Revolutionary Army, to change their soviet in Yanan into a special region of the Republic of China, and to stop the confiscation of landlords' land. In return, the Communists demanded from the Guomindang an end to the civil war, cessation of the killing of Communists, democratic reforms within the Guomindang government, and resistance against Japan.

Thus was forged the second alliance between Nationalists and Communists. For both sides it was a marriage of convenience. It never had, nor did it ever develop, the spontaneity of the original revolutionary alliance. Neither side trusted the other, and Chiang's imprisonment of Zhang Xueliang rankled millions of Chinese. Chiang never forgave either Zhang or Gen. Yang Hucheng for the kidnapping and the humiliation that forced him to fight the Japanese.

But on the surface the coalition seemed real.

Zhou Enlai had indicated that he was ready to go to Nanjing at any time to negotiate with Chiang and the other leaders of the Guomindang in behalf of unity. Thus Zhou emerged in the winter of 1937 as Mao Zedong's spokesman for external relations of all sorts.

Down in Nanjing Soong Chingling, the widow of Dr. Sun Yatsen, called upon the Nationalists to return to the San Min Zhu Yi. Chiang often spoke of these three principles of the people, but he was usually just giving lip service to concepts that he did not practice. But Madame Sun was joined by others in the Guomindang, He Xiangning and Feng Yuxiang, in particular. All three had strong ties to the party and much influence with the people.

So in Nanjing the debate began, but the talks were mostly acrimonious. Madame Sun, He, and Feng advocated cooperation with the Soviet Union, cooperation with the Communists, and support of the workers and peasants, while the right wing talked about noncooperation and ignored the issue of public welfare. Finally, however, the center won out and a resolution was passed which substantially accepted the Xi'an points.

Zhou Enlai came south. He began negotiations that involved shuttling between Yanan, where Mao's headquarters lay, and Xi'an, Hangzhou, and Lushan Mountain. He talked with various Guomindang leaders and several times with Chiang Kaishek.

The negotiations did not get very far. Chiang demanded that the Red Army be disbanded and that the Red Army soldiers and officers enlist as individuals in the National Revolutionary Army. This was the same tactic he had used in 1926 to eliminate Communist influence in the Guomindang, and it was recognized in Yanan for what it was. Once the officers and men enlisted and were widely dispersed, it would be no trick for Chiang to "eliminate" them. Chiang also demanded that Mao Zedong and Zhou Enlai leave China and go into exile. In June 1937 he made these proposals as part of a plan for a National Revolutionary League, with himself at the top, holding dictatorial powers.

Zhou took these demands back to Yanan. He returned with a rejection. The discussions, he said, were supposed to consider the methods of cooperation between the Communist party and the Nationalist party. The issue was not whether the Chinese Communist party should surrender to the Nationalists—which it would never do—but how the two parties could effectively fight against Japanese aggression.

It seemed that the two parties were really at an impasse.

But the difficulty was resolved by the Japanese. On July 7, 1937, Japanese troops suddenly attacked Chinese troops near Lugouqiao, southwest of Beijing. It was known to the world as the incident at Marco Polo Bridge. The attack was the extension of the Guandong Army's plan to capture and control all China, a plan that had now spread into the upper reaches of the Japanese army and had become national policy, as the army gained oligarchic control of the Japanese government.

The Marco Polo Bridge incident was a natural outcome of Japanese policy toward China. Early in the summer of 1937 Gen. Tojo Hideki, chief of staff to the Guandong Army, sent a report to army headquarters in Tokyo. The Chinese in north China were strengthening their forces, he said. What he meant was that the Communists were pushing in the northwest and that the "coalition" was possibly going to work out. All this Chinese activity threatened the position of Manchukuo as an "independent" state supporting Japanese policies, said Tojo. The Chinese had just recently signed a mutual-assistance pact with the Mongolian People's Republic, which was very much under Soviet influence. Since the Japanese had been moving steadily into Inner Mongolia, which abuts the republic, the pact threatened further Japanese expansion.

The Soviets, concerned about the Berlin-Rome-Tokyo alliance which was in the offing, were encouraging a united front in China to further their own purposes. Tojo, whose main politico-military interest was in the Soviet Union and the attack he hoped some day to launch against it to wrench away Siberia, foresaw the signing of a Soviet-Chinese defense alliance which would be even more destructive to Japan. Further, the United States and Britain had now shown a new interest in supporting Chiang Kaishek, and that created new problems for Japan's influence in north China.

Some 2200 Japanese citizens lived in Beijing, and there were more in Tianjin and other cities, in Hubei Province, and, particularly, in Shandong Province, where the Japanese had interests that ranged from coal mines to a brewery. Tojo advocated a preemptive strike against the Nanjing government. That matched the thinking at army headquarters and in the War Ministry. The Japanese had exhibited the same sort of thinking at Port Arthur in 1904; they would exhibit it again in 1941.

Foreign Minister Hirota Kaki opposed this view and wanted seriously to negotiate the differences between the Japanese and Chinese. But even Hirota's position called for more concessions from China, and now these concessions were not going to be forthcoming.

Therefore the Guandong Army, in particular, was chafing for action. For years the soldiers of this army had behaved very badly toward the Chinese. They made it a matter of policy to mistreat Chinese civilians, intending to cow the Chinese into submission to Japanese demands. Now, Foreign Minister Hirota heard that the Japanese army garrison in north China was planning an incident "around the time of the Festival of the Weaver," July 7.

Lt. Gen. Tashiiro Koichiro was conducting maneuvers of the north China garrison along the Beijing-Hankou railroad on the night of July 7. This area was part of the training ground of the Chinese Twenty-ninth Army and should have been out of bounds to the Japanese. General Tashiiro knew that as well as anyone, but his young staff officers had deliberately laid out the route for the training to help force an incident.

One company of Japanese soldiers came to the Marco Polo Bridge, which crosses the Hu River at the city of Lugouqiao. On the bridge the Japanese passed a Chinese company going the other way. Somehow a shot was fired—probably by one of the young Japanese officers. So edgy were the soldiers of both sides that just the one shot led to general shooting, and a pitched battle broke out. Both sides scurried off the bridge onto the approaches and began a firefight. Before dawn the firing stopped and the two columns moved back to their barracks. Tokyo was informed of the incident by an officer of the army's Military Affairs Bureau; he had come over from Tokyo to north China specifically to stop just such an incident, but he had arrived after the fact.

When Foreign Minister Hirota was informed of the incident, he was furious. But what could he do? He complained to the war minister, who smiled and shrugged. The Chinese had fired first, said the army.

The army command at Tianjin was more cautious than the Guandong Army command or the officers in Tokyo. The Tianjin army counseled patience, and a cease-fire was arranged with the Chinese. Foreign Minister Hirota resumed his efforts to negotiate the differences.

But the Japanese garrison sent reinforcements to Beijing, just as Gen. Song Zheyuan was negotiating a peace with the Japanese. Gen. Sugiyama Hajime, the Japanese war minister, went to the emperor with the argument for war with China. The Japanese army could subdue China in less than a month, he said, and that would put an end to the string of incidents (most manufactured by the Japanese) of mistreatment of Japanese nationals by the Chinese. The emperor was not impressed and said so. But the army had public support. Rally followed rally in Tokyo. The newspaper headlines screamed for action.

General Sugiyama then went to Prime Minister Prince Konoye. The army did not want war, he said. The army wanted a show of force to maintain peace. Prince Konoye allowed himself to be convinced by this specious argument. The army would employ the Guandong Army for "pacification," said the war minister. That should have been a tipoff. The Guandong Army did not want to pacify anybody; it wanted to conquer China.

And so the negotiations deteriorated, while the Japanese mobilized five divisions for dispatch to China.

Chiang Kaishek saw the writing on the wall, but he made one last effort to give the Japanese an out.

"Six years have passed since the loss of Manchuria," he told the Chinese people, "and now the battle is drawing near Beiping." He averred that the Chinese had sought peace steadily for the past two years without success. There were people who believed that the Lugouqiao incident was an accident, he said, but he did not. For a month the Japanese had been making threatening statements. For several months he had heard rumors that the Japanese were going to forget the various agreements with China, enlarge the east Hebei government they had established in China, drive out the Twenty-ninth Army from north China, and force the resignation of Gen. Song Zheyuan. The only way to avoid trouble would be to let the Japanese armies come and go as they wished and to restrict Chinese troop movement within China. This was patently an impossible situation.

If the Chinese allowed the Japanese to occupy Lugouqiao, then Beijing (which Chiang always called Beiping) would become a second Shenyang. Then Hebei and Qahar would share the fate of the three northeast provinces. And would not Nanjing become a second Beijing? he asked.

Whether or not the Lugouqiao incident developed into war now depended on the Japanese, said Chiang. He announced four principles from which the Chinese would not budge:

1. Settlement must not infringe on China's territorial integrity or sovereign rights.

2. The status of the Hebei-Qahar Political Council must not be changed.
3. Local officials appointed by the central government (Song Zheyuan, chairman of the Hebei-Qahar Political Council) could not be deposed.
4. The Twenty-ninth Army would not be disturbed.

Naturally, these were the four areas in which the Japanese insisted on taking action in their drive to take over north China. The reinforcements to the Japanese army from Tianjin marched up to Lugouqiao, bent on occupying the place, and they opened fire once more. It was July 10. Again the Chinese troops of the Twenty-ninth Army fired back. They held their ground.

Back to Japan went the news. The Chinese were all at fault, the army told Prince Konoye.

"Fight," shouted the people in the streets.

Prince Konoye wavered, but came around. On July 11 he authorized the movement of the Guandong Army south across the Great Wall and into north China. Three divisions, including General Itagaki's Fifth Division, set out for China, with bands playing, flags waving, and people cheering.

Generalissimo Chiang Kaishek was pushed into final action: He ordered the general mobilization of the Chinese armies.

In Changchun General Tojo moved into action personally, which he had been itching to do for some time. He led a brigade up through north China, north of Beijing.

In Tokyo General Ishihara warned Prime Minister Konoye that Japan was about to embark on a suicidal war. He suggested that the prime minister go to China and meet with Generalissimo Chiang to try to settle their differences.

But the army was obdurate. The military and the *zaibatsu*, the industrial clique, wanted to exploit Inner Mongolia, and they were brooking no interference. Prince Konoye had the idea of sending to China a personal envoy, Miyazaki Enten, son of a man who had been a personal friend to Dr. Sun Yatsen. Miyazaki got his orders and accepted the mission. He went to Kobe to take a steamer to China and was on the pier when a squad of the army *kempeitai* ("military police") arrived. They arrested Miyazaki and prevented him from making the prime minister's mission. So it was quite apparent who was controlling Japan.

———

In July, General Tojo was marching into Qahar Province. He moved to Changbei, and Changyuan, and then down toward Zhangjiakou, which was uncomfortably close to Beijing. The idea was to cut off Inner Mongolia from China and further Japanese ambitions in this region.

In the Beijing area General Tashiiro died of natural causes and was replaced by Gen. Kotouki Kyoji. The change of command created a hiatus in military activity around Lugouqiao. Some people thought a cease-fire might really work.

But then the three divisions loosed by Prince Konoye began to arrive, full of war slogans and Japanese patriotic fervor. Japanese troops attacked Langfang, halfway along the Tianjin-Beijing road. Army airplanes also began to arrive, about 200 of them, and they started to bomb Langfang. One brigade of the Japanese Twentieth Division attacked the Guang An gate in Beijing but was driven off by the Chinese.

On July 27 the Japanese attacked again in the Beijing area. The war was definitely expanding. The fighting around Langfang was particularly severe. The Japanese attacked the Fengtai railroad station, and the struggle moved back and forth. But having captured the station, the Chinese retreated back to the far bank of the Yong Ding River.

Chiang Kaishek had already predicted the sort of war it would be. In an address to Chinese leaders at Kuling, Jiangxi, on July 17 he had laid it out:

> If it should turn out that we have reached the limit and a conflict is unavoidable, then we cannot do otherwise than resist and be prepared for the supreme sacrifice. But our attitude will be simply one of resistance: we have not sought war, it will have been enforced upon us. We will resist because there is no other possible way of meeting the situation, when the limit of endurance is reached. All our people must have confidence in the National Government and realize that it is in the process of making comprehensive preparations for the defense of the country. We are a weak nation, and our policy is to maintain peace; it is impossible for us to seek war. We are weak yet we must fight for the elite of our race, and shoulder the historic responsibilities handed down

to us by our fathers and all the generations before us. When there is no alternative, we shall have to resist. Let us realize, however, that once the war has begun, there will be no opportunity for a weak nation to seek a compromise. If we allow one inch more of our territory to be lost, or our sovereignty to be again infringed, we shall be guilty of committing an unpardonable offense against our race. There will then be no way left but to throw all the resources of our nation into a grim struggle for ultimate victory.

Long-winded though it was, it was still a definite warning to the Japanese that if they extended the war in China, they would be moving into a morass. Some people, like General Ishihara, Admiral Yonai, and Admiral Yamamoto, knew this to be true. But the army, generally speaking, had on its blinders. All that the generals and the young lieutenant colonels and majors could see was victory and conquest. They did not envisage an army of millions of men trapped on the Chinese continent as surely as if there were a wall around them, sitting, waiting, unable to win, unable to move, while the tides of war surged elsewhere.

On July 30 the Japanese captured Tianjin. The city was looted and burned. The idea, a product of the Guandong Army's way of thinking, was to show the Chinese that it did no good to resist the Japanese juggernaut. Better to cooperate with them and avoid such treatment.

On August 4 the Twenty-ninth Army evacuated Beijing, and within a week the Japanese had established a puppet government. Another wave of the future was shown to the Chinese.

Although the Japanese kept winning and occupying more countryside, something strange was happening: The Chinese lost, but they did not quit. They retreated, they attacked again, they lost again, they retreated again. But they attacked a third time, and a fourth. The Japanese quickly began to realize that a "victory" was nothing. It meant only more territory to police and more problems to solve. Soon the three divisions sent over from Japan were not enough. The call went out for still more troops to police the growing area of China that was coming under Japanese control.

On August 7 the Chinese National Defense Council adopted a strategy of attrition. In other words, the earth would be burned for the Japanese invaders.

Still, the Japanese army was supremely confident. Did it not have seventeen active divisions, with 380,000 men? Did it not have twice as many reservists, men who had served their three years and been discharged, but who could be called again? Was not Japan's army the strongest in Asia?

All these statistics were correct, but there was one statistic the Japanese forgot. Theirs was a country of 105 million people. China's population numbered 450 million, at least.

By the second week of August 1937 many wise heads in Tokyo knew that their country was embarked on disaster. There might be a way to stop it. The emperor had spoken up strongly to Prince Konoye: He did not like this war, he did not think it was just, nor did he believe it could be won.

And the army was growing a little uneasy. The troops had not cut through China so smoothly as they had expected. At the battles of Qianbian and Hengling, the Chinese had taken casualties of more than 50 percent, but they kept coming on. Japanese casualties were far fewer, but they were still significant. And once those battles were won, there were simply more battles.

The future was there for all to see: 450 million people fighting 105 million people.

In that second week of August Foreign Minister Hirota struggled desperately to find a political solution to a problem that the Japanese army said had to be military. Hirota proposed a demilitarized zone, and the reduction of Japanese forces in China. The Japanese would also disband that hated puppet government called the East Hebei Autonomous Region.

Foreign Minister Hirota's plans seemed to hold hope. The emperor approved. So did Prince Konoye. On August 10 the plans were taken by a Japanese envoy to Nanjing for discussion. The Chinese were most impressed by the proposal to disband that government in Hebei.

But then in Shanghai a Japanese marine lieutenant was killed by Chinese guards in an incident at Hongkou airport. The Japanese army knew what was happening in Nanjing and was determined to stop it. So the Japanese in Shanghai made new demands of the Chinese; the Chinese refused, and the Chinese National Defense Council ordered three divisions up to Shanghai.

The fighting began again, and it spread all around Shanghai. The Chinese bombed the Japanese cruiser *Idzumo*, and Japanese and Chinese aircraft clashed in air battles. Communications between Shanghai and Nanjing were cut off by the Japanese army, which wanted no part of peace.

The Japanese bombed Nanjing. On August 12 the Japanese cabinet authorized the dispatch of two more divisions of troops to China. A new expeditionary force was authorized. No one bothered to ask how many troops this problem would demand or how long it would last. There were no answers to those questions. Japan had just mired itself in the China war.

One month, said General Sugiyama to the emperor in July, one month was all it would take to end the China incident. Now that month had passed, and the China incident had become a China war. Ten thousand Japanese troops had been sent to Shanghai alone. The Guandong Army was fighting in Inner Mongolia, resisted by the Chinese Communists. Three divisions were moving south of Beijing.

Everywhere the Japanese moved, the newspapers were filled with tales of Japanese victories. They won, and won, and won. But they did not win a decisive victory. The Chinese fought and bled and died, and then moved back to fight again.

"Full Annihilation Said in Sight for 29th Army" said a Japanese headline about the fighting in north China. But that army had been "annihilated" several times already, and although it would be "annihilated" again and again in the future, it would keep coming back to fight.

20

The Nationalist War

We must remember that real victory will be won only by a long per-
severing struggle, not by any lucky accident. International sympathy,
though greatly encouraging to us, should not be allowed to foster a
spirit of reliance upon others. We must first help ourselves; only then
will others help us.

Let our people cultivate a willingness to face unprecedented suffering, to begrudge no sacrifice, to fight undaunted and unyielding to
the end. Let us overcome all perils, and endure suffering and hardship. Let us, through this war, train and discipline ourselves, trans-
form our race, and create new life for our nation.

—Chiang Kaishek in a broadcast from Nanjing on October 9, 1937,
celebrating the Double Ten national holiday, which marked
the twenty-sixth anniversary of the Chinese Republic.

In north China the superior Japanese forces swiftly drove the Chinese army
back from Tianjin and Beijing to the line of defense along the Huang He
and the Longhai railway. The Japanese bombed Nankai University in
Tianjin. The Japanese navy began occupying coastal territory: Shantou and
the islands of Hangzhoo Bay. Japanese bombers raided Hangzhou, Nanjang,
Nanjing, Suzhou, Jinjiang, and the Shanghai-Nanjing railway.

After occupying Shanghai, the Japanese forces rapidly drove the Chinese
back up the Yangtze River. By December the fighting had nearly reached
Nanjing. The Japanese were carrying out a war of terror everywhere. Under the Japanese military system the local commander, be it of an army,
corps, or division, was basically responsible for the conduct of his troops,
and higher authority did not often interfere with his methods of discipline.
In China the word was out, spread by the Guandong Army, that against
the Chinese civilians any sort of conduct was acceptable. Consequently,
rape, murder, and pillage became the rule. The most striking example was
at Nanjing.

The Chinese had made a strong stand outside Nanjing, and the Japanese had countered with every sort of attack. By the end of the first week of December 1937, the Japanese were planning to make an all-out assault on the city.

On December 12 Japanese planes bombed several vessels in the Yangtze River, including three military vessels: the American gunboat *Panay*, which was sunk, and the British *Ladybird* and *Bee*. The man responsible for this attack was Col. Hashimoto Kingoro, who was already notorious in China: When he had arrived at his headquarters at Wuhu weeks earlier, he had torn an American flag from the gateway of an American mission compound, ripped it to shreds, and trampled it underfoot with his hobnailed boots.

The incident aroused Americans and British more than anything that had happened before. It was an indication of things to come, although the Japanese government disavowed the Hashimoto stance and apologized to Britain and America. Admiral Yamamoto Isoroku, the vice minister of the navy, made a personal apology to Ambassador Joseph C. Grew in Tokyo. But once again the signals were deceptive. Admiral Yamamoto's apology was sincere—he dreaded the thought of a Japanese-American conflict—but the Japanese government was now in the hands of the military oligarchy; there was no stopping it short of strong military action by the United States and Britain, which was not forthcoming.

In China the *Panay* incident was dwarfed by the fall of Nanjing the following day, December 13, 1937, and the subsequent "rape of Nanjing" carried out by the Japanese army. The entire city was pillaged and an estimated 100,000 captured Chinese soldiers were machine-gunned, bayoneted, or killed in target practice by the Japanese. It was the worst debacle inflicted on a city in the twentieth century.

The Chinese moved their capital back upriver to Hankou, in the Wuhan complex. So once again, for a brief time, Wuhan became the center of Chinese government activity. Actually, the seat of government—Chiang Kaishek's headquarters—moved 1500 miles up the Yangtze River to Chongqing, which would be the Nationalists' capital for the next eight years. Chiang was anticipating a continued Japanese drive inland.

But the Japanese had already discovered the high cost of taking and holding Chinese territory. Each week, each month, more Japanese forces were being committed to a China that seemed to swallow them up. So Tokyo and the headquarters of the China Expeditionary Army decided upon a new policy. They would stop the drive inland, and consolidate the Japanese victory along the important coastal sector. Holding that part of China, they would achieve a political victory. The army moved from north and south along the railway that connects Tianjin with Pukou on the north bank of the Yangtze opposite Nanjing. Their goal was the city Xuzhou, from which another railway runs east and west and intersects the Beijing-Hankou line.

The Japanese crossed the Huang He in December and took Jinan, the capital of Shandong Province. The Chinese fought a splendid battle at Taierzhuang, where they defeated the superior Japanese forces. It was their most famous military victory in the entire war. But it delayed the Japanese only momentarily; they marched on and reached Xuzhou in March 1938.

In October 1938 the Chinese had to abandon the Wuhan complex. They moved back into the mountains of Sichuan Province.

The Japanese moved into Guangzhou, and now they held the whole of the Chinese coastline, from Manchukuo to the Pearl River in the south. They were capable of driving a column of troops anywhere within 500 miles of the coast. But those penetrations were really meaningless in terms of military victory: Wherever the Japanese went, the people moved out and the local militia and warlord forces scattered; and when the Japanese retreated back to the coast, the people returned and the local forces took command again. So the Japanese controlled China, but they had not won their war. Instead, they were being sapped month after month by the high cost of occupying part of that vast country.

Their deepest penetration inland was north of the Huang He, where the Japanese had moved west of Taiyuan. From Changzhou to Hankou they had been able to move only as far west as the Beijing-Hankou railway. They held the Yangtze valley from Wuhan to the sea. South of the Yangtze their control was much spottier. They held the north end of the Wuchang-Guangzhou railway and Guangzhou, but in between was a no-man's-land. In this area, particularly in Mao Zedong's old stamping ground of Hunan, Communist guerilla forces began to emerge and exercise control.

In 1938 Chiang Kaishek's status gained immeasurably. Britain and America elevated China to their own level in a series of agreements, most important of which was the ABCD (American, British, Chinese, and Dutch) defense pact. In that year, too, Chiang was made "leader" of the Guomindang political section as well as commander in chief of the military forces. From the summer of 1938 on, the government was controlled by the People's Political Council, which included Communists and representatives of groups other than the Guomindang. A sort of national unity had been achieved, even if it was not very deep.

The fact was, as was shown in Chiang's reluctance to carry the war against the Japanese in those areas where he might have, that he was more interested in maintaining his military forces for future use against the Communists than he was in fighting the Japanese. From the beginning Chiang was certain that the war would expand to become global. When, in February 1939, the Japanese occupied Hainan Island off the south coast of China, Chiang said, "This is the 18th of September of the Pacific War." He was referring to the day the Japanese began their attack on Manchuria at Shenyang in 1931.

Chiang believed that the war would envelop the western powers and that ultimately they would win the war, thus defeating Japan and leaving Chiang in control of a China for which he would have to contest with the Communists once again. This was the cornerstone of his war policy.

In late 1939 Chiang became concerned with the growth and extension of Chinese Communist power in the Shaanxi-Ningxia-Gansu border region. He was, in effect, blockading the Communist forces in the Yanan stronghold of northern Shaanxi. The Guomindang Army commander in the area attacked the Communist Eighth Route Army, but the effort failed. Then, early in 1941, Chiang ordered the Chinese Communist New Fourth Army to move from its position south of the Huang He to a position north of the river, hoping to eliminate that Communist army. The army did move—the Communists had placed all their forces under Chiang's command. The front-line troops moved first, then the headquarters and rear echelon. They were passing through a mountainous region when they were ambushed by a vastly superior force of Nationalist troops. This fight became known as the "southern Anhui incident," and it destroyed whatever confidence existed between Communist and Nationalist forces. Chiang accused the New Fourth Army of having fomented the trouble, and he ordered it disbanded. The Communists held it together, but the army received no further supplies or support from the Nationalist government.

From that point on the suspicion between Communists and Nationalists was renewed. Chiang prepared for the future—which meant saving his best troops and keeping them along the borders of the Communist territory so that they could strike when the Pacific war ended. The Communists had the same idea.

*   *   *

When the war did indeed come to the western powers in December 1941, Chiang Kaishek was immediately appointed supreme allied commander of the China theater, which included Indochina and Thailand and later Burma. Brig. Gen. Joseph W. Stilwell was sent to China as Chiang's military adviser, and American material was sent toward the Burma road, the one remaining method of entering Free China overland.

The Chinese did send an army into Burma to try to hold the Burma road open. It fought around Mandalay, but ultimately the Japanese triumphed and closed off the Burma road in 1942. Thereafter, for three years all the military and civilian goods that were sent to China by the Allies came by airplane across the Himalaya Mountains.

The Japanese advance stopped in northern Burma and along the eastern border of India's Assam Province. Yunnan Province of China was the central defense position. Gen. Claire Chennault's Fourteenth U.S. Air Force (the descendant of the American volunteer group called the Flying Tigers) was located at Kunming. That city and most of the province were controlled by the Long Yun, whose troops under his half-brother Gen. Lu Han had only token loyalty to Chiang Kaishek's government. Indeed, during the war, Long Yun showed his independence of the Guomindang by keeping Yunnan Province on standard time while Chiang's Free China went on daylight savings time. There was no earthly reason for it; it was a matter of defiance.

In the spring of 1944 affairs were going very badly for the Japanese in the Central Pacific. The Gilbert Islands and Guadalcanal had fallen, the northern Solomon Islands and the Bismarck Archipelago were being bypassed, the Marshall Islands had fallen, and the Marianas were obviously going to be next.

In Tokyo General Tojo decided on a major offensive in China to put an end to the "China incident." If he could drive west and capture Chongqing, and bring Chiang Kaishek to a point of surrender, the Allies would have no further impetus to continue the war, Tojo reasoned. Then a negotiated peace could be arranged, which would allow Japan to keep its empire. To this end a major Japanese offensive was launched in June along the Wuchang-Guangzhou railway, and it moved steadily forward into Guangxi Province to the capital city of Guilin. There it stalled, and would go no further, because in July 1944 the Americans attacked Saipan, and Tinian and Guam islands in the Marianas, and thus breached the inner line of the Japanese empire. From that point on it was apparent that all

Japan's resources must be devoted to defense of the inner empire. There was nothing left to expend on a new China offensive. The opportunity had been lost and would never emerge again.

In September General Stilwell, who recognized Chiang's reluctance to fight the Japanese and the reasons for it, was replaced in China by Gen. Albert C. Wedemeyer, who was much more sympathetic to Chiang's point of view. A limited offensive of Chinese, American, and British troops was launched in northern Burma, and by the end of the year the Burma road was reopened and connected with the Ledo road, which brought supplies up from the terminus of the Assam and Bengal railway at Ledo.

In 1937, when Chiang moved the capital of Free China to Chongqing, a spirit of unity and resistance dominated that city. In Yanan Mao Zedong was undoubtedly as cynical about the future as was Chiang, but on the lower levels some Communists and certainly many liberals and intellectuals truly foresaw a united China. The spirit was made stronger by Japanese bombings of Chongqing.

But gradually the spirit of unity and hope began to diminish. The cutting off of western China from the coast, and the serious shortage of every sort of consumer good, brought inflation and scarcity.

Inflation was used to finance the war economy. The government wanted money, so it printed money. In 1937 the Nationalist government issued 2.06 billion yuan. The price index that year was 100. The yuan was 3 to the U.S. dollar, or 33.3 cents.

In 1941 the government printed 15.81 billion yuan. The price index jumped almost twenty times, to 1980. The yuan dropped to 30 to the U.S. dollar, or 3.3 cents. In 1945 the government printed 1.03 trillion yuan. The price index was 249 times that of 1937. The yuan dropped to 3250 to the U.S. dollar. By this time it took a satchel full of money to buy a meal.

Even worse than the currency inflation was the outright manipulation of the currency and the gold reserves by H. H. Kung, the minister of finance, and by T. V. Soong, Chiang's principal adviser.*

---

*I was in Chongqing in 1945. I recall that one evening I gave a dinner party at a restaurant and did not have enough cash with me to pay the bill. I promised to return the next day. Overnight, Finance Minister Kung manipulated the currency, the dollar dropped temporarily about 30 percent, and my restaurant bill became enormous. Within two days the dollar had bounced back to its real level, H. H. Kung was much richer, and I was much poorer.

Their peculations became notorious. It was common knowledge that the "Big Four" families—the Kungs, the Soongs, the Chiangs, and the Chen brothers—were enriching themselves at the expense of the people and that millions of dollars given to China by America were disappearing into private coffers. It was said that one day, when Madame Chiang was returning from one of her visits to America, one of the cases in her enormous pile of luggage burst open at the Kunming airport and out spilled a king's ransom in furs and jewels. This sort of story raced across Free China, and was anathema to unity.

As the war went along, the Guomindang became more oppressive. Chiang and his advisers were looking to the future and the civil war. The secret police of the party and the army pressed down on intellectuals, many of whom had fled to Chongqing, Kunming, and Chengdu. The intellectuals responded by moving to Yanan to join the Communists. As China historian John King Fairbank put it:

> Strong arm methods against students, publishers, and other seeming enemies steadily widened the split between the intellectuals and the government that hoped to rely upon them in the future.

Conscription for the Nationalist armies became a national disgrace. It was widely known that many of Chiang's generals were corrupt; they enriched themselves by padding the army payroll mercilessly. A Chinese division officially consisted of 10,000 men, but many divisions actually had as few as 2,000 soldiers and the remaining 8000 were "name soldiers" on the list. Needless to say, the pay allotted these latter was scooped off into the pockets of the general and his officers.

A common sight on the roads of west China was a band of ragged young men, chained or roped together, stumbling along under the control of half a dozen soldiers in padded yellow uniforms. These were conscripts, yanked abruptly from life in the village or on the farm, being taken to a faraway camp where they would be chained or penned up until they realized there was no hope of escaping and returning to their villages. Then they became "soldiers."

Equally destructive was the sale of supplies, equipment, and rations. The Nationalists often sold to the Communists, and sometimes they sold to warlord troops. Even the Japanese were approached. An enormous black-market network stretched across all of Free China from Chongqing to Shanghai, at the other end of the Yangtze River.

*   *   *

The demands of the Guomindang government upon the farmers were enormous. As long as the crops were good, the demands could be borne, although the farmers felt the pinch and resented it. But as the inflation
continued, the Nationalist government stopped collecting taxes in the worth-
less paper money and instead collected them in crops. Once more the peasants found themselves paying 50 percent of their crops to the tax man, just
as in the worst of the old warlord days. The Central Agricultural Bank of
the Guomindang had been set up to help farmers; instead, it became an
instrument of usurers and landlords, providing a way for them to foreclose
on poor farmers and put the land back into the hands of the landlords.

When the crops did not come in, as when Henan was struck by drought
in 1942, the result was famine. The government was unalterable in its tax
policy: People starved, and the troops got the food; and the Guomindang
got the hatred of the people. Not only in Henan but in other provinces,
too, the Guomindang lost its reputation as a revolutionary party of the
people, and gained a new one as an oppressor. This reputation, spreading
through Free China, would have an enormous effect on the future of
China.

In foreign relations, the Chongqing government assumed a stance quite
out of keeping with its real world position. At American insistence, Chiang
Kaishek was elevated to the ranks of Roosevelt, Churchill, and Stalin. It
was patent nonsense, as Winston Churchill observed. Stalin kept his own
counsel on the matter, and President Roosevelt pretended that China was
really a world power.

But then the whole American stance regarding China was illusory. Most
of the field representatives of the U.S. Department of State in China were
knowledgeable men, and most of them appreciated the true state of affairs
in China. The Chinese Communists were Communists, as they had certainly proved in the Wuhan government and in the Jiangxi soviet. For
the time being they had submerged basic Communist policy in the interests of the common front against Japan, but they had given no promises for the future. It was certainly known by the knowledgeable that the
Communists were far more than "agrarian reformers," yet some liberal
Americans within China and outside the country tried to whitewash the
Communists as being just that. This stance was more notable because of

its sneering use by the supporters of the Guomindang than for its effect on American thinking.

As the war wore on, however, the thinking about China tended to crystallize. Worst of all for the American position, the Americans both inside and outside China really began to believe that they could control the country as a puppeteer controls puppets. They knew very little of Chiang Kaishek's definite antiforeign bias, and not much more about the Communists.

21
Japan's China

The Japanese Government attaches the utmost importance to the maintenance of peace and order in Manchuria, and is prepared to do all it can to prevent the occurrence of any such state of affairs as may disturb that peace and order, or constitute the probable cause of such a disturbance.

In these circumstances, should disturbances develop further in the direction of Beijing and Tianjin and the situation become so menacing as to threaten the peace and order of Manchuria, Japan may possibly be constrained to take appropriate effective steps for the effective maintenance of peace and order in Manchuria.

—Prime Minister Baron Tanaka to the Chinese Nationalist
government on May 28, 1928

Perhaps alone among the world's chiefs of state, Chiang Kaishek had the omniscience to predict that the war in China would soon become a general Pacific war. After all, he knew the Japanese better than all the other leaders: He had studied in Japan, and he had met with various Japanese ministers in the middle and late 1920s. Chiang knew his Japanese like a cardsharp knows his spades.

Until 1926 Japanese policy toward China had followed what was known as the Shidehara line, after Baron Shidehara, the foreign minister of that period. That line represented Japan's acceptance of the status quo of the 1920s, with western powers dominating China. It was a policy that called for Japanese cooperation with the western powers, but it depended on Chinese acceptance of foreign manipulation of their currency and taxes. When the northern expedition of 1927 succeeded far beyond anyone's expectations, the Japanese confidence in the Shidehara line was shaken. Prime Minister Tanaka Giichi held a different view. He wanted a weak China, and by 1927 he insisted that a unified China must not include Manchuria. Already, the Japanese financial interests in Manchuria were such that Japan considered those northeastern provinces of China to be Japanese territory. Tanaka was prime minister three times in 1927 and 1928, and each time he came to office he sent troops to China to prevent the unification of the country.

The views of the Guandong Army in Manchuria are well known: It demanded the physical possession of Manchuria and got it in 1931. The real reason for the Army's move in September 1931 was Zhang Xueliang's adherence to the Nationalist cause and his plan to build an alternative harbor and railroad system in Manchuria to lessen the effects of Japanese influence there. From that point on the army and the civil government of Japan pursued two different China policies.

In 1932 the Guandong Army invaded China across the steppes of Inner Mongolia. In 1933 it attacked Shanhaiguan. Thereafter the Japanese dominated north China. The Tanggu truce of 1933 set up a demilitarized zone of twenty-one districts on the Chinese side of the Manchurian frontier.

The truce provided for Chinese policing of the districts with a constabulary. But two factions developed within the constabulary, one loyal to the warlord Yu Xuechung and one loyal to the Japanese Tianjin garrison. As in Manchuria, it was younger officers who forced the issue. When the commander of the Japanese garrison left for Changchun, capital of Manchukuo and headquarters of the Guandong Army, Colonel Sakai, his chief of staff, served notice on the Nanjing government to withdraw all Nationalist forces from Hebei Province and to move General Yu elsewhere.

With this, the government in Tokyo panicked. If the Guandong Army was going to expand further, the Tokyo government must be in control, even though it had no part in the planning. So the Japanese navy sent ships to Tanggu to show support for the military, and thus keep the initiative in Tokyo's hands, not Changchun's. Chiang Kaishek thought this represented a considered Japanese policy and sent He Yingqin to north China to negotiate an agreement with the Japanese. The result was the He-Umezu agreement of 1935, which put power in the hands of the warlord Song Zheyuan. Then came the organization of the North China Autonomous Movement, which was designed to separate north China from Nationalist China. It was not a very successful movement.

For the next two years the government in Tokyo struggled to reestablish control over the Guandong Army, but failed. Rather, the Guandong Army took over the Tokyo government, as can be seen in the emergence late in the decade of Hideki Tojo, chief of staff of the Guandong Army, who ultimately became prime minister. With that move, Tojo then took over the

Guandong Army, which, amid the greater concern over the Pacific war, ceased to be a major element in Japanese politics.

After the Marco Polo Bridge incident of 1937, the Japanese army in China became stronger and more independent of Changchun. In August the army was renamed the North China Army and was strengthened with the addition of a number of divisions of troops. Control of north China then passed to Tokyo, which established rule of the occupied areas in Chinese hands to keep it out of the hands of the Guandong Army.

A provisional government was established in Beijing; it was controlled by the China Affairs Board, which was a part of the Japanese prime minister's office. (Ultimately, in 1941, General Tojo put the responsibility under a cabinet ministry, the Ministry of Greater East Asia.)

In 1937 and 1938 Gen. Kita Seiichi was sent to China to supervise a special-service section of the North China Army and to establish puppet administrations for the government of north China. By 1938 the Japanese controlled north China through the provisional government at Beijing and the provincial governments of Hebei, Shaanxi, Shandong, and Henan.

After the fall of Nanjing to the Japanese, the provisional government of the Republic of China was established at Beijing. The Japanese were careful to follow Chinese forms, and thus they observed the separation of powers demanded by Dr. Sun Yatsen. The most important figure in this provisional government was Wang Kemin, chairman of the Executive Committee.

Soon after the outbreak of war in 1937, the Japanese government in Tokyo had sought an accommodation with Chiang Kaishek. He was willing; but the people had spoken up, in the form of the Xi'an incident, and Chiang was forced to carry out a real war against the Japanese. Despite his own predilections—even his wife Soong Meiling sensed the public will long before Chiang did—he had to give up his hope of first eliminating the Communists and then dealing with a Japan that he understood quite well.

On November 3, 1938, Prince Konoye, the prime minister of Japan, announced a "new order in Asia." This was the beginning of the hopeful Japanese experiment in attaining Hakko Ichiu, all the eight corners of the world under one roof, a federation of Asian nations under Japanese control and protection. Hakko Ichiu had no place for an independent China, so all thought of negotiating with Chiang Kaishek was abandoned by the Japanese.

There was, however, one caveat. The new order was dedicated to the eradication of communism. If, at some future date, Chiang Kaishek had a change of heart and stopped cooperating with the Communists, then Japan would reconsider the whole matter.

What a blow that had to be for Chiang Kaishek. So near and yet so far. He had dedicated the years since the northern expedition to the eradication of communism in China; yet now that the Japanese, with all their immense economic and military power, shared his goal, Chiang could do nothing to take advantage of all the assistance Japan would be ready to give in the furtherance of his ambition. So far, Chiang had shown no reluctance in dealing with foreign capitalists who were exploiting the Chinese; why would he be reluctant to deal with the Japanese if they protected his political power?

There was benefit to China in the Japanese action. The United States granted China a loan of $25 million. Britain was also generous, with a loan of £500,000.

———

Meanwhile, however, the Japanese were not idle in trying to resolve the political aspects of the "China incident." They began dealings with Wang Jingwei, the old left-wing Guomindang leader who had vied for so long, and so unsuccessfully, for control of the Guomindang. After several years in France he had returned to China in 1937 and rejoined the Guomindang leadership. Wang was finally convinced that Japan held the key to Asia's future, and he cast his lot with Japan.

In December 1937 he left Chongqing, and on December 21 he surfaced in Hanoi and sent an open telegram to Chiang Kaishek and the world press. He called on Chiang to stop his resistance against the Japanese and, for China's sake, to join Japan in the new era in Asia.

Chiang seemed to ignore the telegram, but the Japanese sent emissaries to talk to Wang. He remained in Hanoi in comfort for three months, but he indicated that he was about to return to his favorite place, France, where he would wait until Chiang had exhausted China in the struggle against Japan. Then Wang would offer himself as the force of unification and return to China with Japanese backing.

On March 21, 1939, agents of Dai Li, Chiang Kaishek's secret police chief, raided Wang Jingwei's house in an attempt to assassinate him. They killed his private secretary by mistake. Wang was shocked and outraged, and he immediately accepted the Japanese proposals that he return to China and assume command of a Japanese-sponsored government.

In March 1938 the Japanese had tried to fill the power vacuum caused by the fall of Nanjing and the move of the Guomindang government to the west by establishing a reformed government of the Chinese Republic at Nanjing. The Japanese tried to get Wu Peifu, the old warlord who had retired to Beijing, to come down and run this government, but he pleaded age and illness and refused. So the Japanese were reduced to using unknowns and politicians who for years had been known to be Japanese pawns.

Then Wang appeared on the scene in the spring of 1939. The next few months were taken up with negotiation. For although Wang was to go down in history as a "puppet" of the Japanese, he was not the sort of puppet whose strings could be visibly displayed. His history was honorable. He had been Dr. Sun Yatsen's closest associate. He had been instrumental in the revolution of China in the 1920s and had parted company with Chiang Kaishek only when Chiang showed that he did not want to share power with anyone. Wang was a great find for the Japanese, or so it seemed. But they had to be very careful about how they employed him, lest the whole scheme backfire in their faces. What if he suddenly rose up and defected to the west or, worse, to Chongqing? The blow to Japanese prestige would be worse than if they had never employed Wang. Furthermore, he had to be convinced that Japan would win and would let China rule itself in the future. His distrust of Chiang Kaishek was complete after the assassination attempt, but Wang still had many ties to the government out in west China.

By March 1940 the Japanese had assured themselves that all was well. That month they announced that Wang Jingwei had come to Nanjing to restore there the reins of national revolutionary power, and they stated that Chiang Kaishek and his government were the defectors from the revolution.

This point of view, oddly enough, was precisely that of the Communists in Yanan. Many Chinese who had been told the same thing by the Communists believed what the Japanese said.

The blow to Chongqing was a big one. Wang had his following among the politicians of the Guomindang. The Japanese hoped that the blow would bring Chiang around to negotiation, but Chiang was in no position to revert to his old policies, having given assurances to the western world and to the liberals within the Chinese establishment that he would cooperate with the Communists to fight Japan.

Therefore, in November 1940, Japan extended formal recognition to the Wang Jingwei government; recognition followed very soon by Germany, Italy, and then Spain.

Wang Jingwei had bargained well with the Japanese. Soon a treaty of alliance between Japan and the new government was drawn up, providing that Japanese troops would be withdrawn from central and south China within two years after Chiang Kaishek's "rebellion" had been suppressed. Wang had to agree, under pressure from the Guandong Army, to allow Japanese troops to remain in north China for the purpose of suppressing the Communists. Wang claimed control over north China, however, and over all China except Manchukuo and the independent administration the Japanese had established in Inner Mongolia.

There was a certain dichotomy in all this. With the advent of the Wang Jingwei government, Wang Kemin, an admirer of Wang Jingwei's, had stepped down as chairman of the executive of the provisional government in Beijing. The provisional government disappeared and was replaced by the North China Political Council, with Wang Itang in charge. This was a new manifestation of Japanese control, made necessary by the establishment of the Wang Jingwei government.

The relationship of the Wang Jingwei government to the people of eastern China has been largely misunderstood by westerners, because of the propaganda of the Chiang Kaishek government, on the one hand, and the propaganda of the Communists, on the other. Wang was highly regarded in east China. His government, which was seen as a buffer between the people and their Japanese conquerors, was actually quite popular.

Still, dichotomy once again appeared. The foreign press and broadcasts let the people know that Chiang Kaishek was out there in the west, resisting the Japanese. Therefore, Chiang became a greater hero in east China than he was in west China, where the people had to live under the repressions of his government. In the big cities of Free China, Chiang's Guomindang was in effective control, but in the countryside the *laobaixing* ("common people") were exposed to the Guomindang largely through its taxation and brutal recruitment of troops and labor forces. There was no great love lost in the west for Chiang and the Guomindang.

But the one thing that all Chinese could agree on was the need to conquer China for themselves and put an end to Japanese domination of their land. In fact, the Japanese were simply the latest manifestation of foreign imperialism, although of course the most vigorous one of all. Had it been Britain or the United States that occupied east China, the Chinese reaction would have been the same. For Britain and the United States represented imperialism to the Chinese people just as much as did Japan. The whole

American history in China, in spite of such fine-sounding themes as "open-door policy," had been imperialist in nature. Imperialism was the way of the western powers in the nineteenth and early twentieth centuries; the U.S. brand was less forceful than most, but it was still imperialism: the manipulation of one people for the benefit of another.

In fact, Chiang Kaishek was on record as opposing imperialism as much as did the Chinese Communists. If he had been able to control his Guomindang party, wipe out venality and greed, and secure the adherence of the *laobaixing*, ultimately he would have thrown the imperialists out of China himself, and that would have included the United States.

Americans have a lot of myths in their minds about China. They have always had a highly romantic view of that country, tempered in the 1940s by a ridiculous paranoia about the Soviet Union and communism, caused by a lack of confidence in their own political system.

It all seemed much simpler in the late 1930s, when the Japanese set out to conquer China for themselves. The other foreign powers could be as pious as they pleased, but it is notable that none of them actually moved to stop Japanese aggression on the two occasions when they could have succeeded: the days following the Shenyang incident and the days following the incident at the Marco Polo Bridge. Thereafter the Japanese knew that the other foreigners had given them the green light to go ahead with their colonization of China.

22
Mao's Way

The secret of Mao's success at Yanan was his flexibility in combining short term and long term goals. In the short term he espoused in 1940 the New Democracy as a united-front doctrine that would embrace all the Chinese people who would subscribe to CCP [Chinese Communist party] leadership. For the long term he steadily developed the party organization, including its control over intellectuals. Meantime the real sinews of power grew up in the CCP mobilization of the peasantry in North China.

—John K. Fairbank, China scholar

During the Long March of 8000 miles across China to Yanan, Mao Zedong had proposed the united front to stop the civil war and concentrate all Chinese effort on expulsion of the Japanese from China. By 1937 the Communists were already fighting the Japanese in the north, and they continued to do so. After Chiang was pushed by his associates into accepting the truce and the united front, the question remained: How would this united front work? Down from Yanan to Xi'an and Nanjing came Zhou Enlai, the chief Communist negotiator, already a diplomat, to work out the issues.

Mao, who knew Chiang Kaishek very well, did not trust him a bit, and neither did Zhou Enlai. There is probably no schism quite so deep as that between parted revolutionaries; like a divorced couple, they are too much aware of one another's faults.

But in 1937 there were also many tensions and many frictions within the Communist party. Wang Ming, the author of the disastrous military policy of Jiangxi days, returned to China from Moscow in 1937 full of ideas. He was the one who forced the issue and made the Communists offer to serve under Chiang Kaishek in a united front. That was the Kremlin line, as laid down to the Comintern. Mao did not like it, but he was outmaneuvered in the Central Committee. The offer was made, and it was accepted by a Chiang Kaishek who was as skeptical of its outcome as was Mao.

*   *   *

The Communists placed themselves under Nationalist command, at least nominally, and the Red Army's name was changed to "Eighth Route Army of the National Revolutionary Army."

In the Eighth Route Army, Zhu De was appointed commander in chief. Peng Dehuai was deputy commander in chief, and Ye Jianying was chief of staff. Zuo Quan was deputy chief of staff. Ren Bishi was director of the political department, and Deng Xiaoping was deputy director. The Eighth Route Army consisted of the 115th, 120th, and 129th divisions.

At that time the Red Army numbered 32,000 men. Four thousand of them were sent to the Shaanxi-Gansu-Ningxia border to defend the Communist area.

The 115th Division, under Lin Biao, was the old First Front Army, with 14,000 men. The 120th Division was the old Second Front Army, with 6000 men. He Long was commander. The 129th Division was the old Fourth Front Army, with Liu Bocheng in command of the 8000 troops.

Wang Ming insisted that the united front was real, because the Comintern wanted Chiang Kaishek won over to follow an anti-Japanese, anti-German policy. Wang succeeded in both cases: Chiang did agree to fight the Japanese, and he did break with the German military advisers who had been so helpful to him in rebuilding the Nationalist armies after the quarrel with the Communists removed the Red forces from Guomindang control.

In the fall of 1937 several victories were won by the Eighth Route Army over the Japanese Itagaki Division at Pingxingguan Pass and at Yangmingbao airfield, where the Communists burned some twenty-four Japanese planes. But the Japanese troops occupied Taiyuan.

Still, the two victories helped the Communist prestige in the north. More and more people joined the Eighth Route Army, and Zhu De and Peng Dehuai never lost sight of the necessity of retaining strong ties with the peasants and recruiting soldiers from among them.

In November, after the Japanese occupation of Taiyuan, the Eighth Route Army headquarters moved from the Wutai Mountains to southern Shaanxi Province. Then, one day in December, General Peng was summoned back to Yanan to represent the Eighth Route Army at a meeting of the Political Bureau of the Central Committee.

At the meeting Wang Ming and Kang Sheng seemed to be in charge.

Wang Ming delivered the first speech; then Mao spoke. Both leaders called for resistance to Japanese aggression, but there the divergence began.

Wang Ming, speaking with the authority of a representative of the Comintern, repeated his claim that resistance against Japan was the only important matter. The Guomindang and the Communist party were equals, he said, and the Communists must subordinate themselves to Chiang Kaishek at every step. Cooperation with the Guomindang had to be retained at all costs. Wang's oratory rose in tenor and volume as he praised Chiang Kaishek's leadership.

Mao and others who had lived like hunted rats during those years when Chiang was mounting his five Communist extermination campaigns listened in silence. For years the Communists had fought against the C. C. Clique and the Fu Xing society, as "Fascist organizations within the Guomindang," used by Chiang to maintain the oligarchic rule of the big landlords and the big bourgeoisie. The C. C. Clique was so called because its leaders were Chen Guofu and Chen Lifu, the notorious Chen brothers, intimates of Chiang Kaishek and two of the richest men in China. The leaders of the Fu Xing society were He Zhonghan, Kang Ze, and Dai Li, the chief of Chiang's secret police and terrorist force.

Now, Wang Ming said with a straight face that these two organizations were perfectly democratic and not Fascist, because they resisted the Japanese. The Japanese, he said, were the Fascists. It was as it had been in Spain, where the party had to resist the Nazis and the Italian Fascists. They fought in the international brigades alongside Americans and Frenchmen and Britons, few of whom were Communists. So it must be in China. The Communists had to accommodate anyone who fought the Japanese.

Mao Zedong found it impossible to accept this ridiculous Kremlin line. Finally he spoke up.

He said that Wang Ming's arguments were specious and self-defeating. When Wang Ming cited Spain, he was talking about failure. In China failure meant failure to keep close to the mass of people. The Communist party could win only if it maintained its leadership of the common people. Also, in terms of the army, the Communist party had to maintain its absolute leadership and control of the Eighth Route Army at all times. This also applied to the new Fourth Army. Chiang was already trying to change the nature of the Communist armies and bring them under his control. That way lay party suicide, said Chairman Mao. It must be resisted at all costs. If Chiang had his way, it would be impossible to maintain the bases and democratic government in the war zones of the Japanese rear.

Peng Dehuai recognized the importance of the arguments he was hearing, but he was not sure of his course. So when he spoke, he did not support either faction, but related the experiences of the Eighth Route Army in the field. He did say, however, that it was vital that the Communist party maintain absolute leadership of the army. Already there were dangers. The soldiers had been forced to give up their red-star caps and wear Guomindang caps. Chiang was changing the nature of the Eighth Route Army in his attempt to assimilate it.

The meeting had begun early in the evening, and it lasted until dawn. Wang Ming insisted that every action of the Chinese Communist military be approved first by Chiang Kaishek as supreme commander. "Everything must go through the united front" was his slogan.

Peng Dehuai returned to the Eighth Route Army a confused man. He had asked Luo Fu, the general secretary of the party and chairman of the meeting, for instructions on reporting to his comrades in the army. Luo had told him not to worry; he said he would supply an outline of the salient points of the meeting. But after Peng got the outline, he saw that the problems had not been solved.

So, when Peng returned to the army, he added some warnings to his report:

1. The army must ensure and strengthen its Communist party leadership.
2. The leaders must ensure the predominance of soldiers from worker and peasant families.
3. The army must continue political effort and political study.

The outline itself, however, followed the Wang Ming line, and Peng had to communicate it. He hedged by saying that the subordination to the Guomindang must "be carried out in accordance with actual work." Through the use of such gobbledygook the middle-level Communist party leaders tried to protect themselves against the day when the party line would change.

Not long afterward the army restored the system of political commissars and political departments. By the spring of 1938 this was done, and the Eighth Route Army began to expand. Chiang Kaishek had no provisions for its expansion and moved to try to stop it, but the leadership of the army added training brigades, organizational brigades, provisional brigades, and replenishment brigades as a way of getting around the Guomindang restrictions. Each section of the new army—the Wutai mountain area, the 115th Division, the 120th Division, and the 129th Division—could add as many brigades as it wished, and then report to Yanan and to the Eighth Route Army headquarters. Chiang Kaishek need not know a thing about it.

Nor would the new army depend on the Guomindang for its pay and allowances. To do so would be suicide. Chiang could starve the army to death unless the army set up a base area and collected taxes. If there was no base area, then the army would depend on donations and confiscation of the property of traitors.

By October 1938 many cracks had opened in the column of unification. At a meeting of the Central Committee, Mao gathered his forces and insisted that the united front had not led to any real broadening of the Nationalist government to include democratic elements. Chiang, he charged, was maintaining his personal dictatorship over the Guomindang and the government.

Mao attacked Wang Ming's policy. If it was continued, he said, the Communist party would be no better off than it was in 1927 when Chiang turned on the Reds and began killing them. To leave the Red Army under the control of Chiang Kaishek was to welcome that army's destruction.

During the months just past, he said, some officers had run away in disgust at the Wang Ming line. Some had turned traitor. And the Guomindang had tried to impose restrictions on the growth of the Eighth Route Army and the Communist party. In spite of this, the Eighth Route Army had grown to 250,000, all because it had refused to go through the Guomindang control processes.

That session of the Central Committee repudiated the Wang Ming line. "Our policy," said Mao Zedong, "is one of independence and initiative within the united front, a policy of unity and independence." This became the new party line.

Once the struggle within the party was resolved, Mao was able to follow his own policy and renew efforts to gain the adherence of the people. The Communists were very careful not to follow their natural bent: They knew that if they began seizing landlords and taking their lands, they would be subject to criticism not only from the Guomindang for destroying the united front but also from outside China. So they contented themselves at that time with forcing the landlords to lower rents, leaving the ownership of the land undisturbed. They waited.

Some foreigners, and particularly Americans, fooled themselves into believing that the Chinese Communists were not Communists at all, but "simple agrarian reformers" who wanted the landlords to behave themselves. It was easy to believe this line, and at the moment the Communists did nothing to discourage it. As a result, outsiders failed to understand the course of the Chinese revolution.

Mao's hunch about the intentions of Chiang Kaishek toward the Communist armies was borne out in the spring of 1941 at the southern Anhui incident, already described, when Xiang Ying, leader of the rear echelon of the New Fourth Army, was ambushed by Guomindang troops who decimated the Communist force and killed Xiang.

The incident resulted in a real breach.

Never again would the Communists trust the Nationalist military command for a single inch. From that point on the Communists accepted the inevitability of future civil war, and they acted accordingly. Unlike Chiang's forces, however, the Communists did continue to fight the Japanese.

And the Communist army commanders were very shrewd. They confined their distrust of the Guomindang troops to the high officers. They were kind and friendly to lower-ranking officers and soldiers, trying to win them over to the Communist side. In Yanan, Mao laid down a policy of cooperation with peasants and workers and with the middle bourgeoisie and "enlightened gentry." It encouraged a new organization of liberal intellectuals that called itself the "Democratic League." This organization, which existed in many parts of China, was celebrated by Americans and other foreigners as the hope of China's future. The trouble with the league, however, at that time and later, was that it had no army.

As time went on, the Mao policies began to pay off in the north. The Red armies—Eighth Route and New Fourth—rose to 500,000 men by the summer of 1940. Mao had pioneered in the development of a people's militia, organized along village and county lines, to police its own areas and fight the Japanese when possible. This force had grown to 200,000 men and women. The "liberated areas" of north China had grown until they included 100 million people, and it was in these areas that the struggle against the Japanese continued unabated, even as it came to nothing in the areas controlled by Chiang Kaishek.

The Communists took full advantage of the peculiar nature of Japanese control. The Japanese controlled the cities and big towns but not the countryside. So all through the Japanese rear areas Communist infiltrators moved. They set up schools. They collected taxes and reapportioned the money among the needy. They befriended the people, whether Communist or not. By the middle of the anti-Japanese war they had gained a reputation for probity that was in direct contradistinction to the known corruption of the Guomindang.

In 1940 and 1941 an exasperated Japanese Expeditionary Army command embarked on a new policy toward the Chinese of the "liberated areas." The Japanese were unable to persuade the people to accept Japan. They were unable to control the Red armies; the militias fought brief actions and then vanished in the night. The Japanese were unable to control their lines of communication in the field.

So the Japanese embarked on a scorched-earth policy. Wherever they went, they not only looted, raped, and murdered but also burned. The Communists estimated that in two years the Japanese killed 30 million civilians by this method.

At the same time, Chiang Kaishek, sensing the growth of the Communist strength, stopped all subsidies to the armed forces and the government of the Red area and began an economic blockade of that area.

So the Red Army and the Communist party tightened their belts.

By 1941 the Communist Party of China had grown to number 800,000 men and women. It had grown too fast, Mao decided, and in 1941 he launched "the rectification movement," which was aimed at teaching the new party members the essentials of the party's theory and method of operation. It had another purpose, not generally discussed: the rooting out of traitors and self-serving members of the party who had joined in the looser moments.

"Rectification" began in May 1941 with a speech by Mao, "Reform Our Study," and the opening of a central party school in Yanan. The students were to study some twenty documents, including speeches by Mao and party theorist Liu Shaoqi and writings by Lenin, Stalin, and the leader of the Comintern, Dimitrov, a Bulgarian.

Party leaders began to outdo each other in self-criticism. Zhou Enlai, who had been spending most of his time in Chongqing as liaison man with the Nationalists, returned to Yanan and criticized his own previous "leftist" errors. He was referring to the period during which he was closely associated with the twenty-eight Bolsheviks who gained control of the Communist party after the collapse of the Wuhan government. This undoubtedly saved Zhou's career, because all the old Communists were aware of his previous allegiances. By self-criticism, Zhou removed the grounds for criticism of his actions by others.

And that was important because party leaders did begin to criticize one another, which was a dangerous situation. As it turned out, some enmities were created that lasted for years.

In 1943, through "rectification," which included the seeking out of secret Guomindang agents and the mistreatment of many loyal party people, Mao Zedong purged the Communist party of most of the elements that disagreed with his views. Thereafter, he was constantly alive to problems of "deviationism" and took steps to see that it did not go far. A political meeting in March established a central secretariat for daily work. The membership watched for deviations.

A commission for propaganda was established to keep firing away on the party line. A committee for organization was established to keep the party free of error. "This collective leadership," said historian Su Kaiming, who returned to China in 1953 after years in America, "ensured free discussions of burning problems and helped keep revolutionary actions along the correct line."

Necessity is the mother of invention, and it served the Communists well. With the shortages, everyone—including Mao Zedong—planted his or her own vegetables and learned such peasant skills as spinning and weaving. Government organizations began to grow their own food. So did schools. All army units were ordered to engage in agriculture. All this brought the Red Army and the Red organization closer to the people than the Guomindang had been since the days of national revolution. According to historian Su:

> An outstanding example was the 359th Brigade under General Wang Zhen, which undertook the reclamation of Nanniwan, a barren, hilly area southeast of Yanan. *

---

*For anyone who has seen northern Shaanxi Province and Yanan that is saying a great deal. The whole area is barren, hilly countryside—one of the most formidable environments in all China.

When they first arrived there were no caves or houses to live in nor tools to work with. The Border Region was so poor that soldiers could not bring enough food with them. From the very beginning they had to provide almost everything they needed with their own hands. They cut wood for primitive shelters and dug caves in the hillsides. They each reclaimed a bit of land to grow food crops. By 1943 they had reclaimed over 10,000 hectares of farmland, which yielded more grain than they needed. Meanwhile the soldiers learned how to make practically everything, such as clothes, blankets, shoes, tables and chairs, paper and charcoal. They became completely self-supporting, receiving no subsidy from the government. The "spirit of Nanniwan" inspired many other army units at the time and has become a virtue treasured by the Chinese people.

In the Communist areas the Red government followed a policy almost diametrically opposed to that of the Guomindang in west China. Cooperatives were encouraged. Pay was based on labor and investment, a system which benefited the working poor as well as the prosperous. By 1943, 80 percent of the peasants in the Communist areas belonged to cooperatives.

The Communists created industries to make iron and to refine oil. They built machine shops, arsenals, pottery kilns, and factories to make cloth, soap, and other necessities. The government encouraged home weaving.

By the end of World War II, the Yanan region of Shaanxi Province, unbelievably poor ten years earlier, had become relatively prosperous. Everywhere that the Communists took control, the peasants were better off than they had been before. And by war's end, this word had begun to seep through all China.

23
Postwar Crisis

How should we hold high the banner of Mao Zedong Thought? This is a really big question. Many people, both inside and outside the Party, and both at home and abroad, want the banner to be held high. What does that mean? How are we to do so? As you all know, there is a doctrine known as "the two whatevers." Hasn't it become famous?

According to this doctrine whatever documents Comrade Mao Zedong read and endorsed and whatever he did and said must always determine our actions, without the slightest deviation. Can this be called holding high the banner of Mao Zedong Thought? Certainly not. If this goes on it will debase Mao Zedong Thought. The fundamental point of Mao Zedong Thought is seeking truth from facts, and integrating the universal truth of Marxism-Leninism with the concrete practice of the Chinese revolution. Comrade Mao Zedong wrote a four-word motto for the Central Party School in Yanan: "Seek truth from facts."

These four words are the quintessence of Mao Zedong Thought. In the final analysis, Comrade Mao's greatness and his success in guiding the Chinese revolution to victory rest on just this approach. Marx and Lenin never mentioned the encirclement of the cities from the countryside—a strategic principle that had not been formulated anywhere in the world in their lifetime. Nevertheless, Comrade Mao Zedong pointed it out as the specific road for the revolution in China's concrete conditions. At a time when the country was split up into separate warlord domains, he led the people in the fight to establish revolutionary bases in areas where the enemy's control was weak, to encircle the cities from the countryside and ultimately to seize political power. Just as the Bolshevik party led by Lenin made its revolution at a weak link in the chain of the imperialist world, we made our revolution in areas where the enemy was weak. In principle the two courses were the same. But instead of trying to take the cities first, we began with the rural areas, then gradually encircled the cities. If we had not applied the fundamental principle of seeking truth from facts, how could we have raised and solved this problem of strategy? How could the Chinese revolution have been victorious?

—Deng Xiaoping

As seen from China, the Pacific war ended with a big bang at Hiroshima. In Chongqing no one was really quite ready for it. For three years the Nationalists had been waging desultory warfare against the Japanese. In the last days of the war some captured territory in Guangxi Province was recovered by the Nationalists. But by and large the Nationalists moved back into territory once the war had ended, by simply marching in and taking over from the Japanese. They were not prepared politically or economically to manage these areas.

The Communists, on the other hand, had prepared very well. In August 1940 the Communist armies had begun a widespread attack on the Japanese. Peng Dehuai originated the Hundred Regiments Offensive, in which the Communist forces cut Japanese communications to shreds. The Japanese had retaliated in force, cutting up the Red Army's base area and burning much of the countryside. There were two results: first, the depletion of Japanese strength by enormous expansion of their occupying army force, and second, the withdrawal of the Communists to interior positions. For the next four years most of Mao's time was spent reflecting on events and planning for the future. At Yanan he had plenty of leisure to do so.

In March 1945 it was estimated that of 914 counties theoretically held by the Japanese in eastern China, 678 were actually controlled by the Communists. The Communists divided their China into nineteen separate liberated areas, and the population of these areas was 100 million people. The Eighth Route Army numbered 330,000 men and women; the New Fourth Army numbered 150,000. In south China the Communist guerillas behind the Japanese lines numbered around 30,000.

Government in the liberated areas was developed along Mao Zedong's guidelines. What the Communists called the "Three Three Three system" was based on Mao's theory that the government must always rest in the hands of the Communist party. But to achieve democracy that gave the peasants a feeling of participation, the government was built on the pyramidal pattern, the base being the publicly elected village councils. The councils then chose representatives to the county level, and so forth. The difference under the Three Three Three system was that one third of the people elected at every level *had to be* members of the Communist party. This third became the leaders and directors. Another third were Communist supporters, but not party members for one reason or another. The final third were liberals and nonaligned persons. Thus the form of democracy was retained, while party control was ensured by the discipline of the Communist one-third. The Communist representatives were a unit, thinking and acting as one person, and they could always find enough people to vote with them in the other two-thirds to maintain control.

In the liberated areas and the border areas of China, land reform had been treated very carefully by the Communists during the war years. Three factors had to first be established: military control by the Red Army, economic improvement of the area, and recruitment of villagers to carry out the reforms.

In the old days, before the second coalition, the Communists had no qualms about seizing landlords, executing them, and redistributing their land. But with the coalition had come a change. To placate the bourgeoisie of Nationalist China, the dispossessing of landlords had ceased. Now, in the liberated areas, it began again as the Japanese surrendered. But it came in a new guise. The landlords were suddenly discovered to have been "collaborationists" and for that reason were not entitled to any consideration. It was certainly true that many of the landlords had collaborated with the Japanese, but it was also true that many had not. The distinction was not very clearly made in the Communist areas, and sometimes was not made at all.

In the spring of 1945 the Chinese Communists held their Seventh National Congress, which adopted a new constitution. Mao Zedong got more power as chairman of the Central Committee and Political Bureau.

As the Pacific war drew to a close, Chiang Kaishek and Zhou Enlai—with American encouragement—were trying to negotiate the future of China. Mao Zedong agreed to go down to Chongqing for a meeting. The American idea was to set up a triangular system, with a committee that consisted of one Nationalist, one Communist, and one American, deciding on supply and logistics for all the armies in China. The plan was given reluctant approval by Chiang. The Communists were noncommittal. Mao noted that all would be well if the Guomindang would end its one-party rule and create a real Nationalist government, including the Communists, the Democratic League, and other elements.

So, when the Japanese suddenly surrendered, only the Communists were ready for it; as noted, they had been planning for this event for a long time. A complicating factor was the eleventh-hour entry of the Soviet Union into the war. The Russians, who had stayed out all during the hard days, sud-

denly rushed in and conquered Manchuria in a few days, defeating the
remnants of the Japanese Guandong Army. (Most of that army had been
shipped to Taiwan for defense of the homeland.)

The Russians immediately began dismantling the industries of Manchuria and shipping them home to replace the dreadful damage wrought
in the Soviet Union by Hitler. At the moment, there was no major complaint from either Communists or Nationalists, for the fate of Manchuria
was very much in the balance.

The Communists took over the countryside. Chiang Kaishek, with
American naval assistance, took over the cities. The Nationalist government of China was the "legitimate" government, recognized by the Big
Three powers and sanctified by the United Nations. The Communists complained from the beginning, but Chiang had called on the Americans to
ship his troops around China to take over from the Japanese.

Chiang played a canny game. He ordered Gen. Lu Han, of the dissident Yunnan warlord regime, to go to Indochina and occupy that country
north of the 16th parallel. (The British occupied south of the parallel.) This
had been decided at the Yalta Conference, but Chiang's employment of
Lu Han was Machiavellian. He lured Lu Han and his Yunnan troops out
of Kunming with the great prospects of loot in Hanoi. Once the Yunnan
troops were out, they were replaced by other troops loyal to Chiang. Lu
Han's half-brother, the warlord who governed Yunnan, awakened to find
himself Chiang's captive. Thus was another area of Nationalist China pacified.

Immediately after Japan's announcement of surrender at Tokyo, mis-
understandings and complications began. Chiang sent a message to Zhu
De, commander in chief of the Red Army, telling him not to accept any
surrenders from the Japanese and not to move any troops. But the Communists held that this was a violation of the Potsdam agreement and that
their armies had as much right to accept Japanese surrenders as anyone.

After Japan's surrender, American Ambassador Patrick J. Hurley accompanied Mao Zedong to Chongqing for forty days of meetings with Chiang
Kaishek. Out of their meetings came a set of principles which were supposed to govern the transition of China. The Guomindang and the Chinese
Communist party would cooperate in establishing a representative assembly. They would put their armies into a common pot. They would guarantee civil liberties all over China.

Nice words, but neither meaningful nor accurate representations of the emotions and policies involved. Since the earliest days of the revolution, the Guomindang and the Chinese Communist party had each expected to emerge victorious from the ultimate revolution in China. These expectations continued. The difference in 1945, however, was that the Chinese Communist party had retained its revolutionary spirit, but the Guomindang had not. The Guomindang had by that time assumed the mantle of the old republic, whose economic policies catered to the western imperialist powers. Americans do not like to think of their country as imperialist; yet in relationship to China it most definitely was imperialist, and the overtones of that policy remained in 1945.

———

The Chinese Communists moved across north China to take the Japanese surrenders and to reap the harvest of weapons and supplies that the Imperial Japanese Army held. The Nationalists—as the official government of China, recognized by the powers—ordered the Japanese to fight the Communists and hold the territory to surrender to the Nationalists. In Manchuria both sides and the Russians competed for territorial control—the Russians only temporarily so that they could strip the factories of Shenyang and the other cities of the Japanese industrial complex of Manchuria. Soon the Communists controlled northern Manchuria, with Li Lisan emerging once more from Moscow to take charge as political officer. The Nationalists moved into southern Manchuria. The stage was set for a major confrontation there.

The Americans also took a hand. They were constrained—or thought they were—by their responsibilities to Chiang Kaishek as one of the Big Four. The basic error of that policy, pointed out earlier by Winston Churchill, came home to roost in China in 1945. The Nationalist government of China never was a "power," and treating it as one created endless complications for the Big Three.

The Americans suffered most from the charade, because it affected basic American policy and removed all flexibility. The American navy, having finished fighting the Japanese, now became a sort of supertransport system for the Chinese. The Nationalists insisted on having armies moved. For example, Lu Han's Indochina Expeditionary Force was moved the next year up to Taiwan to occupy that island and to keep General Lu away from Yunnan. Other Nationalist forces were moved to Weihaiwei, as well as to other points in north and central China where they came smack up against

the Communists. Thus the Americans seemed to be aiding the Nationalists in the struggle for control. Their reputation of one-sidedness was not
entirely earned at that time, however, for a large number of Communist
guerillas from south China were transported to north China by the American
navy.

The Americans saw China as a world political battlefield. As American-
Soviet relations worsened (beginning a few days after the American occupation of South Korea) the American military political experts foresaw a
struggle in China involving American and Soviet interests.

The Russians had occupied Port Arthur and did not give any indications of moving out soon. Therefore, 53,000 U.S. marines were sent into
north China to hold Beijing and defend Tianjin. What business did they
have there? None whatsoever, except the old imperialist concept of China
as a place of special foreign interests.

At Yalta, the Soviets and Americans had agreed that Nationalist China
was the legitimate government of China. This agreement became something of a yoke for the Russians when the Chinese Communists moved so
quickly at the end of the war.

So in 1945 and 1946 the China situation was very mixed up as far as
the big powers were concerned. In the end, the Chinese Communists lost
out to a large extent. They did not get the industrial empire that the Japanese
had built up; except for such immovable objects as the Anshan coal mines,
everything transportable was taken off by the Russians over the Trans-
Siberian railroad. The Communists did get a lot of Japanese arms and munitions and military supplies, but so, for that matter, did the Chinese
Nationalists. Because of the prior commitments of the big powers, there
was no simple capitulation of the Japanese to a Chinese government.

As these moves were being taken in the field, in Chongqing the Nationalists and the Communists continued to talk, with an eye to promoting the
coalition government that the Americans and others hoped to see. But neither side had its heart in such negotiations.

On October 10, 1945, the anniversary of the Double Ten holiday, an
agreement was signed. It guaranteed the convening of the People's Consultative Conference; the legality of all parties, including, of course, the
Communist party; and the disbanding of Dai Li's secret police.

The Nationalist armed forces were about twice the size of the Communist Red Army. The agreement called for the reduction of the Com-

munist forces from forty divisions to twenty. But two major problems were not dealt with: the fate of the liberated territories under Communist control and the fate of the Red Army.

So October 10, 1945, was the banner day of the mediationist in China. The Guomindang, the Communists, and the Democratic League (the "third force")—went the theory—ought to get together and work out a joint government and everybody ought to live happily ever after. The problem of the real third China force—Wang Jingwei's pro-Japanese government—had been resolved when Wang died from natural causes in 1944. Had he lived, affairs might have taken a different turn, since Wang had an army.

After the surrender of the Japanese at Nanjing that autumn, there was nothing left of Japanese influence in China. In a sense it was as if they had never been there. Before October ended, the Nationalists and the Communists were at each other's throats in north and central China, as they had been in 1936, and the Americans were being blamed by the Chinese Communists for intervening on the side of Chiang Kaishek.

The Americans then sent one of their most talented and persuasive leaders to China to try to work out an agreement between Nationalists and Communists. He was Gen. George C. Marshall, former chief of the American army and a man whose probity was unquestionable. Even the Communists were impressed by this gesture, although they had many reservations about American policy.

Zhou Enlai came down from Yanan to Nanjing and Shanghai to engage in the negotiations. On January 10, 1946, General Marshall persuaded the Nationalists and Communists to sign a cease-fire. That day the all-party People's Consultative Conference met. In three weeks the conference decided that a National Assembly would meet in May to draft a new constitution and that in the interim a state council, with half the members representative of the Guomindang, would administer the government.

Once more the future appeared bright. It was even being said that the incidents of the autumn of 1945 were all mistakes and that the difficulties between the Guomindang and the Communists could be worked out.

But already, at the beginning of 1946, disillusionment with the Guomindang was beginning to spread eastward in China. In the first euphoric weeks the people of the parts of China occupied by Japan had welcomed Chiang as a liberator. After a few weeks of Guomindang government they were beginning to see the corruption and the confusion that existed in the Guomindang. The Communists played very cleverly on the people's concerns. They showed themselves as peace-loving people whose aim was to build a democratic society in China.

And as they did so, the Big Four families moved in style to the lower Yangtze valley once more. The Soongs and Kungs and Chens went into big mansions. The bankers took over control of the Japanese banks and industries. The ill-paid and underfed troops of Chiang's armies, cheated by their generals, took to raping the countryside.

Soon the inflation that had troubled the Guomindang all during the war spread to the eastern provinces, bringing food shortages as well as official corruption. The United Nations Relief and Rehabilitation Administration came into China with an aid program. But somehow almost all the assistance stayed in the Yangtze valley and along the coast; it did not get into the Communist-held areas.

Further, in the spring of 1946 the United States sent a military advisory group to China to help Chiang Kaishek. Again, the assistance was provided because Chiang's government was the "official" government of China. But, in reality, what need was there to take such an action if not to help Chiang against the Communists? The Nationalists had no other enemy. The fact was that the American attitude toward China was colored mostly by the American attitude toward the Soviet Union. U.S.-Soviet relations, which had apparently been friendly during World War II, immediately reverted to tension at the end of the war. All the American paranoia about international communism and its threat to the United States returned, twice as strong as before. The Chinese Communists had always been controversial in America. Some of their American friends still tried to characterize them as "nothing but agrarian reformers," even after the terror began in the liberated areas in 1946. That was far from the truth, and any of the Communist leaders would say so. The Chinese Communist party was determined to build a socialist society in China, though it did not trumpet this fact in 1945 and 1946 while various negotiations were going on.

In the fall of 1945 the American Export-Import Bank loaned $83 million to the Guomindang. Too much of it went into the hands of the corrupt governors. In the spring of 1946 the Guomindang got another $500 million from the bank, and later that spring the U.S. government gave Chiang an additional $52 million in credits. The Communists, who enjoyed none of this, watched with growing envy and distrust. In August, when the Americans sold the Nationalists an enormous stock of war-surplus material, the Communists had no further illusions. All that equipment could be and, they were sure, would be used to fight a civil war. In September Zhou Enlai complained to the Americans that they had moved nearly 2 million Guomindang soldiers into the Communists' liberated areas.

On the face of it, all this assistance ought to have ensured for the Guomindang government easy mastery of the political and military situations. But the corruption of the Guomindang existed at every level. Generals were still stealing their soldiers' pay, and they were still selling off the equipment they received.

By midsummer, 1946, the stage was set for an explosion. Although the Guomindang seemed to have all the cards in its hand, the one thing it lacked was public support. In the summer of 1946 I visited the Ming tombs outside Beijing with James Grant, the son of a well-known American medical missionary, who spoke fluent Chinese. At the tombs we were met by villagers, who soon enough introduced a Communist political officer of the Red Army, whose task there was the organization of a militia force. He was having no trouble. That area, not 50 miles from Beijing, was "liberated territory." The landlords had been displaced, rents had come down, interest was low, and the peasants were happy. They felt that they now lived under a democratic government, and they were willing to fight to support it. On that day the young Communist lieutenant smiled and waved and was very pleasant, but he left us with a knotty question: Why did the United States insist on intervening in the internal affairs of China? No one present could answer.

A few weeks later I spent some time with Li Lisan in Harbin; he asked the same question rhetorically, since I was a newspaper correspondent. Of course, there was really no question in his mind. Duly, I transmitted his words to America. But from America came no answer except continued support of the Chiang government.

The one thing I wanted to do in the liberated area of the northeast was see Zhu De's great Red Army there, and this was the one thing I was not allowed to do. By August 1946 the Communist party leadership had developed a great distrust of things American.

During that summer of 1946 I also visited several villages around Harbin in Heilongjiang Province, once the center of Zhang Xueliang's control. The Chinese Communists had gone in there on the heels of the Japanese surrender and had organized the villages. Already, the peasants reported, their way of life had become much easier. They had suffered for years under warlord taxation and then strict and onerous Japanese control, but all that had been supplanted by what to them was the most democratic way. To be sure, the Three Three Three system was in place, but it seemed fair enough to them. They said they were being taught the essentials of democratic society by the Communist leadership.

And so the time bomb smoked that summer of 1946, smoked and sizzled, until it finally exploded.

24

The Civil War

Q. Sir, do you consider that the U.S. effort to mediate in the Chinese civil war has failed? If the policy of the United States continues as at present, what will it lead to?

A. I doubt very much that the policy of the U.S. government is one of "mediation." Judging by the large amount of aid the United States is giving Chiang Kaishek, to enable him to wage a civil war on an unprecedented scale, the policy of the U.S. government is to use the so-called mediation as a smokescreen for strengthening Chiang Kaishek in every way and suppressing the democratic forces in China through Chiang Kaishek's policy of slaughter so as to reduce China virtually to a U.S. colony. The continuation of this policy will certainly arouse the firm resistance of all patriotic people throughout China.

Q. How long will the Chinese civil war go on? What will be its outcome?

A. If the U.S. government abandons its present policy of aiding Chiang Kaishek, withdraws its forces now stationed in China and carries out the agreement reached at the Moscow Conference of the Foreign Ministers of the Soviet Union, the United States and Britain, the Chinese civil war is sure to end at an early date. Otherwise it may turn into a long war. This would of course bring suffering to the Chinese people but on the other hand, the Chinese people would certainly unite, fight for survival and decide their own fate. Whatever the difficulties and hardships, the Chinese people will certainly fulfill their task of achieving independence, peace and democracy. No forces of suppression, domestic or foreign, can prevent the fulfillment of this task.

—A. T. Steele, China correspondent for the New York *Herald Tribune*, interviewing Mao Zedong, September 29, 1946

In the summer of 1946 the government of the United States was so arrogant that it believed it could exert decisive pressure on the course of events in China. It heeded not the warnings of many of its most competent public servants in the Department of State that American policy would in the end turn out to be irrelevant to the outcome of the Chinese revolution.

Between the Japanese surrender in August 1945 and August 1946 the Chinese people had a good look at Nationalist policies, and most of them did not like what they saw. The economy of China was shattered by inflation. The Nationalist leaders had rushed into the Chinese coastal cities to seize the assets of Japanese companies and even those of Chinese companies. Nationalists with money speculated in the occupation currency, with its inequitable exchange rate, and made fortunes. The industries of Free China ceased to function as people moved back east, but the industries of the old occupied areas were not brought into production. The army descended on the east like a swarm of locusts, taxing and requisitioning what it wanted. Historian John K. Fairbank has called this movement of the Guomindang back to the China previously occupied by Japan "one of the great carpetbagging operations in history."

Chiang immediately lost the confidence of many of the Chinese people by employing Japanese troops to help put down the Communists. Further, Chiang and his friends completely misread the public mind in the matter of the people who had lived for eight years under Japanese rule. Most Chinese outside the occupied areas were sympathetic to the people who had to live with the Japanese. Indeed, a number of American fliers were rescued from the Japanese by people in occupied China; after the Doolittle raid of April 1942 the Japanese conducted a reign of terror in China that cost about half a million lives because of that help to Americans. But when the Nationalists returned, they treated the people of the occupation area as "collaborationists" and gave them no sympathy. Many students and intellectuals were arrested and brainwashed. So the students turned against the Nationalists.

The Chiang government brought new high taxes to the people, while letting its officials and profiteers with influence remain untaxed. Everywhere it could be seen that the Guomindang officials were corrupt and venal.

Chiang Kaishek had grown completely away from his own people. The Chinese, above all else, wanted peace and national unity. The Nationalists, however, treated this public demand as manifestation of a Communist plot; they suppressed the peace movement and punished the participants. Most Chinese wanted the U.S. forces and influence to get out of China, as the British and French had been forced to do by their own economic circumstances after the war.

*   *   *

The two worst aspects of Guomindang rule were incompetence and venality. The incompetence stemmed down from the top. Chiang Kaishek had some great virtues. He was a splendid military commander, and he recognized his political problem. He could defeat the Communists in battle, and he had. He knew that Mao Zedong's Chinese Communist party was bent on creating a Communist revolution in China, and he knew that any coalition government of the sort the Americans and the "third-force" element in China wanted was bound ultimately to fail because the Communists would never share power for long with anyone. They had shown that in their management of the Wuhan regime. But Chiang knew nothing of government administration, and during the war years he had been too busy to learn. Nor did he have anyone in his administration, since Wang Jingwei had defected and then died, who had such abilities. Chiang's supreme arrogance prevented him from seeing these truths, although Gen. Joseph Stilwell saw them and warned the U.S. government about them.

The second great problem, venality, had emerged fully by the end of 1945. The Big Four families—the Chiangs, the Soongs, the Kungs, and the Chens—controlled virtually every element of Nationalist China life through government monopolies. They were siphoning off millions of dollars for themselves each month. On the military level the generals were taking the money for their armies and using it for themselves, thus weakening the armies. On the civil level the officials found it impossible to live on their salaries because of inflation, so they turned to all sorts of corrupt practices. Bribery was so common that it did not cause a raised eyebrow. If you wanted something from an official in Nationalist China, quite naturally you had to be willing to pay the price.

So in one short year Chiang Kaishek had managed to alienate every element of Chinese society: the workers, because they had no work; the peasants, because they were overtaxed, cheated, and mistreated by officials and the armies; and the middle class, because the Guomindang policies prevented industrial and business profitability. By the summer of 1946, as Chiang planned once again to destroy the Communists, he had already lost the backing of the Chinese people.

Meanwhile, in May 1946, the Chinese invoked their most potent weapon for the civil war. On May 4 the Central Committee of the Communist party issued its "Directive on the Land Question." The title of the paper belittles the content, which was truly revolutionary. Seeing that the civil war was now inevitable, the Communists had decided to revoke their "war of anti-Japanese resistance" land policy, which had insisted on reduction of rents and interest by landlords but had left the landlords in control of their property. In May the Communists changed all that. In the future the landlords would be dispossessed and the land would be distributed to the peasants.

Military activity before the summer of 1946 had been sporadic and more or less desultory. Under the influence of the Marshall mediation mission, an executive headquarters had been established in Beijing. There, representatives of the Nationalists, the Communists, and the U.S. army met to try to resolve local problems as they came up. If an attack or a skirmish was reported, a Communist general, a Nationalist general, and an American colonel would be sent into the field to see what had happened and why. For a time the plan seemed to work, but that was only because Chiang was not yet ready for his all-out offensive against the Communists.

The action began in May 1946. The Russians had completed their occupation duties by then, raping Manchuria of an estimated $2 billion in industrial plants that were transferred to the Soviet Union. That was an enormous loss to Chiang Kaishek, and it would later be felt by the Communists.

Meanwhile, the Nationalists and Communists had both tried to move in to fill the vacuum that would be left by the Russian departure. In November 1945 the U.S. navy was asked to move a Chinese Nationalist army to Yingkou, Manchuria. When the ships approached the port, they found it occupied by the Communists, who refused them permission to land. Rather than risk an open conflict, the Americans withdrew. General Wedemeyer recommended that Chiang give up all thoughts of reoccupying Manchuria at that point, but Chiang knew what the Communists would do. They held the countryside around the cities occupied by the Russians. They would move into the cities too.

When the Russians began to pull out in May, Chiang Kaishek sent troops to Shanhaiguan. They fought their way through the pass into Manchuria. One by one the cities of Manchuria fell to them, including Shenyang and Changchun, the capital of the old Manchukuo.

On June 17 Chiang ordered the Communists to withdraw from a big list of liberated areas, starting at the Yangtze River and including parts of Manchuria. On June 24 an attack was begun against the Communist bases in central China. The Communists retaliated by attacking the Nationalists in Shandong Province. They took in short order ten towns on the Qingdao-Jinan and Tianjin-Pukou railways.

The Nationalist attack was more formidable. This began in July 1946 when the Guomindang army started an invasion of the Jiangsu-Anhui liberated area. Fifteen brigades—about 120,000 men—under Gen. Tang Enbo began the march. The Communist forces consisted of eighteen regiments commanded by Su Yu, Tan Chen, Lin Chen, Liu Bocheng, and Deng Xiaoping. In July and August the Communists and Nationalists fought seven battles in central Jiangsu Province. The Communists claimed to have wiped out six enemy brigades and five other battalions.

In August Liu Bocheng and Deng Xiaoping beat off an attack in the Shaanxi-Hubei-Shandong-Henan liberated area. By that time the civil war was going full blast.

The awkward American presence was revealed soon enough. One day in August the American marines ran a jeep convoy up the road from Tianjin to Beijing, as much at home there as they were in California. The Americans passed through many villages that were held by the Communists. In the past the convoys had gone through easily enough, for the policy laid down by Mao had indicated hands off the Americans. But on this day the local commander decided that he had had enough of American arrogance, and as the American marine convoy came through the village of Anping, it was attacked; one marine was killed in the fighting that followed.

The uproar in the United States was considerable and, as was usual in those days, misguided. The American politicians, the American military, and a considerable section of the public took the position that American interests had been abused and Americans sacrificed. They were, then, easy prey to the propaganda of Chiang Kaishek and his "China lobby" in America, whose purpose was to perpetuate support of the Guomindang against the Communists. Chiang claimed "the Communist problem can be settled by military means within five months." The American military and political leaders believed him, unfortunately for American policy.

*   *   *

By June, according to Communist count, Chiang Kaishek had moved 80 percent of his military force of 2 million men* into position for attacks against the Communist areas. In August the civil war began in earnest.

Chiang's troops moved ahead swiftly, capturing the cities and towns in several of the liberated areas. They took Huaiyin, Heze, Chengde, and Zhangjiakou.

On October 1, 1946, after three months of fighting, Mao Zedong assessed the situation for the Central Committee of the Communist party. The inner-party document he prepared was quite free from propaganda, as Mao followed his own policy of learning from the facts. And what were the facts? Here is Mao's view:

In three months the Communists had destroyed 25 of Chiang's 190 brigades. Further, because of the nature of Chiang's armies and the feeling of the people in the countryside against the Guomindang, half the Guomindang army had to be occupied with garrison duties. This was extremely important. Chiang had already put himself into the position of the Japanese: Operating in an unfriendly environment, they could capture and hold the cities, and sometimes hold the roads (although these could be cut easily enough and transport halted for a time), but they could not control the countryside because of the hatred of the people.

So, Mao judged—and he went into some detail about the generals whose armies had been hard hit—the Communists could defeat the Nationalists in this civil war.

Somewhat tentatively, on July 20, the party's Central Committee had told the party, "We can defeat Chiang Kaishek. The whole party should be confident of this." Obviously, the party had not been very confident, for Mao now felt it necessary to prove the point, and to his own satisfaction he did.

In the next three months, he said, the task of the Red Army would be to destroy another twenty-five enemy brigades. By doing so, the Red Army would recover some of the territory given up to the Nationalists in those first three months.

Particularly impressive was the performance of the Central Plains Liberation Army, led by Li Xiannian and Zheng Weisan. At the end of June the army had been surrounded by 300,000 Guomindang troops, who set out to

---

*That was Mao's estimate at the time. Later, Nationalists and Communists used figures of 4 million, but these must have included some local troops and militia.

annihilate the force. But the Communists fought their way out of the trap and moved into southern Shaanxi and western Hubei provinces. There they were back in the old liberated areas that had once been given up to Chiang's force, and the people were behind the Communists. Where the Nationalists held territory, they faced guerilla fighters.

Because of the greater size of the Nationalist armed forces, Mao laid down a new strategy for the Communists. They would concentrate forces so that they could put three to six times as many troops into any one engagement as the enemy force could muster. They would completely destroy that force and then stop, regroup, and find another element to attack.

> The experience of the past three months has proved that in order to wipe out 10,000 enemy troops we have to pay a price of 2,000 to 3,000 casualties of our own. This is unavoidable. To cope with a long war (and everything everywhere should be considered with such a war in mind), we must expand our army in a planned way, ensure that our main forces are always kept at full strength and train large numbers of military cadres. We must develop production and regulate finances according to plan and firmly put into effect the principles of developing our economy and ensuring supply of unified leadership and decentralized management and of giving consideration to both the army and the people and to both public and private interests.

In those first three months the new land policy of the May 4 directive had been put into effect—in some places with great alacrity, in some places only in a desultory way. Mao found that in the areas where the land had been confiscated from the landlords and redistributed, the Communists had unremitting peasant support. In the other areas, where the action was slower, the peasants were taking a "wait and see" attitude, and they could not really be counted on in a pinch. So the land policy was going to be thoroughly implemented everywhere.

Summing up, Mao Zedong in the autumn of 1946 was optimistic, in spite of the enormous amount of assistance Chiang Kaishek was receiving from the United States.

> It must be made clear that the enemy still has strength, that we ourselves still have some weaknesses, and that the struggle is still a long and cruel one. But we can certainly win victory.

Thus did Mao confirm his view that the Communists would ultimately triumph in the civil war in the name of the Chinese people.

25

The Long War

All circumstances now show that the situation in China is about to enter a new stage of development. This new stage is one in which the country-wide struggle against imperialism and feudalism will develop into a great new people's revolution. The task of our Party is to struggle for the advent of this high tide and its triumph.

—Mao Zedong, assessing the Chinese civil war on February 1, 1947

In September 1946 Mao Zedong had told correspondent A. T. Steele that it would be a long war if the United States continued to help the Guomindang. And despite Mao's determined optimism during the autumn of 1946, Chiang Kaishek's numerically superior military forces, with their superior military equipment, continued to hold the initiative. They drove the Communists back in several areas.

Assessing the situation again in February 1947, Mao saw on the plus side proof that the Communist armies had done what he asked: They had destroyed another thirty-one brigades of Nationalist troops. But on the minus side was the fact that Chiang's offensives in southern and western Shandong Province, in the Shaanxi-Gansu-Ningxia stronghold of the Communists, along the Beijing-Hankou railroad, and in southern Manchuria were all more or less successful. The Communists were driven from the towns, although they still held most of the countryside. What Mao had said about Chiang's problem of garrisoning was true: Chiang had now almost duplicated the Japanese problem of the late 1930s. But he was still very strong.

The People's Consultative Conference was held, but it was a farce. When the National Assembly was convened in November 1946, no Communist members bothered to attend. Zhou Enlai had remained in Nanjing and Shanghai to keep in touch with General Marshall, but in November he gave up and went back to Yanan.

The breach was irreparable. The decision in China would be made through civil war.

*   *   *

Chiang's position seemed very strong. He had captured many of the cities of Manchuria, thus apparently proving wrong General Wedemeyer's assessment of Communist power. Chiang was also preparing to attack Yanan, the stronghold of the Communists. Capturing that city would be an immense blow to Communist prestige.

But inside Nationalist China the rot was beginning to show. In Shanghai in the summer of 1946 the Guomindang's police began to crack down on street vendors, who were taking business from the merchants licensed by the Nationalists. Three months later the street vendors were still operating, so the police began a program of mass arrests. On November 30 3000 street vendors staged a demonstration and surrounded the Huangpu police station. The police opened fire, killing seven demonstrators and wounding many others. Still more were arrested. The next day, December 1, 5000 street vendors came out. The firing began again, and this time ten were killed and a hundred wounded.

On December 2 all the shops in Shanghai closed down to show sympathy for the street vendors. The action turned into a general strike, and Shanghai was paralyzed.

In what seemed to be his usual fashion in postwar China, Chiang Kaishek misread all the signs. The Guomindang announced that the troubles in the cities were instigated by the Communists. The Nationalists refused to believe that the people wanted peace badly enough to change sides if that was necessary. No longer the revered hero of the anti-Japanese war, Chiang was seen as the oppressor; and the Americans, so lately popular, were seen as his willing helpers. Anti-American sentiment came to a head on Christmas eve, 1946, when a girl student at Beijing University was raped by American soldiers. The result was a student strike that spread across Nationalist China. Half a million students quit classes and demonstrated against Chiang Kaishek and "American imperialism." They demanded the withdrawal of all American forces from China. Once again, Chiang's people shouted that this was all part of a Communist plot.

A few weeks later Chiang ordered the middle-of-the-road Democratic League disbanded, calling it a menace to public safety. By that time Chiang was beginning to understand the erosion of his political position. On January 16, 1947, he approached U.S. Ambassador Leighton Stuart. The ambassador proposed to the Communists that they accept a delegation of Nationalist leaders at Yanan to discuss peace terms.

The Communists set two conditions: (1) The constitution framed in the previous few months without Communist participation had to be scrapped, and (2) the Nationalists had to withdraw from all the areas held by the Communists as of January 1946. These conditions were unacceptable to Chiang Kaishek, whose only real stock-in-trade at that point was his collection of military victories, none of them decisive. The negotiations failed. Chiang ordered all the Communist representatives who had come to Nationalist China to leave, and the Communists in Chongqing, Nanjing, and Shanghai moved out to liberated areas. The breach was now total, and Chiang put his campaign to capture Yanan into full operation.

The Communists had been expecting the attack since November. As they had only about 20,000 troops there, while Chiang had amassed some 250,000 men, the outcome seemed predictable. On March 19, however, when Chiang captured Yanan, he won a victory over a ghost city; the Communist leadership had moved to Qinghuabian in northern Shaanxi Province. Mao decided that his troops would remain in that Shaanxi-Gansu-Ningxia liberated area. It was mountainous and bleak; and they knew the country, while Chiang's forces did not. Also, the people were friendly to the Communists.

The Communists then launched a campaign of attrition of the sort they had used so successfully against the Japanese. It was hit and run; let the Nationalists have the cities and the towns, but strike them again and again. Mao deduced that the Nationalist armies were growing tired, that the Guomindang corruption was eroding Chiang's ability to fight, and that ultimately the Nationalists would collapse.

This was tough thinking in the spring of 1947 as the Nationalists achieved victory after victory, driving the Communists ahead of them. In April Chiang's major effort was devoted to driving the central Communist army across the Huang He. The Red armies melted before the Nationalists, but they moved around, reassembled, and fought again. Said Mao:

> There is no need for our main force to hurry north to attack Yulin or south to cut off the enemy's retreat. It should be made clear to the commanders and fighters and also to the masses that this method of our army is the necessary road to the final defeat of the enemy. Unless we reduce the enemy to extreme fatigue and complete starvation, we can not win final victory.

Therefore the "Northwest People's Liberation Army" sent out a small force to lure the Nationalists up toward Ansai, northwest of Yanan. The main Red Army force remained at Qinghuabian, northeast of Yanan.

On March 25, 1947, the headquarters and one regiment of the Nationalist Thirty-first Brigade walked into the Communist trap, which was sprung by the northeastern force. The regiment, surrounded by vastly superior Communist units, was wiped out in a battle that lasted just one hour. Mao's theory of massing forces to attack relatively small units had been proved correct again.

On the face of it, Chiang was still winning. His armies swept across China, into the liberated areas between the Yangtze and the Great Wall, and beyond the wall. South Manchuria and Rehe, and the city of Kargan, were all occupied by Nationalist troops.

But in the main centers of Guomindang power, all was not well. On May 4, 1947, students in Shanghai demonstrated against the civil war. They were joined by workers, and soon 8000 people besieged police headquarters. The movement spread to many nationalist cities. On May 18 the Guomindang issued a document, entitled "Provisional Measures for the Maintenance of Public Order," that prohibited demonstrations and forbade all strikes. On May 20 students demonstrated in Nanjing and Tianjin. The police in both cities opened fire, and a hundred students were wounded. More were arrested.

In that summer of 1947 the tide of war changed. For months the Communists had been building their forces, recruiting from among the peasants and from among their prisoners, the Guomindang troops who had fought against them. But these Guomindang troops were not the soldiers of the 1920s and 1930s, indoctrinated in revolutionary fervor by leaders who truly believed what they were saying. These were mercenary troops or forcibly conscripted troops; most were the latter, and they felt no loyalty to the Guomindang. By June 1947 the Red Army numbered 2 million men.

In July the Communists were ready to take the offensive against a worn-down Guomindang army. The main Red force under generals Liu Bocheng and Deng Xiaoping crossed the Huang He from north China and drove south. One after another the old liberated areas fell again to the Communists.

On September 1, Mao Zedong assessed the new situation. In the first year of fighting, he said, the Communists had wiped out 1,120,000 Guomindang troops. Admittedly, the Communists had taken 300,000 casualties of their own, but Mao had been prepared for that. The important matter was that the Red Army had maintained its core and its interior lines, and had not broken under the strain. The ranks had been thickened, and it was time now to move faster.

But the fighting was not all of it:

In all the new and old Liberated Areas, we must resolutely carry through the land reform (which is the most fundamental requirement for supporting a long war and winning country-wide victory), develop production, practice economy and strengthen the building of war industry—all for victory at the front.

The war results now had a different tone:

Southern Shaanxi... May 4... captured twenty-two towns including two important crossings of the Huang He... wiped out 18,000 enemy troops.

Northern Henan... May 28... captured Zexian, Zounxian, Huaxian, and Tangyin... wiped out over 45,000 enemy troops.

Southwestern Shandong... July... in the region of Heze, Yuncheng, Chuye, Dingtao, Qinxian, Zaoxian, four KMT division headquarters and 9.5 brigades... 56,000 men wiped out.

By October Mao Zedong was beginning to scent victory. That month he issued a manifesto of the People's Liberation Army. "Overthrow Chiang Kaishek and liberate all China" was the slogan. The manifesto contained eight basic policies:

1. Unite the people.
2. Arrest Chiang Kaishek and the other civil war criminals.
3. Abolish Chiang's dictatorship and establish people's democracy with freedom of speech, press, assembly, and association.
4. Clear out corruption.
5. Confiscate the property of the Big Four families and other war criminals.
6. Abolish exploitation and distribute the land.
7. Recognize the rights of minorities.

8. Repudiate Chiang's foreign policy. Unite in a common struggle with all nations which treat the Chinese as equals.

Above all, said Mao, let the men and women of the Red Army remember:

> We are the great People's Liberation Army, we are the troops led by the great Communist Party of China. Provided we constantly observe the directives of the Party, we are sure to win.
> "Down with Chiang Kaishek!
> "Long live New China!"

So there it was at last. New China. A new concept, dedicated to overthrowing Chiang and forming a democratic coalition government. By the fall of 1947 the concept was more than an idle dream.

By January 1948 the Guomindang itself was beginning to fall apart. That month a group of Chiang's former associates organized the Guomindang Revolutionary Committee in Hong Kong. This new group declared itself opposed to Chiang and in favor of the Chinese Communists and "other democratic parties." Also, the Democratic League, outlawed in China, moved to Hong Kong and flourished once more, issuing statements of policy that were heard by many on the mainland.

The Communists concentrated their military efforts in Manchuria and north of the Yangtze River, and steadily they began to get the upper hand. Town followed city, falling into Communist hands. The problems facing Mao changed; no longer was he concerned with survival of his party and his army. The topics of his writings show the change:

- A reiteration of the eight principles of Red Army discipline
- A program for setting up a system of reports
- The problem of combating erroneous tendencies within the party
- The problem of state power
- The problem of the relationship between those who lead and those who are led in the revolutionary united front
- The democratic movement in the army
- The question of the national bourgeoisie and the enlightened gentry

By March 1948 the Red armies had taken much new territory, and within the new liberated areas there were people of means to be dealt with. The radicals wanted to destroy them all and turn their assets over to the masses. But Mao intervened:

> We should not abandon the enlightened gentry who cooperated with us in the past and continue to cooperate with us at present, who approved of the struggle against the United States and Chiang Kaishek and who approve of the land reform. Take people for instance like Liu Shaopai of the Shaanxi Suiyuan Border Region, Li Tingming of the Shaanxi Gansu Ningxia border region. Since they gave us considerable help in the hard times during and after the War of Resistance against Japan and did not obstruct or oppose the land reform when we were carrying it out, we should continue the policy of uniting with them. But uniting with them does not mean treating that as a force that determines the character of the Chinese revolution.

To Mao, on the eve of victory, it was apparent that the Communist party of China had created a new sort of revolution, applicable to China's situation:

> The forces that determine the character of a revolution are the chief enemies on the one side and the chief revolutionaries on the other. At present our chief enemies are imperialism, feudalism, and bureaucratic capitalism, while the main forces in our struggle against these enemies are the people engaged in manual and mental labor who make up 90 percent of the country's population. And this determines that our revolution at the present state is a new-democratic, a people's democratic revolution in character and is different from a socialist revolution such as the October Revolution.

Already the problems of government were beginning to take precedence over the military problems in Mao's mind. His generals were handling the military side very nicely.

In the summer of 1948 Chiang Kaishek's slippage began to show. He controlled the cities north of the Yangtze but they were falling one by one. His control of the railroads was at best nominal. Northern Manchuria was solidly in the hands of the Communists and provided a powerful base for movement south. In September the Communists began what they called the Liaoxi-Shenyang campaign. To the outside world it was known as the battle for Mukden (Shenyang).

As the forces of battle mounted, the Nationalists put four armies into the field. That meant forty-four divisions. They were placed in three sectors, isolated from each other, at Changchun, Shenyang, and Jinzhou. All the Nationalists were in fixed defensive positions.

The Communists now brought up fifty-three divisions, or 700,000 men. The key to their success, they decided, was Jinzhou, on the Beijing-Liaoning railroad. So it was there that they fought the main battle. Lesser forces continued the siege of Changchun and Shenyang, to keep reinforcements from moving into Jinzhou.

The fighting began on September 12 with an attack on Ihsien, on the outskirts of Jinzhou. Ihsien fell. Chiang Kaishek saw what was happening, hurriedly flew up to Jinzhou from Nanjing, and summoned another six divisions from north China for reinforcement.

On October 12 the Nationalists counterattacked at Tashan. The Communists held. Down from Changchun came the Ninth Nationalist Army, under Gen. Liao Yaoxiang. His eleven divisions and three cavalry brigades were intercepted by the Communists northeast of Heishan, and the relief of Jinzhou was not accomplished.

On October 14 the Communists began their attack on Jinzhou. The battle lasted thirty-one hours, and it resulted in the defeat of the Nationalists and the capture of 100,000 prisoners.

With the fall of Jinzhou, the Nationalist troops at Changchun rebelled and refused to fight. Thousands of them surrendered to the Communists. Chiang still hoped to recapture Jinzhou and ordered General Liao to resume his advance on that city. Liao did so, but the Communists who had taken Jinzhou now swung back north. Liao's force was caught in the Communist pincers near Heishan, and after two days of fighting the Nationalists were defeated. Liao was captured, and so were three corps commanders and another 100,000 troops. On November 2 the Communists attacked Shenyang, and the Nationalist defense fell apart. Another 150,000 troops were lost by Chiang's armies.

With the victory at Shenyang the whole of Manchuria fell into Communist hands. Chiang had lost all his northeastern armies, a total of 470,000 men.

So strong was the Communist military force by November 1948 that it had to be reorganized. Five field armies were set up in various parts of the country, each consisting of two or more armies. The Red Army numbered more than 3 million men, and for the first time Mao's forces outnumbered Chiang's.

Now the unravelling of Chiang's China came much faster. In November and December battles were fought for Xuzhou, a railroad junction halfway between Tianjin and the Yangtze. The Nationalists held out grimly. But elsewhere there were even grimmer indications of the end to come.

On November 8, 1948, Gen. He Jifeng and Gen. Zhang Kexia rebelled against Chiang and came over to the Communists with 20,000 men. On November 27 Liao Yunchou rebelled and brought 5500 more men. Then came Sun Liangcheng, deputy commander of the Guomindang First Pacification Zone, with his troops. General followed general: Chao Pipang, Zeng Zesheng, and Huang Zehua. The rats were deserting the sinking ship.

Earlier, Nationalist troops besieged at Changchun had all surrendered. But Nationalist troops at Xuzhou, under Generals Du Luming, Qiu Qingquan, and Li Mi, refused to surrender. To try to shorten casualty lists and speed the process, Mao Zedong himself prepared a message to the defenders of Xuzhou, which shows how completely the military situation had changed in the past year:

You are now at the end of your rope. Huang Wei's army was completely wiped out on the night of the 15th. Li Yannian's army has taken to its heels and fled south, and it is hopeless for you to think of joining them.

Are you hoping to break through? How can you break through when the People's Liberation Army is all around? During the last few days you have tried to break through, but what came of it? Your planes and tanks, too, are useless. We have more planes and tanks than you, that is artillery and explosives which people call our homemade planes and tanks. Aren't they ten times more formidable than your foreign-made planes and tanks? Your army under Sun Yuanliang is finished, and more than half the men in your two remaining armies have been wounded or captured. You have brought many miscellaneous and idle personnel of various organizations and many young students from Hsuchow [Xuzhou] and forced them into your army, but how can these people fight? For more than ten days you have been surrounded ring upon ring and received blow upon blow, and your position has shrunk greatly. You have such a tiny place, only a little more than ten li [a sixth of a mile] square and so many people are crowded together that a single shell from us can kill a lot of you.

Your wounded soldiers and the families who have followed that army are complaining to high heaven. Your soldiers and many of your officers have no stomach for any more fighting. You, as deputy commander in chief, as commanders of armies, corps, divisions, and regiments, should understand and sympathize with the feelings of your subordinates and families. Hold their lives dear, find a way out for them as early as possible and stop sending them to a senseless death.

Now that Huang Wei's army has been completely wiped out and Li Yannian's army has fled towards Bengbu, we are able to concentrate an attacking force several times your strength. This time we have fought for only 40 days and you have lost 10 divisions under Huang Potao, 11 under Huang Wei, four under Sun Yuanliang, four under Feng Jian, three under Sun Liangcheng, one under Liu Juming, one division in Suxian and another in Lingpi. Altogether you have lost 34 divisions. Of these, 27.5 divisions were completely wiped out by our army, the only exceptions were the 3.5 divisions led by He Jifeng and Zhang Kexia and one division led by Liao Yunchou which revolted and came over to our side, and one division led by Sun Liangcheng and the two half divisions led by Chao Pikuang and Huang Zehua which surrendered. You have seen with your own eyes the fate of the three armies under Huang Potao, Huang Wei, and Sun Yuanliang. You should learn from the example of General Zheng Dongguo in Changchun and from the current example of corps commander Sun Liangcheng and division commanders Chao Pikuan and Huang Zehua and immediately order all your troops to lay down their arms and cease resistance. Our army will guarantee life and safety to you, high ranking officers and to all officers and men. This is your only way out. Think it over. If you feel that this is right, then do it. If you still want to fight another round, you can have it, but you will be finished off anyway.

After the Nationalist officers heard this broadcast message, they refused to consider the course Mao proposed. They continued to resist, desperately, but it did no good. The whole army inside the square was wiped out. Du Luming was captured, Qiu Qingquan was killed, and only Li Mi managed somehow to escape.

By the end of December the Communists held most of north China. The hold was cemented in January, when Tianjin was attacked. The garrison, under Gen. Chen Changchieh, refused to surrender, so the whole garrison of 130,000 men was destroyed and Chen was captured.

Next was the city the Nationalists still insisted on calling Beiping, but

which the Communists and the residents always called Beijing. Gen. Fu
Zuoyi was in charge at Beijing, and with the fall of Tianjin he saw what
was coming. Completely surrounded by an enormous Communist army,
Fu surrendered the garrison of 200,000 and the Communists walked in
peacefully on January 31, 1949.

By the end of this campaign, more than half a million of Chiang's troops
had been lost, killed, or wounded or had surrendered to the Communists.
The Nationalist troops now swelled the Communist ranks. Only one garrison of north China, that of the Tanggu forts, managed to escape. Fifty
thousand men were carried out by ship and moved south to fight for Chiang
Kaishek again.

The Communists held all China north of the Yangtze by 1949. Those who
still talked of Nationalist survival, and there were some, liked to think of a
revival of the old Ming northern and southern dynasties, north and south
of the river. But there really was no hope. No hope at all.

26

The Chinese Conquer China

Even our enemy no longer doubts the outcome. . . . In our struggle we shall overthrow once and for all the feudal oppression of thousands of years and the imperialist oppression of a hundred years. The year 1949 will be a year of tremendous importance. We should redouble our efforts.

—Mao Zedong to the party on December 30, 1948

Winter, 1949. Nanjing and Shanghai, the heart of Guomindang country, were virtually in a state of siege. The Communists stood north of the Yangtze River. When were they going to cross?

For months the Nationalists had tried to prop up the economy that the Big Four families had so mercilessly raped. In August the Guomindang government made a desperate attempt to halt the inflation by throwing out the old yuan and introducing a new currency. Along with these new paper notes came orders that every individual and every business must turn in all its old money *and* all its gold, silver, and U.S. dollars. In Shanghai the order was enforced by one of Chiang Kaishek's sons. The enforcers were unyielding and severe. At first, many businessmen and citizens were publicly executed for failing to comply with the regulations. Many of the bourgeoisie gave up all their savings for the new banknotes. What recourse did they have? If they were caught with other money, they would be killed. But within three months the new currency had been so debased that it was no more valuable than the old.

And who profited? As anyone could guess, the high officials of the Guomindang. It was said in Shanghai that the whole plan had been invented by T. V. Soong as a way to take one last bite out of the wealth of the Chinese people for the Big Four families, who then moved all their assets overseas.*

---

*Even in the 1980s no one knew exactly how much money the Big Four families had looted from China. Much of it was taken to the United States and invested. The Soongs, now of America, are known to be enormously wealthy, but that is all that is known.

This economic terrorism was accompanied by a renewed political terror. Suspected Communists, and even those simply accused of trying to help the Communists, were brought to public places for public hearings, called trials, and then shot through the back of the head. Nearly every day at some busy corner of Shanghai, several such executions were carried out. Most of the people killed were very young, many of them students.

In the United States the China lobby was complaining that the American government was not doing enough for Chiang Kaishek, not bringing in enough guns, enough money, enough supplies. But the fact was that many of those supplies had found their way into the Communist areas. Some of this material had been captured, but much of it had been turned over to the Red Army by Guomindang soldiers and officers who defected.

Brig. Gen. David Barr, head of the U.S. military advisory group, said of the military situation: "No battle has been lost since my arrival due to lack of ammunition or equipment."

No, the fact was that by the beginning of 1949 the Nationalist forces were totally demoralized and the Communist victory was almost complete. As General Barr put it, "The Guomindang's military debacle in my opinion can be attributed to the world's worst leadership and many other morale-destroying factors that lead to a complete loss of will to fight."

Principal among these had to be the total loss of public support for the Guomindang in the three short years since the end of the war against Japan.

With the Communists poised on the north bank of the Yangtze, Chiang searched desperately for some solution that would enable him to buy time. On New Year's day, he called publicly for negotiations that would bring peace to China.

> I have no desire of my own other than that the peace negotiations should not impair the country's independence and integrity but instead should help the rehabilitation of the people; that the sacred constitution should not be violated by my action and that democratic constitutionalism should not be thereby undermined; that the form of government of the Republic of China should be guaranteed and the legally constituted authority of the Republic of China should not be interrupted; that the armed forces should be definitely preserved and that the people should be allowed to continue their free way of life and maintain their present minimum standard of living. If only peace can be realized I certainly

do not care whether I remain in office or retire, but will abide by the common will of the people. *

At first, Mao Zedong simply sneered at the Guomindang's suggestion of negotiations and refuted Chiang's statements one by one.

"As we said long ago," Mao wrote, "Chiang Kaishek has lost his soul, is merely a corpse, and no one believes him any more."

Chiang had spoken of the strength of the Nationalist forces, preparing for "a decisive battle in the Nanjing Shanghai sector." The Communists could laugh at the claim; they knew very well that their armies were much stronger than those of the enemy and that Chiang could not even depend upon the integrity of his armies. General after general was deserting the Nationalist fold. The people of Shanghai, questioned by foreign reporters about Chiang's suggestions, were as derisive as were the Communists. Except for the band of dedicated Guomindang sycophants and officials, Chiang had wasted his power base almost entirely.

No, the Communists sensed their own strength at that point. As Mao said bluntly:

> The present situation is quite clear—the whole structure of the reactionary Guomindang regime will crumble and perish if the People's Liberation Army launches a few more powerful attacks against its remnant forces. Having pursued a policy of civil war, the reactionary Guomindang government is now reaping what it has sown. The masses are in rebellion, its close followers are deserting, and it can no longer maintain itself.

Stripped of the Communist hyperbole, the statement was true. Knowing that, Mao replied to Chiang's suggestion for peace talks with a very tough counteroffer: The Communists would negotiate instead of fighting only on these terms:

1. Punish the war criminals. (Mao had already indicated that in the Communist view, Chiang Kaishek was a war criminal.)
2. Abolish the bogus constitution. (This was the constitution that Chiang called "sacred.")

---

*The integrity of that statement is more than a little undermined by Chiang's actions subsequent to his flight to Taiwan. Never for a day did he give up his authority over the Republic of China until his death.

3. Abolish the bogus "constituted authority." (This was the Guomindang.)

4. Reorganize all reactionary troops on democratic principles. (This meant disband the Nationalist armies and recreate them on the lines of the People's Liberation Army.)

5. Confiscate bureaucrat capital. (This meant arrest the Big Four families, who were listed as war criminals, and force them to return the money they had looted from China.)

6. Reform the land system. (This meant do away with the landlords, who were practically Chiang's sole supporters.)

7. Abrogate treasonable treaties. (This referred to several treaties with the United States, especially the Sino-U.S. bilateral agreement, signed at Nanjing in 1948, which gave the U.S. economic experts an enormous amount of control over Nationalist economic affairs in return for more loans and grants. This had been done at the insistence of a Congress that suddenly began to realize where the American money for China was really going: into the hands of a handful of people. The Communists also frequently mentioned the Sino-U.S. air transport agreement, in which they said Chiang had sold out command of China's airspace to the Americans, letting them land and fly wherever they wanted whenever they wanted.)

8. Convene a political consultative conference without the participation of reactionary elements, and form a democratic coalition government to take over all the powers of the reactionary Nanjing Guomindang government and of its subordinate governments at all levels. (This final provision meant simply that the Communists would not negotiate with the Guomindang's right wing.)

So desperate was the situation of the Nationalist government, however, that even these conditions did not sink the negotiations before they began.

Realizing that Mao's eight conditions were almost impossible for the Nationalists to meet, a Communist party spokesman modified them a bit in a statement on January 31. The new statement was a bit of tortured logic, manufactured to meet conditions:

We have permitted the reactionary Nanjing government to send a delegation for peace negotiations with us, not because we recognize the government as still qualified to represent the Chinese people, but because it still has some remnants of the reactionary armed forces. If that government feels it has completely forfeited the people's confidence and that the remnants of the reactionary armed forces are unable to resist the Powerful People's Liberation Army, and if that government is willing to accept the eight terms for peace proposed by the Chinese Communist Party, then it is of course preferable and beneficial to the cause of the people to settle the matter by negotiations, so as to lessen the peoples' sufferings.

But the Communists made one last jab, refusing to accept certain candidates. Among them was Peng Chaohsien, one of the key figures of the Guomindang C.C. Clique. The Communists called him a war criminal and said he was persona non grata.

Actually the Second and Third Communist field armies had planned to cross the Yangtze in April. Then they announced to Chairman Mao that they would be prepared to move in March. But Mao cautioned them that they had to get ready to take over some very large cities, and they needed study to do so. For years the Communists had concentrated on the farms and villages; now they had to learn how to deal with cities.

The Communists estimated that Chiang's army was down to less than 2 million men. But Mao cautioned his commanders: No matter what he said for public consumption, he still regarded the Guomindang armies as formidable. The generals must be careful. They must prepare, and they must move cautiously.

Embarrassed by the direction in which the discussions were going, Chiang Kaishek in February again abandoned the public scene to go into "retirement." The war against the Communists would be managed by Sun Fo's executive yuan. But by then the Nationalist government was very much in disarray. Li Zongren had taken over as chief executive, and he accepted the Communist demands. But the demands were repudiated by Sun Fo and other diehard Guomindang men. So it was all very murky in Nanjing and Shanghai.

Bai Zongxi, commander of the old bandit-suppression headquarters in central China, decided he could manage affairs better than anyone. He suggested to Chiang that he step down permanently and let the Guangxi Clique take over management of China's affairs.

Chiang appealed to the United States to intervene in the dispute with the Communists. But the Americans, finally, had discovered that they had worn out their welcome in China, so they refused. The delegates of Acting President Li Zongren made ready to go to Beijing to talk. Mao summed up his reactions as of February 15, 1949:

> These reactionaries are the greatest obstacle to the realization of peace in China today. They dream of agitating for a total war under the slogan of "total peace." But as a matter of fact they have neither the power to bring about a total peace nor the power to wage a total war. Total power is in the hands of the Chinese people, the Chinese People's Liberation Army, the Communist Party of China, and the other democratic parties, not in the hands of the badly split and disintegrating Guomindang. One side wields total power, while the other is hopelessly split and disintegrated. And this is the result of the prolonged struggle of the Chinese people and the prolonged evil-doing of the Guomindang. No serious person can ignore this basic fact in the political situation in China today.

By March not much had occurred. Along the Yangtze River's south side, the Nationalists were building fortifications, in the hope of holding the Communists back. How, since they were in their negotiating stance, is subject to opinion. The Guomindang officials were on the one hand the most obdurate enemies of the Communists, on the other the most frightened of the future. The Communists estimated that the Guomindang now had only 1 million combat troops left, dispersed over an area that extended from Xinjiang to Taiwan.

But by March it was apparent that the peace negotiations would be held in Beijing, so the crossing of the Yangtze was deferred.

The Guomindang continued to unravel. Sun Fo resigned. Acting President Li Zongren appointed He Yingqin to succeed him as president of the executive yuan.

On April 1, 1949, the Guomindang delegation headed by Zhang Zhizhong arrived in Beijing. On the same day students demonstrated in Nanjing for peace. The Guomindang police tried to break up the demonstration of about 6000 students, but was unable to. Someone started clubbing the students, and in the end two were dead and a hundred were wounded. The result was more hatred within China for the Guomindang, more tension in Nanjing. After two weeks an agreement was drafted, but when it was presented to the Nanjing government, it was rejected. The old leaders of the Guomindang still had enough power to wreck their country.

The Guomindang was now split. One group insisted on following Chiang Kaishek. Another group wanted to dump Chiang and participate in the Communist-led government. A third group was not sure which road to take.

The Communists' patience was now at an end. They had made all the gestures to world opinion that need be made. On April 21, 1949, Mao Zedong and Zhu De issued a joint statement, ordering the Red Army to cross the Yangtze and complete the revolution.

On April 21, 1949, the Chinese Communists crossed in spectacular force: the Second Field Army, led by Liu Bocheng and Deng Xiaoping, and the Third Field Army, led by Chen Yi. They had their orders, and after the failure of the last negotiations the orders were uncompromising:

1. Advance bravely and annihilate resolutely, thoroughly, wholly, and completely all the Guomindang reactionaries within China's borders who dare to resist.
2. Advance bravely and arrest all the incorrigible war criminals. Pay special attention to arresting the bandit chieftain Chiang Kaishek.
3. Proclaim to all Guomindang local governments and local military groups the final amended version of the Agreement on Internal Peace. In accordance with its general ideas, you may conclude local agreements....
4. After the People's Liberation Army has encircled Nanjing, we are willing to give the Li Zongren government at Nanjing another opportunity to sign the Agreement on Internal Peace, if that government has not yet fled and dispersed and desires to sign it.

The riverfront was 500 kilometers long, extending from a point northeast of Jiujiang on the west to Jiangyin on the east. The Red Army cut through the Nationalists with ease, overwhelmed the defenses, and on April 25 captured Nanjing.

On May 3 the Communists took Hangzhou. On May 27 they captured Shanghai. In June they moved into Fujian Province, took Amoy and Fuzhou. On May 14 Lin Biao took the Fourth Field Army across the

Yangtze and captured the three cities of Wuhan. Then Lin marched south into Hunan, Mao's old home grounds. As the troops advanced, the Guomindang officials fell before them like wheat. Cheng Chien, the governor of Hunan, surrendered and came over to join the Communists. Chen Mingren, commander of the Chinese First Army, Chiang's own troops, renounced allegiance to the Guomindang. The Fourth Field Army then defeated Bai Zongxi and moved into Guangdong and Guangxi provinces. Guangzhou fell, and then Guilin. Nanning was taken on December 4.

In the north Peng Dehuai led the First Field Army into Taiyuan and northwest. Lanzhou, Xining, Yinchuan—all fell. Everywhere the generals either died or renounced their allegiance to the Guomindang. As the battles continued, more renounced their allegiance.

Liu Bocheng and Deng Xiaoping then moved into southwest China, to Guiyang and Chongqing.

Down in Kunming, Gen. Lu Han had succeeded his half-brother as governor. Now he renounced his allegiance to Chiang Kaishek and joined the Communists. Yunnan and Sichuan provinces were both peacefully liberated when the Guomindang officials came over to the Communists. The last big battle was at Chengdu, where the Communists wiped out the Guomindang troops under Hu Zongnan on December 27. The mainland of China was now free, with the exception of Tibet.

The Guomindang moved south, ahead of the advancing Communist armies. At first, Chiang came back to office—nobody ever believed he had intended to let others run his government—and he went down to Guangzhou. He considered moving back to Chongqing to try to hold out as he had against the Japanese, but the Communists were another matter. They had the people almost solidly behind them, and Chiang could not expect support even in his old stronghold, so badly had he abused his government weal.

So he cast his eyes on Taiwan, which had been taken over by Lu Han's troops in 1945 and had been governed by Chen Yi for a time. In 1947 the Taiwanese, who spoke a sort of Fujian dialect, rose up against the Nationalists, whom they detested. The Guomindang responded with a blood bath so severe that the people were terrorized and the rebellion was put down. Thus it was no great trick in 1949 to take over the island. At that time Taiwan was Nationalist territory, the only safe place in the world for Chiang Kaishek.

So there, in Taiwan, the Republic of China government was set up in exile. And there it would remain in exile, with much haranguing and talk about the day when Chiang would "unleash" his forces against the Chinese mainland. But from the beginning there was never a chance of that—unless the United States, which had been so foolish in its perceptions of China for years, would become more foolish and involve itself in a war on the Asian mainland. In 1949 nobody expected that. It was foolish enough that the United States undertook the protection of the Chiang Kaishek government from the Communists, a protection invoking the power of the U.S. Seventh Fleet. This use of power by the United States to interfere in the affairs of China still further was much resented in Beijing, and it would have prevented the normalization of relations with the United States, had the Americans even sought such a course. But in Washington the China lobby had Congress and several administrations convinced that Chiang might possibly make it back to the mainland and that the Communist government would arouse so much opposition that the Chinese people would welcome the Guomindang back.

It was a total pipedream. The Democratic League and the Guomindang left wing, which had set up in Hong Kong, now moved back to Beijing to test the atmosphere. That was just what the Communists wanted; this "third force" gave an added aura of respectability to the revolution. In June 1949 Mao Zedong ordained the formation of a dictatorship of the proletariat, which would be led by the working class through the Communist party. Reactionaries would be deprived of the right of free expression. Only the people could speak.

Mao also announced the Communist party's intention of changing China from an agricultural country to an industrial one. First there would be the new democracy; that would change to socialism; and finally, China would achieve what the Soviet Union had not, true communism, classless and with plenty for all. A law establishing the Central People's Government was passed by the People's Political Consultative Conference in October. The Chinese had conquered China. The revolution was complete. Now the Communists had to govern.

27

The People's Republic of China

Very soon we shall be victorious throughout the country. This victory will breach the eastern front of imperialism and will have great international significance. To win this victory will not require much more time and effort, but to consolidate it will. The bourgeoisie doubts our ability to construct. The imperialists reckon that eventually we will beg alms from them in order to live. With victory certain moods may grow within the party—arrogance, the airs of a self-styled hero, inertia and unwillingness to make progress, love of pleasure and distaste for continued hard living. With victory, the people will be grateful to us and the bourgeoisie will come forward to flatter us. It has been proved that the enemy cannot conquer us by force of arms. However, the flattery of the bourgeoisie may conquer the weak-willed within our ranks. There may be some Communists who were not conquered by enemies with guns and were worthy of the name of heroes for standing up to those enemies, but who cannot withstand sugar-coated bullets; they will be defeated by sugar-coated bullets. We must guard against such a situation. To win country-wide victory is only the first step in a long march of ten thousand li. Even if this step is worthy of pride, it is comparatively tiny; what will be more worthy of pride is yet to come. After several decades, the victory of the Chinese People's democratic revolution, viewed in retrospect, will seem like only a brief prologue to a long drama. A drama begins with a prologue, but the prologue is not the climax. The Chinese revolution is great, but the road after the revolution will be longer, the work greater and more arduous. This must be made clear now in the Party. The comrades must be taught to remain modest, prudent and free from arrogance and rashness in their style of work. The comrades must be taught to preserve the style of plain living and hard struggle. We have the Marxist-Leninist weapon of criticism and self criticism. We can get rid of a bad style and keep the good. We can learn what we did not know. We are not only good at destroying the old world, we are also good at building the new. Not only can the Chinese people live without begging alms from the imperialists, they will live a better life than that in the imperialist countries.

—Mao Zedong, report to the Second Plenary Session of the Seventh
Central Committee of the Communist party of China,
March 5, 1949

Mao Zedong made his triumphal entry into Beijing with his troops riding in American trucks, led by American tanks. Many of the soldiers carried American weapons. All this was the result of the civil war, and the American products, as noted, were either captured from the Nationalists or turned over to the Communists by Nationalist generals and troops who changed sides when they saw the end of the Guomindang's rule of China.

As the Communists took over the south, they moved slowly. In his address to the Second Session of the Seventh Central Committee in the spring of 1949, Mao outlined the pattern. This was Guomindang country, and the Communists must go slow in changing it. They had to form party organizations, arouse the masses, and establish trade unions, peasant associations, and other peoples' organizations. In the cities they had to clean out the Guomindang. In the countryside they had to force the landlords to reduce rents and interest, but they must not seriously disarrange the economy. Not yet. They must wait a year or two to take strong action, establishing control by the People's Liberation Army. Then they could proceed with land distribution and the elimination of the landlord class.

China's modern industry, about 10 percent of its total industry, had already been "socialized" by the Guomindang, although the profits went into the hands of the Guomindang faithful. The Communists simply took this sector over.

China's private capital industry was left alone for the time being—"nurtured" was really the word. According to Mao's guidelines: "In this period all capitalist elements in the cities and countryside which are not harmful but beneficial to the national economy should be allowed to exist and expand."

So all mainland China, except Tibet, was "liberated," and the liberation seemed very mild. To be sure, the foreign journalists in Beijing and elsewhere were kept under house arrest for months and were not allowed to report what was going on. This matter brought some criticism. Ultimately, the journalists were sent back to their own countries.

Nevertheless, the administration of China was benign for the first twelve months. Foreigners who were allowed to remain noticed this and commented that the Chinese Communist revolution was far milder than the Bolshevik revolution had been. The Communists even maintained most local Guomindang officials in their posts. Only the officials who had abused their power were done away with.

What the world did not see was the difficulty Mao and his people were having in assimilating control of this vast country, which really had not been under national management since the early days of the Qing dynasty. Yuan Shikai had certainly not controlled all China, and neither had Chiang Kaishek. So before great changes could be made, the administrative machinery had to be put into place to make them work. The People's Consultative Council turned power over to the Communist party and to the fifty-six-member Government Council, with Mao Zedong as chairman. All civil and military functions were performed under this council's authority. In the beginning the actual administration of the country was carried out by six administrative divisions, from Manchuria to the southwest.

There were immediate changes. Newspapers were closed down or became organs of the state and party, carrying information from the governors but no investigations or comments. Courses in Marxism were mandatory. But all in all, the first few months after the Communist takeover were very mild. It was not until 1950 that all this changed.

Meanwhile, having conquered China, the Chinese had to decide how they were going to deal with the foreign powers who had, until so very lately, exercised so much influence on Chinese affairs. Dealing with the United States and Russia were the first matters of importance.

Mao Zedong had some strong ideas on the subject. In August 1946, in an interview with correspondent Anna Louisa Strong, Mao said that the hope for a peaceful political settlement of China's problems rested with the United States. But he had very little hope that the American government would take the action necessary to bring about this change: the abandonment of aid to Chiang Kaishek.

In Mao's view the United States was preparing for war with the Soviet Union. But like Chiang Kaishek, the Americans, said Mao, were "paper tigers" whose power would erode in time:

Take the case of China. We have only millet plus rifles to rely on, but history will finally prove that our millet plus rifles is more powerful than Chiang Kaishek's airplanes plus tanks. Although the Chinese people still face many difficulties and will long suffer hardships from the joint attacks of U.S. imperialism and the Chinese reactionaries, the day will come when these reactionaries are defeated and we are victorious. The reason is simply this: the reactionaries represent reaction, we represent progress.

The United States had really gotten off on the wrong foot with the Chinese Communists during the immediate postwar months. In the 1930s the Americans had shown some interest in what was going on in the Communist part of China. Maj. Evans Carlson, a U.S. Marine Corps officer, had come to north China and spent some time with the Eighth Route Army, observing their manner of fighting the Japanese. He was enormously impressed with what he saw, both in the military sphere (guerilla warfare) and in the Chinese Communist relationships with the people. When he went back to America, he made several reports on the subject.

Also, for its professional foreign policy staff, the U.S. Department of State depended heavily on men who had experience and long relationships with China. One of the most brilliant was John Stewart Service, the son of American missionary parents, born in Chengdu. His knowledge of China was encyclopedic, his knowledge of the language more than adequate. He was the best type of American diplomat, a man loyal to his own country but totally familiar with the country to which he had been sent.

This one long extract from one of his reports to the State Department, dated July 28, 1944, tells almost all that need be known about the most sensitive American perception of the civil war:

> I called by invitation on General Zhou Enlai on the morning of July 27 and spent about three hours in private conversation with him. General Zhou, who was for several years the Communist representative in Chongqing, is usually referred to in Yanan as "vice chairman." Apparently, however, his only official or party post is that of member of the Politburo or Standing Committee of the Central Executive Committee of the Chinese Communist Party. His influence in the political councils of the party is reputedly second only to Mao Zedong and if the communists had a foreign minister he would be the most likely candidate. Having known him for some time in Chongqing our conversation was from the start on a very frank and cordial basis....
>
> I mentioned that the morning's Chongqing broadcast had carried a statement by the government spokesman that considerable progress had been made in the Guomindang-Communist negotiations. Zhou appeared amused. He pointed out that the Guomindang terms of June

5, what had been presented in answer to the communist proposals of May 22, left little ground for agreement. The communists find particularly unacceptable the Guomindang's refusal of any political commitments, the demand that the communist armies be limited to ten divisions, (100,000 men) and the remainder be disbanded even though they are holding territory against the enemy and that all territory now held by the communists in excess of that authorized (presumably all territory south of the course of the Yellow river [Huang He]) be turned over to the central government. (Even though its ability to hold them has been proved in the past and it now is unable to get forces into them.)

When it became obvious after the Guomindang submitted its terms that a great deal of negotiation would be necessary, the communists asked the Guomindang to send suitably authorized representatives to Yanan to talk with the top communists. The Guomindang refused. The communists then suggested that Lin Tsuhan return to Yanan for consultations. The Guomindang then used every sort of pressure to prevent Lin from leaving Chongqing.

It is apparent that the Guomindang will not make reasonable concessions, that a compromise is impossible and that the Guomindang has entered into the talks primarily for their propaganda value and to make an impression on foreign opinion, especially American. Here and several times later he referred to the Guomindang as completely unrealistic.

In 1944 the Guomindang's two alternatives are to seek compromise on its own terms or to continue to delay. Even though there was little hope of the first being successful, nothing would be lost and there would be gains from the propaganda standpoint.

Delay, in the mind of the Guomindang, means an eventual conflict. The Guomindang hopes that it will be in a position at the end of the war, with newly reorganized, trained and equipped armies, to liquidate the communists in a summary fashion.

The communists do not welcome this delay in settling their difficulties with the Guomindang because their only objective is the speedy defeat of Japan. To accomplish this there must be democratization and mobilization of the country. They will not, therefore, agree to giving up what they have accomplished toward those ends. And if the Guomindang prefers delay to present settlement, the communists do not fear it because they know that they are getting stronger as the Guomindang gets weaker and because the Guomindang as it continues its present course, cannot mobilize the popular support which it will need.

We turned to discussion of conditions in Guomindang China and after Zhou described the tendency there in gloomy but not particularly

new terms, I asked his opinion regarding the likelihood of a collapse.
In reply he suggested that Guomindang China was more like a tuber-
culosis patient than a man suffering from a disease such as cholera,
that there would continue to be a steady decline, but that there probably would be no sudden break or collapse.

Zhou then estimated for Service the Japanese aims in their offensive in
south central China. The situation was gloomy, he said, but it would grow
worse because of Chiang's refusal to take action. Chiang, said Zhou, would
not face any problem until he was forced to, and he cited the Xi'an incident of 1936, where Zhou had been a party to the events. Further, said
Zhou, Chiang was an opportunistic drifter and was surrounded by unbelievably stupid, second-rate people. Chiang's education had been neglected,
and his understanding of such matters as democracy and economics was
absurdly simple. Still, Zhou told Service, there was a possibility that Chiang
would see the light and turn around. But if he did not do it by 1945, then
it would be too late for the Guomindang.

Zhou then told Service about the reforms the Guomindang should carry
out, reiterating all that had been said before by Mao Zedong.

So Service was one sort of American in China during the war years, a
man who understood very well what was happening there. His report was
made in 1944. Everything predicted in it came to pass in the next five years.
Everything.

But there was another sort of American in China, of which the epitome
was Joseph Alsop. During the war Alsop had been a captain in the U.S. air
force; afterward, with his brother Stewart, he was the author of an important political column that appeared in hundreds of American newspapers.
A member of the "eastern establishment" since birth, a Groton and Harvard
graduate, Alsop had an influence in official Washington far beyond his apparent importance as a newspaper columnist.

Here is John S. Service's report of a February 28, 1945, conversation
with Alsop:

Captain Alsop often reflects the sentiments of T. V. Soong and other
important Chinese to whom he is very close. The following view expressed by him in a private conversation on February 24, 1945, may
therefore be of some interest.

Alsop, who had been very critical in the past of both General Stilwell and Ambassador Gauss, was pleased over recent improvement in American political and military relations with the Central Government. He was sure that the Chinese will cooperate 100 percent "as long as they are treated decently."

I suggested that several phases of the situation, the obvious feeling of strength of the Central Government, countered by aggressive actions of the communists, such as moving into South China, did not augur well for "getting on with the war against Japan." Alsop vehemently replied that such concentration on the war against Japan in China is "naive," the issues being much deeper. He explained that Japan will be destroyed by other means. The real problem to be faced by the United States is the rise of Russia and the probable destruction of any balance of power in Asia.

I said that the prosecution of the war against Japan is, however, the chief concern of the American commander in China.

He emphatically refuted this, saying "Any American commander who put this immediate objective and his own personal desire to make a name for himself, ahead of fundamental long-range American national interests should be flogged from his post."

And Alsop then said:

We are childish to assume that the Chinese communists are anything but an appendage to the Soviet Union, that they are really willing to accept any compromise or coalition short of complete control of China, or that they can be swung into cooperation with our interests. Attempts to arrange a reconciliation in China, or to utilize communist military forces, are therefore dangerous and idiotic.

Our only correct policy, accordingly, is to support the Central Government, giving it all possible aid on a much larger scale than at present, helping it to create a strong army, and then assisting by our own forces if necessary in unifying the country, liquidating the communists, and establishing a strong government.

To back up China we must adopt a strong policy toward Russia. Russian dependence on our military supplies and their desire for postwar economic assistance enables us to buy them off. At the same time our political concession to Russia in Europe and our acceptance of Russian prohibitions against, for instance, participation in the war in Finland and the Balkans, gives us basis to tell the Russians that they must stay out of China.

We Americans are alone in failing to realize that all relationships between countries are on a basis of power politics and that we must play the game the whole way in the preservation of our own interests.

Service suggested that the guns of the central government might have difficulty in dealing with the mass opposition engendered by several years of Communist control of most of occupied China. Alsop denied it. He believed that "really capable American statesmanship," which he had not yet seen in China, would be able to persuade the central government of the advantage of progressive liberalism: "American public reaction to our involvement in civil war in China would not be serious when the American people had the true picture—that is, the danger of communism and Russian dominance."

———

In essence those were the two differing views of Americans about the situation in China at the end of the Japanese occupation. Of course, the Alsop view prevailed with the American public and the more educated view failed to gain hold.

American policy turned out just as Joseph Alsop hoped, and the results were just as John Stewart Service feared: an unmitigated disaster for the United States.

The Marshall mission to China was a failure in every way but one. General Marshall returned to the United States in 1947, and he soon became U.S. Secretary of State in the Truman administration. The hawks of America were pressing for the United States to give more and more assistance to the Guomindang, but Marshall knew better and refused to become further involved. This was true even though the Chinese Communists accused General Marshall of being an agent of American imperialism.

Of course, by 1947 the Communists had become totally disillusioned with American policy because although the Americans talked sometimes of a united China, they acted as though they were believers in the Joseph Alsop line, which, of course, the U.S. government was. The year 1947 was the beginning of a whole series of spy scares and espionage cases, many of them involving the "atomic secret," and a campaign of anticommunism began that virtually paralyzed the liberal community of the United States. Anyone who suggested that there was something to be said for the Chinese Communists as opposed to the Nationalists was immediately called "soft on communism," at the very least.

*   *   *

In the summer of 1949, Ambassador John Leighton Stuart of the United States watched as the Communists took over the Yangtze River country. When they came to Nanjing, he remained, hoping to achieve some relationship with the Chinese Communists who now would assuredly control China. But the Chinese had no interest in establishing a relationship with the United States. They were angry and felt betrayed. So Ambassador Stuart went home to America, with the jeers of the Chinese ringing in his ears.

By 1949, when the Chinese were conquering China, their feelings toward the United States were grim. To say the least, U.S. policy toward China had been obstructionist as far as the Communists were concerned. Now the United States would pay the price: America would have absolutely no influence on China, and, even worse, Americans would be completely out of touch with Chinese affairs and Chinese thinking.

"U.S. naval, ground and air forces did participate in the war in China," said Mao Zedong. There were U.S. naval bases in Qingdao, Shanghai, and Taiwan. U.S. troops were stationed in Beijing, Tianjin, Tangshan, Qinhuangdao, Qingdao, Shanghai, and Nanjing. The U.S. air force controlled all China's airspace and took aerial photographs of all China's strategic areas for military maps. At the town of Anping near Beijing, at Qiutai near Changchun, at Tangshan, and in the eastern Shandong Peninsula, U.S. troops and other military personnel clashed with the People's Liberation Army and on several occasions were captured. Chennault's air fleet took an extensive part in the civil war.*

Besides transporting troops for Chiang Kaishek, the U.S. air force bombed and sank the cruiser *Chongqing*, which had mutinied against the Guomindang. These were acts of direct participation in the war, although they fell short of an open declaration of war and were not large in scale. Even so, the principal means of U.S. aggression was the large-scale supply of money, munitions, and advisers to help Chiang Kaishek fight the civil war.

When the Americans threatened a blockade of the Chinese mainland, Mao responded as follows:

What matter if we have to face some difficulties? Let them blockade us. Let them blockade us for eight or ten years. By that time all of

---

*Maj. Gen. Claire Chennault had been commander of the U.S. Fourteenth Air Force at Kunming. Before that he was leader of the Flying Tigers, an American volunteer air group that flew for the Nationalists in the war against Japan until the U.S. entered the war. After the war, Chennault organized the China Air Transport Command, which flew for the Nationalists in the war with the Communists.

China's problems will have been solved. Will the Chinese cower before difficulties when they are not afraid even of death?

Lao Zi said, "The people fear not death, why threaten them with it?"

U.S. imperialism and its running dogs, the Chiang Kaishek reactionaries, have not only threatened us with death but actually put many of us to death. Besides people like Wen Yiduo, they have killed millions of Chinese in the last three years with U.S. carbines, machine guns, mortars, bazookas, howitzers, tanks and bombs dropped from airplanes. This situation is now coming to an end. They have been defeated. It is we who are going to attack them, not they who are coming out to attack us. They will soon be finished. True the few problems left to us, such as blockade, unemployment, famine, inflation, and rising prices, are difficulties, but we have already begun to breathe more easily in these past three years. We have come triumphantly through the ordeal of the last three years, why can't we overcome these few difficulties of today? Why can't we live without the United States?

The truth was that China *could* live without the United States, and it was Mao's intention to do so. One reason was Red China's friendship with the Soviet Union. Beginning with the October Revolution, the Russians had helped the Chinese revolutionaries, including Chiang Kaishek. Russia sent advisers and guns and money to the infant Republic of China in the 1920s, when Guomindang and Communists were united in the Nationalist fold.

The moment the Chinese conquered China, the Soviet Union recognized the new state; in December 1949 Mao Zedong went to Moscow, making his first foreign visit. In February 1950 China signed the Treaty of Friendship and Alliance with the Soviet Union. The Russians promised to return the Manchuria railways and Port Arthur, but the Chinese had to give up their desire to have outer Mongolia returned to the Chinese fold. The parts of China snipped off years ago, along the Manchurian-Siberian border, were not returned either, and an incipient border dispute ran almost all the way along the common border.

But the Russians came in after 1949 to help China build. The architecture of the period shows it. Shanghai, for example, has several Soviet-style buildings, erected during the Soviet-Chinese honeymoon of the 1950s.

So 1950 was ushered in, with the Chinese both moving toward the Soviet Union and preparing to tighten the administrative strings in their own country.

28
The Terror

What is our general policy at present? It is to eliminate the Guomindang forces, the secret agents and the bandits, overthrow the landlord class, liberate Taiwan and Tibet and fight imperialism to the end. In order to isolate and attack our immediate enemies, we must convert those among the people who are dissatisfied with us into our supporters. Although this task is fraught with difficulties at present, we must overcome them by every possible means....

It is undesirable to hit out in all directions and cause nationwide tension. We must definitely not make too many enemies, we must make concessions and relax the tension a little in some quarters and concentrate our attack in one direction.

—Mao Zedong to the Third Plenary Session of the Seventh
Central Committee of the Chinese Communist party,
June 6, 1950

In the beginning the Communists' transformation of China was gradual. One of their first problems was the rehabilitation of the shattered Chinese economy. They accomplished this very nicely and quickly by taking over the banking system and by paying employees in kind rather than money. This brought the inflation rate down to about 15 percent.

Next came the need to extend land reform to the area south of the Yangtze. After the Guomindang troops were disarmed, work teams entered the villages in the south and organized the peasants. The Communist party cadres were joined by more young people. Their task was to observe the class structures of the villages and to become familiar with the local people. Then they organized the peasants into village associations. The associations chose delegates to county congresses, and these, in turn, sent delegates to congresses at the provincial level.

Special people's tribunals were established, and these had enormous power. They could declare a person a "class enemy," and once that was done there was no appeal from the sentence they imposed, even if it was

247

death. The president and half the judges were elected by the peasants' associations, and the tribunal was on circuit around the countryside.

In the villages the Communist cadres showed the way. They began with denunciations of the public enemies, the rapacious landlords and rich peasants. Usually, the crowd grew angry as the cadres detailed the crimes of a landlord. But if they did not, the cadres took the peasants through the landlord's house, showed them the rich silks and porcelains the landlord used, and raised their anger. By the time the trial was held, public indignation against the rich person was at a peak. Sometimes the landlord was simply humiliated and his lands and goods taken. Sometimes he was shot out of hand. Sometimes he was lynched.

Local newspapers had one great freedom: the freedom to report in full the feelings of the peasants and the villagers at these denunciation meetings and trials, including the yells of the mob. The Nationalists on Taiwan claimed that in this period the Communists killed 15 million people, which is an exaggeration, but all other sources agree that the figure had to be about 1 million people. Outside China little was known of this change or the terror that accompanied it. The press, domestic and foreign, was either closed down or under complete government control. Reporters were not moving around China investigating and writing about the events of the day. The sources of information were tightly controlled.

In fact, the terror had begun earlier in some areas. In the wake of the Red Army that crossed the Yangtze, *gongzuodui*, or operations squads of party cadres, began taking land reform and revolutionary terror into the villages. And it was there, at the village level, that the excesses, which Mao called "left deviation," began. The fact was that the party leadership was not in control at that time. The ardent young "reformers" were doing what they wanted to do, and the result was the first wave of terror. This was rectified in 1949 when Mao and the other leaders called for orderly reorganization.

Mao was seeking a policy. He wrote to various bureaus of the Central Committee throughout China asking for opinions on how to deal with rich peasants as opposed to landlords:

> If we leave the semi-feudal rich peasants untouched for the time being and deal with them a few years later, we will stand on stronger ground, that is to say, politically we will have more initiative. We have formed

a united front with the national bourgeoisie politically, economically and organizationally; and since the national bourgeoisie is closely tied up with the land problem, it seems better not to touch the semi-feudal rich peasants for the time being in order to set the minds of the bourgeoisie at rest.

That was Mao's opinion as of March 12, 1950. He wanted this problem solved so that the Communists could put the new land law into effect and make it work after the coming harvest.

The campaign to destroy the landlords began with the Land Reform Law of June 1950. Land owned by landlords, plus their farm implements, draft animals, surplus grains, and surplus houses were all confiscated everywhere across China, and the things were given to the people who worked the soil. Then came a reign of terror: In the next few months the peasant committees began liquidating landlords. Ultimately, they would liquidate about a million of them throughout the country over a period of months.

It began with a speech by Mao Zedong to the Central Committee on June 6:

> We have completed agrarian reform in the northern part of the country with a population of 160 million, and this must be affirmed as an immense achievement. We won the War of Liberation by relying mainly on these 160 million people. It was the victory of the agrarian reform that made possible our victory in overthrowing Chiang Kaishek. In the autumn we shall start agrarian reform in vast areas with a population of some 310 million in order to topple the entire landlord class. In the agrarian reform our enemies are as numerous as they are powerful. Against us are arrayed, first the imperialists, second the reactionaries in Taiwan and Tibet, third the remnant Guomindang forces, the secret agents and the bandits, fourth the landlord class and fifth the reactionary forces in the missionary schools established in China by the imperialists and in religious circles and those in the cultural and educational institutions taken over from the Guomindang. These are our enemies. We have to fight them one and all and accomplish the agrarian reform in an area much larger than before. This is a very acute struggle unprecedented in history.

At that meeting in June 1950, Liu Shaoqi and Mao both demanded that land reform be carried out slowly and carefully.

The peasant council, the *nongmin xiehui*, was the chief instrument of land reform. Nearly all the peasants belonged to the council in each village. Earlier, the wealthy peasants had been denied membership and their heads seemed always on the block. But the new policy from Beijing ended that. Even rich peasants were allowed to join, as long as they worked the land themselves rather than just owning it.

The fate of the well-to-do peasants depended on the community and on the relationship of those peasants with their community. Some well-to-do peasants survived and prospered. Others lost everything, including their lives.

By the autumn of 1950 the land reform had affected 100 million peasants, with landlords constituting 4 percent of the total, or 4 million people. This left another 364 million peasants and 10 million landlords to be dealt with.

The agrarian reform continued through 1952, with its excesses, until the bulk of landlord and rich-peasant lands had been redistributed. The major result was an enormous social change, with the destruction of the old rural gentry class.

At the same time the new government confiscated the holdings of the wealthy Guomindang officials. The Big Four families lost everything left to them in China, as did their sycophants. These people had taken over from the Japanese. On the eve of the Communist victory the capitalists of the Guomindang controlled two-thirds of China's industrial capacity, 90 percent of iron and steel production, 67 percent of electric power, 33 percent of coal production, and all the petroleum and metal industries. The conversion of these assets into state-owned enterprises laid the foundation for the socialization of industry in China.

Within two years of the Communist takeover most foreign businesses had closed down or been turned over to the Communist government. The foreign businessmen found it impossible to continue profitably under Chinese law. But by 1952 China was beginning to show industrial and economic recovery, and even agriculture was improving. This was not difficult, of course, since the structures of the civil war had just about wrecked China's economy.

By 1951 new problems had arisen in the new China. A great deal of zeal had been devoted to the movement to suppress counterrevolutionaries. Too much zeal in fact had been expressed, and this movement became a part of the terror. Party committees were instructed to examine most carefully the lists of persons to be arrested or executed, for in past months many people had been executed as counterrevolutionaries, only to have their erstwhile comrades later discover the charges were false. Mao found it necessary to lay down a ground rule:

> The number of counter revolutionaries to be killed must be kept within certain proportions. The principle to follow is that those who owe blood debts or are guilty of other extremely serious crimes and have to be executed to assuage the people's anger and those who have caused extremely serious harm to the national interest must be unhesitatingly sentenced to death and executed without delay. As for those whose crimes deserve capital punishment but who owe no blood debts and are not bitterly hated by the people or who have done serious but not extremely serious harm to the national interest, the policy to follow is to hand down the death sentence, grant a two year reprieve and subject them to forced labor to see how they behave. In addition it must be expressly stipulated that in cases where it is marginal to make an arrest, under no circumstance should there be an arrest, and that in cases where it is marginal to execute under no circumstances should there be an execution and to act otherwise would be a mistake.

Mao also took away from the village councils the power to sanction arrests and executions and put it back into the hands of the prefectural authorities. There had been too many abuses.

But the terror continued. A batch of bandits, landlords, and secret agents was executed in twenty-one counties in western Hunan late in 1950, and another batch was to be executed in 1951. Mao applauded the executions. "Absolutely necessary," he said.

In 1951 the terror broadened. Mao announced it:

> The struggle against corruption and waste is a major issue which concerns the whole party, and we have told you to give it your serious attention. We need to have a good clean up in the whole party, which will thoroughly uncover all cases of corruption whether major, medium, or minor, and aim the main blows at the most corrupt, while following the policy of educating and remolding the medium and minor embezzlers so that they will not relapse. Only thus can we check the grave danger of many party members being corroded by the bourgeoisie, put an end to a situation already foreseen at the Second Ple-

nary Session of the Seventh Central Committee and carry out the principle of combating corrosion then laid down.

The trouble was that power corrupts. Many of the party members, suddenly thrust into power, with access to funds and the good things of life, had begun to abuse their power. Naturally, the party leaders blamed this corruption on "the bourgeoisie." Still, it had to be rooted out, and it was rooted out with gusto and terror.

On December 8, 1951, Mao stated:

> In minor cases the guilty should be criticized and educated. In major ones the guilty should be dismissed from office, punished or sentenced to prison terms (to be reformed through labor) and the worst among them should be shot. The problem can only be solved in these ways.

The three evils of corruption, waste, and bureaucracy were not yet eradicated when five new evils appeared: bribery, tax evasion, theft of state property, cheating on government contracts, and stealing of economic information. A terrible example, cited in the press, was that of the Thursday Dinner Club, a secret organization of capitalists in Chongqing, which was found to be guilty of all five evils. The organization was exposed, its members were punished, and the organization was banned.

The crackdown came largely in the cities, where it was directed against businessmen and capitalists. For a time these people had been left alone, under Mao's dictum that the bourgeoisie must be encouraged rather than frightened. But in 1951 they saw signs of terror, and then the terror was upon them. In June 1952 Mao announced that with the overthrow of the landlord class and the bureaucrat capitalist class, it was now time for the party to take on the bourgeoisie. The time for tender treatment was over:

> The contradiction between the working class and the national bourgeoisie has become the principal contradiction in China; therefore the national bourgeoisie should no longer be defined as an intermediate class.

No, it was now to be a new enemy of the people.

In 1952 cadres settled in among the workmen in their factories and business firms; denouncing the employers, they started rumors and persuaded workers to rise up against the employers. Accusations were made and then repeated endlessly until the accused "confessed." Then they were punished. In big cities such as Shanghai, hundreds of people committed suicide under harassment. When people confessed, they were given heavy fines but they were not usually killed; Mao's instructions were to harry the bourgeoisie but not yet to eliminate them. The tribunals moved into the towns and cities to do the party's work. But by 1953 all this had ended, and the towns and cities were declared free from corruption. At least the corruption was now better hidden than it had been. And surprisingly, agricultural and industrial production had returned to what it had been in the years before the onset of the Sino-Japanese in 1937. Still, China had a long way to go.

Several areas of revolutionary importance remained to be addressed. In the spring of 1952 the Communists began the occupation* of Tibet. Mao and his comrades had never forgotten or forgiven the harassment by the Tibetan tribesmen during the Long March, and if these memories did not prompt the decision to take over Tibet, they certainly spurred it along.

Tibet presented a new problem. There were no Han people to speak of in the whole country, and the Tibetans were very much opposed to the Chinese. So the army was sent in, and it determinedly went about its business of investing the towns, the cities, and the villages. The soldiers brought their own food and tried hard to make as little negative impact on the Tibetans as possible. But the party was obdurate. Tibet would be a part of China and would be administered from Beijing.

The Chinese faced demonstrations and uprisings. The Dalai Lama refused to cooperate with their takeover and ultimately left the country, never to return.

The question of Taiwan, the last remaining territorial problem (aside from the problems with the Soviet Union, which went back many years), was the most troublesome of all. Had it not been for the presence of the United States fleet off Taiwan shores and the general promise of the Amer-

---

*Originally, I had written "invasion," using the word in the same sense as in the American "invasion" of Crenada. After all, China has always claimed suzerainty over Tibet. But many Chinese friends objected to this usage. The Beijing government is very sensitive to the word "invasion," since it has been critical of foreign invasions for so long. But when I asked my friends what term I should use, most of them were at a loss for an answer. One suggested "liberation." I chose another friend's suggestion: "occupation."

icans to protect Taiwan from attack, the Communists undoubtedly would have invaded the island. But they did not. Instead they continued a propaganda barrage against the United States and the Chiang Kaishek government.

Particularly galling was the continued retention of the Guomindang government's U.N. seat in the name of China. That retention made no sense whatsoever after 1949, and all the world knew it. But the United States insisted on maintaining the fiction that the Republic of China still existed. That insistence created an enormous reservoir of ill will for the United States among the smaller nations of the world, but Washington was obdurate. The veto power in the Security Council (which China also had) prevented any change when change was long overdue.

But until 1953 there was a limiting factor: a war primarily between Red China and the United States, a war that was totally unnecessary and was a reflection of a blind, misinformed American foreign policy and a breakdown in American military discipline. It was never called a war, but the U.N. Korea police action was a full-fledged war nonetheless.

29
The Korean War

The Chinese and Korean Comrades should unite as closely as brothers, go through thick and thin together, stick together in life and death and fight to the end to defeat their common enemy. The Chinese comrades must consider Korea's cause as their own, and the commanders and fighters must be instructed to cherish every hill, every river, every tree and every blade of grass in Korea and take not a single needle or a single thread from the Korean people, just the way we feel about our own country and treat our own people.

In order to support the Korean people's war of liberation and to resist the attacks of U.S. imperialism and its running dogs, thereby safeguarding the interests of the people of Korea, China, and all the other countries in the east, I herewith order the Chinese People's Volunteers to march speedily to Korea and join the Korean comrades in fighting the aggressors and winning a glorious victory.

While in Korea the Chinese People's Volunteers must show fraternal feelings and respect for the people, the People's Army, the Democratic Government, the Workers' Party and the other democratic parties of Korea as well as for Comrade Kim Il Sung, the leader of the Korean people, and strictly observe military and political disciplines. This is a most important political basis for ensuring the fulfillment of your military task.

You must fully anticipate various possible and inevitable difficulties and be prepared to overcome them with great enthusiasm, courage, care and stamina. At present the international and domestic situation as a whole is favorable to us, not to the aggressors. So long as you comrades are firm and brave and good at uniting with the people there and at fighting the aggressors, final victory will be ours.

—Mao Zedong, October 8, 1950

After the Communists had conquered the Chinese mainland and occupied Tibet, there was one more territorial task left to the People's Army: the conquest of Taiwan and the final elimination of the Guomindang.

255

Early in 1950 plans were made for the occupation of Taiwan just as soon as the task of clearing up Tibet was completed. Relations with the United States no longer existed, of course, with the departure of Ambassador Leighton Stuart from Nanjing amidst a chorus of Chinese boos and the failure of the United States to recognize the new government at Beijing as the legitimate government of China.

In America the China lobby was working vigorously to prevent American recognition of Beijing. Despite the millions of dollars of the Chinese people's stolen money that the Big Four families were spending, it is questionable how long the China lobby would have succeeded, save for two factors: (1) the inordinate paranoia of the American public about communism in general and the threat of the new Soviet imperialism that showed itself at the end of World War II, and (2) the emergence of a new threat to the American zone of influence in Asia, the North Korean attack on South Korea.

At the end of 1949 the Americans had begun to have some second thoughts about their support of the Chiang Kaishek regime. Too many facts had come to light showing that Chiang's regime had fallen through its own ineptitude and corruption. There were too many accounts of generals selling out or going over to the Communists, and not even the China lobby could successfully gainsay these. On January 5, 1950, President Harry S. Truman had seemed to indicate a new political climate regarding China when he said:

> The United States will not pursue a course which will lead to involvement in the civil conflict in China. The United States will not provide military aid or advice to the Chinese forces on Formosa [Taiwan].

That statement seemed to indicate a new American policy toward China, a policy which might lead swiftly to the normalization of American relations with the Beijing government. Further, a week later, Secretary of State Dean Acheson made a major policy address to the press corps in Washington, in which he declared that Korea was outside the perimeter of American defense interests.

Those statements gave aid and comfort to the Beijing government, although it was too busy with its affairs in Tibet and with organization of the Chinese government to take advantage of them. Remember that in the spring of 1950 Mao was holding back the ardent left wing from further excesses in the agrarian reform, and at the same time trying to root out a growing corruption in fighting "the three evils" and "the five evils." Indeed, earlier Mao had suggested that it would take the Communist party at least three years to organize the Chinese government to govern the whole of China. The almost immediate public acceptance of the Communist regime in China had come as an enormous surprise to the Communist party. Even the Communists had not known the full extent of the Chinese people's disillusionment with the Guomindang's failed revolution and their desire for peace.

The North Korean attack on South Korea was a surprise to China, but it did not seem very important at the moment. Even when the United States reversed its policy and decided on the spur of the moment to defend South Korea after all, China was not seriously concerned. Of far more concern was a concomitant announcement by President Harry Truman in which he reversed his statement of six months earlier and said that the U.S. Seventh Fleet would be sent to neutralize Taiwan, to make sure that the Nationalists did not attack the Chinese mainland and that the Beijing government did not attack the island.

Given the previous American behavior, this statement was regarded in Beijing as further proof of America's evil intentions toward China, but there was no immediate reaction from the leading officials of the Communist party. The reaction did come a few weeks later, however, when the Americans went further and began to build up the Guomindang army once more by sending equipment and advisers. That seemed to follow the pattern of the American activities during the latter 1940s, when America was helping the Guomindang in the civil war.

But while the Chinese reaction to this switch in American policy was anger, it was a controlled anger. The Communist party was too busy with its internal affairs to spend much time worrying about Taiwan just then. The Beijing government contented itself with rhetoric, announcing to the world that the United States had just begun an aggressive war against China. This line of reasoning spread throughout China and made what was to happen a few months later completely palatable to the public. Most Chinese were aware of the American support of the Guomindang during the war and afterward. Most of them accepted the theme of the Communists: America was the enemy of the Chinese people. It was not hard to accept that theme, given the long history of foreign imperialism in China. Even though American participation in that imperialism had been minimal, Americans had maintained troops on Chinese soil for many years and warships on China's rivers and in her ports. It was easy to forget America's role in the anti-Japanese war because the major fighting was outside China and therefore far from the ken of the Chinese people.

As long as the U.N. forces were on the defensive in South Korea, Beijing did not pay too much attention to the Korean war. But in the fall, when General Douglas MacArthur launched his brilliant counterattack on Inchon and the U.N. forces began moving rapidly northward, the Chinese took another look. MacArthur had earlier made an unauthorized trip to Taiwan to meet with Chiang Kaishek. It was no secret that President Truman was furious with MacArthur, and the truth was soon out: MacArthur wanted to use Chinese Nationalist troops to fight in Korea. He would have liked to have gone north into Manchuria and "unleashed" Chiang Kaishek and, once Korea was decommunized, to have moved right on into China to repeat the process there. MacArthur's views were well known in Beijing; what was not so well known was that most Americans did not sympathize with them and that most Americans, while still suffering from that blind spot about the nature of communism, had little sympathy for Chiang Kaishek.

When General MacArthur announced that he intended to send the U.N. forces all the way to the Yalu River and to wipe out the North Korean People's Republic, the Chinese knew that the next political step would be the reorganization of Korea under the Republic of Korea, a regime that was even further to the right politically than the Guomindang was in the 1930s. The government of Dr. Syngman Rhee was in no sense a revolutionary government. It was totally capitalistic in its economic nature and authoritarian politically.

For more than 1000 years before Japanese occupation of Korea that country had been governed by a kingdom and the king was always a vassal of China. It was traditional Chinese policy to insist that a friendly government exist on the shoulder of Manchuria. And so it was in 1950. The American government did not understand this fact; Washington's political myopia about Asia and the Pacific continued unchanged from the 1940s.

The Chinese issued some warnings. The United Nations must not send troops above the 38th parallel, the old dividing line of the two Koreas. The Chinese indicated that they had no intention of interfering in the Korean civil war. The South Koreans might go north to the Yalu, but no Americans or British or Turks or other troops. That would constitute an interference with China that would not be permitted.

Had U.S. relations with China been different, had not the Americans already shown their animosity toward the Communist government of China, then Beijing might not have become so nervous. But as it was, the Communists of China were extremely worried by the new turn of events. Zhou Enlai went to Moscow to confer with Stalin and other Soviet leaders, and returned with promises of support, short of actual war participation, from the Soviet Union. The Soviets were fully aware of the danger of a Soviet-American war developing out of Korea, and they did not want one.

Thereafter, in late September, Zhou issued several more warnings, in public statements and in talks to neutral diplomats. If the Americans moved above the 38th parallel, he warned, China would send troops into Korea and join in the war.

General MacArthur thought the Chinese were bluffing. Why he thought so was odd; anyone examining the record of Chinese Communist pronouncements over the years knew that they did not say things they did not mean. Yet General MacArthur insisted that the Chinese were bluffing, and he convinced Washington to share his opinion.

When the U.N. forces did cross the 38th parallel, the Chinese did not act immediately; they issued more warnings. Zhou called in the Indian ambassador to Beijing and sent through him another warning by way of New Delhi. More bluff, said MacArthur.

On October 4, 1950, Mao Zedong called a meeting of the Politburo of the Chinese Communist party's Central Committee. It was a hurried call, so hurried that aircraft were sent to get members summoned from far places.

One of those summoned was Marshal Peng Dehuai, military commander of the Northwest Military Region and secretary of the Northwest Bureau of the party. He was very busy just then, and his mind was on anything but foreign affairs. Three days earlier he had participated in the celebration of National Day, the holiday that marked the founding of the People's Republic of China just one year earlier.

Marshal Peng was in his office when Mao's emissary arrived and told him that his presence in Beijing was urgently required that very day. The aircraft was on the Xi'an field, waiting to take him.

Marshal Peng was dressed that day in an old, faded brown uniform, but he took no time to change it. He picked up a few toilet articles and without taking even a change of clothing went to the aircraft. With him went his secretary Lin Qing and his personal bodyguard Zhang Qiudun.

The airplane landed at Beijing's Xiwan airfield at 2:20 that afternoon, and a car was waiting to take him to Yiniantang Hall in Zhongnanhai. The Political Bureau was already in session, but when Marshal Peng entered the room, all the members stood up and shook hands with him. The atmosphere, he sensed, was serious and solemn.

Mao Zedong spoke: "Comrade Peng Dehuai. It's good you came! I'm afraid we had to rush you a little, but what could we do? It was U.S. Imperialism that had you come."

Everybody laughed.

Mao continued: "Our Comrade Zhou Enlai warned them beforehand, telling them not to cross the 38th parallel. We cannot ignore it, he said, if you cross that line. But they simply didn't believe us and have actually crossed it. What can we do about it? We can send troops to fight or let it go unchecked. We are going to ask you, Chief Peng, to be prepared to present your views."

Chairman Mao then lit a cigarette and settled down to listen to the speeches. Two basic views were presented to the meeting. First was the negative.

The Red Army had been fighting continuously for twenty-two years. China's financial condition had not yet recovered from the civil war. The country was not fully unified and the economy was only slowly being rectified and advanced. In two-thirds of the country land reform was just about to begin. Even though the Guomindang had been driven from China, still a million bandits and guerillas remained and had to be dealt with as soon as possible. And the army's equipment was paltry and ancient. If the troops went to war against the Americans, they would be facing the most modern weapons, perhaps even the atomic bomb. Entry into the Korean war could endanger all the strides forward that the Chinese Communist party had made. If the war were lost, it might even bring the Guomindang back to China.

That was the conservative view. The more aggressive members of the committee admitted all these facts, but...

Certainly China was not then prepared to go to war, but neither had the United States been prepared in June. The United States was still not prepared for a long land war in Asia. The Americans did not have enough troops in Korea, and their supply lines were overextended.

If the imperialists won the war, that would encourage reactionaries at home and abroad. The war might come to China. The new people's government would have difficulties with defense and with consolidation of affairs in China. And finally, if China did not go to the assistance of the North Koreans, the world would see China as a selfish nation that looked only after its own narrow interests.

The meeting went on and on, one person after another airing his views. Finally Mao called a halt.

"I think we have to fight U.S. Imperialism and eat, too," he observed. But that was not a definitive statement. They would continue the meeting on the next day. "Comrades, you all have reasons for what you have said, but other people want to conquer a nation. If we stand on the sidelines and watch, regardless of what you say, you will feel bad about it."

The meeting lasted two more days, until every member of the committee and all the observers, mostly military men, had had their say. On October 7 the committee voted to send troops, and Mao appointed Peng Dehuai as commander of what they called the Chinese People's Volunteer Army. Peng would also be political commissar.

There was really no question about the army's consisting of "volunteers." It was the Chinese army that was going to fight in Korea. The volunteer label was strictly propaganda.

It took some days to form the units that would be fighting inside Korea. Under Zhu De's instructions the units were organized and moved. Many of them were troops from Lin Biao's Manchurian command. In fact, Lin had been Mao Zedong's first choice to lead the expeditionary army into Korea, but Marshal Lin had pleaded ill health. He was suffering from insomnia, sleeping only an hour or two each night. He might also have been suffering from a political fever: The military adventure against the Americans had a high chance of failure. Peng knew it but was willing to stake his career on success. About Lin, it was not so certain; he was a far more political creature than Peng Dehuai.

━━━━━

Peng Dehuai led the Chinese Communist army across the Yalu River on October 18, 1950. The troops moved by foot and by cart. Their equipment was extremely primitive, but they had one great advantage, knowledge of guerilla warfare. The Chinese were deep inside Korea in strength for several days before the Americans even suspected their presence. Marshal Peng reached the Ragocho power station on the morning of October 19. He established his headquarters in a gully northwest of Bukjin on October 20. All this time the Chinese troops were moving quietly inside Korea, concealing the evidence of their presence as they advanced. Soldiers with pine branches swept the snow behind the troops to wipe out foot tracks and vehicle ruts. The troops traveled at night, holing up in the forest in the daytime. They did not build fires.

On the morning of October 21 the first Chinese troops, a division of the Fortieth Army, went into action against Republic of Korea troops. At first the Koreans thought they were fighting North Korean troops. But when some of the Chinese soldiers were captured, the Koreans discovered that their prisoners did not speak their language and wore a different sort of uniform. The South Koreans told the Americans, but the Americans did not believe them. It was three days more before the Americans would believe, and that was when the Chinese army struck Gen. Walton Walker's Eighth Army.

As Marshal Peng said: "Our troops displayed characteristic flexibility and mobility and wiped out some Syngman Rhee units in the Unsan area near Bukjin, forcing the pursuing U.S. and puppet troops to retreat."

This fight, which Marshal Peng called "the first campaign," ended in a Chinese victory on October 25.

Outside Korea, the political and military leaders waited, hoping that the Americans would see the light and retreat below the 38th parallel. But it did not happen. General MacArthur stubbornly insisted that the Yalu line would be reached and held. Well, it had been reached, but it was not being held.

The Chinese used the same tactics that had proved so successful against the Japanese and against the Guomindang troops in the civil war. They lured the enemy by an appearance of weakness, until the enemy moved forward deep into their territory. Then they closed around the enemy.

General MacArthur made a flight across Korea. Afterward, Peng heard that the general had told his troops to push to the Yalu and then they would be home in time for Christmas.

On November 20 the Chinese sent several minor units to engage the enemy. The Americans moved into the Unsan-Kusong area. After a day of fighting they were tired and ready to dig in. Just then other Chinese troops hit them from the rear; when they turned to fight, the main body of the Chinese swept down on them from the front.

The Chinese continued their tactics, and they claimed to have destroyed 6000 trucks and 1000 tanks. They would have liked to have captured these vehicles, but they got very few. The Americans burned their vehicles, or sent bombers over to drop napalm and destroy them.

The U.N. forces dropped back below the 38th parallel early in December, and the Chinese called that the end of the second campaign.

The third Chinese campaign involved the crossing of the 38th parallel and the capture of Seoul and Inchon. The war aim of the Chinese had changed since they entered the war. Originally, their intent was to preserve the 38th parallel division line and protect the North Korean government. But Beijing decided that the Americans could be driven out of Korea altogether and that the original intention of the North Koreans could be carried out. So Peng Dehuai's troops set out to do what the North Korean army, with its vastly superior equipment, had failed to do.

The Americans dropped back to the 37th parallel, and there they held. The superiority of their firepower and equipment began to tell. The Chinese were tired from their three campaigns. They had suffered 50 percent losses. Three Chinese armies were now inside Korea, most of them along the 38th parallel and just south of it.

In February 1951 Marshal Peng took a trip back to Beijing to confer with Chairman Mao on the strategy to be followed in Korea. The war had settled down to a slogging match, he told Mao. The chairman agreed that the war would probably last a long time, and he told Marshal Peng to stay in there and fight.

The war continued. The Chinese suffered seriously from supply problems. They also discovered that fighting the Americans was not like fighting the Guomindang troops or the Japanese. The Communist tactic of surrounding a large unit of troops and trying to wipe them out did not work with the Americans. They had too much artillery and too much power. If a surrounded unit could hold out through the night, the next day the unit would be rescued either by troop movement or by air. The Chinese surrounded and finished off a few battalions, but no larger unit succumbed.

The war then became static, with the Communists building complex defense positions along the 38th parallel. (They built 1250 kilometers of tunnels and 6240 kilometers of trenches.) Neither side could defeat the other, given the conditions that applied. The U.S. government had decided to conduct a limited war, keeping the confrontation within the borders of Korea and not bombing Manchurian or Chinese bases. This decision put a premium on the Chinese method of warfare, the employment of vast numbers of troops. The American technological warfare was vastly superior to that of the Chinese, but the Chinese troop strength was so enormous that they could take hundreds of thousands of casualties and still keep fighting.

In the end, the Chinese accused the Americans of using germ warfare, and Mao himself spoke of it, although no proof was offered.

Finally, in September 1953, a truce was signed. Mao Zedong claimed it as a Chinese victory, although it was not: at one point the Chinese had promised to drive the Americans out of Korea. No, the war ended in stalemate, and not even Mao's celebrated rhetoric could conceal that fact.

"Signing the armistice," said Marshal Peng, "I thought that the war had set a precedent for many years to come—something the people would rejoice at. It was a pity, however, that having established our battlefield deployment, we were unable to deal greater blows against the enemy."

It was a matter of a superior military force confronting a numerically superior force right down to the end. And in 1953, after months of haggling, the Chinese and the Americans were ready to quit. Both sides had learned much from the war, including a mutual respect for the fighting capabilities of the other.

Thirty-five years later, the Korean war was almost expunged from the Chinese memory. It was not a matter the government liked to discuss. No books about the war were available in bookstores, either new or used.* The only records were in the Beijing archives and in books tucked away in the libraries. It was as if the war had never happened.

---

*I spent several days in Beijing and Shanghai trying to find books on the Korean war during the spring of 1987, without any success. Previously, I had found a set of histories in Japanese, but in Chinese, nothing. All I found was one book in Chinese about the Red Army; it was Volume One of two volumes, and its story ended with the end of the civil war. Later that spring I also conducted a search in Moscow, with the same results. Still later I did secure a bibliography of some 100 books available in the Beijing public library. In 1987 the government of the People's Republic announced that its national archives for that period would be opened soon. When that happens, some of the major questions about Chinese military decisions can be answered. Until then, the best outside source is the library of the School of Oriental and African Studies of the University of London.

30

Let a Hundred Flowers Bloom

The party's general task for the transition period is basically to accomplish socialist industrialization and the socialist transformation of agriculture, handicrafts and capitalist industry and commerce in the course of three five-year plans.... Make a small step each year, and a big stride every five years, and with three big strides the work is almost done. "Basically accomplished" does not mean "completely accomplished." To say it is basically accomplished is a prudent way of speaking; it is always better to be prudent in everything we do.

At this stage China's agricultural economy is by and large individual in nature and it needs step-by-step socialist transformation. The principle of voluntary participation must be adhered to in promoting the mutual-aid land co-operative movement in agriculture. Failure to promote it will lead to the capitalist road and that would be a right deviation.

—Mao Zedong to the New Democratic Youth League of China,
June 30, 1953

How do counterrevolutionaries employ their double-dealing tactics? How do they succeed in deceiving us by their false appearances, while furtively doing the things we least expect? All this is a blank to thousands upon thousands of well-intentioned people. On this account many counterrevolutionaries have wormed their way into our ranks.

—Mao Zedong, June 15, 1955

The first Five-Year Plan was begun in 1953. Before any transformation could be accomplished, the Chinese had to learn what assets they had, and the fact was that in 1953 nobody knew. Since the days of the Qing empire China had been in such a constant state of ferment that the industrial revolution had never arrived. So the Communist government set out to remedy the situation.

Many things were learned about iron ore reserves, coal, even uranium. Oil fields were discovered in many areas, from Tibet to Manchuria, from Guangdong to Sichuan. But the most important discovery made by the Chinese, though not fully appreciated at the time, was that the population, which the world had been estimating at about 400 million people, was actually nearly 600 million. The projection indicated that by 1980 the population would be 1 billion! A movement began to limit the population, but it was not very successful. Mao Zedong had a peasant mentality, and peasants wanted sons to work the land. The population-control program did not get very far, nor would it in Mao's lifetime.

In the reorganization of the government undertaken at this time, Zhou Enlai became premier and Mao Zedong became chairman of the People's Republic and head of state.

The concept of "mutual-aid" teams was promoted. Neighbors pooled their labor and equipment, and by the end of 1952 there were 6 million such teams, involving 35 million households. At the same time the government was promoting agricultural cooperatives, but the peasants resisted them. The result was that while industrialization of China proceeded rapidly, under state ownership of all major industries, agriculture lagged behind. In 1955 Mao Zedong made a special point of this and demanded that in the next three years at least half the rural population be organized in cooperatives. Actually, by 1957 90 percent of the peasants were organized in cooperatives. Private ownership was eliminated. Only tiny plots of land were kept by individuals to grow vegetables; all else was thrown into the common pot.

The peasants did not like it. At first some slaughtered their animals rather than hand them over to the cooperative. Yet even when the cooperatives were going full blast, agricultural production did not rise as it should have. The resentment of the people grew, but it was kept under wraps, because nearly everyone remembered the terror of the years 1947–1952.

One vexing problem for the party was how to produce educated people capable of leading the country forward in various fields, without upsetting the Communist applecart. The answer in the 1950s was the establishment of a Soviet-style educational system. The liberal arts colleges and universities, an inheritance from the Christian missionary influence by and large, were mostly disbanded. Twenty polytechnic colleges were established, as were twenty-six engineering schools. Of 200 colleges and universities, only 13 were comprehensive universities with schools of art and science. China turned squarely toward the Soviet Union; Russian became the second language, replacing English.

Given the world political situation of the time, it probably would have happened that way anyhow. The Soviet Union had showed itself quick to recognize Communist China. The Americans dillied and dallied, and finally failed to recognize the new China. Then came the Korean war involvement, and no relations between the two countries could possibly be established. The United States signed a treaty of alliance with Chiang Kaishek in 1954, and that put a seal on the bad relationship, making sure that it would last for nearly twenty years longer. There were many in America, like Gen. Omar Bradley, who lamented the blind American policy.*

The spring of 1955 saw trouble developing within the Communist party. Two members of the Central Committee, Gao Gang and Rao Shushi, had disagreed with some fundamental economic policies of the party and had worked against those policies. Rao was in a particularly sensitive position as director of the organizational department of the party. Among other things, he and Gao distributed a list of prospective members of the Political Bureau, with an eye to securing appointment of their followers. When Mao Zedong recognized this threat to his leadership, he acted swiftly and scotched the rebellion. Half a dozen Political Bureau members were ejected.

A campaign of terror was again instituted. This time, however, it was a different sort of terror, and the campaign was carried on against party members who did not conform immediately and totally to the convolutions in the party lines. One victim was Yue Daiyun, a teacher of Chinese literature at Beijing University. During this campaign Yue took leave from her tasks to go home to Guizhou to visit her family. When she came back to Beijing, she stepped into a maelstrom. She was reprimanded for taking leave, called a counterrevolutionary and suspended from her teaching post, and fired as party branch secretary on the campus.

---

*Speaking of the Korean war, Bradley called it "the wrong war, at the wrong place, at the wrong time, with the wrong enemy" and observed that Red China had shown absolutely no inclination to dominate the world.

The terrorization of the intellectuals continued. Beijing University, the showplace, was the center of the campaign. After the civil war, Beida, as the university was called locally, had moved to the campus of the old Yanqing University. There, many intellectuals learned how to manage themselves. "The way to get ahead," said Huang Chaoqun, one of the leaders of the Beida campus, "was to curse yourself, to claim that you were dirty, polluted, to attack other people—your family, parents, the foreigners, to say you were polluted by them. Then you could be considered reeducated."

But there were mumbles of discontent from the intellectuals. Mao observed the Hungarian uprising against the Communists, and he thought very hard about what happened when the party lost touch with the people.

Zhou Enlai warned that the party was not appealing to intellectuals. Only about 40 percent of the intellectuals really supported the party and its actions. Another 40 percent were neutral. The other 20 percent were more or less opposed to the party and socialism.

Mao decided to experiment with public opinion and find out how the party stood in China. "Let a hundred flowers bloom together, let the hundred schools of thought contend," he observed. And the party let it be known that it welcomed criticism.

This remark was taken to be the signal of a new wave of freedom. Mao made the statement in May 1956. By September Yue had been restored to her teaching post—a tacit admission that the charges against her had been trumpery. She was also restored to her post as party branch secretary.

Despite the unpleasant relationship with the United States and the nagging problem of Taiwan which was connected with it, by the mid-1950s Mao Zedong was fairly well satisfied with the progress of the revolution in building a socialist society in China. That was why he had decided to loosen the straps on the Chinese people, not a little but a lot.

On February 27, 1957, Mao Zedong was feeling particularly euphoric about the progress of the past ten years. Speaking to a government group, Mao said:

> Never before has our country been as united as it is today. The victories of the bourgeois-democratic revolution and of the socialist revolution and our achievements in socialist construction have rapidly changed the face of the old China. A still brighter future lies ahead for our motherland. The days of national disunity and chaos which the people de-

tested are gone, never to return. Led by the working class and the Communist Party, our 600 million people, united as one, are engaged in the great task of building socialism.

Mao then repeated the "hundred flowers" theme, and elaborated on it:

> Letting a hundred flowers blossom and a hundred schools of thought contend is the policy for promoting progress in the arts and sciences and a flourishing socialist culture in our land. Different forms and styles in art should develop freely and different schools in science should contend freely. We think that it is harmful to the growth of art and science if administrative measures are used to impose one particular style of art or school of thought and to ban another.

Many times in the past he had said, "Often correct and good things were first regarded not as fragrant flowers but as poisonous weeds," and he cited the Darwinian and Copernican theories as cases in point.

———

At first the criticism was light and tentative. But by May 1957 it became a torrent. The complaints?

- The domineering by the party people on campus
- Too much time spent on political study
- Too many Communist party members without talent in education*
- Too much reliance on the Soviet Union and too slavish a copying of the Soviet educational system
- The shortage of consumer goods and the failure of the Communist party to bring a better life
- Accusations that the Communist party and its officials (and this included Chairman Mao) had forgotten the people and that the people were worse off than they had been under the Japanese

So, after only six weeks, Mao's open invitation brought something he least expected, a real storm of furious criticism from the intellectual community. For years the university people had been chafing under tight party control and favoritism and cronyism within the party. Now they suddenly

———

*At Shenyang college it was said that the head of the Russian language department did not speak a word of Russian.

discovered that the chairman had asked for criticism. They believed he was sincere. Maybe he did too, until the results came in.

Soon a storm of criticism was raging against the party. Intellectuals, who had been fretting at the restrictions on their activity and thought, spoke their minds. One such was Yue Daiyun.

The teachers and students in the Chinese literature department of Beijing University held frequent meetings, and many spoke their minds about what was wrong with party management. As secretary of the university branch of the party, Yue Daiyun wrote all these things down as a matter of course, anticipating that such honest criticism would help the party better itself.

In April 1957 a rectification campaign was begun to eliminate "the triple evils." Those evils, said the party leaders, were "subjectivism, sectarianism, and bureaucratism." Students and professors wrote long and complicated messages, some of which appeared as signed wall posters.. They dealt with such matters as democracy in a socialist system and the importance of rooting out official privilege in a society that is based on equality.

One of Yue's students wrote a stirring poem, "Now Is the Time," which dealt with the need for speaking out against ills within the party. Everyone should speak his mind, said the student, to examine deficiencies so that they could be rectified. The party people, said this student, could then practice self-criticism, and the system would be made better.

But by 1957 the high party members, including Mao, considered themselves to be above criticism, and that is what nettled. As the storm of protest grew, so did the official reaction.

Yue and six other young teachers at Beijing University decided to establish a new literary magazine, an alternative to the Beida *Journal*, a highly academic magazine. They wanted a forum in which young intellectuals could explore contemporary problems.

"Our purpose," said Yue, "was to follow Chairman Mao's call and encourage everyone to develop his own talents for the building of a New China."

At 26, she was the "old lady" of this group of young intellectuals. Her political responsibilities as secretary of the campus branch of the party were such that she could not take on the job of editing the new magazine. So she suggested that Lao Lu, another young teacher, take charge of *Contemporary Heroes*. He agreed.

So the young teachers planned. On May 16 they held a meeting, talking about all the new perspectives they would add to Chinese literary theory. But then, quite suddenly, several members of the group sensed, through other contacts, a change in the party line. Many of the young radicals in the student movement had become strident and quite negative in their criticisms of the party leadership.

Hu Feng was a Marxist literary critic and follower of Lu Xun, the party's most beloved essayist, who had fallen out of favor with Mao Zedong. Mao had personally denounced Hu Feng in 1954 and had led a campaign vilifying the critic. Now some of Hu's students called for a reversal of the verdict.

Other students criticized the 1955 "anti-counterrevolutionary" campaign as excessive. Still other students attacked Chairman Mao personally, charging that he compared himself to the Pope in Rome and that he tried to take personal credit for the success of the Chinese revolution.

This last complaint possibly triggered the reaction. Anyhow, the *Contemporary Heroes* group sensed the wind of change blowing, and they suspended all activity on their new magazine.

Their premonition was borne out completely on June 8. That day an editorial in *Ren Min Ri Bao ("People's Daily")*, the official Communist party newspaper, announced that a serious situation had arisen in China: Counterrevolutionary movements threatened the state and the party. What upset the party was the violence and widespread criticism in "big-character wall posters" that were appearing all around the country.

On that day, too, Mao Zedong reversed himself. He drafted an inner-party directive for the Central Committee:

> The reactionary elements [for that, read dissident students] have been unbridled in their attacks. . . . We needn't worry, for the reactionary elements number no more than a few percent and the most frantic only one percent. Don't be scared stiff just because the sky appears overcast for the time being. . . . Call meetings of the principal cadres and veteran workers in the factories and explain to them that *some bad capitalists, bad intellectuals and reactionary elements in society are mounting wild attacks against the working class and the Communist Party in an attempt to overthrow the state power led by the working class, and that they should make sure not to be taken in by these persons.**
> Stop anyone trying to incite the people. Mobilize the masses to tear down reactionary posters on street walls. . . .

---

*Italics added. This part of the long paper is the key to the shift in policy.

Organize forums at colleges and universities to let the professors speak their minds about the Party, and as far as possible try to get the Rightists to spew out all their venom, which will be published in the newspapers. Let the professors make speeches and let the students respond freely. Better let the reactionary professors, lecturers, associates, and students spew out their venom and speak without any inhibitions. They are the best teachers. When the opportune moment arrives, lose no time in organizing separate meetings of Party and League members to sort out the criticisms; accept those criticisms that are constructive and correct mistakes and shortcomings, but refute those criticisms which are destructive. At the same time organize some non-Party people to make speeches and state the correct views. Then have a responsible Party cadre who enjoys prestige make a summing-up speech that is both analytical and convincing to effect a complete change in the atmosphere. If all goes well a month or so will see the whole process through and we can then switch to the inner-Party rectification, which will proceed like "a gentle breeze and a mild rain."

At a secret meeting of the Beijing University branch of the party this Central Committee report was read.

Its title, "Muster Our Forces to Repulse the Rightists' Wild Attacks," was more inflammatory and frightening than the document itself. Everyone knew that the report came from Mao himself, and what it made clear was that the storm of criticism had frightened him, particularly when some intellectuals called for the abandonment of Marxism altogether. The reaction was swift.

Within three weeks, two important publications, Wen Hui Pao and Kuangming Daily, announced major meetings for staff self-criticism. Kuangming Daily's editor, Chu Anping, was severely criticized, and the newspaper's policy was changed. Wen Hui Pao, Mao Zedong charged, was showing the right-wing orientation of the Democratic League. Mao devoted a long editorial to the matter in Ren Min Ri Bao and demanded "more adequate" self-criticism. Yes, said the chairman, "the rightists' wild attacks" must be repulsed.

A week later, on July 9, Mao spoke to a meeting of cadres in Shanghai and again attacked the "rightists." What he meant was becoming clear: Wall posters continued to appear at Beijing University and elsewhere, but they were no longer critical of the party; rather, they criticized the critics of the party as counterrevolutionaries. Critics who had attacked the official privileges of high party members were now told that they were undermining the party. Those who called for more democracy in the country were told that they were trying to overthrow the state. Those who had attacked the elite in the party were accused of really attacking Chairman Mao.

All these were counterrevolutionary acts and were not to be tolerated.

So those students who had spoken out for change were suddenly isolated, but their words were remembered—they had signed the big-character posters. The other group, the toadies who had waited to see which way the wind would blow, came forth to trumpet the new party line and to attack the critics of the state and party who had been encouraged by Chairman Mao's "hundred flowers" statements.

The Beijing University party branch held several meetings. The leaders were told to separate the critics of the party from the majority and to make it clear that these people threatened the party. Each department was told to select several people to be condemned as "bourgeois rightists." Yue Daiyun was selected to serve on a four-person committee to provide evidence against the "rightists" whose selection would be approved by the Beijing University party committee.

So, six weeks after Mao's latest "hundred flowers" statement, the philosophy was revoked. Tight discipline was again clamped down on intellectual activity.

One dissident against this policy was Deng Xiaoping, general secretary of the Communist party, but as a good follower, he bowed to Mao's indignation and accepted the new line. The antirightist campaign of June 1957 spread very quickly, as Mao warmed to his task.

By November Yue's committee at Beijing University had identified five people to be attacked as rightists. One was Lao Yang, who had been a former secretary to the warlord Feng Yuxiang and then worked at a publishing house before coming to the university. He had spoken out very positively against certain practices of the party, claiming, among other charges, that the party's agricultural policy often made the situation of the peasants worse.

Yue had taken notes of Lao Yang's speeches, with an eye to rectifying party mistakes. But in the new campaign the speeches were read in a different way, and now Lao Yang was to be treated as an enemy of the people and his own words used to establish his guilt.

The second accused was Lao Xie, a young teacher from a peasant family; he was vice secretary of the branch committee. This young zealot had read all the posters and had decided that there was so much truth in them that there must be something fundamentally wrong with the party to have made so many errors. Now this statement was to be used to prove that he wanted to overthrow socialism.

The third victim was a teaching assistant who endorsed Nikita Khrushchev's criticism of Josef Stalin and came out against the blind worship of any leader. The committee saw that he had really been criticizing Chairman Mao.

The fourth suspect was Lao Pan, a member of Yue's magazine organization. He was the son of a landlord, and he had been denied permission to continue his studies in the Soviet Union, so he had burst out with a fatal remark: Every person's destiny was controlled by the file in the university central office that showed his background and "political reliability." Beyond peradventure this was a counterrevolutionary remark, accusing the party of favoritism.

The fifth victim of the new purge was a 23-year-old graduate of the university named Lao Shi. He had heard from a friend about a split over policy between Mao Zedong and Liu Shaoqi, a member of the Politburo Standing Committee. He had spoken of this split to others and was now accused of spreading rumors in an effort to divide the Central Committee of the Communist party and thus threaten socialism.

So all five were ruined, and so also was Yue, who was criticized as a rightist because she had the temerity to try to start a new magazine. She was kicked out of the Communist party and sentenced to hard labor in the countryside.

These were just a handful of the millions of people affected by the latest convolution in the party line. Mao Zedong had made a grievous error; believing that he was as popular as his sycophants told him, he had opened the doors to criticism. The criticism from the intellectuals had come, and it was stinging and often personal and he could not bear it. He turned against China's intellectuals and thereafter he had no use for them. They were to feel the lash time and again in the remaining years of Mao Zedong's life and power.

31

The Great Leap Forward

My views on the domestic situation then were as follows:

I held that an excellent situation prevailed in our country. Led by the Party and guided by the General Line, the Chinese people launched a vigorous Great Leap Forward movement in 1958, at which time people's communes came into existence across the country. The Great Leap Forward movements had unfolded on an extensive scale, and the formation of the people's communes conformed to the interests of the people and their wishes to get rid of quickly the state of being "poor and blank" (economically and culturally backward). This excellent situation created favorable conditions for us to carry out the General Line, consolidate the people's communes, and carry on the Great Leap Forward movement.

—Marshal Peng Dehuai, in his autobiography

"We want flowers, not weeds, in the socialist garden," said the members of the Central Committee, in justifying the purge of intellectuals after the "hundred flowers" honeymoon. They did not seem to realize that they were twisting the words with which Chairman Mao had ushered in the period of freedom that he later repressed. So the critics who had not been ruined now learned to keep their mouths shut. Mao added:

"Right words and actions help to consolidate, not undermine or weaken, the people's democratic dictatorship and then to strengthen, not to cast off or weaken, the leadership of the Communist Party."

The left wing of the Communist party was back in power. As if to get the unpleasant memories of the past few months out of the collective mind, the party began to concentrate on a second Five-Year Plan. Liu Shaoqi predicted that this plan would create a spectacular development in industry. "Faster and better" was the slogan.

The first step in the Great Leap Forward was to put everyone to work. Mao Zedong suggested that the peasants had an enormous amount of free time on their hands—for 100 days each year they were not working in the fields. Why not turn this unproductive time into service for the state?

So the peasants were dragooned to work in the off-season after the 1957 harvest. Using the *bao-jia* organizational structure, millions of men and women were put to work that winter, digging irrigation ditches and canals, preparing railroad rights of way, and laying track. The "backyard furnace" was invented, and 600,000 small steel establishments were set up. The object was to overtake Britain in steel production, and Mao and his advisers predicted that this would be done in ten years.

Of course, when the people left their lands to work on these industrial projects, the lands suffered. There was not enough chemical fertilizer to go around, and the movement of the people cut down on the natural fertilizers that they had always used. At Mao's behest the cooperative farm organizations began to merge into communes. Soon dozens, scores, and hundreds of co-ops were communalized. Cheering the peasants on, Mao made a tour of north China to advocate that they move further and faster.

The communes became all-embracing. They included mess halls, daycare centers, hospitals. In some communes men and women were moved into separate dormitories to further increase their productivity by cutting down on social activity. In Beijing the social planners cheered. It was no great trick, they realized, to mold the peasantry any way they saw fit. A little sacrifice now, they could see with their projections, would produce exponential results. They had discovered the key to the nation's industrial success—human labor!

By the end of the growing season in 1958, 90 percent of the peasantry of China had been organized into some 26,000 communes. The average commune consisted of 5000 households, operating 10,000 acres of land. And what could not be done with this organized labor force?

The leadership voted against the common sparrow, that prodigious eater of grain. An antisparrow campaign was organized, and farmers from Lanzhou to Tianjin, from Yanan to Guangzhou, coordinated their efforts, organizing hunts, beating gongs, and chanting, to frighten the birds and keep them flying until they collapsed from exhaustion. The same sort of campaign was begun against the rat and the common housefly; it was one of the boasts of the party that the housefly would be eliminated completely in China—unlike anywhere else in the world—within a few months.

Since the weather was so good and the harvest so bountiful in the fall of 1958, nobody worried. Everything was going beautifully. Agricultural production next year would double, said the party. So would iron and steel production. China was on its way!

*   *   *

A triumphal meeting began at Zhengzhou on November 2, 1958; it lasted more than a week. Chairman Mao discussed the people's communes and gave advice on how to improve and speed their development. He made a speech against "thc Communist wind," which was a plan for egalitarianism based not on the principle "to each according to his need, from each according to his ability" but on absolute equality in the distribution of goods to every person, including the uncompensated seizure of property from low-level communes by higher-level communes and by government agencies.

A second meeting was held at Zhengzhou between February 27 and March 5, 1959. It set down rules for further speeding the development of communes.

But then came the reaction. Peasants began to drop from overwork or to slack off. The party issued a dictum that no one should be forced to work more than twelve hours a day.

Another meeting took place at Wuchang on November 21, 1958. Mao brought together the Central Committee leaders, leaders of ministries, and first secretaries of party committees to talk about the Great Leap Forward and industrial and agricultural production. One of the people in attendance was Peng Dehuai, one of the ten marshals of the Red Army and at that time minister of defense.

Peng participated in the discussions of the Northeast group of leaders. While talking of grain and cotton production figures for 1958, some of the commune officials said the grain output was more than 500 million tons and the cotton output was 3.5 million tons. Yes, said the commune leaders, they had solved the problems of agriculture, and China could produce as much grain as was wanted.

Marshal Peng Dehuai stood up and said the figures were exaggerated. Army records indicated that the country had not produced that much grain.

"Comrade," said one of the leaders, "you seem to have doubts about everything. What can we say to you?"

"If the figure released is less than the actual harvest," said Peng, "it will be easy for us to add to it later. But if it exceeds the actual harvest, we will get into a fix."

Chairman Mao listened. He suggested that they announce a harvest of 375 million tons. Marshal Peng disagreed; he thought the figure would be much lower, but he kept quiet about that.

Peng then went traveling to Wuxi and Shaoshan and to Pingjiang county. He visited communes, and he came away with the distinct impression that the harvests had been exaggerated. At Pingjiang he learned that the commune leaders had falsified their figures, giving out the high 1957 harvest figure as the 1958 harvest, and the low 1958 harvest figure as the 1957 harvest. He was horrified at this doctoring of statistics, which was easy enough to do because Chairman Mao, in his detestation of anything that smacked of central control, had disbanded the central Statistical Bureau.

Back in Zhuzhou, Marshal Peng worried about the government's proposal to purchase from the communes 60 million tons of grain that year for the army and other uses. That was too much and could not be supplied without wrecking the life of the communes, he said. When the shortages in the communes were discovered, the grain would have to be returned. He said the government ought to buy only 45 million tons in China. Others told him to send a message to the Central Committee, which he did, signing his name.

In April 1959 another meeting was convened at Shanghai. Marshal Peng was there, but he was busy with the uprising in Tibet and was so concerned about moving troops west that he did not get into the agricultural discussions.

That spring Peng toured eastern Europe. When he returned to China in June he found that the agricultural problem had grown more serious, and Gansu Province was once again facing famine. There was grain available elsewhere, but transport was in short supply because of the Tibetan problem and the number of troops employed there.

Another meeting was called in Lushan on July 1. Chairman Mao spoke the next day and reported that although the country had problems, the future appeared to be very bright. But in the meetings of the subcommittees, Peng did not get that impression. One day he met with Zhou Xiaozhou, first secretary of the Hunan Province party committee, who had a confession to make.

"The grain figures for last year were cooked up," he said.

"Why?" asked Marshal Peng.

"It was a result of pressure. When the figures of different areas were made available, the higher authorities said they were not final. The figures were sent up a second time, and they said again 'not final.' As this process was repeated several times, cadres at lower levels came to know that what was wanted was exaggerated figures."

Peng expressed his shock.

"Now people are having their meals in communal canteens," Zhou said. "So large cauldrons and big ranges are used, resulting in a waste of both firewood and labor power. If people cook in their own kitchens, meals can be prepared by women and the weak. But now only the able-bodied can cook. Because of the communal canteens hot water cannot be conveniently obtained by individual households. People have objections to the communal canteens."

Peng told Zhou to inform Mao Zedong. The marshal said he had also had complaints from people in the army and he had informed Mao of these.

"Can it reach the chairman?" asked Zhou.

"Yes, it can," said Peng. He had great faith in Chairman Mao, with whom he had worked for more than thirty years.

Peng attended many meetings at Lushan, and he gained the definite impression that agricultural affairs were not going well. On July 14 he wrote a letter to Chairman Mao to that effect, criticizing the leftish policies of those in charge of agriculture who were exaggerating production claims.

On July 17 Peng received a copy of his letter. It had been meant for Mao's personal attention only, but Mao had handed it over to be printed and distributed by the General Office of the party's Central Committee. Mao had appended in big characters the words: "Comrade Peng Dehuai's Statement of Opinions."

So Peng knew that he had displeased the chairman and that there was going to be the devil to pay.

On July 18 Peng asked for permission to take back the letter, saying it had not been a clear enough statement of his opinions. He did not criticize Chairman Mao for having used the letter for the wrong purpose. But it was too late. Mao was angry; he was looking for a scapegoat for the troubles he was encountering. Peng was going to be that goat.

On July 23 Chairman Mao spoke to a meeting and criticized Peng's letter as "Right opportunist." That was the kiss of death; it put Marshal Peng in the same boat with all those intellectuals who had infuriated Mao by daring to question his actions. Not only was Peng right wing, but he was showing warlordism and great-nation chauvinism.

Friends suggested that day that Peng make a speech in his defense. But Peng did not want to perpetuate controversy, so he refused. On that same day, at the room of Huang Kecheng, the deputy war minister, Peng encountered Zhou Xiaozhou for just a moment.

Party officials called on Peng the next day and asked him if he had spoken to anyone before writing his letter. He mentioned Zhou Xiaozhou.

He went back to the Lushan meeting, where he was asked to confess to rightist tendencies. He said he did not have any.

In August Peng was hailed before a meeting of the Military Commission of the party and accused of being dishonest, insincere, and deceitful and of organizing a "military club," which was trying to take control of the party and the country. So great was Chairman Mao's paranoia!

The matter came to a head on August 16. The Eighth Plenary Session of the Eighth Central Committee passed the "Resolution on the Mistake of the Anti-Party Clique Headed by Comrade Peng Dehuai." Peng was disgraced; he was dismissed from his post as minister of war and from the Central Committee. For the next six years he was unemployed, but he refused to criticize Mao or the party, to commit suicide, or to escape abroad. He was another example of the revolution devouring its children.

———

In the fall of 1959 Premier Zhou Enlai made a startling confession: The Great Leap Forward had been a pipedream. A monstrous fake. As Marshal Peng had indicated, the leaders of the communes, pressed so enthusiastically for results by Chairman Mao, had falsified their figures to show enormous progress. Grain production for 1959 was not 375 million tons, as the party had bragged; it was 250 million tons. The party had said 11 million tons of steel had been produced in the backyard furnaces. Now Zhou said it was only 8 million tons, and for each ton some group of peasants was taking time from the fields to work on the steel.

So the "norm" for 1960 was reduced from 525 million tons of grain to 275 million tons. All other quotas were similarly reduced.

Then nature took a hand. Weather in the summer of 1960 was bad. The party hedged on figures, but it is doubtful whether the country reached even the 1959 production rate. No one could tell after the disbanding of the central Statistical Bureau.

The next year was still worse, and China bought 10 million tons of wheat abroad. The third year was the worst yet, with drought and famine, and more than 20 million people died of malnutrition.

The backyard furnaces continued to turn out steel, but the steel was of such poor quality that most of it had to be junked.

In 1960 Premier Zhou took measures to try to stop the rot.

*   *   *

The political consequences of Mao Zedong's precipitate attack on Peng Dehuai were even more serious. Until that time, the top leaders of the Communist party Politburo had held many discussions and all had spoken frankly. It was understood that this top leadership would act in concert once a decision was made; no questions would be asked. Until the decision was made, however, plenty of questions were in order. But now, in attacking and destroying Peng Dehuai, one of the most honored and loyal of the party leadership, Mao had destroyed the party's unity. The members of the Politburo were running scared; they did not dare question Mao's slightest decision or whim. So the chairman moved from error to error.

Soon enough it became apparent that whatever Mao's abilities as an organizer and inspirational leader were—and he was admittedly a genius— as an administrator he had no talent. He had also failed to heed his own advice, "learn from facts," and had rejected facts supplied by Marshal Peng in favor of falsehoods supplied by his theorists. The enormously talented administrator and diplomat Zhou Enlai had patiently picked up the pieces for years and protected Mao. Now the chairman had gone too far, and his actions threatened to destroy the party altogether. The Chinese Communist party fell into factionalism, and Mao Zedong in the 1960s cloaked himself in the mantle of omniscience and omnipotence.

The leaders of government retreated to statistical analysis to protect themselves. Liu Shaoqi and Deng Xiaoping established programs of planned development. They called on the party to make reforms that would support individual responsibility. Mao stubbornly fought for "class struggle," once again seeking a goat for the party's failures in some minor element within the country. It had worked before because the landlords, the bourgeoisie, and the intellectuals were easy targets. Now that they had all been used, it was becoming harder to find targets for the class struggle.

So began the "two-line struggle" between the modernists in the party, symbolized by Deng Xiaoping, and the old revolutionists who depended on the class struggle and the peasant mobilization for success. The struggle would continue for many years; at the approach of the 1990s it is not yet resolved, as the Maoists fight to hold their ground.

The 1960s saw a basic change in China: the reduction of the unified party leadership into factions. Mao Zedong led the most powerful faction, but he was no longer able to pull the country together for a massive positive effort. The intellectuals had stopped trusting him, as had many of the party leaders. He stepped down as chief of state and was succeeded by Liu Shaoqi.

Mao then began a campaign to retrieve his position in the party and once again to become undisputed leader. He never succeeded, although he retained his position until the end. But from this point on, Mao Zedong was to create enormous confusion and retrogression for the Chinese people and to come very close to destroying the revolution altogether.

32

Quarrels

In the Soviet Union, those who once extolled Stalin to the skies have now in one swoop consigned him to purgatory. Here in China some people are following their example. It is the opinion of the Central Committee that Stalin's mistakes amounted to only 30 percent of the whole and his achievements to 70 percent, and that all things considered, Stalin was nonetheless a great Marxist.

We wrote "On the Historical Experience of the Dictatorship of the Proletariat" on the basis of this evaluation. This assessment of 30 percent for mistakes and 70 percent for achievement is just about right. Stalin did a number of wrong things in connection with China. The "left" adventurism pursued by Wang Ming in the latter part of the Second Revolutionary Civil War Period and his right opportunism in the early days of the War of Resistance Against Japan can both be traced to Stalin. At the time of the War of Liberation, Stalin first enjoined us not to press on with the revolution, maintaining that if civil war flared up, the Chinese nation would run the risk of destroying itself. Then when fighting did flare up he took us half seriously, half skeptically. When we won the war, Stalin suspected that ours was a victory of the Tito type and in 1949 and 1950 the pressure on us was very strong indeed. Even so we maintain the estimate of 30 percent for his mistakes and 70 percent for his achievements. That is only fair.

In the social sciences and in Marxism-Leninism we must continue to study Stalin diligently wherever he is right. What we must study is all that is universally true, and we must make sure that this study is linked with Chinese reality. It would lead to a mess if every single sentence, even of Marx's, were followed. Our theory is an integration of the universal truth of Marxism-Leninism with the concrete practice of the Chinese revolution.

—Mao Zedong, on the "ten major relationships," April 25, 1956

Red China and the United States not only quarreled; because of American foreign-policy myopia they fought a totally unnecessary war until they both learned new lessons. The Americans did not learn fast. It took them still another war in Asia to learn that what American leaders had said many years ago was true: No statesman with a lick of sense will let the country get involved in a land war in Asia. There was another lesson that the Americans may not even yet have learned: Anyone who interferes in an indigenous revolution anywhere is a fool, and such interference is bound to fail. In China and in Vietnam the Americans tried to interfere. These actions cost them billions of dollars and far too many lives, and ultimately the revolutions succeeded in the face of American interference.

The Chinese learned that enormous manpower was not enough when fighting a war in another country against a power with such sophisticated weaponry as the United States had.

Both countries learned from their experiences and emerged from the Korean war-that-was-not-a-war with considerably more mutual respect than they had held before. It would be years before the wounds healed, but they would heal, and that was more than could be said for some other wounds.

In 1956 the Soviet leaders under Nikita Khrushchev began downgrading the memory of Stalin. They did this without consulting the Chinese, and Mao Zedong was miffed. As noted, Mao's ego was driving him to ill-considered action in several directions. The Great Leap Forward, it was suggested in Beijing, would bring China to the leadership of Communist theory; China would leapfrog the Soviet Union, which had never been able to institute a thoroughly socialist society, providing plenty for all.

The Soviets resented this apparent attempt to wrest away their leadership of the Communist world. By 1958 the Chinese had to admit that they had more than a little trouble with their commune system and that the great world of total communism was not as close as they thought, nor did they have the key that they had believed they had. The Russians were reassured enough to offer a new trade program involving $1 billion worth of goods between then and 1967.

But the Russians were soon enough discommoded again. Their resentment returned when China occupied Tibet. Another point of friction with the Soviet Union developed over India, in the border dispute of 1959. The Russians took a determinedly neutral stand in this quarrel.

In October 1959 Khrushchev made a visit to China to warn the Chinese about their militaristic ambitions, which were showing in the India crisis.

In 1960 the relationship between Moscow and Beijing began to unravel. The issue really was Khrushchev's interest in reaching an accommodation with the United States, an interest not shared by Mao Zedong.

On Lenin's ninetieth birthday Lu Tingyi, a member of the Chinese party Politburo, quoted Lenin's remarks of long ago that American imperialism was the most vicious enemy of the world's people. Revisionists, said he, were camouflaging imperialism and describing the American president, General Eisenhower, as a man of peace. Mao Zedong denied this; his thinking "integrated the universal truth of Marxism-Leninism with the concrete practice of the Chinese revolution."

The Russians looked with disfavor on the whole Great Leap Forward as "an infantile disorder," and they considered China's adventurism in India to be the same. The dispute simmered, and in August 1960 Khrushchev ordered all Russian technicians in China to come home and bring everything with them.

Then the Chinese began to recall all the troubles that the Comintern had caused them in years past. Mao's words repeated the old plaints. The breach was soon open, and remained so.

When Nikita Khrushchev fell from power in 1964, some people saw it as a sign that reconciliation could be worked out. But what they did not understand was the depth of disagreement. China had challenged the Soviet Union for leadership of the Communist bloc, not only in the Great Leap Forward but also at the Bandung conference in 1955, when Zhou Enlai emerged as the hero of the hour and the champion of "peaceful coexistence."

China still thinks of itself as the leader of the Third World. It is a stance that does not help relations with the Russians. Mao's belief that the 1960s was a time for world revolution and his attempts to foment that revolution in Africa were not appreciated by the Russians any more than by the Americans. After the promising beginning at Bandung, Zhou Enlai toured Africa again in the 1960s, but this tour was as resounding a flop as the Bandung appearance had been successful. China ended the decade of the 1960s with relatively little influence on the international scene.

Indeed, that decade and the next were marked by internal problems that quite demanded the full attention of all concerned.

33
The Great Proletarian Cultural Revolution

Now, about this university education. From entering primary school to leaving college is altogether sixteen or seventeen years. I fear that for over twenty years people will not see rice, mustard, wheat or millet growing; nor will they see how workers work, nor how peasants till the fields, nor how people do business. Moreover their health will be ruined. It is really terribly harmful. I said to my own child, "You go down to the countryside and tell the poor and lower middle peasants: 'My dad says that after studying a few years we became more and more stupid. Please, uncles, aunts, brothers, and sisters, be my teachers. I want to learn from you.'"

In point of fact pre-school children have a lot of contact with society up to the age of seven. At two they learn how to speak and at three they have noisy little quarrels. When they grow a little bigger, they dig with toy hoes to imitate grown ups working. This is the real world. By then the children have already learned concepts. Dog is a major concept. Black dog and yellow dog are minor concepts. His family's yellow dog is concrete. Man is a concept which has had a great deal of meaning. Man or woman, great or small, Chinese or foreigner, revolutionary or counter revolutionary. All these distinctions are absent. What is left are only the characteristics which differentiate man from the other animals....

We should reform university education. So much time should not be spent attending classes. Not to reform arts faculties would be terrible.... We must reform the arts faculties in the universities. The students must go down and engage in industry, agriculture, and commerce....

Many great inventors, such as Watt and Edison, came from workers' families. Franklin, who discovered electricity, sold newspapers. He started as a newspaper boy. Many of the great scholars and scientists did not go through college. Not many of the comrades in our Party's Central Committee are university graduates....

—Mao Zedong, speech at Hangzhou, 21 December, 1965

After 1957 Mao Zedong's antipathy to the intellectual community of China took on insane qualities. That speech above, delivered in Hangzhou at the end of 1965, is insane. It was part of a long, wandering harangue about education that proved nothing and offered no practical solutions to the many problems of Chinese education. It was an exercise in hatred, and a complete reversal of Mao's earlier statements that China would progress by encouraging experimentation in education.

It was also one of the first shots fired in the Great Proletarian Cultural Revolution, the most destructive policy ever invented by Mao Zedong, and one that will affect China adversely for at least another fifty years. In retrospect it seems almost as if Mao Zedong had set out to destroy the revolution he and his fellows had labored so long to bring about. They very nearly destroyed China. In the process they sacrificed years of progress, innumerable priceless antiquities and works of art, and very nearly the entire culture of China. It was the most disgraceful display of naked brute force since the coming of the Mongol hordes across the steppes. Yet even the Mongols showed a respect for Chinese culture that was not shared by the brainless mob of students, children, and workers who were unleashed upon the land by Mao in the 1960s.

Before the Cultural Revolution ended, 500 million people, or three-quarters of the people of China, were sorely hurt and millions were killed.

Among the factors that brought about the Cultural Revolution was Mao's quarrel with the Chinese Communist party. In the 1960s Mao was in his seventies. Was he senile? Some say he was. Others say he was suffering from concealed rage at the way the party was going, that is, not in the image he had chosen. Mao was still the most revered figure in China, and he still managed to control the Chinese party's Central Committee. He had secured the dismissal of such men as Peng Dehuai on the flimsiest of grounds. In 1966 he mounted a full-scale campaign through the Central Committee to cement his dictatorial power. It came in the guise of a campaign against revisionism.

In less strident terms than mine, China expert John K. Fairbank has analyzed Mao and his motives. Mao, says Fairbank, was like one of the emperors whose mantle he had inherited. True, Mao's power was unassailable in that same fashion, supported by what was then known as the People's Liberation Army, which he controlled through manipulation of its leadership. But if Mao was an emperor, he was Nero, a mad emperor, and what happened in the 1960s and 1970s proves it. For Mao set out to destroy Chinese society, and he very nearly succeeded. This does not mean he set out to change it; that had already been done. What he did, what he assented to, was far more than change—it was the production of chaos.

From the beginning of Mao's career, his strong point had been his ability to manipulate the masses. He believed in the peasant and the worker as the backbone of the society he wanted. He knew a lot about the peasant, for he, himself, came from landlord stock. He did not know much about the worker, and he never learned that the worker is a greater brute than the peasant, for the worker has no ties to the land to humble him. Mao was not wise enough or cynical enough to realize what would happen if he persuaded the masses that they were being abused and then turned them loose against society. Two quotations come to mind in trying to come to grips with Mao's actions and the consequences:

> A revolution only lasts fifteen years, the period which coincides with the effectiveness of a generation. *

and

> The people is a many headed monster. †

Mao's original successes had been based on his manipulation of the peasants. Virtually nothing was needed to convince them that they had been abused for generations by a succession of landlords. With Communist party encouragement, they rose up against the landlords, dispossessed them, and destroyed that whole class of Chinese society.

Fifteen years after the success of his revolution, Mao saw his new society as distinctly troubled. Having destroyed the old ruling class, the Communist party had established two new ones, the intelligentsia and the bureaucracy. Mao had turned against the intelligentsia in 1956 when their criticisms threatened his status as a god, but he had not finished the job of destroying them. Now, when Mao spoke of "revisionism," he was referring to the rise of the new class of governors, the Communist party and government leaders, who had become princes of privilege.

---

*Jose Ortega y Gasset, *The Revolt of the Masses*.
†Epistles I:1, line 76.

Indeed, all Mao needed to do was look west, to the dachas and limousines of the Soviet Union's new aristocracy, to see whither China was headed. So Mao set out to destroy the establishment he had created.

But how to do it? The peasants were busy trying to cope with the natural fallout of the commune system, which had begun with such enormous enthusiasm. They had already learned that combined farming operation does not necessarily mean better operation and that sluggards and disaffected people can hurt production sorely.

The peasants knew, although the party did not, that a political decision mandating grain as the major crop did not produce more grain; they knew that certain lands are good only for certain produce. The politicians still had that to learn, and until they did, China's agriculture would not prosper.

No, the peasants were not to be chosen to carry Mao's new revolution to China. The instrument would be the student youth. Here was an instrument just waiting for an expert to pluck the strings.

In 1966 Mao obviously discussed his concerns over the future of China with his current wife, Jiang Qing. She had been a movie actress before she appeared in Yanan. Mao's choice of a woman whom most of his comrades regarded as a floozy was not popular. In the years since, she had studied politics assiduously. Her aim in life was to become the queen of Chinese culture; she was the Soong Meiling, the Evita, the Imelda of China. In Mao's shrewd recognition of the decay of the revolution she saw her future. In his peculiar twisted view of the urban masses she saw her opportunity.

Mao's second principal supporter in his plan was Lin Biao, who had succeeded the disgraced Peng Dehuai as minister of defense.

In the spring of 1966 it was apparent that the army was well under control. Under Mao's directives and Lin Biao's administration of them, all dissention had been eliminated from the army. Mao was ready to move.

The new campaign against the intellectuals had begun in the summer of 1965. Mao's followers had criticized Beijing University as "a reactionary fortress" where bourgeois ideas were in control. Two university officials, Deng Tuo and Peng Zhen, convened a conference on education at the International Hotel in Beijing. They were attempting to strengthen the position of Liu Shaoqi, the president of China, who supported the university. The result was a campaign of wall posters setting forth the opposing views, gaining in vituperation, and attacking individuals.

*   *   *

In that spring of 1966 Mao found in his own paranoia a reason to attack Wu Han, one of the hated intellectuals, a professor who had risen to the post of vice mayor of Beijing. The reason for the attack was a morality play published by Wu, "The Dismissal of Hai Rui from Office," which criticized one of the Ming emperors for having wrongly dismissed a high official.

Actually, the play had been written in 1961. It told the story of a Ming dynasty official who had tried hard to alleviate the sufferings of the peasants, and for his pains aroused the enmity of other officials, who engineered his dismissal. Mao at the time was smarting from the realization that he had quite improperly destroyed his old and loyal comrade Peng Dehuai and that in so doing he had caused the remainder of the party's old leadership to move away from him.

In the fall of 1965 Peng had written a long letter to Mao in which he was sufficiently obsequious to give the chairman an excuse to right at least part of the wrong he had done. Mao called in Liu Shaoqi, Deng Xiaoping, and Peng Zhen for a meeting with Peng Dehuai. Premier Zhou Enlai was informed of all that went on. Mao then admitted left-handedly to Peng Dehuai what he had known for years, that Peng's criticisms of the Great Leap Forward had been based on solid fact. Mao came as close to admitting error as God could. "Perhaps the truth is on your side," he said. That was all he said about the incident, and he said it privately to Peng. Then he appointed Peng deputy chief of the southwest under Li Jingquan, first secretary of the Southwest Bureau of the Chinese Communist party.

Having done so, Mao announced that this was party policy, and if anyone objected, let him come and see Chairman Mao.

This left-handed exoneration indicated to the intellectual community that it was permissible to praise Peng, as long as one did not praise him too much.

To some others, the incident opened the door for a left-handed criticism of Mao himself. One such was Vice Mayor Wu, obviously. His morality play was bound to be considered (by Mao) an allegory of Mao's behavior, with the wrongly punished official representing Marshal Peng, the most prominent Communist ever disgraced by Mao's whims.

Yao Wenyuan, a Shanghai literary critic and an intimate of Mao's wife, Jiang Qing, criticized the play and the playwright for making an attack on Chairman Mao. Jiang Qing made sure the matter was brought to her husband's attention.

So Mao undertook the punishment of playwright Wu. But Wu was cleared by an investigation, which further infuriated Mao, because the verdict was an insult to him. Now Mao's anger broadened to include Peng Zhen, the mayor of Beijing, who had protected Wu. Mao arranged for a forum in Shanghai, where his wife had much influence. At the forum Peng was denounced as a "revisionist," and in April 1966 he was attacked by the Central Committee, under Mao's direction.

———

The wall poster campaign in Beijing involving Beijing University continued for weeks. The Central Committee finally decided, under Mao's direction, that Beijing University was a hotbed of bourgeois right-wing thinking, and half a dozen officials were dismissed. So was Mayor Peng Zhen.

Mao Zedong now had his sights set: The intellectuals and the bureaucrats were to be the quarry.

The Cultural Revolution had begun. Day after day students rushed to the university to read the wall posters and learn who was under attack. Hundreds of old scores were settled, and thousands of young students suddenly discovered that they had immense power and could attack without danger.

One leader of this movement was a 50-year-old woman named Nie Yuanzi, who had emerged from obscurity by carrying the attack on the Beijing University officials. On May 25 she had put up a vicious poster attacking the officials, and Chairman Mao approved so wholeheartedly that he called her "the first red banner."

One day Nie spoke at the campus: "We must all follow Chairman Mao and pursue to the end the cultural revolution, an event that will affect the whole world."

She was interrupted by wild cheering. She was picked up by a gang of students and carried around on their shoulders as they chanted: "Yes, we will follow Chairman Mao and oppose the capitalist road."

"Chairman Mao has said that I am the first red banner," shouted Nie Yuanzi, "so anyone who opposes me, opposes Chairman Mao."

Amid a chorus of assent the procession moved off.

By this time, June 1966, the Maoists had organized "work teams" of Communist cadres who came onto the campus to try to control the trouble. They were not students; most of them were much older. Mao opposed the work teams' efforts to stop the excesses.

Yue Daiyun, the former secretary of the campus branch of the Communist party, had just returned from her involuntary work service in the south. On June 18 she went to her university department offices, where she had been ordered to appear along with all the other members. At nine o'clock a group of ten students burst into the offices, angry and shouting.

"Chairman Mao says that a revolution is not a time to embroider or serve tea," they yelled. Grabbing Lao Chen, the department party secretary, they shouted, "You are an enemy of the people." They jammed a bamboo wastebasket over his head, slapped his back with library paste, and then stuck a poster on it which read: "Enemy of the People. Follower of the capitalist road."

"Black teeth and claws of the black gang," shouted one of the students. He was referring to the university administration, now called the "black gang" by the revolutionaries. It included the president of the People's Republic, Liu Shaoqi, who disagreed with Mao Zedong's attempts to destroy the university and was now marked for extinction by Mao and his followers.

But the poster would not stick to Lao Chen's blue polyester shirt, and it fell off onto the ground. One of the students picked up the big jar of library paste and dumped the whole mess on Lao Chen's back. The poster then stuck fast.

Yue watched as the revolutionaries seized ten of her associates and decorated them with posters and wastebaskets. There was no talking, no listening—nothing but violence. Finally, the band left the department, warning all the other members to "watch and be educated."

The students were going out to join a mass parade of "enemies of the people" who were being marched around the campus by jeering students. At the head of the line of enemies was Jian Bozai, a close friend of Zhou Enlai's.

The violence spread swiftly, engulfing not only the campus but the entire city. Lao Chen, one of the first to be reviled and humiliated, committed suicide a few days later. The students charged that he had chosen death because he refused to reform. They showed no compunction for their savage behavior.

By July 1 the future of Beijing University was in doubt. All that kept it together was a Communist party work team that held down the violence, but the work team itself was under attack. On July 22 Jiang Qing appeared on the campus and made a radical speech. "All of Beida is under the dictatorship of the academic warlords," she said. "It is time to overthrow the bourgeois academic clique."

With Jiang Qing that day were Kang Sheng, a go-between who carried messages from Chairman Mao to his wife, and several other leaders of the revolutionary committee. One of them, Guang Feng, stated that the principles of the Paris Commune must be followed in this new revolution. It would be a violent revolution, he said. All privilege must be removed from everyone.

There was the crux of it: Chairman Mao's belief that he could create in this fashion a truly egalitarian society.

By the end of July the work team was dismissed, and its members told to stop interfering with the Cultural Revolution. The Beida Cultural Revolution Preparatory Committee was founded, with Nie Yuanzi at its head. The movie actress Jiang Qing was now in charge of the university.

The students began coming to the university wearing olive-green jackets, trousers, and caps and bright-red armbands. At an August rally in Tian An Men Square, Chairman Mao appeared in the same outfit. The children at Qinghua University Middle School invented the name "Red Guards," and they aped their elders in staging their own revolution. Mao was delighted. Here was a new weapon, one he had not counted on: the schoolchildren of China, the easiest of all to lead. Immediately, he took steps to turn the revolution over to the children or, rather, to employ the children to do violence under the guidance of adults. It was as if the youth of Anthony Burgess's *Clockwork Orange* had come to life, with their brutality and excesses.

———

By September the children were on the march throughout China, sanctioned by the highest authority in the land, Chairman Mao himself, and bent on destruction.

What were they trying to destroy?

The targets changed as they went along. In essence the children destroyed anything that did not appeal to them, anything that aroused the irritation of their leaders. "Long live the red terror" was their slogan. At Beida that summer the preliminary aim was established:

Destroy the four olds:

1. Old ideas
2. Old culture
3. Old customs
4. Old habits

That was the license granted the youth of China by Mao Zedong. They adored him.

One of the Qinghua Middle School students received by Chairman Mao after he had been so impressed by the children's revolutionary zeal was a girl named Binbin, which means gentle and refined in Chinese. Chairman Mao told the children they should be militant. So Binbin changed her name to Yaowu, which means militant.

The young Red Guards literally ran amok through Beijing that summer. Traveling in bands for mutual protection and inspiration, they destroyed stores and restaurants. They gave new names to old streets. Perpetual Peace Boulevard, which ran through Tian An Men Square, was renamed East-Is-Red Boulevard.

Mao Zedong cheered.

The Red Guards marched through the streets of Beijing and soon through other towns. They sang as they went:

> We are Chairman Mao's Red Guards
> Tempering ourselves in great waves and winds;
> Armed with Mao Zedong thought,
> We'll wipe out all pests and vermin.

At the town of Yizhen, Red Guards of the local middle school made a foray to rename streets. Four Harmonies Street became Four News Street—to commemorate the attack on the four olds. The Empress Guo Wineshop was renamed Worker-Peasant-Soldier Wineshop.

The Yizhen marchers came to a triple marble archway. It had stood on Four Harmonies Street for 200 years, erected in the Qing dynasty to honor a court minister who had been a native of Yizhen. This archway, the Yizhen Preparatory Committee of children had decided, symbolized feudal oppression and must be pulled down.

"Smash the four olds," shouted the marchers.

One boy climbed to the top of the archway and fastened a rope around it. Others dug away at the foundations. In two hours the magnificent stone structure was rubble in the street.

"Revolutionary comrades in arms," shouted one of the children, waving his red armband, "we have successfully knocked down this feudal relic. This is our first great victory. Let us advance on the crest of this victory to our next target."

So next they attacked the Hui people's mosque and pulled down the onion on the top. They hung a pig's tail around the neck of the imam. The next day, under the guidance of the chairman of their committee, a teacher named Deng Zeng, they attacked the Dafo Temple. But there they had scarcely begun their campaign of destruction (wrecking an ancient statue) when an officer of the People's Liberation Army brought out a platoon of soldiers to stop them.

The girls among these young Red Guards cut off their hair—and then they stood on street corners and cut off the hair of all the women who passed.

. Chairman Deng decided the Yizhen Red Guards should pull down the marble gate on the south end of their own school campus, so they destroyed that landmark. They tore down the bell tower that stood in the center of the campus, a tower that dated from the Song dynasty, a thousand years ago.

That period, from June to August 1966, was known as "the fifty days." Many people were humiliated; some were beaten to death; others were sent away from their homes in disgrace.

In August 1966 the Cultural Revolution moved into a new phase. Liu Shaoqi had been trying to divert the Red Guards from destruction. Mao did not like this, and he engineered a meeting of a segment of the Central Committee, called on short notice so that his supporters would dominate. At that meeting he demoted Liu Shaoqi from his spot as number 2 man in the party and gave that post to Marshal Lin Biao.

Soon there were 10 million Red Guards on the rampage throughout China. Anywhere one goes in the 1980s, one still sees the results of their destruction: statues with their arms and heads chopped off, the ruins of temples and public buildings. In Taiyuan the Red Guards invaded the Shanxi provincial museum, where eighty exhibition rooms were loaded with precious artifacts, and destroyed everything.

Soon enough Liu Shaoqi was under personal attack. So was Deng Xiaoping. Mao had clearly drawn the lines; he, and only he, would control the party.

In January 1967 came the Seizure of Power movement, Mao's big move. He authorized the ousting of officials all over the country and their replacement by young people with no experience and no common sense. Eventually, the Red Guards began to break down into factions and to accuse, beat, and harry one another.

The People's Liberation Army was finally called in to maintain some kind of public control. Mao wanted the army to side with the left revolutionaries against the old (now called right-wing) elements of the party. But the army began to split. Mao, at this point completely insane, ordered the Red Guards to invade the army ranks and wipe out the "capitalist road people" and "the right-wing deviationists." So the army split further, and soon civil war was raising its ugly head in China.

The entire country was immersed in a dirty bath of factionalism. Class origin had started much of the trouble. At Beijing University some of the students who did not do well had complained that their peasant origins worked against them, and it was true that they did not have the cultural background of young people who had come from intellectual families. The result was envy and ultimately a resumption of a sort of class hatred on the new lines.

In the Cultural Revolution children from the families of landlords or capitalists were excluded from the Red Guards. Usually they were targets. The children of parents who were denounced were also denounced. The Red Guards were divided by family backgrounds: poor peasants against well-to-do peasants, peasants against workers and the children of army officers.

The universities closed down. The middle schools closed down. Even the primary schools closed in the period of the terror. All China was deeply affected. A hundred million Chinese were involved in the struggle. Five hundred million were affected by it. How many million died is not known. But the negative consequences to China were enormous. In 1987 I traveled for ten weeks around China by train talking to people. I talked to hundreds of people, and I always had one question: What happened to you in the Cultural Revolution? Everyone had a story:

She was sent from a teacher's job to work in the fields.

His father was reviled and beaten and died of a heart attack.

His restaurant was closed down and it never reopened.

She did not attend school until she was 15 years old.

That last complaint, from young people in their early thirties, was almost universal. Oddly enough, one of the lasting results of the Cultural Revolution, and one certainly not foreseen by Mao Zedong in his madness, is found in the educational process he tried to destroy. The only young people to receive any education during almost ten years of the Cultural Revolution and its aftermath were those who could be educated by their parents and relatives. And those parents and relatives with education were all members of the intelligentsia and the gentry. In other words, Mao Zedong destroyed the landlords in the 1950s, but in the 1960s and 1970s he made

sure that their children, most of whom have the same attitude toward life
as their parents, will be the people running China in the 1990s.

———

In the middle of 1968 so much destruction had occurred, and the threat of
total civil war was so great, that Mao Zedong reluctantly disbanded the
Red Guards and called on the People's Liberation Army, the only element
in China that still had any central control, to restore order.

Mao had achieved his purpose. By destroying the party and disgracing
Liu Shaoqi, Deng Xiaoping, and others, he had apparently ensured his
personal control of the Communist party. Among the victims were many
of the followers of such men as Deng. Zhao Ziyang, a Communist party
official in Guangzhou, was one of these. He was disgraced and sent to the
countryside to work in the fields. There were millions of such cases, as
Mao destroyed the party organization and replaced it with one loyal to himself alone.

At the Ninth Congress of the Communist party, in April 1969, Mao was
officially enshrined, and his little red book of quotations was introduced as
the party bible. Lin Biao was named as the party's vice chairman, and he
was to be the successor. The radicals who had led the Red Guards were
prominent in the Central Committee. Mao declared that the Cultural Revolution had ended, but it was not true. Although Mao did not know it, he
had lost control. He had unleashed the dogs, and they would not march
easily back into their kennels.

Mao ordered the army to form revolutionary committees in all provinces, which it did, but some elements of the army rebelled against their
leadership and continued to fight. The revolutionary committees were dominated by the army, which disbanded Red Guard units and sent the members into the countryside, where they were attacked by the same sort of
people they had been attacking. Chaos threatened all China in 1969 and
1970. Zhou Enlai estimated that the People's Liberation Army alone had
suffered "hundreds of thousands" of casualties.

So did the Red Guards. The army began suppressing the revolutionaries with great vigor. In order to maintain public order, Mao had been forced
to acquiesce in the assumption of party power by many army officers. They
hunted down, tortured, and killed some of those they found.

The peasantry had been largely left alone in this preponderantly urban "revolution." But there was one aspect that did affect the farmers. The Red Guards insisted that they stop maintaining their own private plots of land for raising personal food.

Typical was the case of the Red Guards of Yizhen. At the town's main intersection they encountered some peasants who were selling vegetables out of wooden barrows. The Red Guards assailed the peasants, insisting that their behavior showed capitalist tendencies. The guards tried to take one peddler's cucumbers away from him.

This attitude spread throughout the countryside. Farmers were attacked and assaulted for raising their own pigs or growing rice or vegetables. To grow your own food was to "exhibit capitalist tendencies," so even the farmers were affected, and some went hungry.

Despite Mao Zedong's hope that he could turn off the Cultural Revolution in 1969, he was wrong. All he had done by his latest actions was sow the seeds of a struggle for power.

34
The Gang of Four

I hope that you will practice Marxism and not revisionism; that you will unite and not split; that you will be sincere and open and not resort to plotting and conspiracy.

The correctness or otherwise of the ideological and political line decides everything. When the Party's line is correct, then everything will come its way. If it has no followers, then it can have followers; if it has no guns, then it can have guns; if it has no political power, then it can have political power. If its line is not correct, even what it has it may lose. The line is a net rope. When it is pulled, the whole net opens out.

This Party of ours already has fifty years' history, during which time we have had ten big struggles on the question of our line. During these ten struggles there were people who wanted to split our Party, but none of them were able to do so. This is a question worth studying; such a big country, such a large population, yet no split. We can only say that this means that the Party wants what the people want, and the Party members do not want a split. In view of its past history the future of the Party is full of Hope.

—Mao Zedong, during his provincial tour of 1971

From Mao Zedong's seat of power, the Cultural Revolution was seen as a failure of the Red Guards, but Mao had no real conception of the disaster he had caused. Like the emperors of old, he could do no wrong.

The Cultural Revolution had begun to come apart in January 1967. Zhang Chunqiao and Yao Wenyuan began a rebellion in Shanghai. Wang Hongwen set up a meeting to overthrow the Municipal Party Committee, and he seized power in Shanghai. They called it the "January Storm." Then Lin Biao, Jiang Qing, and their supporters struck back, and violence came to Shanghai once again. That was the first big break in the front of the Cultural Revolution.

Mao Zedong issued a call to the People's Liberation Army to support the forces of the left, which meant the Lin Biao–Jiang Qing group. So the People's Liberation Army supported the left, but not all the units did. The army began to come apart as some units broke away in disgust and pitched battles took place between other units.

In February 1967 in Beijing, at Zhongnanhai's Huairen Hall, the party's Central Committee and the leaders of the Cultural Revolution group held a confrontation, overseen by Chairman Mao. The old party heroes, Tan Zhenlin, Chen Yi, Ye Jianying, Li Fuchun, Li Xiannian, Xu Xiangqian, and Nie Rongzhen, attacked the Cultural Revolution. They were attacked in turn by the Cultural Revolution group, and with Mao's support they were suppressed.

The party had come apart at the top. Mao was so determined to rule China single-handedly that he was willing to destroy the Communist party itself.

The attack on the "olds" became general. Zhou Enlai was censured. Zhu De and Chen Yi were censured. In shock, the Political Bureau of the Central Committee stopped functioning; it was completely replaced by the Cultural Revolution group.

Mao seemed to have had his way entirely. But...

In the summer of 1967 Lin Biao, Jiang Qing, and their supporters took over the Foreign Ministry and created a series of incidents to embarrass the Chinese government with foreign powers.

Mao Zedong watched, unwavering, unwitting.

In 1967 Mao went out into the provinces to try to discover why other party members were saying that China was on the brink of civil war once more. He returned with the comforting word that there was no reason for the working class to split into two irreconcilable factions.

What Mao did not know was that his wife and Lin Biao, perhaps sensing his insanity (but not his megalomania) and certainly sensing his growing weakness, had decided to take power in China.

In March 1968 the Lin Biao–Jiang Qing group manufactured one of the usual "incidents" that marks an attempt to force a change in direction in China. This one was called the "Yang Chengwu, Yu Lijin, and Fu Chongbi incident." These three officers of the army were accused of trying to reverse the direction of the "February Adverse Current"—the party meeting of the year before in which Zhou Enlai and Zhu De had been disgraced. They were important people, these three. Yang was acting chief of staff of the People's Liberation Army. Yu was political commissar of the air force. Fu was commander of the Beijing garrison of the People's Liberation Army.

On March 22, 1968, Lin Biao moved. The three were arrested, and Yu Lijin was ordered to stand trial for treason. Lin Biao replaced the three officers with his own people. At the same time he secured most of the power of the Military Commission, managing the appointment of his followers.

Mao was so bemused by his Cultural Revolution that he scarcely seemed to notice.

That summer, however, Mao became worried because what he said would not happen had happened, and he could not overlook it. From his point of view, the Cultural Revolution had really begun when the children rebelled at Qinghua University Middle School. Now Qinghua University was the scene of bloody battle between opposing factions of students. On August 25 Mao ordered workers' propaganda teams to Qinghua University to try to put an end to the fighting.

Soon such teams were sent to all the schools and colleges in China, but they did not stop the fighting. They took sides, and only increased the chaos. The forces fighting each other were of confused origin; in one area they might represent one group of students, the original Red Guards, being challenged by a new group which had been refused admission to the old. The polarization was proceeding rapidly, and the real danger was that the group that had disassociated itself from Mao would find a leadership committee that would challenge Mao in behalf of the masses and thus create an open civil war. Since Mao had chosen to use the students and workers, he might very well lose the adherence of the peasants if the proper leadership could be found.

Thus Mao acquiesced in the establishment of revolutionary committees composed of "revolutionary cadres," the army, and the "revolutionary masses." In other words, each committee consisted of representatives of the old party people who had not been thrown out yet (and who accounted for only 40 percent of the party cadres), the army, and the "revolutionary masses," which were the Red Guard faction. The Red Guard faction was outnumbered and already shattered into little groups.

By October the Red Guards were under enormous pressure from the army, and Mao disbanded them. He told them to stop whatever they were doing and go down to the countryside to learn from manual labor.

Mao believed they would obey. But what he failed to realize was that the youngsters had as many complications as did the adult members of the party. The unbridled activities of the Red Guards, their arrogance and their beatings and murders, had brought a reaction that could not be stayed.

That October, Liu Shaoqi was expelled forever from the Communist party, and Zhou Enlai and Deng Xiaoping were again condemned as right-wing deviationists. Liu was sent to Kaifeng, imprisoned, and tortured until he died.

But by December Mao was in a box. The army was not going to take any more of the Red Guards. So on December 22 he reiterated his direction that educated young people should go to the countryside to be reeducated by the poor and lower-middle peasants. So the Red Guards were sent to the country, under supervision of the army, and to the peasants who did not like them.

In fact, nobody knew precisely what was going on. On the face of it, Mao said the Cultural Revolution was a great success. Beneath the surface, the original forces of the Cultural Revolution, the mobs of young students, had been supplanted by the army. At the Ninth National Congress in Beijing in April, Lin Biao and Jiang Qing were made members of the Politburo, and Lin Biao, as noted, was named as Mao's heir presumptive. The Lin Biao element could now see its way to eventual control of the Central Committee and power.

The power play of the Lin Biao–Jiang Qing group—which became infamously known as the "Gang of Four"—was made at the Second Plenary Session of the Ninth Central Committee of the Chinese Communist party at Mount Lushan in Jiangxi Province. It began on August 23, 1970.

Mao wanted to keep all power for himself, as chairman of the party. So now that Liu Shaoqi had been destroyed and his office of chairman of the government left open, Mao suggested that there be no chairman of the government. But Lin Biao attacked. Speaking of Lin's "genius," his supporters indicated that he had surpassed Mao Zedong as a leader of the people.

One of Lin Biao's lieutenants, Chen Boda, distributed a pamphlet at the conference which suggested that Lin Biao be made chairman of the state.

Mao countered with a statement of his own, criticizing Chen Boda's views. Mao still had enough power and prestige to stop the Lin Biao move. It died.

Still, Mao was on the defensive now.

At an educational conference in April 1971 Mao stated that his proletarian educational line had not been carried out and that the educational
work in the seventeen years since liberation had been a failure. He said
nothing about the past six years, in which the educational program had
been a total disaster because of his Cultural Revolution.

At the March meeting Jiang Qing, Lin Biao, and their people had decided to set up a coup d'état in September. The principal conspirator was
Lin Liguo, a high officer in the army and Lin Biao's son. But Mao's people
learned of the coup and put a stop to it. Rather than face certain punishment, Lin Biao, his wife Ye Qun, and Lin Liguo fled in a military aircraft,
bound for the sanctuary of the Soviet Union. They were shot down near
Undurkhan, in Mongolia, by Chinese military planes from a unit loyal to
Mao. The exact circumstances are still a mystery.

Jiang Qing tried hard to cover her tracks in this affair, and apparently
she succeeded.

At the time of the failed coup, Mao and Lin Biao were at a crossroads.
Mao was exasperated with the Soviet Union's failure to accept him as the
leader of the world Communist movement, on the correct path, as opposed
to the wrong path of the Soviets. The abrasions had led to more difficulty
and a resumption of the old border dispute along the north edge of China.
To show the Russians how he felt, Mao decided it was time to warm up
the frozen relationship with the United States, and he made some tentative
overtures.

When U.S. President Richard Nixon responded affirmatively, a change
in the Sino-American climate began. A Ping-Pong tournament was arranged, and following that, President Nixon accepted an invitation to visit
China, where he met with Mao Zedong and Zhou Enlai.

A few months later China reopened relations with Japan. This move
seemed to represent a victory within the Chinese establishment for the mod-
erates, as represented by Zhou Enlai and Deng Xiaoping. In the beginning
of 1972 Mao reversed some of his old statements at a memorial meeting
after the death of Chen Yi, vice premier, who had been the subject of an
attack by the left wing in February 1968. In October 1972 Zhou told the
People's Daily to publish three articles criticizing the leftists, and the paper
did, thus showing that Mao was losing his influence.

The three articles were criticized by Zhang Chunqiao and Yao Wenyuan, close associates of Mao's wife. Another fight was in the offing. But this time Mao was not taking any sides. Indeed, Zhou and Deng Xiaoping had gained control of the Central Committee, and while they certainly did not attack Mao, they did as they pleased. On March 10, 1973, Deng took over the day-to-day work of the Central Committee, supplanting Mao.

That summer, the Central Committee dealt with the Lin Biao case, expelling him (in absentia, since it was not generally known that he was dead) and his cohort from the party.

About two weeks later, at the Tenth National Congress of the party in Beijing, the Jiang Qing faction seemed to gain control again.

This time the faction came out into the open, reaffirming the left-wing statements of the Ninth Congress. Zhang Chunqiao was elected to the Standing Committee of the Politburo, and Wang Hongwen became vice chairman of the Central Committee. Thus came into being the Gang of Four: Jiang Qing, Zhang Chunqiao, Yao Wenyuan, and Wang Hongwen. They were the inside group of the Politburo.

In January 1974 the Gang of Four made its first move for power, presenting an allegorical criticism of Confucius which was really an attack on Zhou Enlai. In the charade the gang gave great praise to the empress of the period, which was an indication of Jiang Qing's desire to become the new "empress" of China and to succeed her husband in power.

By July 1974 even Mao had to take cognizance of his wife's bid to supplant him. He warned her and the other three members of her coterie not to form a "four member small clique." Thus did China become aware of the Gang of Four.

In the fall the ailing Mao went down to his home country of Jiangxi and visited Changsha in neighboring Hunan Province. Wang Hongwen, of the Gang of Four, came down to complain about Zhou Enlai, hoping thus to get an endorsement from Chairman Mao. But Mao sent Wang away with a sharp rebuke. A few weeks later Mao was telling people that Jiang Qing was obviously seeking power and that he opposed it. He warned her to stop pressing.

By the time the Second Plenary Session of the Tenth Central Committee was held in Beijing, in January 1975, Zhou Enlai and Deng Xiaoping had done some planning to retrieve their balance of power from the Gang of Four. Over the objections of Jiang Qing, Deng was elected vice chairman of the Central Committee and member of the Standing Committee of the Politburo. Five days later, at the First Session of the Fourth National People's Congress, Zhou delivered the keynote speech. The delegates elected Zhu De as chairman of the Standing Committee and appointed Zhou as premier and Deng Xiaoping as his first vice premier. The Gang of Four got nothing.

Quietly, without any special mention, Marshal Peng Dehuai died, apparently the victim of torture and mistreatment by Mao's sycophants. He had lived in obscurity for several years, a victim of the excesses of the Red Guards and Mao Zedong once more, after his apparent rehabilitation. The new attack on Peng in the 1960s could not have been made without Mao's knowledge and concurrence. It was another indication of Mao's megalomania.

In 1975 Zhou Enlai became seriously ill—cancer—and had to give up most of his activity. Deng Xiaoping, his heir apparent, took over the day-to-day work of the Central Committee and the government. He began straightening out some of the mess made by the Cultural Revolution, but Mao took violent exception to the characterization of the revolution as the disaster it obviously was. Trying to interfere, Mao launched a movement to criticize Deng Xiaoping as a rightist. The shadow of the Cultural Revolution again fell over China, with Mao's supporters—now admittedly fewer than in the past—trying to stage a comeback and seize power.

Perhaps they would have succeeded, except for the death of Zhou Enlai. With his death all China suddenly realized what a great man he was—always submerging himself in the shadow of Mao Zedong while ameliorating Mao's worst errors and holding the party and the country together. His death was the signal for an intensive campaign against Maoism, masked as a struggle against the Gang of Four. Millions of mourners came to Tiananmen Square to lay wreaths and poems against the Gang of Four. The army, however, was still largely in Maoist hands, and it suppressed this movement violently. A large number of people were killed, wounded, and arrested.

Mao continued to control the party mechanism as chairman. On April 7, 1976, Hua Guofeng was appointed chairman of the party's Central Committee and premier of the state council. He was Mao's man. Deng Xiaoping was removed from all government and party posts, which was a serious demotion.

*　　*　　*

In selecting Hua Guofeng, the Central Committee was kowtowing to Mao Zedong. The country and the party still did not know quite what to do. Life was changing rapidly, and a power vacuum threatened. Now it was kill or cure.

The Gang of Four made its move to seize power but failed. The party's Central Committee, engineered by Deng and manned by Hua Guofeng, Ye Jianying, and Li Xiannian, moved swiftly. Hua Guofeng was in a dangerous position. If he opposed the Deng faction, most certainly the Gang of Four would seize power; everyone concerned was aware that the advent of the four would mean a new sort of dictatorship over China. Jiang Qing's ambition knew no bounds; she had no strong or long ties to the party. So the party caused the arrest of Jiang Qing, Zhang Chunqiao, Yao Wenyuan, and Wang Hongwen. The threat of violence ended, and for the first time in ten years, following the death of Mao, there could be peace in China.

In October Hua Guofeng was appointed chairman of the party, so party affairs were apparently settled. Now the party and the government could turn their attention to other matters.

The Cultural Revolution and the turmoil that lasted for more than ten years had cut the Chinese economy to ribbons. The third and fourth Five-Year Plans never got off the ground. What was needed was a program that would undo the wrongs and errors committed by the left in the preceding few years.

35
The Rise of Deng Xiaoping

The whole Party must now give serious thought to our country's overall interest. What is that interest? The Reports on the Work of the government at the first sessions of the Third and Fourth National People's Congresses both envisaged a two-stage development of our economy:
The first stage is to build an independent and relatively comprehensive industrial and economic system by 1980.
The second will be to turn China into a powerful Socialist country with modern agriculture, industry, national defense, and science and technology by the end of this century, that is, within the next twenty-five years. The entire party and nation must strive for the attainment of this great objective. This constitutes the overall national interest.
Chairman Mao has said that it is necessary to make revolution, promote production and other work and ensure preparedness in the event of war. I am told that some comrades nowadays only dare to make revolution but not to promote production. They say that the former is safe but the latter dangerous. That is utterly wrong.... We should bear the overall interest of the country in mind and solve these problems without delay. How much longer can this task be put off? How can we afford to delay in advancing the cause of Socialism?

—Deng Xiaoping, March 5, 1975

On the day that Deng Xiaoping made the above speech to the Communist party secretaries in charge of industrial affairs at the provincial, regional, and local levels, he was deeply engaged in the struggle against Mao Zedong's excesses and the chaos that had resulted from the Cultural Revolution.

Deng and his mentor, Zhou Enlai, had begun to make inroads into the Central Committee against the left-wing revolutionaries, but the issue was still in doubt. Zhou was ill with cancer and Deng was carrying the administrative load, which had become enormous because of the schism within the party. Zhou and Deng could not trust the Maoists even to carry out assigned tasks of administration.

Mao was still proclaiming the virtues of the destruction he had caused. Soon he would launch the movement to "criticize Deng and counter the Right deviationism trend to reverse correct verdicts." Mao's influence was still such that this campaign would plunge China into a new turmoil in 1976. But whereas ten years earlier Mao's campaign would certainly have resulted in Deng's ouster from his posts and his exile to some remote farming area, in 1976 too many people were aware of the disaster Mao had brought on the nation. Thus, his mischief-making created turmoil, but not wreckage. Within the year 1976 Zhou and Mao both died, and the Gang of Four were arrested. Now China could turn back to the road toward progress.

The focus of Deng Xiaoping's speech on March 5, 1975, was a dreadful situation in the Chinese railroads. It was an epitome of the damage the Cultural Revolution had brought.

The railroad system the Communists had inherited from the Nationalist government was primitive on the whole, and yet excellent in parts, particularly in north China and Manchuria where the Japanese had built it up. In the beginning the Communists had operated the system as a national system, as had the Guomindang before them. But under Mao's insistence that everything be decentralized, except his own power, the central control of the railroads had been destroyed. Provinces and localities were given some of the general responsibilities for their areas. Consequently, while the number of railroad employees had increased in the decade of the Cultural Revolution, and so had the amount of equipment, track, and rolling stock, the system was actually worse off. In fact, it was not a system at all anymore but a whole group of minisystems. With their equipment and manpower, Chinese railroads should have been able to load 55,000 freight cars per day, but they loaded only 40,000 cars.

That statistic was only the first indication of the trouble of the railroads. In 1964 there had been 88 railroad accidents, whereas in 1976 there were 755 major railroad accidents, most of them caused by human negligence. But "negligence" is not precisely the right word. "Nihilism" is a better one; the nihilism of the Cultural Revolution had wrecked the railroads.

In 1964 engineers had to bring their lunch boxes with them as they were not allowed to leave the engine during hours of operation. In 1976 engineers left the trains when and where they wished, and the result was absolute chaos in the railroad schedule. Many accidents occurred due to this factor alone. Also, the rule against drinking on duty was not enforced. Consequently, engineers and switchmen sometimes pulled the wrong switch, causing more terrible accidents with enormous loss of life.

Such discipline problems had to be solved immediately. But before they could be solved, said Deng Xiaoping, the railroads must first rid themselves of "factionalism." That meant that Mao's revolutionaries must be brought sharply into line. Those who would not reform would be removed from their jobs and sent away for reeducation.

And who were they? According to Deng, they fell into two categories:

[The first consists of] persons who are obsessed with factionalism, have engaged in factionalism for several years, and have lost their sense of right and wrong. . . . They should be educated. If they correct their mistakes, then we will let bygones be bygones, but if they refuse to mend their ways, then they will be sternly dealt with.

The second category consists of a few bad elements. They can be found in all lines of work in every province and city. They fish in troubled waters by capitalizing on factionalism and undermine socialist public order and economic construction.

Deng singled out one particularly bad apple, a ringleader of a railroad faction in Xuzhou who was exercising a virtual dictatorship, lining his pockets and creating trouble. Deng gave him one month to get into line. After that, warned Deng Xiaoping, the offender would be treated as a criminal.

The answer to factionalism, said Deng, was the transfer out of individuals who were causing trouble. This meant the ringleaders:

What if a new ringleader emerges following the transfer of the previous one? Transfer him too. Do it two or three times and the problem will ultimately be solved. We won't arrest anyone, of course, except counter revolutionaries.

And what if a factional leader refused to be transferred?

Stop paying his wages until he submits. Since his trade is factionalism, why should we keep him on our payroll?

*   *   *

So Deng declared war on Mao's revolutionaries. After that speech the railroad men knew what was going to happen. If they did not toe the line, they would ultimately be declared counterrevolutionaries, and they might even be executed.

The warning was clear to all workers in all industries. Although Deng was speaking in the teeth of Mao Zedong that day, he showed his confidence in the outcome:

"Which do you think there are more of," he asked, "people who favor the Central Committee's decision or people who are against it?"

It was a plain warning to Mao and his supporters that Deng and Zhou now controlled the Central Committee.

"If 80 percent of the people concerned support the decision, then it can be carried out."

Deng said he thought virtually all the people concerned supported the decision. He was referring to people within the party.

So the "mobilization drive" for the railroads was on, and the issues were going to be explained to everyone, including the family members of railroad personnel and the peasants living along the railroads. Then, if the railroad workers did not fall into line, they would be dealt with ruthlessly.

The death of Zhou Enlai on January 8, 1976, brought an abrupt switch in the balance of the Central Committee. By early April the Maoists had seized control. Deng and his followers tried hard to stem the tide, but Mao exerted his every effort to continue the chaos he had created. As noted, the first big test was a demonstration organized by Deng's people. Ostensibly, it was a meeting to honor Zhou Enlai's memory. Actually, it was a display against the Gang of Four and Mao's revolution, although, of course, Mao was never mentioned, never reviled. One could not criticize God.

The demonstrators laid their wreaths and displayed their poems against the Gang of Four. The Maoists retaliated by attacking the demonstrators. Tian An Men Square erupted in violence, and the army sent troops to quell it. They sided with the Maoists.

Throughout China similar situations developed, and the army came out for the Gang of Four and helped the group gain power in the party. The army was the only integrated force in China still loyal to Mao and to his memory, as exemplified by Chairman Hua Guofeng.

By April Deng Xiaoping had been stripped of all his posts and sent away from Beijing. Ruthlessly, the Gang of Four rooted out Deng's followers from high office. It also went after the followers of Zhou Enlai, and they too were banished from the seats of power.

The emergence of Hua Guofeng as first vice chairman of the party's Central Committee indicated that Mao still had the reins of power and that he was able to prevent Jiang Qing and Wang Hongwen from seizing control.

The factionalism continued unabated wherever it had not been dealt with by army action, and it returned to the railroad and other areas where it had been corrected. China again moved toward chaos.

In September 1976, when Mao Zedong died, the Gang of Four made its power play—and lost. Hua Guofeng and the other leaders of the Central Committee had the four arrested immediately and clapped into jail.

How was Hua to maintain power? Having no plan of his own, he had to follow the Maoist line. But what was the Maoist line? As Mao himself had said, policy was the result of the study of the facts and then their interpretation. To be careful, Hua began an "on the one hand and then on the other hand" approach, telling the party and the people that this was Mao Zedong thought. But Deng Xiaoping recognized Hua's flounderings for what they were and contemptuously titled the policy "the two whatevers."

In October 1976 Hua's power base was apparently confirmed: He manipulated the Politburo into appointing him again as chairman of the Central Committee and also as chairman of the Military Commission, the two sources of Mao Zedong's power.

But Deng was not finished. In April 1977 he wrote a letter in which he criticized the two-whatevers policy as worse than no policy at all. Consequently, in July Deng was brought back into the government again, as a member of the Politburo, vice chairman of the Central Committee, vice chairman of the Military Commission, vice premier, and chief of staff of the army. These appointments gave Deng a very powerful position.

Hua Guofeng remained in power through the Eleventh National Congress held in Beijing in August 1977. Hua still represented what was left of the Maoist line, a defense of the Cultural Revolution. But in the minds of the people the Cultural Revolution was a dreadful, destructive error, and most of them had suffered needlessly because of it. The party, of course, never admitted such error.

Even so, forces were at work to rectify some of the error, if possible. Deng Xiaoping's protégé Hu Yaobang was appointed head of the organizational department of the party's Central Committee, a most important post. He announced that he was going to follow the Maoist principle of "seeking truth from facts." Who could complain about that? So Hu conducted studies of the Cultural Revolution's excesses, and he began reversing decisions. Ultimately, nearly a million such reversals were made and the accused were rehabilitated.

By February 1978 Deng Xiaoping was ready to challenge the Maoists. Deng offered a positive program to undo the wrongs of a dozen years. Hua Guofeng offered only floundering—and searching in Mao Zedong's writings of the past for a policy for the future. With the people's growing knowledge of the fact that Mao had visited disaster upon China, there really was only one choice. At the First Session of the Fifth National Committee of the Chinese People's Consultative Conference, Deng Xiaoping was elected chairman.

Swiftly now came another opportunity for Deng. The Fifth National People's Congress was convened, and Hua Guofeng made an opening address. He made some serious mistakes. Following the old Mao line of allowing the commune leaders to estimate production, he came up with totally erroneous production figures. He proposed a quick fix: 120 giant new industrial projects in the next seven years. The congress accepted his idea, and the work began.

Deng worked behind the scenes. He got the word "rightist" removed from the record of half a million party members.

By December 1978, while Hua Guofeng was still chairman of the party, the two-whatevers policy had been rejected, the need to correct the "left deviation errors" of the Cultural Revolution was accepted in the Central Committee, and the concept of the class struggle forced by Mao Zedong was no longer regarded as Mao Zedong thought. The Central Committee declared for "socialist modernization."

That was really the end of Hua Guofeng. The Maoist terrorists were either trembling in their boots or suffering the rigors of "reeducation." The Shanxi provincial museum was being put back together again with artifacts collected from all over China, and other destruction was repaired where possible. Of course nobody could put back together the buildings that had been torn to rubble, or revive the people beaten to death by the juvenile delinquents called Red Guards, or bring back the dead Peng Dehuai and other real heroes of the revolution to the honor they deserved. No one could even speak his or her mind about the monstrosities perpetrated by Mao Zedong in his later years. Even dead, he was still God. But his wrongs could be righted for the living, and they were.

———

In 1979 Deng Xiaoping, speaking at a national conference, laid out a new approach to China's problems. He did it within the framework of Maoist talk, speaking of the four fundamental principles: the Socialist road, the dictatorship of the proletariat, the leadership of the Communist party, and Marxism-Leninism and Mao Zedong thought. But what he was really telling the conference was that China must be emancipated from the narrow policy interpretations of the past. Month after month Deng gained strength and prestige in party matters, and by the middle of 1979 he had made great strides in wiping away the manifestations of that dreadful decade-long nightmare, Mao Zedong's Great Proletarian Cultural Revolution.

Yue Daiyun, the young Chinese literature teacher from Beijing University, was rehabilitated in 1966, sent away again in 1969 as a "rightist," rehabilitated again in 1970, sent to do physical labor again in 1972, attacked again in 1974, assigned to a work farm in 1975. She struggled, in and out of favor as the Gang of Four fought for national power and the balance of power surged back and forth, and was finally rehabilitated and had her party membership restored in 1979.

By that time Deng Xiaoping was in real control and his reforms were being felt. The old class warfare was officially ended, and the epithets "landlord," "rich peasant," "counterrevolutionary," and "bad element" were removed from people's dossiers. Contact was made with Taiwan, and a regular mail service established. Deng Xiaoping went to America and talked with President Jimmy Carter. Relations with the United States took on a new bright look; diplomatic ties were established in December 1978, and the United States cut off its diplomatic contact with Taiwan. China now had the U.N. seat and was recognized as the real China, not just the Beijing government or "Communist China."

Americans were no longer reviled in China, and in America the China lobby was forgotten.

In China big projects began to take shape. The Baoji-Chengdu railroad was electrified. An oil pipeline was built from Daqing to Beijing, and another from Hebei Province to Jiangsu Province, serving the Renqiu oil field in central Hebei.

China launched a satellite of its own into space. The Huangpu Bridge in Shanghai, China's first doubledecker bridge, was opened, and a highway completed that linked Xiaguan in Yunnan Province and Markam in Tibet. The Huang He was spanned by a 3400-meter-long highway bridge at Luoyang.

The Anshan steel mills were rehabilitated and a large new blast furnace began operation—a far cry from Mao's backyard furnaces. Another rail line was built, this one linking Xiangfan and Chongqing.

China was on the march, industrially. The fifth Five-Year Plan was in effect. (It was really only the second Five-Year Plan, because three intervening plans had been destroyed by the Cultural Revolution and its death throes.) Industrial production was up nearly 14 percent, but it was very spotty and not all goods produced were available in all places.

Agriculture did not do so well. In 1979 the Central Committee recognized the need for serious reforms in the commune system which Mao had hailed as the solution to all China's problems. Something had to be done to bring a new spirit to the disgusted peasants, who had expected utopia and suffered with the rest of China through fifteen years of chaos.

In many ways, the year 1979 marked the end of the old era and the beginning of a new one. In November Deng Xiaoping made a speech at a national congress of writers and artists in Beijing, and publicly refuted all the slanders against intellectuals of the past. These, he said, had been spread by Lin Biao and the Gang of Four. He did not charge Mao Zedong, but of course everyone who heard him could remember the cause of the Cultural Revolution and the primary victims of it. Education, which had suffered and stopped entirely for years, was revived, and standards for college degrees were established in 1980. But so terrible had been the rigors of the past that by 1983 only twenty nine people had received doctor's degrees (in fields other than medicine) from Chinese institutions. It was going to take a long time to catch up and repair the damage done by Mao.

Virtually everyone who had been damned by Mao Zedong was rehabilitated by 1980, including Liu Shaoqi. A symbol of the change was the fact that Hua Guofeng continued in office as premier of China, although his views had been rejected; in Mao's day he would have been disgraced.

From time to time there came a fleeting reaction reminiscent of the past. In August 1980 Deng Xiaoping made a speech to the Politburo of the party's Central Committee and invited guests. He talked about reforming the system of leadership so that leading personnel would become "revolutionized," but he also said "better educated and more competent," which was a far cry from the Mao idea. Deng also spoke of "opposing the bourgeois ideological corrosion and eliminating the pernicious vestige of feudalism, politically and ideologically." But that was just a bone thrown to quiet the leftists while he tamed them.

China was still China. In 1980 the Central Committee announced that Kang Sheng and Xie Fuzhi had been members of the Lin Biao–Jiang Qing clique; it posthumously expelled them both from the party and "revoked" the laudatory memorial speeches made at their funerals. In 1981 the members of the Gang of Four were convicted. Jiang Qing was sentenced to death; so was Zhang Chunqiao, who had aspired to be Chairman Mao's successor. From the grave, Mao Zedong saved their lives. Following Mao's edict years earlier, the death sentences were accompanied by a two-year reprieve. In 1983 the death sentences were commuted to life imprisonment.

The others of the gang, including Yao Wenyuan, whose review of a play had turned Mao Zedong against intellectuals and opened the Cultural Revolution, were sentenced to life imprisonment.

By 1981 the shock of the past had worn off enough for the leaders of China to assess what had happened between 1957 and 1976, when the arrest of the Gang of Four had put an end to the violence of twenty years. The Sixth Plenary Session of the Eleventh Central Committee of the Chinese Communist party met and solemnly revoked Mao Zedong's godhood.

Mao, they said, was a great Marxist and a great strategist and revolutionary theorist. But he had made "gross mistakes" during the Cultural Revolution. The committee gave Mao the same grade Mao had given Stalin: 70 percent right, 30 percent wrong. Perhaps history will give a slightly different estimate, for in ten years Mao very nearly destroyed what he and the other revolutionaries had spent forty years in building.

Hua Guofeng was pushed out of power at that same meeting; thus the last vestige of Mao's influence was eliminated. Deng Xiaoping was in charge as chairman of the Central Military Commission, the key post in China, and Hu Yaobang, his protégé, became chairman of the Central Committee. Zhao Ziyang, another Deng protégé, was chosen as premier. The oligarchy had been totally restored for the first time since Mao took over dictatorial control. The total assessment of Mao's excesses is not in yet, but a look at the record will show that the virtual destruction of the old Communist party began on the day that Mao degraded Peng Dehuai and in a moment destroyed the old comradeship that had glued the party's major leaders together.

The year 1982 put the seal on all the changes. That year Hua Guofeng disappeared from the top leadership altogether, deprived of his final post as vice chairman of the Central Committee. The committee was heavily loaded with Deng Xiaoping's supporters. The new era of China had been established. Now it was confirmed.

36

Toward New China

To show the superiority of socialism, we must undertake reforms of the economic and political structures. The road ahead will be tortuous, and mistakes are hardly avoidable, but we will always draw lessons from our experiences so as not to commit serious mistakes.

In the first seven years after the founding of the People's Republic of China in 1949, there was healthy development. But policies departed from people's practices from the last half of 1957 until 1976.

During the socialist construction period, China suffered mainly from the leftist mistakes since 1957. We ran counter to the path set by the Party's Eighth Congress in 1956, mainly because of leftist mistakes. The mistakes cost China nearly 20 years and have taught us a lesson. We summarized the historic lesson in this period of time and freed people's minds from dogmatism, carrying out Mao Zedong's theory of seeking truths from facts and the four cardinal principles.

But China can overcome these leftist errors. In 1935 at the notable Zunyi meeting the Party redressed leftist errors and assured the leadership of Mao Zedong.

—Deng Xiaoping, in an interview with Hungarian Communist leader
Janos Kadar, October 13, 1987

Eleven years after Mao Zedong's death his name is still cited in noting the correctness of given Communist policies, even when the citation invokes an implied criticism of Mao's actions, as in the above statement by Deng Xiaoping. Mao, and Mao alone, was the instigator of the serious "leftist errors" that marked China's road from 1957 to 1976. As long as Mao lived, he tried to continue the destructiveness of his Cultural Revolution.

But while the Cultural Revolution is now accepted by the party as the greatest disaster of its history, Chinese politicians are careful even yet not to link Mao's name with the destruction. No one is fooled, of course, but the care in dealing with the memory of Mao is indicative of the continued existence of a left-wing (sometimes called "conservative") faction in the

Chinese Communist party which advocates the sort of dictatorship Mao invoked in the name of decentralization of power.

In 1987 Deng Xiaoping's "reform" movement was clearly ascendant in China. His whole concentration was on practical lines as the Thirteenth National Congress of the Chinese Communist party opened in Beijing.

Zhao Ziyang, Deng's heir apparent, would carry out these reforms as premier and chairman of the Communist party. Deng, who decided in 1987 not to stand again for election to the Central Committee because of his age, retained basic power as chairman of the Military Commission.

The aim of the party for the rest of the twentieth century, said Deng and Zhao, would be to better the way of life of the Chinese people through economic, industrial, and agricultural reforms.

Some of these reforms had already been undertaken: the encouragement of farmers and farm communes to improve their agricultural standards and the permission to sell their produce locally and keep the profits. This change made the farmers happy and provided them with extra income. But the real agricultural change was just beginning in 1987, in moves to take millions of people off the land and mechanize farming procedures to increase productivity. Where it had been tried, as in the enormous Beijing suburban area, it had worked; productivity improved by 10 to 15 percent.

The problem, as Zhao and Deng put it, was the expansion of scientific, technological, and educational work.

However, in 1987 there occurred a perceptible repression of intellectual freedom.

In the spring of 1986 Deng's program for liberalization had been extended to intellectual matters. Deng, and his protégés Communist party Secretary Hu Yaobang and Premier Zhao Ziyang, spoke enthusiastically, inviting criticism of possible party errors. The performance was reminiscent of Mao's "hundred flowers" period. As Deng indicated, the party hacks had to be removed from productive enterprises and made to stop interfering. As far as he was concerned, it was almost entirely a practical economic problem. But, of course, there can be no such thing as a practical economic problem without political overtones in a Communist society.

The leaders called for a debate on the road ahead, and promised not to take action against any who took part in it, no matter what their expressed views. So all sorts of suggestions were made for bettering China. Some called for checks and balances in the party. Some called for laws safeguarding human rights. Some called for a multiparty system.

Deng was in favor of many of these reforms, including separation of the functions of the party and government and competitive local elections with a number of candidates.

But when the Sixth Plenum of the Twelfth Central Committee met in September 1986, the struggle began. Opposing Deng and his followers were Chen Yun, the economic planning expert, and Peng Zhen, president of the National People's Congress. They regarded Deng's actions as a threat to the party and the bureaucracy. Chen and Peng were joined by the generals, who were very cool to Hu Yaobang because he was cool to the military. They also did not like his extreme tolerance of dissent.

Thus the end result of the Sixth Plenum was meaningless. The final statement spoke of "socialist spiritual organization" and spoke against "bourgeois liberalism." The latter phrase became part of the new slogan of the old left, or new conservative, elements in the party: "Stamp out bourgeois liberalism!"

Then came the dramatic student demonstrations of December 1986 and January 1987. The students demonstrated for more freedom. They clashed with police. Playing into the hands of the conservative-leftist faction, they forced Deng's hand.

Deng was a most pragmatic political leader, and how he stood on intellectuals was a matter of considerable doubt. He had led the campaign against rightist thought in the 1950s under Mao, although he had opposed it until it became party dictum. He had carried out a campaign against intellectuals in 1983 and accused them of "spreading spiritual pollution." But in each case it must be seen that Deng was a moderating force; his campaigns never reached the witch-hunt stage, and they usually petered out quickly. This indicates that he did not have his heart in them, but was merely responding to the political climate of the moment.

After the Tian An Men Square demonstrations of January, the neoconservatives rushed to the attack. Peng Zhen, one of their leaders, complained:

We need thought rectification in today's reforms. The ideological trends of bourgeois liberalization and its influence have been reflected in literary and art circles, and some erroneous points of view have become rampant.

Deng Xiaoping apparently switched his whole viewpoint. He came out against "bourgeois liberalism" and launched a campaign to eradicate this evil. Hu Yaobang was the scapegoat, because he had encouraged the spread of new ideas in the intellectual marketplace. Hu was fired as Communist party secretary, and on a temporary basis, his job went to Zhao Ziyang.

Young people throughout China, particularly in the colleges and universities, moaned their disappointment. "We had hoped that China could approach Japan in matters of productivity and freedom within twenty-five years," one student in Taiyuan told me. "Now, with the sacking of Secretary Hu, we have lost our confidence."

Yet the campaign against "bourgeois liberalism" never did anything except let off hot air.

Wait a minute, someone will say. What about Liu Xinwu, Liu Binyan, and Wang Ruowang?

Liu Xinwu was suspended from *People's Literature*, a leading magazine. The magazine was already in trouble for describing in vigorous detail the sexual practices and living conditions of Tibetan herdsmen. Politically this article violated the party rule that minorities had to be coddled at all times. Liu was fired because he was an indefatigable gadfly, stinging the party politicians in their sensitive egos. But he remained on the payroll. It wasn't anything like the Cultural Revolution.

Nor was the expulsion of Liu Binyan from the party and from *Ren Min Ri Bao*, the *People's Daily*. He too had become a gadfly, needling the party about policy. But he simply moved from the payroll of *Ren Min Ri Bao* to that of the Chinese Writers' Association, where he is vice chairman. When the party got after the writers, they showed total solidarity with Liu, and the Party backed away.

Wang Ruowang was expelled from the party for personally taunting Deng Xiaoping—saying that more and more Deng resembled Mao Zedong.

That reaction reminds one that China is not like any other country, not even the Soviet Union. The Chinese oligarchic dictatorship of the party is extremely quick to respond to criticism.

Nonetheless, it is hard to believe anything other than the fact that Deng's protestations on the subject were more for effect with the leftist, or neo-conservative, element of the party than they were real. A few days after the expulsion of the intellectuals from various jobs, Zhao Ziyang made it known that there would be no witch-hunt and that local officials had best be sure that no campaign began. In May 1987 Zhao announced that the situation was under control. After that, very little was said about "bourgeois liberalization," except by foreign reporters, who could not understand what had happened to it.

When the Thirteenth National Congress assembled in the fall of 1987, the party and the government could show a great deal of positive change in the time just past. The issues of Hong Kong and Macao had been settled; both foreign colonies would be returned to China at the end of the century. Thus China's territorial pride had been restored, yet the old colonies were assured that business interests would be protected for many years. It had been an admirable solution to a knotty problem, requiring forbearance and trust on both sides.

The question of Taiwan was nearing solution, too. Earlier in the year Deng had come out in favor of "one China, two systems," which would guarantee the Taiwanese their own form of government and economic life. At the time of the congress the Guomindang government of Taiwan responded positively to many overtures of the preceding months, and it announced that for the first time people who lived on Taiwan would be free to travel on the mainland.

The Thirteenth Congress went along with Deng Xiaoping and his multitudinous reforms. Indications were that the 1987 struggles of the leftist-conservative movement had not been very successful and that Peng Zhen and his friends are not the wave of the future, but ghostly voices from the past.

All sorts of changes were in the air, mostly regarding reforms of systems. The Communist party cadre system was due for an overhaul; the problem, as in the government, was the perpetuation of a bureaucracy that prevented progress.

As one student put it, "Many party cadres are government officials at the same time, managing both political and economic affairs. So the party's direct involvement in all governmental issues reduces the initiative of government organizations and enterprises and tends to create power abuse and bureaucracy."

That was, in general, the view among students. A poll conducted by the Communist Youth Leagues of Beijing and Qinghua universities showed that 93 percent of students said political reforms were necessary.

*   *   *

The move toward more private enterprise was indicated by Zhao Ziyang at the time of the congress when he stated that in two or three years China would maintain only about 30 percent of its economy under central planning. Nine years earlier it had been 100 percent; in 1987 it was 50 percent. As of the end of 1986 some 18 million people were engaged in private enterprise in China, and this area is bound to expand if the policies of Deng Xiaoping remain the same.

Most visible to a traveler is the burgeoning of small restaurants in China's cities, a real reversal of trend. In the People's Republic the restaurant had nearly disappeared. One reason for this was the change in economic conditions that the Communists brought. Industries and businesses were expected to feed and sometimes to house their employees. Since the employees ate in mess halls and company dining rooms, there was not much need for restaurants. The big hotels served foreign travelers. In 1987, for example, in Qingdao, only four big restaurants survived, and these existed for party functions, bureaucratic functions, and business parties. Everywhere, virtually all restaurant tables were big ones that could seat a dozen people.

Another reason for the disappearance of the restaurant in China was the Cultural Revolution. Restaurants were considered decadent and were closed down by the Red Guards; the cooks were sent to become farmers and learn Socialist humility. Many did not come back to the cities; many escaped the country.

But in the 1980s, as some people had a little more money and a little more time, small restaurants, seating perhaps six or eight people, began to proliferate in the cities. Free enterprise was finding its own way, and as a result Chinese cuisine, nearly destroyed in China proper in the middle of the twentieth century, was beginning to revive.

The Chinese language was another area of puzzlement to China. On a visit to China in 1987 I happened to be talking to the floor boy on my floor at Shanghai's Peace Hotel.

"*Wuzi liu ling jiu,*" I said, as I asked for the key to Room 609.

"*Liu ling zhu,*" said the boy.

"*Jiu,*" I said. "*Nage shi Beijing hua.*" ("That is Beijing standard Chinese.")

"*Zhu,*" he said. "*Zhege shi Shanghai. Women shuo Shanghai hua. Women bushuo Beijing hua. Buyao.*" ("*Zhu.* This is Shanghai. We talk Shanghai language. We don't talk Beijing talk. We don't want it.")

And that is why in 1988 a radio station that is broadcasting in Guangzhou, the capital of Guangdong Province, can be understood by only half its listeners. It broadcasts in Guangzhou dialect (Cantonese), not in *putonghua*, or standard Mandarin, Beijing talk. The reason: This station is pioneering in economic broadcasts, aimed at the Guangdong people.

"First of all," said the *China Daily* in an editorial, "it is up to the leadership to see that standard Chinese is used. Leading cadres should understand that the unity of the nation and the progress of society call for a common spoken Chinese language."

But it has not yet come to China. Mao Zedong tried to change the people but failed, and the indications are that a common language will be a long time in coming.

That is the sort of problem that will dog this immense country for years. That and birth control. In 1986 the Chinese awakened to discover that their nation numbered 1.2 billion people. Too many, said the leadership. And a campaign to limit families to one child per couple, already undertaken, was stepped up. It involves carrot-and-stick techniques. Families that comply receive many benefits: education, food, money, and guarantees for the single child. But the second child, unless produced with government permission, gets none of these perquisites; instead, the child is the subject of government discrimination.

The problem was and is that rural families want sons to work the land. Since 1984 governments in Shaanxi, Shandong, and Liaoning undertook some relaxation of the planning program. In fact, rural families ignored it by the millions. Third and fourth children became relatively common, although frowned upon. It was going to take more than frowns to resolve the population problem.

But as with so many problems in China, the one is a part of another. For example, Deng Xiaoping's agricultural changes were expected to take 100 million people off the land and put them into industry in about ten years. That change would also remove the economic spur to farm families to harvest more than one child.

The 1987 congress of the Communist party showed indications of sprouting a whole new set of freedoms in China, freedoms much wanted by the intellectual community, and in growing numbers by the business and government communities as well. At that meeting Deng Xiaoping passed the mantle to Zhao Ziyang, retaining only the vital office of chairman of the Military Commission as a bridle on power. The talk was about such matters as a civil service system for China, an end to bureaucratic control, and a general loosening of the bonds of the Chinese people.

It all seemed almost too good to be true. In fact, could it be true? Could a Communist party actually become democratic? That is the real question China faces going into the 1990s. The nature of the Communist party is a "dictatorship of the proletariat," which in effect means an oligarchy that might at any time develop into a personal dictatorship, as Russia did under Stalin and as China did under Mao Zedong. The oligarchy lends itself far more to this trend than to the development of democracy.

Yet in 1987 in Beijing, for the first time, the party put up more candidates for office on the Central Committee than there were posts. That meant a freedom of choice. If that trend continues, the infighting against the lessening and decaying influence of the leftist-conservatives of the Communist Party will not matter. In a generation or two, China could truly develop into a democratic society.

The world is watching the emergence of Asia as the prime mover in affairs. The United States has faltered and taken a secondary position economically. Only militarily does it remain strong, and how long that will continue is debatable in view of the American failure to come to grips with its national deficit.

But, more than that, the United States has run out of gas politically and philosophically. Any nation that converts from a dynamic economy to a service economy, which the United States did in the years after the Korean war, finds that it loses that precious quality of initiative. The American government is still posturing itself in the world as the defender of the status quo. It is hard to consider a less dynamic and less appealing posture for a nation that once boasted of its revolutionary spirit.

It is even harder to realize, sometimes, that the United States is the father of all these revolutions, yet having achieved a fairly reasonable society and one that is willing to accommodate itself to its own citizens—the United States has grown impatient with other people's revolutions.

As for the Soviet Union, it is showing new signs of life in its willingness to learn from China. Gorbachev's economic reforms, including a new attitude toward agriculture, are based on those of China. With all its poverty and all its problems, China has seized the lead in the revolution.

I have written before of the "political evangelism" that has guided American foreign policy for the past century. It is a failed policy, as the events in Central America show beyond doubt. Indeed, in almost every aspect, American attitudes toward the rest of the world are lacking in dynamism. Our politicians—I do not call them statesmen—continue to look upon the world around them without considering the aspirations of the people in these countries, or their fears.

China, in the last quarter of the twentieth century, has virtually no fears. Its people have weathered every conceivable disaster in this century past. Starting from a decadent monarchy, moving into a republic whose leader wished to be an emperor, moving from that into a true revolution led by Dr. Sun Yatsen and assisted by the Russians and no others, China set out on the long road to freedom. The country was at that time, the 1920s, harried by the western powers, including the United States. China's revolution was fragmented when it became apparent to Chiang Kaishek that the Communists would seize control of the country if he did not act. But in acting, he put himself into the hands of the western powers and the Shanghai gangsters, and thus, indeed, betrayed the revolution. But what could one expect? Sun Yatsen was the man who realized that the revolution stemmed from the people. Chiang was a soldier and an opportunist.

Then the revolution, or what was left of it, fell into the hands of the Chinese Communists, who did not forget the people. Mao's base of power was the Chinese peasantry, not the urban workers that appealed so much to Li Lisan and Wang Ming. But after he had brilliantly led his revolution to victory, Mao Zedong also betrayed the revolution, in his madness. To be sure, by the mid-1950s the Communist party was riddled with corruption and self-serving officials. So was the government. But Mao's betrayal of the people assumed that to save the revolution one must destroy the spirit of the nation. He took China into what was really its second civil war. Zhou Enlai and others tried to stop him and later to restrain him, but only when Mao died could the pieces be put back together. Then the power struggle was relatively short and relatively painless. Mao had dealt with one great threat: Lin Biao's attempt at a military coup. He had informed others of the ambitions of his wife Jiang Qing, and when she and her accomplices tried to seize power at the hour of his death, they were dealt with swiftly. The final chapter in the paroxysm, that of Hua Guofeng, was relatively peaceful and he passed out of the picture without violence.

In the 1980s China continued to face a struggle for power within the Central Committee. As with any oligarchy, there is always the danger that one man will decide that he can become the dictator. Peng Zhen, the leader of the conservative-leftist group, seemed to be the most likely candidate for strong opposition. Obviously, by 1988 he had generated a following of his own that would hope to topple the Deng Xiaoping crowd.

The real problem of China in the 1990s will be achieving a true stability of government. Mao proved one thing: The Chinese revolution did not and could not follow the path of the Russian revolution or the American revolution. China has always had its own ways.

In the century to come, what I call the "Age of Asia," the leadership of the world will pass into Asian hands, as it has already done in the sphere of economy. Japan is today the world's banker and the most powerful industrial force. As Japan does, so does the rest of the world. Korea, particularly the Republic of Korea, has shown itself to be potentially an important force too, if it can resolve its political problems. But above all China can take leadership in a new world, where general war is unlikely and the military posturings of the two great superpowers look more and more ridiculous as the decades pass.

What China needs is a good quarter-century of stability. Under the successors to Deng Xiaoping, with the nightmare of Maoism in its excesses as a constant reminder, it seems likely that China will get it.

NOTES

I am indebted to many people for help in the writing of this book on China, not least of them the officials of the U.S. Office of War Information who sent me to China more than forty years ago during World War II and thus awakened my interest in China and things Chinese. In 1987 I returned to a China which was physically very much like the one I had known (except for the modern highways and burgeoning skyscrapers) but which was socially as different as it could possibly be. The China of the 1940s was an oligarchic state, with political and economic power resting in the hands of the leaders of the Nationalist "clique." I don't like to use that word—it has been tarnished by propaganda for years—but it is the truth. The Chiang-Soong-Kung bloc controlled the Republic of China and milked its resources for personal gain for ten years. Then the Soongs and Kungs fled to America with their wealth, and Chiang Kaishek fled to Taiwan with the vestiges of his power.

Out of the economic wreckage left by the fleeing Guomindang, the Chinese Communists have begun the creation of a modern state. It did not happen easily, nor overnight. Mao Zedong, in his mad years, very nearly destroyed all that he and thousands of other loyal party members had created by starting the wrong-headed Cultural Revolution, which did nothing *but* destroy. Thousands of buildings, monuments, and cultural additions were effaced or ruined by the excesses of children, unleashed by Mao, misguided into thinking that everything old had to be destroyed to begin something new. Mao's worst crime of all was the continuation of the carnage long after it had become apparent that it was destructive to China and had set the country back fifty years in its progress. But that is another story. Suffice it to say here that China survived Mao Zedong at his worst and that the new China which has emerged with the transition of the Fourteenth National Congress in the fall of 1987 is moving toward modernization as well as away from a concentration of political power and toward a more free society. There will be ups and downs; the hard-line members of the Communist party will look upon every increase in freedom for the people with revulsion and will try to retain party control of all aspects of Chinese life. But it will no longer work; the revolution has gone too far for that, and the reforms being carried out in China in the late 1980s are ever more far-reaching.

327

The intention is to produce a better life for the Chinese people, and as long as that intention holds, it is bound to succeed.

But it is a mark of the tentative nature of Chinese freedom today that I am not mentioning by name scores of Chinese people who contributed to this book in my ten-week railroad tour of China in 1987. Whether or not disclosing their identity would today jeopardize their jobs or their positions in the community is perhaps questionable, but they are concerned; and since that is so, I would not embarrass them in any way. Thus, although I rode on trains with dozens of people and met scores of others who talked very freely to me on almost every subject, I am not mentioning many Chinese names. I am grateful to Zhang Yan, vice editor of *China Reconstructs*, and to Dong Tianmin, Liu Yalin, Yeh Nienlun, Qu Cuicui, Xu Xiangmin, and Xu Jian for reading the manuscript and for their comments. Among the few westerners with whom I came into contact, I wish particularly to thank James R. Schiffman, at that time the Beijing correspondent of the *Asian Wall Street Journal*, for much assistance while I was in Beijing.

Also, I want to thank various officials and guides of the China International Travel Service in Shanghai, Qingdao, Harbin, Changchun, Beijing, Shaanxi Province and Shenxi Province, Xi'an, Yanan, Chongqing, Guiyang, Guilin, and Wuhan. That procession of names more or less indicates the nature of my rail journey around the core of China. We came in by sea from Japan to Shanghai, and we left by rail across the Trans-Siberian Railroad. Every inch of the trip was instructive, and every experience is in some way a part of this book.

I also want to thank Gladys Justin Carr, vice president and publisher of McGraw-Hill General Books Division; editor Leslie Meredith, for shepherding the idea for this book through the maze of the McGraw-Hill corporation and securing adequate financial backing to make it possible; and her successor, Lisa Frost, who took the book the rest of the way through the production processes.

I am already in the process of two more books that originated on this trip: a study of Mao Zedong's rise to leadership in China and of his corruption at the end; and *The New China*, which is the exciting tale of the China that has emerged since Mao's fall, through the patient ministrations of Deng Xiaoping and other spiritual heirs to Zhou Enlai, who was, to my mind, the leading spirit in the whole Chinese revolution.

1

For this chapter I relied largely on half a dozen histories of China and Chinese political affairs, several of them by John K. Fairbank, a leading western scholar. For the modern official view I used *An Outline History of China*, edited by Bai Shouyi; Hucker's *China's Imperial Past*; and Su Kaiming's *Modern China*.

2

For this chapter, like the first, I relied on published histories, including Bai's *Outline History*. In the discussion of Russian penetration of China, I used a good deal of research I had amassed for one of my own books, *Russo-Japanese War*.

3

Much of this chapter came from studies I made earlier for my book *The Boxer Rebellion*. I also used Warner here, as well as studies I made for my book *Japan's War*. Extremely useful were Bai's *Outline History* and the biography of Admiral Togo. Su's *Modern China* was helpful, as were several biographies of Dr. Sun Yatsen and his own writings.

4

Bai's Chapter X and McAleavy were useful here for setting the scene. Sheridan's *China in Disintegration* was also helpful.

5

For the story of China's warlords I went back into research I had done for my studies of colonial China, which led to the books *The Boxer Rebellion* and *The Fall of Qingdao*, including biographies of Yuan Shikai, Feng Yuxiang, and Chiang Kaishek. Nien's book was helpful for this chapter too, as were several topical books by foreigners, including Sam Ginsburg and J. B. Powell. Mao Zedong's reminiscences of his boyhood and Edgar Snow's *Red Star over China* were also helpful.

6

The Fall of Qingdao was useful for establishing the background of Shandong Province. The memoirs of Mao Zedong and biography of Zhou Enlai were also very important for study of the establishment of the Communist movement in China.

7

J. B. Powell's memoirs were helpful in showing foreign attitudes and foreign stances in China during the 1920s. So was Seagrave's *The Soong Dynasty*.

McAleavy was very helpful. The notes of a volunteer showed events in Shanghai from a Chinese point of view.

8

The story of the Communist party is put together from several sources, including J. B. Powell's memoirs, the works of Mao Zedong, and Snow's *Red Star
over China*. The story of the Guomindang comes from the biography of Sun
Yatsen, from Bai and Su, and from Fitzgerald's *Revolution in China*.

9

The story of the northern expedition is from Fitzgerald and Su and from Mao
Zedong and Snow. Powell tells of some incidents he observed. Sam Ginsburg,
a young Russian refugee in Shanghai, also was a keen observer of the China
scene.

10

The story of the confrontation of the Communists and Nationalists comes from
Ginsburg, Fitzgerald, Powell, Su, the works of Chiang Kaishek and Mao, and
the Fang profile of Zhou Enlai. The story of the Green Gang participation in
the Shanghai doings is from Powell and from Seagrave. The story of the Japanese
confrontation with Chiang comes from research done for my own book *Japan's War*.

11

Mao's works and the Fang profile of Zhou were valuable for this chapter on
the rise of the Communists. Mao told the tale of his narrow escape from death
to Edgar Snow. The autobiography of Peng Dehuai was also useful here. Mao's
precepts and slogans have been widely reprinted by many authors.

12

Sheridan's biography of Feng Yuxiang was a valuable adjunct to the writing of
this chapter on warlords and the power of Chiang Kaishek.

13

For all the historical chapters I relied on many sources, listed in the bibliography. Mao's writings and the biographies of him are basic to the study of the

Communist movement, of course, but so are works about Li Lisan, who represented the left wing of the party in those days. Peng Dehuai's memoirs were very useful here, particularly for the tale of Huang Hanxiang.

14

Sam Ginsburg's reminiscences were valuable for this chapter. The story of the Guandong Army comes from my book *Japan's War*. Chiang Kaishek's dilemma—and his failure to resolve it cost him China in the end—was how to deal with the Japanese and the Communists at the same time. He never trusted the Communists enough to go into a real alliance with them, then or afterward. And by this time Chiang had lost his own revolutionary zeal.

15

The Powell and Ginsburg books were valuable for this chapter. The story of the Shanghai incident comes from various sources, including some Japanese, as used in my work *Japan's War*. Mao Zedong's works and Peng Dehuai's autobiography were very valuable. Sheridan's *China in Disintegration* has some interesting analyses of Chiang's problems.

16

Mao Zedong, Zhou Enlai, and Peng Dehuai were all valuable for the story of the Long March, and so was Anthony Lawrence's beautifully illustrated *China: The Long March*, issued in 1986. Su described the Zunyi conference too.

17

The best source for the story of the Xi'an incident is Peng Dehuai. I visited Xi'an and the little hot-spring complex in which Chiang Kaishek was incarcerated, and I felt the wind of history as I looked into the long narrow room where Chiang spent most of his time in bed. Seagrave was valuable for part of the story of Zhang Xueliang. The biography of General Yang Hucheng was also very valuable for this chapter.

18

The biography of General Yang was very valuable for this inside view of the Xi'an incident, as were works by Su Kaiming and Peng Dehuai. In *China Shall*

Rise Again Madame Chiang Kaishek (Soong Meiling) makes some allusions to her role.

19

Mao and Peng were useful here, as well as material from my research for *Japan's War* and also my *The New Militarists*. The official Guomindang history of the early days of the war was also valuable. So was Foreign Minister Hirota's memoir.

20

The Guomindang war history was valuable here. The story of the incidents along the Yangtze River comes from research done for my book *The Lonely Ships*, the story of the U.S. Asiatic fleet, which deals at length with the Panay incident. The war of the 1940s is easy for me to describe, because during that period I was in west China. I can remember seeing young men walking along a road, arms bound and nooses looped around their necks and held by their captors. These were "recruits" for the Nationalist army.

21

Again, the discussion of the Japanese is from *Japan's War*. Su was useful, as was Fitzgerald and Fairbank.

22

John K. Fairbank's analysis of Mao's successes was vital to this chapter. So were Mao's works. Some feeling for the Eighth Route Army and Communist tactics was gained through Evans Carlson's reports to the U.S. Marine Corps about the time he spent with the Communist armies in the late 1930s. Peng's autobiography was also used here. So was *Showashi*, the multivolume history of the Hirohito era.

23

Deng Xiaoping's writings were valuable for this chapter, and so were Mao's works. Su outlines the progress. I was in China during this period and reported on many of these events for United Press Associations and the *Denver Post*.

24

Again, this chapter covers a period during which I was in China as a reporter, and much of the material has been derived from recollections and notes. Mao deals with this period at some length. So does Peng Dehuai.

25

During this period A. T. Steele's dispatches to the now defunct *New York Herald Tribune* were probably the best journalism coming out of China. The rot of the Guomindang was definitely showing, nowhere more tragically than on Suzhou Creek, just below the windows of the Broadway Mansions Hotel, the press hostel for the correspondents. From the windows of their comfortable apartments, they could look out on the steaming mass of humanity crowded into the sampans on the creek, and slopping over onto the sidewalks of the street, where whole families lived in the open because they had nowhere else to go. It did not take long to get numbed to such sights; they were commonplace in the cities, and no one could see any efforts being made by the Guomindang to alleviate the suffering of the people. Under such conditions, Guomindang support and thus power eroded rapidly.

26

The collapse of Nationalist China was detailed in the daily newspaper reports from Shanghai and other cities in the summer of 1948, but in Washington the signs were steadfastly ignored. I saw such men as John S. Service hounded out of the U.S. Foreign Service for being soft on communism, when what they had done was report correctly on what was going on in China and predict what was going to happen: a Communist victory over Guomindang corruption. As many American reporters in China agreed, in Washington American politicians had so forgotten the history of our own rebellion against England that they believed the United States could arrange affairs in China. Nothing could have been further from the truth. George Weller, correspondent of the Chicago *Daily News*, put it succinctly: "What America did in China was irrelevant to Chinese history." America's support of the failing Guomindang did only one thing: It prolonged the Chinese agony and ensured the Chinese Communist distrust of America that militated against reasonable relationships for the next twenty-five years. The best single account of this failure that I know of is John Service's memoir *Lost Chance in China*.

27

Su, the works of Mao and Deng Xiaoping, the Fang biography of Zhou, and various accounts by younger Chinese, as listed in the bibliography, were all valuable to this chapter. The Service book was invaluable here. Joseph Alsop, through the column that he and his brother wrote, was extremely influential in behalf of the China lobby. As a newspaper editor in that period I recall the enormous influence the Alsop brothers had. We used their column regularly in the *Denver Post*, although I tried as editor of the editorial page to counterbalance it with other materials. But by 1948 other materials were quite hard to find. I remember that I used to use quite a bit of material from Julian Schuman, a free-lance correspondent in China, who later became closely associated with the Chinese Communists. He is now a member of the staff of the *China Daily*, the official English-language paper published in Beijing, New York, and London simultaneously (by satellite transmission). I had to defend this search for "the other side" against the protests of the China lobby and sometimes against the people who owned the *Post*, some of whom, I think, suspected that I was a Communist. In all this I was stoutly supported by the newspaper publisher, Palmer Hoyt, not because he was my father, but because he really believed in freedom of expression and telling all sides of a story. He was an early and steadfast enemy of McCarthyism, that poison that spread across America in the late 1940s, and the *Post* retained a liberal view of the China question until the very end, when the Communists conquered China and then broke off relationships with the United States.

28

As noted by John K. Fairbank and others, following the conquest of China by the Communists, the period of terror was virtually unknown to the outside world. Mao Zedong first arrested all foreign journalists and then ejected them from China. The extent of the early terror only started to become known in the 1980s, through the fall of Maoism, typified by the tearing down of Mao statues in many parts of China. By the late 1980s the chairman's excesses were being uncovered and reexamined. The first of these, but by no means the worst, occurred during the early 1950s when the landlord class was rooted out of China, largely by extirpation, and Mao laid down the ground rules. Woe to any landlord who had ever angered any of his peasants. In the 1980s, slowly, various leaders are beginning to refer to Mao's excesses, led by Deng Xiaoping

29

The Chinese phase of the Korean war is one of the most tragic periods of modern history, because it was totally avoidable and came about only because of the ego of one man, General Douglas MacArthur. I have written three volumes about the Korean war, and I am working on another, *The Day the Chinese Attacked*, which is a study of the fallible American policies that led to the situation in which General MacArthur's view came to cause total misdirection of the American war policy and forced the Chinese into the war against the United Nations. The Chinese side of this war has been described by Russell Spurr in *Enter the Dragon*. The result of the MacArthur error was two long years of attenuated struggle and loss of life, which ended in stalemate with the two Koreas right back where they had been in June 1950, and where they could have been stabilized in October.

For this chapter I relied on my own research and knowledge of such people as President Syngman Rhee of the Republic of Korea, whom I had known well when I was a correspondent in Korea in 1945 and 1946. The memoirs of Marshal Peng Dehuai, the leader of the "people's volunteers" who were sent into China, were of some value, but not very much. Also, in 1987 it was impossible to find any books about the Korean war in bookshops in China or in the Soviet Union. The subject has been "closed." Only in 1988 did some Chinese historical magazines begin publishing articles about this period.

30

Mao's writings are essential to this chapter, as are Deng's. Various personal accounts of the period were very helpful, as is noted in the text. As noted by Deng Xiaoping in his collected writings, the "hundred-flowers" statement turned out to be the beginning of the end for a growing sense of intellectual freedom in China in the 1950s. The 1960s and early 1970s turned out to be a period of confusion and repression, and almost the undoing of the whole Chinese social fabric, as a result of the madness of Mao Zedong.

31

The madness continued. Russell Spurr tells how Mao attacked and destroyed his old friend and supporter Peng Dehuai, for no reason except to feed his own ego. In so doing, he broke the bonds that held together the old leaders of the revolution, and from that point onward every man had to look to his own skin, a matter confirmed to me by several old revolutionaries. It was the old story of the revolution destroying its children. Peng's story is one of the great tragedies of China, and his writings show how the Great Leap Forward was an economic disaster.

32

What emerges in this chapter is a picture of Mao Zedong, the revolutionary, as a failed administrator. As the *China Daily* shows in its daily pages, his policies after the Communist victory turned to dross, and most of them brought hardship to the Chinese people. But Mao was not ready to quit and give the reins of power to administrators. He hoped to achieve by a new revolution what he had failed to do by administration, and he wrongly blamed the intellectuals for his troubles. This is all given credence by Thurston in *Enemies of the People* and Yue in *To the Storm*. But that blame led to the many quarrels within the leadership of the party, where such men as Deng Xiaoping bobbed up and down, in disgrace one year and back in favor another.

33

Mao's abuse of his power became final in the Cultural Revolution, in which he turned over the reins of party and social destruction to children, knowing that they would act, believing and not thinking. Gao's *Born Red* tells the whole tale. It was, in a sense, like the disastrous "children's crusade" of the European middle ages, when thousands of children went to destruction carrying what they thought was a holy cause. The Cultural Revolution lasted more than a decade, and left virtually no family untouched by some bitter sting. On my ten-week trip to China I verified that fact to my own satisfaction. The effect was so terrible and so drastic that the Chinese themselves are numb to it now. They have begun to recognize that Mao had gone mad, but the excesses were so great that virtually everyone was equally hurt. Thus has set in a sort of national acceptance and willingness to forget. No one is seeking to right old wrongs by punishing the perpetrators of the past, and they have quietly disappeared into the greater framework of Chinese society. As one Chinese now in his twenties said to me in the spring of 1988 about the Red Guards:

"We were all Red Guards. We all had the red armband; it was a kind of peer pressure to be a Red Guard." And everyone in China seems to understand that fact.

34

Knowing that Mao was mad, his wife and several associates sought to transfer his power to themselves, but they underestimated the old man's craft and his continued influence as a god. His writings show how he put down the attempts of the Gang of Four to seize power at about the same time that Richard Nixon effected a thaw in Chinese-American relationships.

35

The rise of Deng Xiaoping, through the labyrinths of Chinese Politburo politics, is one of the most remarkable stories of the Chinese revolution. His collected works hint at all the important facts. He was eclipsed time and again, only to come back and finally to emerge as the single greatest force in China, a successor to Mao Zedong, without the urge for personal power. His rise to power is shown in the daily pages of the *China Daily*. Deng put China on a new tack, as is indicated in this chapter.

36

Deng's struggle against the leftist revolutionaries of the Chinese Communist party lasted until 1987, when he took control at the Thirteenth National Congress and set in motion a series of reforms that will change China enormously in the next few decades. The proceedings of the Thirteenth Party Congress show this. The changes were profound, and they began immediately. As of 1988 the party was having some difficulty in rearranging terminology to accommodate the new ways, but the new ways were definitely in effect in virtually every aspect of Chinese life. Wages rose, prices rose, conditions grew better, economic freedom improved, and economic opportunity did too. The purpose of these changes was to improve the quality of Chinese life, and the objectives were clearly stated by the leadership.

The changes were coming so fast that already by the middle of 1988 they showed the way of the future. They will be the subject of the sequel to this book, which is already on my drawing board, along with a study of the rise and fall of Mao Zedong.

BIBLIOGRAPHY

Abend, Hallett. *Chaos in Asia*. New York: Ives Washburn, 1939.
Bai Shouyi. *An Outline History of China*. Beijing: Foreign Languages Press, 1982.
Bergamini, David. *Japan's Imperial Conspiracy*. New York: Pocket Books, 1972.
Bodde, Derk. *Peking Diary, a Year of Revolution*. New York: Octagon Books, 1976.
Borg, Dorothy. *The United States and the Far Eastern Crisis of 1933–38*. Cambridge, Mass.: Harvard University Press, 1964.
Chen Changfeng. *On the Long March with Chairman Mao*. Beijing: Foreign Languages Press, 1972.
Chiang Kaishek. *Resistance and Reconstruction*. New York: Harper, 1943.
Chinese Communist Party. *Proceedings of the 13th Party Congress CCP*. Beijing. 1987.
Chu, Godwin C. *Radical Change through Communication in Mao's China*. Honolulu: University of Hawaii Press, 1977.
Clark, Elmer T. *The Chiangs of China*. New York: Abingdon-Cokesbury, 1942.
Cochran, Sherman, and Andrew C. K. Hsieh, with Janis Cochran. *One Day in China, May 21, 1936*. New Haven, Conn.: Yale University Press, 1983.
Cohen, Warren A. *America's Response to China*. New York: Wiley, 1972.
Corr, Gerard H. *The Chinese Red Army*. Reading, England: Osprey, 1974.
DeFrancis, John. *The Chinese Language*. Honolulu: University of Hawaii Press, 1984.
Deng Xiaoping. *Fundamental Issues in Present-Day China*. Beijing: Foreign Languages Press, 1987.
———. *Selected Works*. Beijing: Foreign Languages Press, 1984.
Fairbank, John K. *The Great Chinese Revolution, 1800–1985*. New York: Harper & Row, 1986.
———(ed.). *Chinese Thought and Institutions*. Chicago: University of Chicago Press, 1957.
Fang, Percy J., and Lucy Guimong Fang. *Zhou Enlai, a Profile*. Beijing: Foreign Languages Press, 1986.
Fitzgerald, C. P. *Revolution in China*. London: Cresset Press, 1952.
Fraser, John. *The Chinese*. New York: Summit Books, 1980.
Gao Yuan. *Born Red*. Stanford, Calif.: Stanford University Press, 1987.

Ginsburg, Sam. *My First Sixty Years in China*. Beijing: New World Press, 1962.

Gittings, John. *The Role of the Chinese Army*. London: Oxford University Press, 1967.

Griffith, Samuel B. *Mao Zedong on Guerilla Warfare*. New York: Praeger, 1961.

Hsu, Francis L. K. *Americans and Chinese*. Honolulu: University of Hawaii Press, 1981.

Hsu Longhsuen and Chang Mingkai. *History of the Sino-Japanese War, 1937–1945*. Taipei: Chungwu, 1971.

Hu Sheng, Liu Danian, et al. *The 1911 Revolution*. Beijing: New World Press, 1983.

Huang Ji Shu et al. *Dai Yi Ge Zong Tong* (a Biography of China's First President), 3 vols. Beijing: Bai Hua Wen Yichu Ban, 1984.

Huc, M. *The Chinese Empire*. Port Washington, N.Y.: Kennikat Press, 1970.

Hucker, Charles O. *China's Imperial Past*. Stanford, Calif.: Stanford University Press, 1975.

Karnow, Stanley. *Mao and China*. New York: Viking, 1972.

Kent, P. H. B. *The Twentieth Century in the Far East*. London: Edward Arnold, 1937.

Lawrence, Anthony. *China: The Long March*. London: Merehurst Press, 1986.

Lee Chongsik. *Revolutionary Struggle in Manchuria, 1922–45*. Berkeley: University of California Press, 1983.

Lewis, John W. (ed.). *Party Leadership and Revolutionary Power in China*. Cambridge, England: Cambridge University Press, 1970.

Li, Lincoln. *The Japanese Army in North China, 1937–1941*. Tokyo: Oxford University Press, 1975.

Liang Heng and Judith Shapiro. *After the Nightmare*. New York: Knopf, 1986.

Llewellyn, Bernard. *I Left My Roots in China*. New York: Oxford University Press, 1953.

MacInnis, Donald E. *Religious Policy and Practice in Communist China*. New York: Macmillan, 1972.

Mainichi Shimbun Sha (eds.). *Showashi*, 17 vols. Tokyo: Mainichi Publishers, 1987.

Mao Zedong. *Selected Works*, 5 vols. Beijing: Foreign Languages Press, 1977.

McAleavy, Henry. *The Modern History of China*. New York: Praeger, 1967.

Mi Zanchen. *The Life of General Yang Hucheng*. Hong Kong: Joint Publishing, 1981.

Michener, James A. *The Voice of Asia*. New York: Random House, 1951.

Myrdal, Jan. *Report from a Chinese Village*. New York: Pantheon, 1965.

Nee, Victor, and James Peck. *China's Uninterrupted Revolution*. New York: Pantheon, 1975.

Nielsen, Krarup. *The Dragon Awakes*. New York: Dodd, Mead, 1928.

Nien Cheng. *Life and Death in Shanghai*. London: Grafton Books, 1986.

Payne, Robert. *Forever China*. New York: Dodd, Mead, 1945.

Peng Te Huai (Dehuai). *Memoirs of a Chinese Marshal*. Beijing: Foreign Languages Press, 1984.

Powell, John B. *My Twenty Five Years in China*. New York: Macmillan, 1945.

Qi Wen. *China. A General Survey*. Beijing: Foreign Languages Press, 1984.

Quigley, H. S. *Far Eastern War, 1937–1941*. Boston: World Peace Foundation, 1943.

Scalapino, Robert A. (ed.). *Elites in the People's Republic of China*. Seattle: University of Washington Press, 1972.

———— and George T. Yu. *Modern China and Its Revolutionary Process*. Berkeley: University of California Press, 1985.

Schramm, Stuart (ed.). *Chairman Mao Talks to the People*. New York: Pantheon, 1974.

Schurmann, Franz. *Ideology and Organization in Communist China*. Berkeley: University of California Press, 1970.

Seagrave, Sterling. *The Soong Dynasty*. New York: Harper & Row, 1985.

Service, John S. *Lost Chance in China*. New York: Random House, 1974.

Sheridan, James E. *China in Disintegration*. London: Free Press, 1975.

————. *Chinese Warlord, the Career of Marshal Feng Yuxiang*. Stanford, Calif.: Stanford University Press, 1966.

Snow, Edgar. *Red Star over China*. New York: Random House, 1938.

Soong Meiling (Mme. Chiang Kaishek). *China Shall Rise Again*. New York: Harper, 1940.

Spurr, Russell. *Enter the Dragon*. New York: Newmarket Press, 1988.

Su Kaiming. *Modern China, a Topical History*. Beijing: New World Press, 1986.

Terrill, Ross. *800,000, the Real China*. Boston: Little, Brown, 1972.

Thurston, Anne F. *Enemies of the People*. New York: Knopf, 1987.

Warner, Marina. *The Dragon Empress*. New York: Atheneum, 1986.

Weiss, Ruth F. *Lu Xun*. Beijing: New World Press, 1985.

White, Theodore H., and Annalee Jacoby. *Thunder Out of China*. New York: Sloane, 1946.

Wilson, J. Tuzo. *One Chinese Moon*. New York: Hill and Wang, 1959.

Yang, Martin C. *A Chinese Village*. New York: Columbia University Press, 1945.

Yue Daiyun and Carolyn Wakeman. *To the Storm*. Berkeley: University of California Press, 1985.

Zhong Wenxian. *Mao Zedong*. Beijing: Foreign Languages Press, 1986.

Zhang Xinxin and Sang Ye. *Chinese Profiles*. Beijing: Panda Books, 1986.

Index

Other DACAPO titles of interest